International Financial Markets

Volume III in the Bush School Series in the Economics of Public Policy

Edited by James M. Griffin

International Financial Markets

The Challenge of Globalization

Edited by

Leonardo Auernheimer

The University of Chicago Press
Chicago and London

Leonardo Auernheimer is professor of economics at Texas A&M University.

The University of Chicago Press, Chicago 60637
The University of Chicago Press, Ltd., London
© 2003 by The University of Chicago
All rights reserved. Published 2003
Printed in the United States of America
12 11 10 09 08 07 06 05 04 03   1 2 3 4 5

ISBN: 0-226-03214-0 (cloth)

Library of Congress Cataloging-in-Publication Data

International financial markets : the challenge of globalization / edited by Leonardo
Auernheimer.
    p. cm. — (Bush School series in the economics of public policy ; v. 3)
    Extensive revision of papers from the third Conference on Public Policy held at the
Bush School of Government & Public Service, Texas A&M University.
    Includes bibliographical references and index.
    ISBN 0-226-03214-0 (cloth : alk. paper)
    1. International finance. 2. Capital movements. 3. Foreign exchange.
    4. Globalization—Economic aspects. I. Auernheimer, Leonardo, 1936– II. Series.

HG3881 .I607286 2002
332'.042—dc21

2002032044

Contents

v

Acknowledgments

A conference and the editing of a volume require the contributions of many people. At the risk of forgetting and offending, I would like to mention a few names. My greatest indebtedness is to my friend Guillermo Calvo, who provided many suggestions as to format and participants, and to Michael D. Bordo and Allan Meltzer. Their initial agreement to participate undoubtedly served as an incentive for the others to join. Bob McTeer, president of the Dallas Fed, graciously agreed to chair and to add his wit to one of the sessions. The Bush School of Government provided magnificent facilities, and the staffs of both the Bush School and the Department of Economics assured a smooth operation. My colleague James Griffin shared many of the "organization blues" and was generous with his suggestions, and Chris Ball provided invaluable assistance in the editing of the volume.

L. A.

International Capital Markets and the Challenge of Globalization: A Touring Guide to Some of the Issues

Leonardo Auernheimer

The purpose of this introduction is, first, to describe the aims and the rationale for the Third Conference on Public Policy, dedicated to the question of international capital markets and the challenge of globalization, and second, to provide the reader with both a sketch of the background of some of the conference's topics, and a brief comment on the presentations and the final roundtable. As indicated by its title, this introduction is written, to a large extent, with the noneconomist reader in mind, although the author has included some reflections that may be useful to economists. It is obviously not intended as a survey, but rather as an appetizer that will hopefully not ruin the reader's appetite.

When deciding on the topic for the Third Conference on Public Policy, globalization of capital markets was at the top of almost everyone's list. The increasing opening of trade in commodities since the inception of the General Agreement on Tariffs and Trade (GATT)—now evolved into the World Trade Organization (WTO)—the upsurge in international capital movements during the last ten years, together with the crisis episodes in Mexico, the Far East, and Russia, and the concretion of the European Monetary Union (EMU), has ignited the interest of academic economists, policy makers, and the press in an unprecedented way.

The phenomenon of globalization in both commodities and capital markets can be traced to some easily identifiable events, some of which are more predictable than others, and all of which have converged upon and reinforced each other. First, there are the collapse of the Soviet Union and the resultant opening of the economies of Eastern Europe, and the gradual transformation and opening of China. Independent of specula-

Leonardo Auernheimer is professor of economics at Texas A&M University.

tion about the demise of the socialist model, these two events of tremendous historical significance have meant, in the language of the economist, that many new large countries now or will soon participate in the mechanism of international exchange of goods and financial assets, which did not exist before.[1] Second is the significant change in economic policies in most Latin American countries. The end of World War II started decades of uniformly disastrous economic policies (high chronic inflation and periodic hyperinflation resulting from government expenditures financed by monetary expansion, pervasive controls on prices and interest rates, and outrageous levels of trade protection and financial repression). After a series of failed attempts during the 1980s, the decade of the 1990s finally brought about, in most of the Latin American countries, successful stabilization and, to various degrees, a reduction in controls and the size of government as well as the opening to international markets, both in goods and services and in financial assets. Finally, the process of integration was undoubtedly facilitated by the advent of the unprecedented change in the technology of information and communications.

Integration and globalization were not without growing pains. Among other minor episodes, some specific shocks reverberated significantly throughout world markets. At the end of 1994 the Mexican peso collapsed, sending shock waves especially to other Latin American economies (the familiarly called *tequila effect*) prompting an eventually successful rescue package initiated by the U.S. government. Thailand, Indonesia, and Korea suffered important crises in 1997, and in October of that year speculative attack descended on Hong Kong (the so-called *Asian flu*). Finally, in August 1998, Russia declared a moratorium on its external debt. In an episode of more restricted geographical significance, the Brazilian crisis of 1998 and its devaluation in January 1999 seriously affected some Latin American financial markets, particularly Argentina's. Concern over contagion and herd behavior once more increased the intensity of the discussion and the number of academic and policy papers seeking an explanation for the events, the possible rationale for controls, and the appropriate role of international organizations (in particular the International Monetary Fund [IMF]).

Against this background, the organization of the Third Conference on Public Policy sought to strike a balance between rigorous analytical work and policy-oriented discussion, with a series of papers useful to academicians, policymakers, and lay persons. Fortunately, interest in the topics related to international financial markets has generated ample demand for clarification on the part of policymakers and the public at large, and the economics profession has responded. The researchers who push the frontiers of analytical research are the same ones who have been generating policy prescriptions as well as the serious but less theoretical work that is widely reported in the specialized press and is accessible to the educated general public. The papers presented at the conference and included in this volume are authored by researchers who in different areas have contributed heavily to the theoretical literature and in some cases have, at the same time, occupied important advisory or executive positions in the making of policy. The conference concluded with a roundtable, moderated by Guillermo A. Calvo, with panelists drawn from academia, the private sector, and the specialized press.

In the design of the conference and the choice of topics to be covered, we also needed to strike a balance between depth and coverage, and the final choice includes four main themes that are at the same time well defined and open-ended, in the sense that they relate to almost any of the questions on balance-of-payments adjustment and international capital mobility. The first chapter is authored by Michael D. Bordo and, as a natural introduction, presents the first theme: a careful analysis of the historical record since 1880, in particular concerning capital movements and the origin and characteristics of various crises that took place during that period. The second topic is capital movements, and chapter 2, by Michael P. Dooley (coauthored with Carl E. Walsh), argues the case for limited capital controls.[2] Chapter 3, by René M. Stulz, not only presents a lucid analysis of the benefits and costs of capital movements, but examines some of the evidence suggested by primary data on equity markets. The last chapter within the same topic, chapter 4, belongs to Guillermo A. Calvo, who elaborates on some of the flaws of capital movements (the maturity profile of international debt and problems derived from possible herd behavior and imperfect information, among others) and provides abundant insight into the nature of the Asian and Latin American crises—making a nice transition to the following theme.

The titles of all four chapters on the first two themes, incidentally, contain question marks. Answers to the problems posed by capital flows are to be provided by the two following topics: the choice of exchange rate regime (including multicountry coordination) and the structure and functions of international institutions—among them, and foremost, the IMF. Two chapters deal with exchange rate regimes. The first (chapter 5), presented by Pablo E. Guidotti (coauthored with Andrew Powell), argues the case for fixed exchange rates in the most extreme form—dollarization—with the prospects for Argentina, under a currency board, as the case study. The next (chapter 6), discussed by Agustín Carstens (coauthored with Guillermo Ortiz Martinez) relies on Mexico's experience since 1995 with the other extreme form—floating exchange rates. Both chapters discuss the reactions of the economies in question (Argentina and Mexico) to the recent international financial crises, and provide valuable, detailed accounts of the institutional environment and the concrete operational rules guiding the actions of each central bank. These two chapters, together, have an added value greater than the sum of the parts, because they describe two concrete experiments, each in one of the two types of arrangement that seem to be emerging as the ones favored by the professional consensus and by some opinions voiced by the IMF (the *bipolar view*). Furthermore, both experiments are simultaneous in time and implemented in relatively large Latin American economies.

The theme of chapter 7 and of the roundtable (chapter 8) relates to the second set of solutions to problems brought about by capital flows (capital-flow "flaws," in the words of Calvo), and is the role of international financial institutions. The chapter is a revised version of previous work by Charles W. Calomiris that had already received wide attention in the profession and the specialized press. It discusses the basic reforms that, in his view, should be introduced into the purposes and operational mechanisms of the IMF. There is, then, an almost seamless continuity between chapter 7 and the following roundtable, the focus of which was the report of the International Financial Institutions Advisory Commission that had just been released at the time of the conference.[3] In fact, we were fortunate to host Allan Meltzer, chair of the commission (of which Calomiris was also a member) and a high-profile academician and policy advisor, as one of the members of the roundtable, which was coordinated by Calvo. We were also fortunate to have Matthew Bishop, T. Britton Harris, and John Lipsky as panelists in the roundtable.

The Historical Background

The historical background is provided by Bordo's chapter 1, which presents a careful and exhaustive analysis of both capital movements and the occurrence of some of the crises since 1880. The unique value of the historical perspective over a rather long period of time is, simply, to remind us that the trees should not obscure the forest, and the chapter does an excellent job of putting the recent globalization of capital markets in perspective. The historical evidence points to a U-shaped pattern of financial integration, with current levels appearing to be higher than before the decline that began with World War I and continued through the twenties and thirties. The paper gets high marks in another respect, i.e., in bringing historical evidence to bear on the analysis of very current issues—a task seldom accomplished in historically oriented pieces. Drawing on this blending of past evidence and current discussion, there is no timidity in some of the prescriptions: sustainable globalization has been and can be obtained only among countries with macroeconomic stability; controls are not an answer, and intermediate forms of exchange rate arrangements other than either floating rates or hard pegs are not to be undertaken—a set of prescriptions remarkably like those in the papers to follow.

Capital Movements, Crises, and Capital Controls

At the inception of the IMF, by the end of World War II, the Bretton Woods articles of agreement were clear in the objectives of the institution: freedom of movements in the trade in goods and services (i.e., in the trade account). Now, more than fifty years later, the discussion both within and outside the institution is whether similar freedom of movements for the capital account—i.e., for capital movements—should be institutionalized as an objective of the new international financial architecture.

The role of capital movements (lending and borrowing, or the sale and purchase of financial assets) among residents or governments of different countries responds to the same rationale, and basically provides the same benefits as the lending and borrowing among individuals in any economy. The exchange of promises to pay is, essentially, the equivalent of exchanging current goods for future goods. Borrowing allows the purchase of goods today, rather than tomorrow, at a cost; lending allows the postponement of purchases in exchange for a reward (interest).

There are, indeed, two closely related but distinct functions of this lending and borrowing process. In its purest form it allows borrowers to consume today rather than later, and lenders to postpone consumption. In another form it allows borrowers (entrepreneurs) to purchase investment rather than consumption goods, and thus permits a division of labor between those who simply wish to save and those who invest. Among countries, lending can take the form of generic *portfolio capital* (deposits in commercial banks and other financial institutions, or private and government bonds), with borrowers being either consumers acquiring consumption goods (mostly consumer durables) or, more frequently, business firms purchasing investment goods. The second form that capital inflows can take is *foreign direct investment* (FDI), i.e., the direct investment in physical capital owned and often operated, at least partially, by foreigners.

As mentioned before (and as Stulz's chapter carefully explains), all the benefits that we recognize from this trade in financial assets among individuals in a country also apply to the case of individual residents of different countries. As always in economic analysis, government intervention and the imposition of controls in capital movements need to be justified by the presence of inherent market imperfections (externalities, free-rider problems, and the like) amounting to market failure. In the case of capital movements there is a well-accepted argument for controls (at least at the theoretical level) when a higher stock of debt held by borrowers increases the risk of default, so that lenders must consider that stock of debt when assessing the risk-adjusted appropriate interest rate. If international lenders cannot verify every individual borrower's debt in a certain country, but they have information about the whole country's debt (that of both the country's residents and its government), then a market imperfection will develop: individual borrowers will borrow too much because they will not take into account ("internalize") the effect of their own borrowing on the rest of the country's residents' (and the government's) interest rates. Theoretically, then, the presence of this distortion would call for a tax on the holding of foreign debt (see, e.g., Bardhan 1967 and Aizenman 1989).

This is certainly not the kind of argument that current proponents of capital controls have in mind, however. The various crises occurring during the last decade have provided ample ammunition for the argument that some kind of control needs to be imposed over capital movements; moreover, independent of whatever truth there is to such arguments, appearances and even catchy qualifications seem to make them self-evident. The usual statements are to the effect that "hot" (short-term) portfolio capital tends to move quickly out of a country on the basis of unfounded rumors, herd behavior, and contagion, or that speculators who "smell blood" gain millions on one-sided bets against central banks that try to defend their currencies, and so on. Independent of the validity of arguments for the imposition of controls, it is clear that crises have a cost, although very little work has been done to identify exactly its components (other than an eventual fall in output and employment), and much less to measure those components. A run on the central bank reserves often translates into a twin banking crisis, with banks recalling loans and jeopardizing business firms' investments and even their very existence; the ensuing fall in employment and output; and eventually a devaluation that otherwise would not be justified by the fundamentals. The welfare benefits of capital flows, some arguments go, can therefore be substantially lessened (if not eliminated) by the risks of sudden withdrawals and the ensuing crisis, and that, hence, some form of control is in order.

Since there is general agreement on the allocation benefits of capital movements, the discussion of those capital movements turns out to be, largely, a discussion of crises. The question of whether the benefits of capital movements exceed the (real or imaginary) costs is then at the heart of the discussion on whether controls should in principle be imposed, and if so, on what form should they take. This is, essentially, a cost-benefit analysis of capital movements—which is precisely what Stulz's chapter undertakes. It may be useful, however, to elaborate on the general question and add a few comments, after some clarifications.

1. Individuals (or governments), not countries, borrow and lend. Of course, it is possible and sometimes useful to measure the total borrowing or lending by the residents of a country and of their government, but capital movements, when allowed, imply that residents can hold international financial assets (debt or credit). *Capital flight,* or the withdrawal of foreign funds, can perfectly well be (and often is) the result of actions by the country's own residents. A related clarification is that the meaningful distinction is not between domestic and foreign debt, but between debt denominated in the domestic currency and that denominated in a foreign currency. In many of the recent crisis episodes, a substantial part of government debt that was denominated in (or indexed to) foreign currency was being held by residents of the country in question.

2. It is important, in principle, to distinguish between exchange rate crises and banking crises, although one very often leads to the other (resulting in what are sometimes called *twin crises*) and it can be difficult to draw the distinction. An *exchange rate crisis* is initially motivated by the expectation (justified or not) that the central bank is likely to devalue the domestic currency (i.e., to increase the predetermined level of the exchange rate). Holders of domestic currency then convert their currency to foreign exchange, thereby lowering central bank reserves. As a result, there is a fall in the domestic monetary base (of which currency is one of the components, with commercial bank reserves being the other), and hence in the money stock (currency plus demand deposits). In the process, banks are then forced to recall or not refinance loans; hence the banking crisis. A *banking crisis* occurs when an abrupt withdrawal of deposits (in the anticipation of either a failure by banks or a devaluation) motivates depositors to obtain currency that can be ex-

changed for foreign currency. Once again, banks are forced to recall or not refinance their loans to business firms.

3. The problem with sudden international capital outflows (*sudden stops,* as Calvo calls them) essentially derives from the asymmetry between borrowing and lending by business firms or from the (mis)matching between maturity of lending and borrowing. Usually, business firms borrow to finance the purchase of physical capital or inventories, and they hold debt with relatively long maturity (i.e., debt that need not be repaid for some time) or in the understanding that refinancing for shorter term debt will be available at some predictable and manageable interest rate. If loans are recalled and firms are forced to liquidate real assets abruptly, more often than not those assets fetch a market value much lower than they would have in the long run, so that not only is further investment halted, but firms can fall into a state of insolvency, and so will the banks.

4. In the discussion of crises and the effects of sudden capital outflows it is important to distinguish, in the case of exchange rate crises in particular,[4] between solvency and liquidity problems. *Solvency problems* often occur due to an inconsistent set of government policies, which shows up in the framework of the government budget constraint and more often than not is caused by a level of government expenditures (including service on the government debt) requiring a relatively high level of *inflation tax* (financing via money creation). This is probably the most common occurrence of the fundamentals not being right, and hence the lack of solvency. There is a rather uniform consensus in the profession that in such instances crises are unavoidable. It is even possible to argue that in such instances the early warning of a crisis may be a positive development in that it is a warning that the inconsistency needs to be resolved.[5]

The relevant discussion on the nature of crises, on the roles of rescue packages and of lenders of last resort, and on the eventual need for controls thus takes place in the context of sudden capital outflows that may occur even when the fundamentals are in place. This can happen in two different situations. The first is the case of a temporary lack of confidence that brings about a liquidity crisis (i.e., a case in which there is solvency, but there is either a mismatch in the maturity of assets and liabilities or a fire sale of real assets that otherwise would have fetched a substantially higher price). This phenomenon has been well studied in the case of banking crises, for which the natural solution has traditionally been the idea of a *lender of last resort* (the central bank) that is able to provide transitory liquidity on short notice. Here, the usual case is that of short-term deposits and long-term loans in commercial banks.[6] This type of liquidity crisis is analogous to a case in which government policies are consistent but a temporary lack of confidence prompts a sudden run on the central bank's foreign exchange reserves.[7] The equivalent of the lender of last resort is, in this case, the rescue package provided by international banks, foreign governments, or the IMF.

The second instance, in which a crisis can take place in spite of solvency, is more dangerous. This is the case usually referred to as the case in which "dreams become reality," or the case of "multiple equilibria." Indeed, what may initially be no more than a liquidity crisis might evolve into such a case. In simplest terms, *multiple equilibria* will exist in situations in which initially unfounded negative expectations become self-fulfilled, in the sense that the market reaction to those expectations is sufficient to change the fundamentals and to make a situation of initial solvency develop into true lack of solvency. Here again is an analogy between the banking crisis and the exchange rate crisis. If, in the case of the initial liquidity crisis in the banking system, banks are forced to recall loans and firms that otherwise are perfectly viable are forced to liquidate their assets, it will most likely be true that the solvency of firms and of creditor banks will be jeopardized. At the level of exchange rate crises, a classic example is the expectation of a default in government debt. This expectation will immediately increase the interest rate at which the government can refinance its liabilities, substantially increasing financing costs and transforming an initially sound fiscal and monetary policy into an unsustainable situation and thus validating the initially unjustified expectation.[8] Cases of multiple equilibria or the reasonable possibility that they can take place are well documented in the literature, at least at the theoretical level, for the case of both banking and exchange rate crises, and it is fair to say that much of the discussion on the eventual need for capital controls takes place within this context. Empirical findings are, unfortunately, much harder to come by, and solid evidence beyond casual observation is rather scant.

Closely related to the case of multiple equilibria is the question of *herd behavior* and *contagion:* the possibility that groups of international lenders base their expectations on other lenders' behavior, or that a crisis in a particular country may spread to other countries that initially were not in any kind of compromised-solvency situation.[9] Unfortunately, it is possible to envision scenarios in which either herd behavior or contagion is quite possible, even in the context of perfectly rational economic behavior. For this to be possible it is necessary only to assume asymmetry of information—for example, the existence of informed and uninformed international investors—or liquidity constraints for some lenders who are forced to withdraw deposits or sell financial assets in one country in order to cover losses in another (see, e.g., Calvo and Mendoza 1998). Here, again, hard empirical evidence is not abundant.

Another point often brought into the discussion of international indebtedness and crises is the question of the maturity of government (and private) foreign debt. Indeed, the short-term maturity of a large part of government foreign debt is usually identified as one of the culprits of the Mexican crisis of 1994–95. Calvo has emphasized this aspect in several of his works, including his paper at the conference. All other things being equal, it seems evident that a short-term structure makes for a more vulnerable position. The basic question, of course, is the relative cost of short-versus long-term debt. Additionally, it could be argued provocatively that revealing a strong preference for long-term borrowing may signal to the market a lack of resolve to keep the fundamentals under control.

Finally, some comments may be in order concerning the more specific question of crises, their anatomy and their mechanics.

It is customary to group the various analytical treatments of crises as models belonging to the first generation, followed by those of the subsequent generation or generations. Briefly, the so-called first-generation models—beginning with the seminal piece by Krugman (1979)—consider a totally passive government (central bank) engaging in an inconsistent policy, perhaps a fiscal deficit that will eventually require a rate of monetary expansion incompatible with the stability of prices and the fixed level of the exchange rate. In this context it is relatively easy to show, in a very simple model, that if there is a minimum level of international reserves at which the central bank will "give up" and let the exchange rate float, there is a point at which a generalized attack on the currency occurs, in such a way that the free-floating exchange rate right after the collapse is the same as the previously fixed parity. Throughout the process there is perfect foresight (i.e., rational individuals are certain about the future of the process). Indeed, the condition in which the new floating exchange rate immediately after the crisis is the same as the previously fixed rate is what eliminates anticipated capital gains or losses—i.e., it assures the fulfillment of the *price continuity principle*. The problem with these first-generation models is in the passivity and the perfectly transparent behavior of the monetary authority, which is therefore perfectly known to speculators—hence the perfect knowledge that speculators have about the monetary authority's behavior. "New crisis models," as they are called by Krugman (1996; see also, e.g., Obstfeld 1994, 1996) begin by recognizing that the decision of whether to defend a fixed parity is, at each point during the process, a decision emerging from the costs and benefits of doing so: losses of international reserves, the effects of the decision on future credibility, and so on. It is, then, a policy decision, and at times a political one. The result of such cost-benefit computation on the part of the central bank will depend on the monetary authority's preferences and priorities. Since these are not perfectly known to speculators, the question is how to model the mechanism those speculators use for signal extraction (i.e., for figuring out the central bank's intentions). In turn, the central bank has no perfect information about the behavior of speculators, so that a complete analysis ultimately requires the modeling of the reciprocal interaction between speculators and the central bank—not an easy task to accomplish.

Beyond the behavioral model of how crises occur, one simpler aspect of crises that has not received sufficient attention in the profession and in policy discussions is the change in balance sheets (i.e., the gains and losses to all participants) brought about by crises, both in the case in which the parity is successfully defended and in the case in which there is a devaluation and collapse.[10] The usual popular version is that the smell of blood is sensed by international speculators who then proceed to raid the central bank and seize its reserves in a no-lose operation. This rather simplistic account needs to be modified in at least two important aspects.

The first is that participants in a crisis are not simply the central bank and speculators at large, as is often assumed, but the central bank and at least two groups of speculators: those believing that ultimately the central bank will successfully defend the parity, at least for some time, and those who anticipate an immediate or soon-to-follow devaluation. The latter borrow (usually at very high interest rates) in terms of domestic currency and acquire foreign exchange at the parity rate (i.e., they "short" the domestic currency) in the hope that a devaluation soon will allow them to repay their domestic currency debt, which would require only part of their acquisition of foreign exchange. The former lend (at the same high interest rates) in the hope that a devaluation will not take place, and that if it does, it does not occur soon. High interest rates in an exchange-rate crisis situation, then, is the natural market outcome of the interaction among speculators with different expectations who therefore take different positions. I should also add, incidentally, that in this context it is unclear the extent to which a "high interest rate defense of the currency," to use a very common expression, reflects a specific policy by the central bank or simply a market reaction. As a result, the process and the eventual resolution of an exchange rate crisis involves important transfers among speculators. Of course, transfers among speculators do not influence a government's fiscal position, and it is important to realize that references to huge gains made by some of those speculators (Mr. Soros and the British-pound crisis come to mind) do not necessarily imply that the counterpart of those gains are losses to the monetary authority.

The second—and more important—aspect is one in which the usual description of the effects of crises needs to be qualified by a consideration of what happens *after* the crisis is resolved, via either a devaluation or a successful defense of the parity. In both cases, and providing that the post-crisis policies are consistent, the central bank will be recovering its reserves, sometimes at nearly the precrisis levels. If this is the case, then, financial losses to the monetary authority would be limited to the loss of the interest on the reserves temporarily lost during the period of the crisis.[11]

I turn now to a brief comment on the conference papers on capital movements. The first (chapter 2, presented by Michael P. Dooley and coauthored with Carl E. Walsh) is the paper most specifically focused on capital controls and alternative policies to reduce the frequency and intensity of crises. The authors take the fruitful approach of drawing on the analogy between exchange rate crises and banking crises (on which there is a vast literature and the experience of long-dated traditional regulatory policies). They review first-, second-, and third-generation models of exchange rate crises, and observe that different, equally plausible models have widely different implications for crisis prevention or alleviation (i.e., for the justification of capital controls or other means of intervention). Next, drawing on the classic Diamond-Dybvig (1983) model among others, they review some of the proposed remedies in the banking literature, concluding that—perhaps with the exception of the temporary suspension of convertibility—none of those arguments make a strong case for controls. In considering the role of a lender of last resort, or deposit insurance, in the last part of their chapter they present an insurance model in which the negative effects of moral hazard take the concrete form of some well-defined financial transactions between domestic depositors and foreign investors, and conclude that, at least for the case of developing economies, a transaction tax on capital inflows can indeed be welfare enhancing. Of course, the limited role of these capital controls is to eliminate, at least partially, the moral hazard distortion introduced by deposit insurance—no minor accomplishment.

Chapter 3 ("Should We Fear Capital Flows?"), by René M. Stulz, is of a wider scope. It is, in my opinion, a masterful and authoritative guide to the benefits and costs of financial globalization. In a style that is at the same time clear and meticulous, the chapter discusses the benefits of financial globalization both for the case of perfect foresight and in the presence of risk, and points out that those benefits go well beyond the usual argument of allowing the encounter between savers and investors located in different countries. In its second section the chapter analyzes the costs of financial integration, asking first whether either equity or debt flows are destabilizing. This is particularly interesting, because most economists restrict their discussion to debt, rather than equity. The analysis concludes that short-term flows can indeed lead to crises, but it rejects the idea of controls on short-term flows as the appropriate response, not only on the basis of the unintended negative effects on expectations, but also from the viewpoint of business firms that find it impossible or too expensive to rely on long-term rather than short-term debt. The solution is, instead, to enhance the particular country's financial structure (prudential regulation, well-defined and quickly enforceable property rights, etc.). The chapter ends with a statement I find significant:

> The appropriate policies to eliminate the fragility of emerging economies are policies that foster better financial structures, so that long-term contracting can be supported. Such better financial structures *can neither be developed nor can they survive* in countries that choose to close their financial markets off from the rest of the world. [emphasis mine]

I find this sentence significant because it advances the hypothesis that even if stringent controls were advisable in the short-run, they carry the additional cost of delaying the implementation of long-run structural policies. I believe this hypothesis is rather plausible.

Guillermo A. Calvo contributes the fourth chapter in the volume and the last in the session on capital flows, also with a suggestive title in the form of a question: "Capital Flows or Capital Flaws?" Calvo reviews both some of the common misconceptions about recent crises and the real evidence, as well as some of the panic-driven recommendations induced by the suddenness and apparent lack of a common explanation for those crises. After a look at some of the reasons behind the explosion in capital inflows to emerging market (EM) economies during the 1990s—a fall in interest rates in the United States and, in the case of Latin America, the introduction of Brady bonds—it is shown how the existence of these bonds, in a framework with informed and uninformed investors, can lead to "a situation in which 'errors' in the capital market give rise to sudden and basically unjustified runs against EM securities." The extent of crises, though, would not have been so pronounced without the vulnerability and lack of strength of the financial sector in emerging economies. In considering palliatives or solutions, bailout packages get a qualified nod of approval in the chapter, with the reminder of a distinction that is often forgotten: Moral hazard problems are likely to develop for private creditors, but are much less likely for governments. The important point is to preclude (perhaps by the IMF, if it is in charge of the package) the government in question from "socializing" the debt, by indiscriminately transferring the rescue to private debtors. After discussing the problems of implementing monetary policy under floating rates—perhaps, more specifically, under an inflation-targeting scheme—the paper briefly considers the case for dollarization, which is found to be a more attractive alternative than many of the other exchange rate arrangements. Capital controls are seen as a recourse to be used, if at all, as an exceptional tool in times of "exuberant expectations," which at any rate are extremely difficult for the policy maker to diagnose on time. The author's own summary of his conclusions are, in a nutshell:

> The strategies underscored in this chapter are highly pro-market and pro-openness of financial markets, e.g., internationalization of the banking sector, lengthening of the maturity of public debt, and dollarization. Capital controls were not ruled out but they were deemed, at best, as transitory policies.

The summary continues with a sentence remarkably reminiscent of the paragraph by Stulz that I quoted before:

> If EMs have to rely on capital mobility controls on a more permanent basis, these controls are likely to eventually permeate the whole economy with highly detrimental effects.

Exchange Rate Regimes

The third theme of the conference, covered by the following two chapters, refers to exchange rate regimes, in particular as possible arrangements that could lessen the intensity and frequency of crises.

The academic and policy discussion on exchange rate regimes is extremely alive nowadays, both in terms of the general features of alternative systems as far as the manner in which they adjust to shocks, and in terms of their robustness to crises. Both the recurrence of puzzling exchange-rate and financial crises in the new world of high capital mobility, and important changes in how economists view macroeconomic phenomena (rational expectations and some of its implications, such as multiple equilibria and time inconsistency) are the driving forces behind this renewed interest.

Economists have been analyzing the differences among alternative exchange rate regimes for a long time—in particular the differences between fixed and floating regimes. Although the results of the analysis have differed depending on the degree of capital mobility, or on whether prices (in the classical view) or real income (in the Keynesian view), were adjusted, the conclusions of the traditional analysis seemed quite straightforward. In a fixed exchange rate system the monetary authority fixes the nominal exchange rate and (indirectly, since the price of tradable goods is directly linked to the exchange rate) the general price level. The adjustment to shocks then takes place through changes in the nominal money stock: An excess of nominal money, for example, brings about an initial balance-of-payments deficit; the central bank is then forced to sell foreign exchange to keep the exchange rate at the fixed parity, which automatically decreases the nominal money stock—and so the process continues until the excess supply of money has been eliminated. With perfect capital mobility the process can be very quick through the adjustment of financial assets; without it, it will take a longer time, through adjustment in the balance of trade (see, e.g., Auernheimer 1987 or Calvo 1987). There is then an automatic adjustment process, which is in fact identical to the process operating in a nation that uses the same money as the rest of the world—as in the case of the gold standard, for example. Strictly, then, there is no scope for monetary policy; an increase in the quantity of money will merely result, sooner or later (depending on the degree of capital mobility), in a loss of international reserves. Persistent attempts to maintain a money stock above the equilibrium level (driven, e.g., by the desire to decrease unemployment, or by the need to finance government expenditures via monetary expansion) will lead to a liquidation of international reserves and the need for devaluation. Under a floating exchange rate system, the monetary authority lets the exchange rate be determined by market conditions and controls the nominal money stock. In this case the adjustment to shocks takes place through changes in the exchange rate and, depending on the case, in prices or real income. One important general conclusion of the early conventional wisdom was that fixed exchange rates facilitated the propagation of shocks, both real and nominal, among nations in the same currency area (i.e., pegged to the same currency), whereas a floating system assured the maximum possible degree of independence.

Although many of the basics in this rather straightforward analysis remain correct, there are several important ways in which some of the traditional conclusions are currently being revisited and reexamined. In particular, and most relevant for some of the themes in the conference, much of the analysis addresses the question of how alternative exchange rate systems stand up to speculative attacks in an environment of high capital mobility. In a sense, then, the adoption of an exchange rate system based on this criterion allows the classification of a system as one of possible solutions (other solutions being the adoption of internal policies such as prudential regulation and the actions of international institutions) to problems that, together with their blessings, capital mobility can bring. This is basically the spirit of chapters 5 and 6, which analyze both the rationale and the experience of two Latin American economies under two polar-opposite regimes. Before commenting on these chapters, however, it seems relevant to elaborate on the general question of exchange rate systems, beginning with a very brief reference to the institutional environment.

The recent historical background can be contained in a nutshell. The Bretton Woods agreement of 1944, in establishing the IMF, opted for a fixed exchange rate system with a particular twist: individual countries would peg their currencies to the U.S. dollar, and the United States would peg the dollar to gold. After much agonizing, the official end of the mechanism came in the early 1970s; during the nearly twenty-five years that it lasted, the familiar story, at least for the developing countries, was one of cycles of monetary expansion incompatible with the fixed rate, followed by periodic devaluations. Another twenty-five years, approximately, have passed since the demise of the dollar standard, and today most European countries have given up their national currencies and adopted the Euro; many Latin American countries are pegged to the U.S. dollar in various degrees (soft pegs, as in the Bretton Woods agreement, hard pegs as currency boards, and in some cases direct dollarization); and the yen appears to have taken its place as the third important world currency.

An equally brief reference to some of the main conceptual issues, admittedly conforming to my own biases and preferences, could be attempted along the following lines.

Fixed versus Floating, or Rules versus Discretion?

The traditional polarity of a fixed versus a floating system is highly misleading for two reasons. First, a fixed exchange rate system is a sufficiently complete description of a set of policies, at least for as long as the central bank simultaneously abides by the rules of the system and abstains from trying to control other variables—that is, if it behaves as a currency board. A floating system is not a complete description, other than to say that the central bank does not set a fixed parity; to be complete, the description needs to specify which variable the central bank fixes or what rule it follows for deciding the value of those variables it can control. It is sometimes customary in economic analysis to assume that when the central bank does not control the exchange rate, it fixes a level or a path of the nominal money stock (i.e., it follows a monetary rule), as we assumed in our previous short description of the classical analysis of floating rates. This is not necessarily the case however—in fact, it seldom is—and in most discussions the question is left unanswered. Second, and more important from the viewpoint of interpreting some reactions to a hard peg such as a currency board (in particular among central bankers), one should note that such a hard peg is a rule (as opposed to a matter of discretion), whereas the insufficiently specified alternative of a floating system does not, by itself, necessarily imply the existence of a rule. Although economists often see another rule (such as a monetary rule of fixing a monetary aggregate) as the alternative to the exchange rate rule given by the fixed parity, policymakers often see the alternative not as a rule, but rather as a matter of discretion.[12] And, of course, policymakers—in particular central bankers—have a strong preference for discretion.

Two additional considerations should be made in connection with this point. First, as is clear from the analysis in several of the papers, although most recent crises have been exchange rate crises with an attack on the currency parity fixed by the central bank, banking crises can occur also under a system in which the exchange rate is left to be determined by the market. Second, if the alternative to the exchange rate rule is another hard rule (say, a monetary rule), it will also be possible for an attack on the rule to occur, forcing government to abandon the rule—a very close analogue, and with no less damaging effects, than the attack on the exchange rate that forces government to abandon the fixed parity (see, e.g., Auernheimer and George 2000).

Currency Areas, Currency Boards, and Dollarization

Currency areas, currency boards, and dollarization are variations on the single theme of fixing the value of a country's currency in terms of some other currency, and the adjustment process to real or nominal shocks proceeds in the same manner in all three of them—in short, as briefly described before, via changes in the nominal money stock. A *currency area* is simply an area (which can be integrated by more than one country) using the same money.[13] Under a *currency board* (which is nothing other than a hard peg, in which the central bank does not intervene other than in passively buying or selling foreign exchange at a fixed parity), the outflow (inflow) of nominal money takes place when it is retired (introduced) by the central bank when it needs to sell (buy) the foreign currency in order to preserve the parity. Within two countries in the same currency area (as with Texas and California, both using the dollar, or—in the near future—Italy and France, both using the euro) there is no central bank acting as an intermediary, and the inflow or outflow is direct. *Dollarization,* of course, is the colloquial expression for the process of a country's adoption (in most cases, unilaterally) of a foreign currency (often the U.S. dollar, hence the name) as its own money. The typical classroom example, for the case of Latin American economies, has been the case of Panama, which has been dollarized for many years. New examples in the same region are Ecuador, since 2000, and, more recently, El Salvador.

The classic argument for whether two or more countries should share the same currency is credited to Mundell (1961). The argument (a very elegant one, as with most of Mundell's work) can be easily summarized. There are gains for a group of individuals to use the same currency rather than several currencies, due to more efficient payment and exchange among individuals. On this account, the optimum currency area is the world, with all individuals using the same money. Monetary policy, however, is a useful instrument to counteract real shocks—a temporary fall in output brought about by a natural event or a fall in aggregate demand, for example. If we take regions to be subject to simultaneous real shocks in the same direction, then different regions will, by definition, be subject to shocks that are either unrelated or that go in opposite directions. Then, the monetary policy (expansionary or contractionary) that is appropriate for one region will not be adequate for another—in fact, it can be the opposite. From this viewpoint, then, the optimal currency area will be the region.[14]

If one demands a very high degree of correlation of shocks within a region, then the definition of a *region,* for which it would be appropriate to have an independent money (and therefore an independent monetary policy), can indeed be very narrow, and the resulting region very small. The design of optimum currency areas, then, needs to strike a balance between the benefits of a money used widely enough so as to take advantage of the exchange gains from using the same numéraire (unit of account) and the same medium of exchange, and the benefits of having a money narrowly tailored to the shock characteristics of regions. In the evaluation of the gains and losses of the EMU, for example, these arguments (among others) are still prominent in the discussion.

The current globalization of capital (and commodity) markets, and the recurrence of periodic crises, have revived the interest for countries adopting a hard peg by either establishing a currency board or dollarizing. Before commenting on such alternatives as compared to others, it seems appropriate to discuss briefly the differences between these two options. As mentioned before, a currency board is nothing other than a well-behaved central bank: the institution (whether called *currency board* or *central bank*) is prohibited from acquiring or selling assets other than monetary base or foreign currency, so that the practice of sterilization (i.e., counteracting the basic adjustment mechanism of changes in the money stock brought about by sales or purchases of foreign exchange via purchases or sales of domestic assets, such as government bonds) is eliminated. The central bank has only one "window": the foreign exchange window.[15] Dollarization brings about the same adjustment mechanism, except that the same currency flows in and out of the country without the exchange intermediation of the central bank. However, there are three distinct differences between the two arrangements.

The first difference is that a country that adopts a foreign currency as its own loses *seigniorage,* i.e., the real revenues derived from the creation of fiat money that costs nothing to produce. Roughly, a measure of such loss is the flow of interest payments received from the holding of international reserves. One of the papers presented at the conference (Guidotti and Powell's discussion of the experience of Argentina with its ten-year-old currency board [chapter 5]) performs a calculation of those losses. The losses to the country would accrue as gains to the country issuing the currency to be used. Of course, if dollarization were to come about not unilaterally, but as a result of an agreement, then in the case of Argentina the United States could share in those gains.[16]

The second difference is that dollarization would imply the loss of the lender of last resort—i.e., the ability of the central bank to lend to commercial banks in times of liquidity crises in order to avoid a collapse of the banking system.[17] Increasingly, the profession is beginning to take this argument with a grain of salt, and correctly so. Banking crises, in most cases, have a heavy insolvency component besides their pure liquidity character, and the eventual bailing out of banks involves a transfer of resources. If the monetary authorities are going to implement such a transfer, it is far preferable that the transfer be financed via borrowing (and eventually via taxation) rather than via monetary expansion (the inflation tax). The former is far more transparent and the subsidy component of the transfer is made clear, and it is of course preferable from the view of price stability. Indeed, an initial banking crisis often extends to an exchange rate crisis because it is anticipated that the bailout will be financed via monetary expansion (the "socialization of private debt" mentioned in Calvo's presentation). The arrangement of contingent international credit lines (as those negotiated in Argentina) offer a healthy possibility, and one could even argue that the loss of the lender of last resort may be seen as a benefit of dollarization.

The third, and probably most important, difference between a currency board and dollarization is the removal, in the case of the latter, of *country risk*—i.e., the risk that, even though a currency board (and often the parity) is created by law, the law could be changed, or convertibility suspended, or the parity changed unexpectedly, with the resulting capital losses. Dollarization could also be reversed, of course, but at least as far as holdings of high-powered money (currency) are concerned, there would be no capital loss.[18] The chapter by Guidotti and Powell contains some estimates, which are certainly not negligible, of the gains that the elimination of this risk would entail in the case of Argentina.

The current discussion of the benefits and costs of a hard peg, either through a currency board or through dollarization, centers on one of Mundell's themes—the loss of the ability to use monetary policy as a countercyclical device—and, fundamentally, on the gains in credibility. There is a rather generalized agreement on two points: first, that the hard peg requires a consistent set of fundamentals (i.e., the elimination of the need for inflationary finance); and second, that a hard fix can be an appropriate device for a stabilization program that, satisfying the previous condition, is imposed in a country with a history of high inflation, and probably one that has experienced a recent hyperinflation.

The question of the loss of the ability to conduct monetary policy is a coin with two faces: on one side, the fact that the record of most developing economies as far as the conduct of monetary policy is dismal; and on the other, that the loss can in fact be an advantage. The chapter by Guidotti and Powell discuss these arguments in detail.

Floating Rates

The rationale for floating exchange rates, of course, is the reverse of the arguments used in favor of hard pegs: the possibility of using monetary policy, and the avoidance of exchange rate crises—although, as argued earlier, banking crises are still perfectly possible, and attacks on whatever rule the monetary authority has set can also take place.

Chapter 6, by Agustín Carstens (coauthored with Guillermo Ortiz Martinez), makes a strong argument for the polar opposite arrangement—floating rates, with an inflation target implemented via the control of short-term interest rates. This is the regime followed by Mexico following its 1994–95 crisis. The diagnosis? So far, so good. The paper is not only an excellent analysis of the more general aspects of the system, but also a lucid exposition of the operational methods used by the central bank (Bank of Mexico). Concerning inflation targeting, however, one could meaningfully argue that the procedure boils down to something essentially quite similar to a soft peg in disguise. In principle, inflation targeting consists of adjusting the monetary variable to be controlled (most directly, a monetary aggregate; or, as in the case of Mexico, indirectly, using short-term interest rates as a means to affect the monetary aggregate) following the behavior of prices. Since it is obvious, however, that there is a very close link between the exchange rate and the price level (both directly, through the price of tradable goods, and indirectly, via the effects of exchange rate behavior on inflationary expectations), then the quantity of money will change in the same direction as it would in the case in which the exchange rate is being pegged. As expressed by Calvo,

> Inflation targeting deserves a brief comment, given its increasing popularity. Is this system very different than a fixed exchange rate? The answer is *no*. With a fixed exchange rate, the target is the exchange rate; under inflation targeting, the target is a price level, that is, the "exchange rate" of a basket of commodities. If foreign exchange were the only component of that basket, the two systems would be identical. In practice, of course, they are not, and that is why the exchange rate fluctuates. *But this is a system very different than the textbook version of free floating, in which the anchor is the quantity of money.* . . . To the extent that the movement is toward inflation targeting, it is a bit misleading to say that we are moving toward more floating. (Calvo 2000; my translation from Spanish, and my emphasis)

The argument is reinforced (as pointed out in Calvo and Reinhart 2000) by the empirical evidence that countries under a floating regime exhibit what the authors aptly call *fear of floating*—i.e., an evident reluctance to let the exchange rate freely move beyond some well-defined boundaries.

The (apparent) Consensus on "Bipolarity"

There seems to be emerging at least a limited consensus, both in academic works and in policy discussions, about the undesirability of mixed systems (soft pegs not backed by a firm and demonstrable commitment to the parity, crawling pegs, and the like): the regime should be either a hard fix (currency board, dollarization) or a pure float.[19] There are some indications that this consensus may be shared by some of the officials of the IMF, albeit with many qualifications, even after some previous speculation on the need for an exit strategy away from currency boards. The problem, in my opinion, is that such dichotomy (perhaps a prettier name than *bipolarity*) does not resolve the basic omission pointed out in the first paragraph of this section—that floating, per se, does not define a regime or a policy prescription, unless there is a definition of what variable the monetary authority is going to control and how (i.e., unless there is some well-defined rule).

The Role of International Financial Institutions

The final theme of the conference is the role of international financial institutions, in particular the IMF, as representative of the second type of solution or remedy for the blues from capital flows. The topic is covered by two contributions: Charles W. Calomiris's chapter 7 on blueprints for a new global architecture, and the roundtable (and ensuing discussion). The two complement one another rather well because, in the latter, the discussion focuses on current proposals for changes in the scope and operational rules of the IMF, at the center of which is the report of the International Financial Institutions Advisory Commission, of which Calomiris was a member and Allan H. Meltzer, one of the panelists, its chairman. The report, which received wide attention among economists, policymakers, and the specialized press, had been released shortly before the conference. In addition, the panel of the roundtable, moderated by Guillermo A. Calvo, was integrated by two highly visible members of the financial community—T. Britton Harris, chief executive officer at GTE Investment Management, and John P. Lipsky, chief economist at the Chase Manhattan Bank and former official at the IMF—and by Matthew Bishop, finance editor of *The Economist*.

Both the Calomiris chapter and the presentations at the roundtable, as well as the discussion that followed, make their points very clearly, and in a sense most of the arguments go back, in one form or the other, to the points covered in the previous papers and in this introduction. It is natural for this to be the case because whatever the functions of the IMF, they need to be dependent on the answers to more basic questions, such as the reasons for crises, the distinction between liquidity and solvency, the importance of domestic institutions and resilient domestic financial markets, and the role of a lender of last resort (LOLR).

The set of proposals in chapter 6 (which to a large extent coincides with the Meltzer Commission's recommendations) is of course one of several others that have been put forward in the immediate past and will undoubtedly continue to be; the reader may wish to consult some works that contain some of these proposals and that review others.[20] In planning the conference, and hence this volume, we opted to give more in-depth coverage to the Calomiris-cum-Meltzer-Commission rather than try to strike a balance either with one paper serving as a survey or with the set of papers reflecting alternative views. We made this choice for three reasons: first, because of the physical impossibility, in a conference format, of the latter option; second, because of the existence of some excellent existing papers surveying previous proposals; and third, because of the public attention, and prospects for at least partial implementation, received by the report of the Meltzer Commission. Additionally, we hope that both the Calomiris chapter and the discussion at the roundtable will be an important source for the reader (scholar or otherwise) seeking clarification and further elaboration of some of the less evident points raised in that report.

Two additional pieces may serve the reader as references concerning other proposals for the reform of international financial institutions. The first is Goldstein (1999), containing the Report of the Independent Task Force sponsored by the Council on Foreign Relations. Some of the six final recommendations in this report coincide with the conclusions of various chapters in this volume, and a few with those in the Meltzer report. The second, dated after the conference, is the proposal of an international bankruptcy court by Anne O. Krueger, first deputy managing director at the IMF (Krueger 2001); the position occupied by Krueger suggests, even though this paper is not an official proposal, that the idea probably marshals some support at the institution.

Conclusion

Reading the conference papers and the roundtable discussion suggests a series of conclusions that seem to have been the consensus at the conference. The reader of this volume is eventually the one to judge precisely what those conclusions are, but at the risk of introducing my own personal inter-pretations, my appraisal of the conclusions would include the following.

1. With different degrees of intensity, all presenters conclude that capital controls are not an answer to the crisis problem, except in very extreme circumstances and under conditions of credibility about their transitory nature. One exception is the treatment of the insurance model ana-lyzed by Dooley, but this seems to be a rather special case in the sense that a tax on capital inflows (which in itself would generate a distortion) is geared to counteract the moral-hazard distortion brought about by deposit insurance or an assured LOLR;

2. A sound domestic financial structure is of paramount importance. Al-though this is explicitly recognized in all the chapters, the point is made more explicitly and with the most force the chapters by Stulz and Calvo;

3. Hybrid or intermediate exchange regimes should not be adopted—i.e., the bipolar paradigm also seems to have a consensus among the partic-ipants to the conference, although some doubts about the true nature of inflation targeting seem to linger (for Calvo, and—less importantly—for me);

4. The functions of LOLR of either central banks (in the case of banking crises) or the IMF (in the case of exchange rate crises) seem to be ac-ceptable and necessary to preserve (even in the new structure of the IMF as envisioned by the Advisory Commission), although with very different degrees of qualification, in particular given the problem of moral hazard; and

5. The IMF has a role to perform, but in the opinion of some, such a role should be far more limited and subject to very transparent ex ante rules.

Notes

1. The "appearance" of new countries opened to trade, by itself, will in general make it possible for all countries to be better off than before.

2. The interested reader may profit by consulting Dooley (1996) as background material.

3. The International Financial Institutions Advisory Commission was insti-tuted by an act of the United States Congress with the purpose of studying the role and mechanisms of the main institutions (the IMF, the World Bank of Re-construction and Development, the International Finance Corporation, and the regional development banks of which the United States is a member).

4. Note that the distinction is not important in the case of banking crises, but simply that it is much more straightforward and always acknowledged.

5. Indeed, restrictions on international capital movements are sometimes an attempt by government to delay the resolution of the policy inconsistency. This is, at the international level, exactly the equivalent of the internal financial repression so prevalent in some developing economies, taking the form of control on interest rates.

6. See below for some remarks on the significance of the loss of this domestic lender of last resort when a country opts for dollarization.

7. It is both analytically convenient and realistic, in these analyses, to think of government and the central bank as a unified entity.

8. This is the case first analyzed in Calvo (1988).

9. Notice that the notion of contagion does not refer to the case in which a solvency crisis in one country may effectively bring about insolvency in another—either via financial channels or due, perhaps, to close trading partners among which a recession could be quickly transmitted. The emphasis in the case of contagion is that, regardless of whether the crisis is justified in the first country, it is in principle not justified in the second. As expressed in Stulz's chapter, "It is important to distinguish between contagion that rationally takes place as the price mechanism works its way to digest shocks to fundamentals and contagion that cannot be justified based on fundamentals."

10. Such an analysis should include, of course, the costs of a policy of "defending the parity with a policy of high interest rates." See below for some remarks on how misleading this expression may be.

11. Consider, for example, the case of the Bank of England following the crisis of October 1992. Just prior to the crisis, reserves were at a level of approximately $43 billion. In three months, during the continuance of the crisis, they fell to around $38 billion, and continued at that level for about a year. At the beginning of 1994 they began climbing steadily, to reach a level comparable to the precrisis level by the end of 1994.

Of course, I am talking in this section about financial gains and losses to the monetary authority. A different kind of loss brought about by crises, and probably the most important one, is the disruption of and eventual fall in output in the real sector.

12. Indeed, empirical works trying to classify stabilization programs according to whether they were based on an exchange rate anchor or a monetary anchor have failed to detect cases in which the latter really existed, despite the frequent use of the label. See, for example, Calvo and Végh (2000).

13. When the currency area includes more than one country, it is sometimes called a *monetary union*—the European Monetary Union (EMU), for example.

14. In his original paper, Mundell's example was that of Canada and the United States, with the Eastern region of both countries being subject to the same shocks, and the Western region of both being subject to opposite shocks.

15. As always, the institutional reality is a bit more involved, but the basic mechanism is essentially as just described.

16. In fact, at the time of this writing there is a proposal in the United States Senate (Senator Connie Mack's proposal) in which the United States would indeed share its gain in seigniorage.

17. Strictly, this would also be the case under a currency board. In reality, how-

ever, the currency board has some limited possibilities to increase the money supply when needed, for example, by reducing reserve requirements (this is, indeed, one of the instruments used in Argentina in 1995, when due to the tequila effect bank deposits were reduced by a considerable amount).

18. Of course, deposits could be frozen, or redeemable at a changed parity, but this would be tantamount to confiscation, with still a higher political cost.

19. For an excellent account on this point, see Fischer (2001).

20. In particular, see Eichengreen (1999a,b).

References

Aizenman, Joshua. 1989. Country risk, incomplete information, and taxes on international borrowing. *The Economic Journal* 99:147–61.

Auernheimer, Leonardo. 1987. On the outcome of inconsistent programs under monetary and exchange rate rules. *Journal of Monetary Economics* 19 (March): 279–305.

Auernheimer, Leonardo, and Susan George. 2000. Bad dreams under alternative anchors: Are the consequences different? *International Monetary Fund Working Paper* 00/20.

Bardhan, P. K. 1967. Optimum foreign borrowing. In *Essays on the theory of optimal economic growth,* ed. Karl Shell, 235–53. Cambridge: MIT Press.

Calvo, Guillermo A. 1987. Balance of payments crises in a cash-in-advance economy. *Journal of Money, Credit, and Banking* 19 (1): 19–32.

———. 1988. Servicing the public debt: The role of expectations. *American Economic Review* 78 (4): 647–61.

———. 2000. Política económica en aguas Borrascosas: Vulnerabilidad financiera en economías emergentes. Lecture delivered as recipient of the King Juan Carlos of Spain Prize in Economics, October, Madrid. Available online at [http://www.bsos.umd.edu/econ/ciecalvo.htm].

Calvo, Guillermo A., and Enrique Mendoza. 1998. Rational contagion and the globalization of securities markets. *Journal of International Economics* 51 (1): 79–113.

Calvo, Guillermo A., and Carmen M. Reinhart. 2000. Fear of floating. NBER Working Paper no. 7993. Cambridge: National Bureau of Economic Research, November.

Calvo, Guillermo A., and Carlos A. Végh. 1999. Inflation stabilization and balance of payments crises in developing countries. In *Handbook of macroeconomics,* vol. 1C, ed. John B. Taylor and Michael Woodford, 1531–614. Amsterdam: North Holland Elsevier.

Diamond, Douglas, and Philip Dybvig. 1983. Bank runs, deposit insurance, and liquidity. *Journal of Political Economy* 91:401–19.

Dooley, Michael P. 1996. A survey of literature on controls over international capital transactions. *IMF Staff Papers* 43 (4): 639–87.

Eichengreen, Barry. 1999a. Policy-making in an integrated world: From surveillance to . . . ? In *Rethinking the international monetary system,* ed. Jane Sneddon Little and Giovanni P. Olivei, 205–26. Boston: Federal Reserve Bank of Boston.

————. 1999b. Toward a new international financial architecture: A practical post-Asia agenda. Washington, D.C.: Institute for International Economics.

Fischer, Stanley. 2001. Exchange rate regimes: Is the bipolar view correct? Distinguished lecture delivered at the Meetings of the American Economic Association, 6 January, New Orleans, La.

Goldstein, Morris. 1999. Safeguarding prosperity in a global financial system: The future international financial architecture. Report of the Independent Task Force, sponsored by the Council on Foreign Relations. Washington, D.C.: Institute for International Economics, September.

Krueger, Anne O. 2001. International financial architecture for 2002: A new approach to sovereign debt restructuring. Address given to the National Economists' Club annual members' dinner. American Enterprise Institute, 26 November, Washington, D.C.

Krugman, Paul. 1979. A model of balance of payments crises. *Journal of Money, Credit, and Banking* 11 (3): 311–25.

————. 1996. Are currency crises self-fulfilling? *NBER macroeconomics annual 1996,* ed. Ben S. Bernanke and Julio Rotemberg, 345–78. Cambridge: MIT Press.

Mundell, Robert A. 1961. A theory of optimum currency areas. *American Economic Review* 51 (November): 509–17.

Obstfeld, Maurice. 1994. The logic of currency crises. *Cashiers Economiques et Monétaires* 43:189–213.

————. 1996. Models of currency crises with self-fulfilling features. *European Economic Review* 40:1037–48.

Chapter One

The Globalization of International Financial Markets: What Can History Teach Us?

Michael D. Bordo

Introduction

Globalization has become the buzzword of the new millennium. It is viewed both as the cause of many of the world's problems and as a panacea. The debate over globalization has been manifested in public demonstrations against the World Trade Organization (WTO) in Seattle in the fall of 1999 and against the International Monetary Fund (IMF) and the World Bank earlier. It also has led to a spate of both scholarly and not-so-scholarly books on the subject (e.g., Friedman 1999; Soros 1998; O'Rourke and Williamson 1999; Davis and Gallman 2000).

Until three years ago, economists' consensus view on the international integration of financial markets was very positive. The benefits of open capital markets that have been stressed include optimal international resource allocation, intertemporal optimization, international portfolio diversification, and discipline on policy makers (see Obstfeld 1995). However, the recent spate of crises in Latin America and Asia has led some to argue that the costs of complete liberalization of financial markets for emerging countries may outweigh the benefits (Rodrick 1998; Cooper 1998, 1999).

This chapter focuses on the globalization of financial markets from the historical perspective of the past 120 years. In the next section, "The Dimensions of Capital Market Integration," I summarize the empirical evidence on the international integration of financial markets from 1880 to the present, based primarily on my research with Barry Eichengreen and on the research of Maurice Obstfeld and Alan Taylor. This research shows

Michael D. Bordo is professor of economics and director of the Center for Monetary and Financial History at Rutgers University and a research associate of the National Bureau of Economic Research.

that globalization has followed a U-shaped pattern for both stocks and net flows of foreign investment relative to gross domestic product (GDP) over the period 1880–1998. The ratios of both stocks and net flows of foreign investment relative to GDP in the period before World War I were comparable to or even higher than today's, collapsing to almost negligible magnitudes in the interwar and post–World War II periods, then recovering from the early 1970s to the high levels observed today.

In "Explanations for the Historical Pattern of Financial Market Integration," I consider whether the globalization of financial markets is indeed much more pervasive today than it was before 1914, noting that although net flows relative to GDP may be less today than pre-1914, the markets are broader and deeper. The greater extent of globalized capital markets today largely reflects institutional innovations' overcoming the barriers of asymmetric information.

The flip side of open capital markets for emerging economies is the problem of financial crises—the pattern of lending booms and busts, massive capital inflows and equally massive reversals. This was a problem in the earlier golden age of liberal capital markets, and is once again today. In "Financial Crises Then and Now," I examine the evidence on the incidence and severity of financial crises (currency crises, banking crises, and twin crises) before 1914 and since 1973. The record suggests that crises are slightly worse, on average, for today's emergers than those of the past, although there were several famous episodes where the collapse in output greatly exceeded the recent experience of the Asian tigers. Explanations for this pattern include the international monetary regime followed (the classical gold standard) and institutional differences (the advent of lenders of last resort and the international financial institutions).

Crises in both golden ages led to international rescues. In the earlier period they were arranged between advanced-country central banks by private investment bankers, whereas today they are arranged by international financial institutions. In addition to a change in the character of the lenders, as I discuss in "International Rescues," the nature of the loans has changed from relatively small amounts to cover temporary current-account shortfalls to today's much larger packages to cover massive capital outflows.

An offshoot of the recent crisis problem is a backlash in favor of shutting off or slowing down the process of capital market liberalization. This is discussed in "Globalization, Crises, and Backlash." Many have argued for the reimposition of capital controls (some on inflows, others on outflows) while others favor the sequencing of liberalization for those countries that are still not completely open. The evidence, both contemporary and historical, on the effects of capital market liberalization and controls on growth and welfare is mixed.

The debate over capital controls is part of the more general debate on globalization. O'Rourke and Williamson (1999) provide comprehensive and convincing evidence that the integration of capital, labor, and goods markets in the 1870–1913 period led to factor price equalization as well as the convergence of real wages and real per capita incomes in the Atlantic economy. This process led to a political backlash in the early decades of the twentieth century in Europe and the Americas in the form of tariff protection, restrictions on migration, and growing nationalism. A backlash against capital movements followed in the 1930s in an attempt to protect monetary sovereignty. The question arises whether similar forces are at work today.

The paper concludes with some policy lessons from the historical record. The benefits of financial market integration are long-run whereas the costs of financial crises are short-run phenomena. The role for policy is to provide an environment for markets to work efficiently and to allow private capital flows to seek their best use in an unfettered manner. Such an environment can mitigate the incidence of crises but not prevent them entirely. In that eventuality there may be a role for the emergency provision of liquidity on classical Bagehotian lines.

The Dimensions of Capital Market Integration

In this section I review the empirical literature on financial market integration from 1880 to the present.[1]

Stocks

Recently, Obstfeld and Taylor (1998, 2001) have compiled the existing data on the stocks of foreign assets relative to world GDP as well as foreign liabilities relative to GDP at benchmark years over the period from 1825 to the present. The sample of countries covered before 1914 are many of today's advanced countries and a number of other countries. The picture portrayed by this data, although it is fragmentary for the early years, is of a U-shaped pattern. At its pre-1914 peak, the share of foreign assets to world GDP was approximately 20 percent. It declined from that level to a low of 5 percent in 1945 with the pre-1914 level not being reattained until 1985. Since then it has risen to 57 percent. A similar picture emerges from the ratio of liabilities to world GDP.[2]

The British held the lion's share of overseas investments in 1914, 50 percent, followed by France at 22 percent, Germany at 17 percent, the Netherlands at 3 percent, and the United States at 6.5 percent. This compares with the United States' holding global foreign assets in 1995 at 24 percent. These funds in turn represented up to one-half of the capital stock of one of the major debtors (Argentina) and close to one-fifth for Australia and Canada.

Finally, the gross asset and liability positions were very close to net positions before 1914, in contrast to today, when (for example) the United States is both a major creditor and debtor. This reflects the prevalence of unidirectional long-term investment from the core countries of Europe to the countries of new settlement.

Net Capital Flows

The fifty years before World War I saw massive flows of capital from the core countries of western Europe to the overseas regions of recent settlement (mainly the rapidly developing Americas and Australasia).[3] At its peak, the outflow from Britain reached 9 percent of gross national product (GNP) and was almost as high in France, Germany, and the Netherlands (Bairoch and Kozul-Wright 1996).[4] Private capital moved essentially without restriction. Much of it flowed into bonds financing railroads and other infrastructure investments and into long-term government debt.[5] Figure 1.1 shows five-year moving averages of the mean absolute value of the ratio of the current account balance to GDP for twelve countries.[6] Figure 1.2 shows current account balances for one large capital exporter (the United Kingdom), one large capital importer (Canada), and the largest "emerging market" (the United States).[7] A striking feature of these data is the size and persistence of current account deficits in the pre-1914 period, especially in Australia, Canada, Argentina, and the Nordic countries, and of the current account surpluses of the United Kingdom and France.[8]

For comparison, figure 1.3 shows the mean absolute value of the ratio of current account to GDP for twenty-three of today's emerging markets (countries whose GDP exceeded $30 billion and were classified as indebted countries by the World Bank) using data from the IMF's *International Financial Statistics* for the period 1949–96.[9] These countries have been running current account imbalances under the recent managed float averaging 4.1 percent of their GDPs, which is similar to the average for the prewar sample of 3.9 percent, which includes both capital importers and exporters.[10]

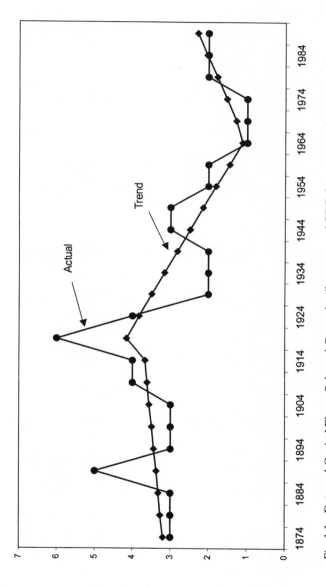

Fig. 1.1   External Capital Flows, Selected Countries (in percent of GDP, five-year moving averages)
SOURCE:
See the data appendix in Bordo, Eichengreen, and Kim (1998).

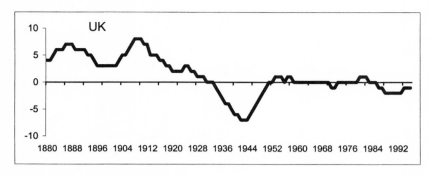

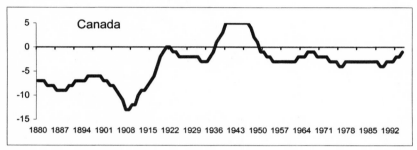

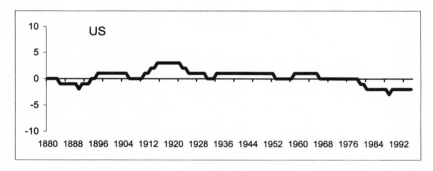

Fig. 1.2 Ratio of the Current Account to GDP, Selected Major Countries
SOURCE:
See the data appendix in Bordo, Eichengreen, and Kim (1998).

Capital flows for the thirteen prewar countries are also considerably less variable (the standard deviation in 1880–1913 was 2.7 percent, versus 4.1 percent under the managed floating regime). In the interwar period, Group 1 countries' current account ratios were about as variable (standard deviation of 3.8 percent) as for the Group 2 countries under the float

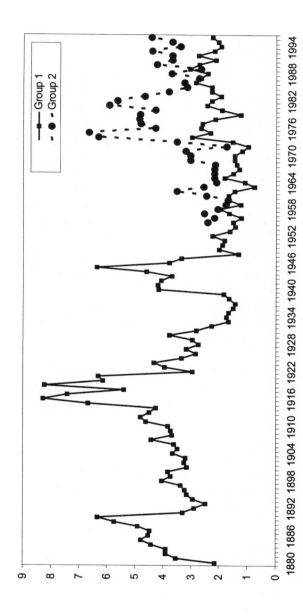

Fig. 1.3 Ratio of the Current Account to GDP Mean of Absolute Values
SOURCE:
See the data appendix in Bordo, Eichengreen, and Kim (1998).

(standard deviation of 4.1 percent; see Bordo, Eichengreen, and Kim 1998, tables 1–2).

Savings-Investment Correlations

A widely used measure of financial integration is the correlation between national savings and investment rates. In a 1980 article, Feldstein and Horioka argued that if international capital markets are well integrated, this correlation should be low because investment can be financed by foreign capital flows. Their regression results for the 1960s and 1970s found a high coefficient from regressing the investment rate on the savings rate for a cross-section of Organization for Economic Cooperation and Development (OECD) countries.[11] They interpreted this as evidence of low capital mobility in a period when conventional wisdom posited the opposite. An enormous literature followed, some of it historical.[12] Bayoumi (1990) extended the Feldstein-Horioka approach to the classical gold standard, finding a much lower correlation and inferring from this that capital markets were better integrated prior to 1913. Similar results are provided by Zevin (1992). Eichengreen (1992) uses a larger sample of countries and concludes in favor of lower overall capital mobility than Bayoumi, although even in his extended data set the correlation of national savings and investment rates is significantly below that reported by Feldstein and Horioka.[13]

Recent research by Taylor (1996) and by Obstfeld and Taylor (1998) goes some way toward reconciling these findings for different periods and samples. Using data for twelve countries from 1850 to 1992, Taylor's estimated coefficients trace out an inverted U shape over time. On this basis he concludes that capital markets were well integrated before 1914, that they then ceased to be so except in the short period of time during which the interwar gold-exchange standard prevailed, and that they have become gradually more integrated since the 1950s, with coefficients in the 1990s again reaching the levels of the pre-1914 period (see fig. 1.4).[14]

Covered Interest Parity

Another indicator of capital mobility is a comparison between interest rates on assets in different financial centers.[15] Marston (1993, 1995) presents evidence based on this approach for key advanced countries following the demise of the Bretton Woods system. Obstfeld and Taylor (1998) apply his methods to the longer period from 1870 to 1990 for the United

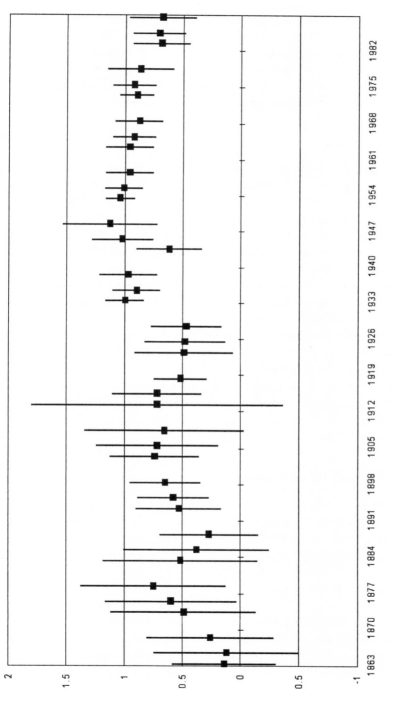

Fig. 1.4 The Feldstein-Horoika Coefficient in History (FH coefficient ±2 standard errors)
SOURCE:
Taylor (1996), table 3.

States and the United Kingdom. As reproduced in figure 1.5, their results, based on sixty-day bank bills and other instruments, indicate a negligible differential in the years before 1914. A similar pattern is observed under Bretton Woods in the 1960s and again in the most recent decade.[16]

Thus, these results are consistent with the null of relatively high levels of financial integration both prior to 1914 and recently.

Real Interest Parity

A more stringent test is real interest parity, which requires both uncovered interest parity and purchasing power parity (Obstfeld 1995). A recent study by Lothian (1995) of divergences in ex post short-term and long-term real interest rates for a panel of ten countries from 1880 to 1995 finds low divergence under the classical gold standard, Bretton Woods, and the recent float alike, but the lowest divergence is in the most recent ten years of the float.

Deviations from real interest parity are shown in panel A of figure 1.6, which plots the dispersion (standard deviation) of annual ex post real long-term bond yields for our sample of twelve countries from 1870 to 1994.[17] Panel B presents a similar calculation using monthly data on the ex ante real interest rate for short-term securities (three-month bank bills) for the four core countries of the gold standard (United Kingdom, United States, France, Germany).[18] A similar pattern is observed for long-term securities. Both figures show clear evidence of capital market integration before World War I and in the most recent decade, bracketing a period of massive disintegration.

Other Dimensions of Financial Market Integration

Gross versus Net Flows   Although integration measured in terms of net capital flows as a percentage of GDP is quite similar in the post-1975 and pre-1914 periods, gross flows are greater today. Bank for International Settlements (BIS) data on turnover in the foreign exchange market suggest that gross flows are in the range of $1.25 trillion a day, or more than $250 trillion a year (see BIS 1997).

Short-Term versus Long-Term Capital Flows   It is not possible to compile the data to give a clear picture of the long-run pattern of the breakdown between short-term and long-term capital flows. According to

Percent Per Annum

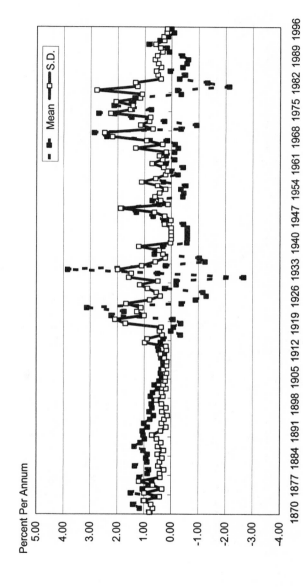

Fig. 1.5 Nominal Interest Parity Since 1870 (U.S.-U.K. covered domestic interest differential, annual)

SOURCE:

Obstfeld and Taylor (1998), table 11.2.

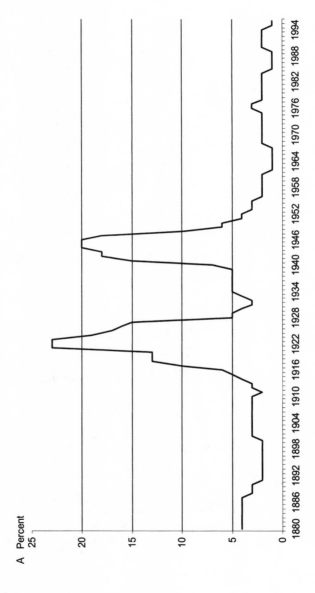

A   Percent

B Percent

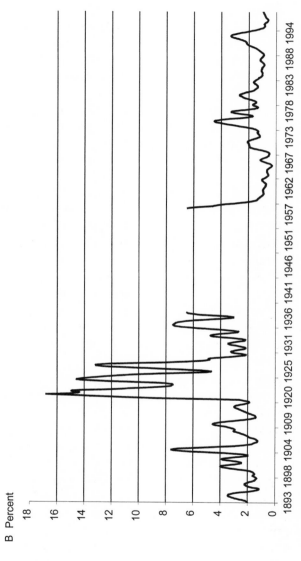

1893 1898 1904 1909 1920 1925 1931 1936 1941 1946 1951 1957 1962 1967 1973 1978 1983 1988 1994

Fig. 1.6 Dispersion of Real (CPI) Interest Rates: Panel A, Long-Term, Ex Post Rates, Group 1 Annual Data, Five-Year Moving Averages; Panel B, Short-Term, Ex Ante Real Rates, Group 4 Monthly Data, Eleven-Month Moving Averages

SOURCE:

See the data appendix in Bordo, Eichengreen, and Kim (1998).

Bloomfield (1963) and Wilkins (1998), based on the very limited data on commercial bank foreign obligations and on official reserve movements, short-term capital flows, while crucial to the adjustment mechanism of the classical gold standard, were small relative to the long-term capital movements. In the interwar period, limited data in United Nations (UN; 1949) and Nurkse's (1944) narrative suggests that short-term capital movements during the turbulent years of the 1930s swamped long-term movements. In the postwar Bretton Woods period in the presence of capital controls, private short-term capital flows were limited. Of greater importance were changes in official reserves to accommodate balance-of-payments disequilibrium. Since 1971 short-term capital movements, especially bank loans, have increased in size and importance (Kregel 1994). However, because many short-term bank credits are routinely rolled over, it is difficult to make the distinction between short-term and long-term capital movements.

The Composition of Foreign Investment   Although data on the composition of pre-1914 portfolio investment are incomplete, probably the best (although still limited) estimates are those for Great Britain, the leading creditor of the period. (British investors held about 50 percent of the stock of long-term foreign investments outstanding in 1913 according to conventional estimates. In terms of composition, there is no reason to think that Britain is grossly unrepresentative.) These estimates suggest that, circa 1913, fully 30 percent of British overseas investments in quoted securities were in the issues of governments and municipalities, 40 percent in railways, 10 percent in resource-extracting industries (mainly mining), and 5 percent in public utilities.[19]

Fishlow (1985) summarizes the conventional wisdom on this subject as follows. In the overseas regions of recent settlement to which the bulk of European lending flowed, external resources were invested in infrastructure projects which enhanced the borrowing country's capacity to export. Foreign funds were used to construct port facilities, railway networks, and other internal improvements. At the same time, the lending countries (particularly Britain) provided open markets for the raw materials and agricultural commodities produced and exported by these newly settled regions.[20] In this way, foreign borrowing generated a stream of export revenues sufficient to service and repay the borrowed funds.

Governments, too, had voracious appetites for external finance. A nonnegligible share of public spending took the form of subsidies for the construction of railways and infrastructure projects, but governments which

Table 1.1   Bank and Bond-Market Lending to Emerging Markets

Functional Sectors	Number of Bonds	Value of Bonds (US$ millions)	Number of Loans	Amount of Loans (US$ millions)
Central bank	77	18,155.85	147	24,897.091
Other government	368	128,080.44	294	39,121.941
Infrastructure investment	385	67,695.01	879	110,844.658
oil, coal, gas	153	28,047.07	315	56,226.715
energy-utility	107	21,951.10	233	30,414.017
others	125	17,623.310	331	24,203.918
Mining	10	664.04	87	10,717.272
Finance (banks, etc.)	1,302	161,610.12	1,769	132,049.471
Manufacturing	415	38,504.02	946	66,996.553
Service	241	26,261.95	867	76,545.381
Total	3,183	508,592.91	5,868	572,017.017

SOURCE: See Bordo, Eichengreen, and Irwin (1999).

borrowed abroad typically did so (as Fishlow emphasizes) not to finance public investment but to underwrite public consumption.

Data for portfolio capital flows to emerging markets in the 1990s paint a different picture. Bordo, Eichengreen, and Irwin (1999) tabulated these by recipient sector for both bank lending and bonds from Capital Data's Bankware (see table 1.1). Admittedly, one way of reading these figures is "the more things change, the more they remain the same." To many readers, however, they will suggest the growing importance of lending to the financial-services sector (banks, etc.), to enterprises producing commercial services, and to manufacturing.

Debt versus Equity   The relative importance of debt and equity has changed, reflecting the recent expansion of emerging stock markets. The most recent issue of the World Bank's *Global Development Finances* estimates that stocks and bonds are now of roughly equal importance. Prior to 1913, the vast majority of portfolio capital flows took the form of bonds, not equity.

Portfolio versus Direct Investment   The balance between portfolio and foreign direct investment (FDI) has changed. Whereas today direct investment is as important as portfolio investment, this was not the case before 1914. According to O'Rourke and Williamson (1999), 79 percent of

British investment to Latin America was in this form, and 85 percent to Australia and North America. In contrast, since World War II direct investment has consistently exceeded portfolio investment. Although securities markets have grown explosively in recent years, around half of all capital flowing to emerging markets is still in the form of direct investment.

The Nature of Foreign Direct Investment   The nature of FDI has also changed. Before 1914, according to Wilkins (1998), FDI was undertaken mainly by free-standing companies—companies incorporated in the United Kingdom, France, Belgium, and a few other Western European countries for the purpose of investing and doing business in an emerging market.[21] These enterprises proliferated in mining, agriculture, and transportation, as in the cases of, inter alia, Rio Tinto and the Suez Canal Company. Today, in contrast, FDI is done through multinational enterprises, whose operations involve the extension across borders not only of financial capital but of the firm's preexisting managerial and productive capabilities.[22]

Explanations for the Historical Pattern of Financial Market Integration

Three salient features of the record need explanation: the high level and persistence of capital flows before 1914; the U-shaped pattern from 1914 to the present; and whether we are indeed back to the future.

The High Level and Persistence of Capital Flows before 1914

A number of factors could explain the larger size and greater persistence of current account imbalances in the pre-1913 period.[23] One is the greater credibility of policymakers' commitment to stable monetary and fiscal policies as manifested in adherence to the gold standard. The gold standard provided a signal that the borrowers followed the same rules as lenders in the metropolitan centers and hence were unlikely to default on their debts. Bordo and Rockoff (1996) evaluate this hypothesis for nine recipients of British capital in the period 1870–1914 and find strong evidence that good gold-standard adherents paid lower interest rates on sovereign debt than those with spottier records. Flandreau, Le Cacheux, and Zumer (1998) find similar results for a different panel of European peripheral countries, as do Sussman and Yateh (2000) for Japan. Insofar as the gold standard proxied for fiscal rectitude and for adherence to similar norms among both the capital recipients and the senders, the failure of the international monetary system to support equally persistent deficits after World War I may reflect a shift to less credible policies.

A related and possibly important determinant of the extent and persistence of British capital exports was the fact that most British investment went to former colonies where the British heritage was strong. These countries (e.g., the United States, Canada, and Australia) shared a common language, culture, legal system, and accounting system. British capital also went to countries such as Argentina and Uruguay, where Britain had long had a strong commercial presence and considerable political influence, or to colonies under direct British control. The French also directed their lending to countries where they had a strong political influence and close cultural ties (e.g., Italy, Spain, and Russia; see Fishlow 1985 and Flandreau 1998). By comparison, today's capital recipients tend to be very different in the above respects from the capital exporters. It follows that the latter may be less willing to maintain foreign investment in the face of adverse shocks.

Another explanation may lie in the nature of the investment itself. Much of the capital flowing to the New World went to finance railroads and other infrastructure. This investment required a long-term commitment because of its very nature: the returns accrued only when the project was completed, rendering it costly to terminate early. Although there is considerable infrastructure investment in today's emerging countries, it does not dominate to the same extent.

Moreover, insofar as prewar investment—British investment in particular—was investment in traded-goods-related sectors (as emphasized by Fishlow 1985), it went into export-related infrastructure and natural-resource-related projects that in the normal course of events generated a stream of foreign exchange revenues sufficient to pay the money back. That is, it did not give rise to balance-of-payments problems. The fact that pre–World War I lending took place in an environment of relatively free multilateral trade allowed countries that engaged in significant amounts of external borrowing to expand their exports as needed to amortize those debts.

A final explanation may lie in the flexibility of nineteenth-century economies. Insofar as their markets were less structured and institutionalized and adjustment was less constrained by policy and powerful interest groups, a shift in capital flows (which implied the need to reallocate resources between sectors producing traded and nontraded goods) could be accommodated easily. Bayoumi and Eichengreen (1996) and Calomiris and Hubbard (1996) provide econometric evidence consistent with this interpretation.

The U-Shaped Pattern of Financial Market Integration

The U-shaped pattern of global financial market integration documented previously has been well explained by Obstfeld and Taylor (1998) in terms of the policy trilemma of open capital markets, pegged exchange rates, and independent monetary policy. Only two of the three elements hold at the same time.

The golden age of financial market integration and capital mobility described above was also the era of the classical gold standard. In that regime, member countries (most of the world) were locked together by making their currencies convertible into gold. Credible gold-standard adherence, in the sense of subsuming domestic monetary and fiscal policy to the dictates of gold convertibility, was enforced for the emerging countries by the desire to have access at favorable terms to the capital markets of the core countries of Western Europe (Bordo and Kydland 1996). Credible adherence to gold also meant that short-term capital movements would be stabilizing. The classical gold-standard era was characterized not only by free capital mobility but also by mobility of labor and goods.

The golden age ended with World War I. The belligerents imposed capital and exchange controls in order to pursue expansionary financial policies and still maintain their parities. The war also changed the political economy of many countries in favor of democracy and the interests of labor—factors which would make it difficult to always subsume domestic policy goals to the dictates of external balance (Eichengreen 1992).

After a period of extreme monetary instability in Europe, the gold standard was restored as a gold-exchange standard with full capital mobility. However, flaws in its architecture (too low a price for gold, maldistribution of gold) and the fact that key members (the United States and France) followed policies inconsistent with long-run external balance meant that the trilemma was stretched. Nevertheless, capital flows did resume in the 1920s with the United States succeeding the United Kingdom as principal lender.

The Great Depression, caused by inappropriate U.S. policies in the deflationary environment of the restored gold standard, spread among countries joined by the links of gold. Adherence to gold also prevented policymakers from following expansionary policies in the world of open capital markets. As a consequence, some countries left the gold standard and allowed their currencies to float, whereas others imposed capital controls but kept their parities.

By the end of the 1930s, capital controls and exchange controls were nearly universal—a development that was reinforced during World War II.

After the war, the Bretton Woods system of 1944 was based on pegged exchange rates with an indirect link to gold, activist stabilization policies, and continued capital controls.

It was only by the late 1960s that private capital flows resumed as a consequence of the restoration of current account convertibility. This development revived the trilemma and, in the face of massive speculative attacks, led to its resolution by the abandonment of the par value system in 1973. Since then, capital controls have been eliminated in the advanced countries and reduced considerably in the emerging nations. Floating exchange rates are compatible with monetary independence and an open capital account.

Back to the Future or Beyond?

The evidence presented earlier suggests that, in some respects, international financial markets may have been at least as integrated before 1914 as they are today (if not more), and that we are in a back to the future scenario.[24] On the other hand, in many other respects international financial markets are clearly more integrated now than they were before 1914. These developments include the greater depth of the markets seen in the number and variety of lenders and borrowers and in the much wider range of securities traded and sectors financed. The vast majority of bonds sold before 1914 were railroad and government bonds; today, industry, finance, and the service sector in emerging markets are all important candidates for foreign portfolio investments. A second important development is the shift from debt to equity. Finally, FDI has expanded considerably from that employed by the free-standing companies of the earlier era.

These differences in the scope of market integration were consequences of information asymmetries, contracting problems, and macroeconomic risks that limited the extent of capital and commodity flows prior to 1914 and that continue to limit them (albeit to a lesser extent) today (see Bordo, Eichengreen, and Irwin 1999). By *information problems* is meant the difficulty of determining product, project, and borrower quality; by *contracting problems,* difficulties of detecting fraud and of attaching collateral; and by *macroeconomic risks,* mainly exchange risk.

Information Problems

Any discussion of information flows must begin with the communications technology of the day. The transatlantic cable was laid in the 1860s, coming into operation in 1866. Prior to its opening, it could take as long as three weeks for information to travel from New York to London (Garbade and Silber 1978). With the inauguration of the cable, this delay dropped to one day. By 1914 the time for cable transmission was down to less than a minute. Garbade and Silber (1978) compare the London and New York prices of U.S. bonds four months before and four months after advent of the cable and find a significant decline in the mean absolute difference. There is every reason to think that the cable had a comparable impact on other markets.[25]

The radio telephone was the next breakthrough. Like the telegraph, it first linked the national financial center (e.g., London) to the hinterlands and regional exchanges before linking it to other centers internationally (linking Europe with North America by 1900). It should be apparent why this information and communications technology translated into a smaller volume of short-term capital flows. Today, currency traders respond almost instantaneously to minute-to-minute changes in currency values. Prior to 1870, when it might take weeks for this information to cross the Atlantic, and even after the advent of the cable and the radio telephone, news arrived at longer intervals than it does now.

Long-term lending to manufacturing, commercial, and financial concerns was deterred not so much by the limitations of the communications technology as by the difficulty of assembling and evaluating the information to be communicated. Lenders were reluctant to lend because of the difficulty of distinguishing good and bad credit risks. This information asymmetry created adverse selection (in which the average credit quality of the pool of borrowers declines with increases in the interest rate) and therefore credit rationing. Overseas investors were further deterred by the difficulty of monitoring and controlling management's actions ex post— of detecting malfeasance and rent dissipation, and preventing owner-managers whose downside risk was truncated by limited liability from devoting borrowed funds to riskier projects.

Several already noted characteristics of late-nineteenth-century international capital markets are explicable in terms of obstacles to information flows. For example, asymmetric information can explain the disproportionate share of railway bonds in foreign investment portfolios. The manufacturing, financial, and commercial sectors of the U.S. economy were growing every bit as rapidly as transportation, but foreign investment in these sectors was less; information asymmetries explain this fact. It was relatively easy to monitor the actions of a railway company's management: Investors could verify how much track had been laid, where it had been laid, and how much traffic it carried more easily than they could verify and evaluate the investment decisions of managers of concerns in these other sectors.

Obstacles to the flow of information can also explain the disproportionate importance of debt as opposed to equity in foreign investment portfolios (Baskin 1988), because debt reduces the risk to investors when imperfect information creates agency problems. The pattern persists today (see, e.g., Eichengreen and Mody 1998), but a century ago it was, if anything, more pronounced.[26]

Information asymmetries can explain the disproportionate importance of family groups (e.g., the foreign branches of the Rothschild and Morgan families) and of the merchant and investment banks that grew out of them, which underwrote foreign bond issues and served as conduits for foreign investment, acting as delegated monitors and emitting signals of borrower creditworthiness. They can explain the well-known Kuznets cycle pattern, in which immigration and financial capital tended to flow in the same direction (a phenomenon to which Hatton and Williamson 1992 refer as the tendency for capital to chase after labor), as the migrants provided the European sending countries with valuable information about local conditions. They can explain the sovereign credit rating departments established by intermediaries like Credit Lyonnais (Flandreau 1998). They can explain the development of investment trusts (the nineteenth-century analog of modern mutual funds), to whom investors delegated information-gathering and analysis functions. They can explain the explosive growth of insurance companies, investments which interested households partly because they could offer an attractive rate of return as a result of their comparative advantage in gathering information from far-flung regions (Snowden 1995). They can explain the popularity of specialized publications like *The Investor's Monthly Manual, Burdett's Stock Exchange Official Intelligence, Poor's Manual of Railroads,* and *Herapath's Railway Journal.* They can explain established railroads' practice of guaranteeing the bonds of feeder lines.

Finally, information asymmetries can explain the surprisingly limited importance of FDI prior to 1914 and the importance of the free-standing company as the vehicle for FDI. A considerable majority of foreign investment prior to 1914 took the form of portfolio investment, whereas direct investment and portfolio investment are of roughly equal importance today (Bloomfield 1968). Moreover, whereas nineteenth-century FDI was undertaken mainly by free-standing companies (companies incorporated in Britain, France, Belgium, and other Western European countries for the sole purpose of investing and doing business in an emerging market), it takes place today through the agency of multinational enterprises that establish foreign branches and foreign subsidiaries.[27] Free-standing companies, in the words of Wilkins,

> were structured to solve the problem posed earlier; business abroad was risky; it was hard to obtain adequate and reliable information about firms in distant lands; returns were unpredictable; but there were clearly opportunities abroad; a company organized within the source-of-capital country, with a responsible board of directors, under source-of-capital country law, to mobilize capital (and other assets) and to conduct the business in foreign countries could take advantage of the opportunities, while reducing the transaction costs by providing a familiar conduit. (1998, 13)

Contracting Problems

Information problems may have been the key explanation for the relatively limited scope of late-nineteenth-century capital flows, but they were not the entire story. Beyond the immediate problem of geographical ignorance, distance made for problems of control. It was difficult to monitor actions taken by management thousands of miles away when round-trip communication could take a month.

Foreign investors were also deterred by the uncertain legal security of their claims. For example, because the United States was a federation, corporations were chartered by the states, not the federal government, and governed by the laws of the state in question. States prohibited foreigners from serving as directors of the corporations chartered there. In response, some British investors hired American citizens to represent them on the board, but this extra layer between ownership and control had the predictable effect of adding principal-agent slack.

Foreign investors also had reason to fear that they would not be treated fairly under American bankruptcy law. They worried that companies might be wound up and their assets sold off to other claimants, to the detriment of foreign investors.

Thus, America's experience before 1914 points out the importance of transparent and equitable bankruptcy laws for emerging markets seeking to attract foreign investment. This, of course, was the attraction of investing in the colonies, where bankruptcy law was familiar and creditor rights were relatively secure. Direct investment through free-standing companies was another solution. Wilkins emphasizes not only the difficulty of obtaining "adequate and reliable information" but also the advantages of establishing the country doing business abroad under "source-of-capital country law" to minimize contracting problems. British shareholders could be confident of their rights because the free-standing company was subject to British law.

The Absence of Adequate Accounting Standards   While difficulties of contract enforcement may have been a significant deterrent to foreign investment, asymmetric information was the overwhelming important obstacle to international capital flows.[28] These information problems were compounded by the inadequacy of prevailing auditing and accounting standards. In particular, British investors were deterred from investing in the United States by the underdevelopment of American accounting practices.

In the U.S. case, both market discipline and regulatory intervention were needed for the adoption of generally accepted accounting principles (GAAP). Market discipline was applied by British investors, who insisted on the transfer to the United States of accounting practices accepted in Britain. Their preferred agent for the transfer was the British-chartered accountancy firm. Another source of market discipline was the New York Stock Exchange (NYSE), which from the turn of the century required the publication of standardized balance sheets by all entities whose securities were accepted for listing.

Market discipline, however, was not enough. There was also the need for regulatory intervention, starting with the Interstate Commerce Commission (ICC), which required the railroads it regulated to provide information using standardized accounting practices from the 1880s, and culminating in the regulations imposed by the Securities and Exchange Commission (SEC) in 1933. The United States' own experience suggests that the development of a uniform, transparent accounting standard is no mean task, and that both market discipline and government intervention are needed to yield the desired result. International investors can be an important source of that market discipline, and international accounting firms can be efficient agents of technology transfer. Until that transfer is effected, however, the integration of the domestic financial markets with their foreign counterparts will necessarily remain incomplete.

Macroeconomic Risks

A number of observers emphasize exchange risk, unstable and uncertain monetary and fiscal policies, and political risk as factors limiting pre-1913 international investment flows. Madden (1985, 255) emphasizes the importance of a stable standard of value, stating that it is "of course common knowledge" that British investors viewed securities issued by countries not on the gold standard as riskier than those of countries that were. Many foreign securities issued in London were denominated in sterling and specified that principal and interest were payable in sterling (or in foreign currency convertible into sterling at a fixed rate of exchange), but in this case exchange rate fluctuations created credit risk instead of currency risk. (Currency depreciation might push the borrower into bankruptcy by raising the value of the borrower's debt-service payments relative to his or her income stream.[29]) In the case of government bonds, the fear was that governments off gold would succumb to the temptation to live beyond their means. For example, Baring's had unusual difficulty in placing U.S. government bonds in the second half of the 1860s, because investors feared that profligacy of the government operating under a fiat money regime would precipitate a financial crisis and force it to repudiate the debt. The Bland Bill of 1877, which raised the specter of large-scale silver coinage, similarly caused British investors to liquidate their U.S. government securities in favor of colonial bonds with interest and principal guaranteed in sterling. Again in the early 1890s, the possibility of free silver coinage led foreign investors to liquidate their holdings of U.S. securities and to a rise in the premiums on U.S. bonds and foreign exchange. Bordo and Rockoff (1996) and Bordo, Edelstein, and Rockoff (2002) find that the effect was general: loans to countries with a fluctuating standard of value commanded significantly higher interest rates in both the 1870–1914 gold-standard and 1925–31 gold-exchange-standard periods.

Financial Crises Then and Now

The recent experiences of international crises in emerging markets in Latin America and Asia lead to the impression that financial crises are a phenomenon of the current age of globalizing capital markets. In fact this is not the case; the world has seen waves of crisis since the advent of capitalism and the earlier era of globalization before 1914 witnessed similar patterns of capital inflows and lending booms followed by capital outflows and lending busts.[30]

Historical Narrative

The classic case with resonance for today is Latin America's experience with lending booms and busts prior to 1914 (Marichal 1989). The first wave of British capital flows to the new states of the region to finance infrastructure and gold and silver mines ended with the crisis of 1825. British investors had purchased Latin American stocks and bonds, some of which were in companies—even countries—that did not exist, with gay abandon (Neal 1998). The boom ended with a stock market crash and a banking panic. The new countries defaulted on their debts and lost access to international capital markets for decades, until they renegotiated terms and began paying into arrears (Cole, Dow, and English 1995).

The second wave of foreign lending to Latin America in the 1850s and 1860s was used to finance railroads and ended in the 1873 financial crisis. Faced with deteriorating terms of trade and a dearth of external finance, countries defaulted on their debts.

The third wave, in the 1880s, involved massive flows from Britain and Europe generally to finance the interior development of Argentina and Uruguay; it ended with the crash of 1890, leading to the insolvency of Baring's, the famous London merchant bank. Argentine state bonds went into default, a moratorium was declared, and flows to the region dried up for half a decade. In the wake of the Barings crisis, financial distress in London and heightened awareness of the risks of foreign lending worsened the capital market access of other emerging markets such as Australia and New Zealand. The next wave of capital flows to emerging markets started up only after the turn of the century, once the former wreckage had been cleared away.

Latin experience may be the classic, but the United States also experienced lending booms and busts (see DeLong 1999). The first wave of British capital in the 1820s and 1830s went to finance canals and the cotton boom. It ended in the depression of 1837–43 with defaults by eight states, causing British investors to shun U.S. investments for the rest of the decade.

The second wave followed the U.S. Civil War and was used to finance westward expansion. The threat that the country would abandon gold for silver precipitated capital flight in the mid-1890s but, unlike the Latin case, did not lead to the suspension of convertibility or an extended reversal of capital flows.

Financial crises in this period were precipitated by events in both the lending and the borrowing countries.[31] A number of crises began in Europe due to harvest failures. On several such occasions (1837, 1847, 1857) the Bank of England raised its discount rate in response to an external drain of gold reserves. This had serious consequences for capital flows to the New World. Thus, the 1837 crisis spread to North America via the

British intermediaries that financed the export of cotton from New Orleans to Liverpool, leading to the suspension of specie convertibility by the United States and to bank failures across the country.

Not all crises originated in the Old World. Some emanated from Latin America, where they were precipitated by supply shocks that made it impossible for commodity-exporting countries to service their debts, and by expansionary monetary and fiscal policies adopted in the effort to protect the economy from the consequences. Some were triggered by financial instability, especially in the United States, a country hobbled by a fragile unit banking system and the lack of a lender of last resort. These crises in the periphery in turn infected the European core. Classic examples include the Argentine crisis of 1889–90 and the U.S. crises of 1893 and 1907.

A fourth wave of flows to emerging markets (and to the "reemerging markets" of Europe) occurred in the 1920s after leadership in international financial affairs shifted from London to New York (Bordo, Edelstein, and Rockoff 2002). It ended at the close of the decade with the collapse of commodity prices and the Great Depression. Virtually all countries, with the exception of Argentina, defaulted on their debts. Private portfolio capital did not return to the region for four decades.

These interwar crises were greater in both severity and scope. They were tied up with the flaws of the gold-exchange standard. Compared to the prewar gold standard, the credibility of the commitment to gold convertibility was weak, and capital flows were not as stabilizing. This fragile system came under early strain from changes in the pattern of international settlements, reflecting the persistent weakness of primary commodity prices and the impact on the current account of reparations and war-debt payments.

Hence, when the Great Depression hit, banking panics spread via the fixed exchange rates of the gold-exchange standard. Countries were spared the ravages of depression only when they cut the link with gold, devaluing their currencies and adopting reflationary policies.

The Bretton Woods system established in reaction to the problems of the interwar period placed limits on capital mobility. In response to the interwar experience with banking crises, governments created elaborate systems of regulation to reduce risk-taking in the domestic financial sector and constructed a financial safety net in the form of deposit insurance and lenders of last resort. The result was virtually no banking crises for the better part of four decades.

Crises under Bretton Woods were strictly currency crises, in which speculators attacked countries that attempted to defend exchange rates inconsistent with their domestic macroeconomic and financial policies. These attacks ended either in devaluation or, on occasion, in a successful rescue mounted by international authorities (the IMF and the Group of Ten [G10]). This contrasts with the Victorian era, when there were fewer pure currency crises (unaccompanied by banking crises) except at the outbreak of wars.

Incidence and Severity of Crises

How does the record of recent emerging-market crises compare with that of earlier times? Bordo and Eichengreen (1999) provide an answer to that question. They show the behavior of real GDP growth in a window five years before a crisis and five years after a crisis for fifteen emerging countries and six advanced countries in the period 1880–1913—a period when capital flowed as freely as it does today[32]—compared with a sample of ten emerging market countries experiencing crises in the past twenty-five years.[33]

Crises are defined as both currency and banking crises[34] that were identified from historical narratives. In addition, as an alternative indicator of a currency crisis, Bordo and Eichengreen used an index of exchange market pressure.[35] They included twenty-two crises in emerging market countries (and seven in their advanced industrial counterparts) prior to 1914. For the period since 1972, they identified thirty crises in ten emerging market countries.

The incidence of emerging market crises today is considerably higher than in the earlier period, at 11.5 percent per country year versus 4.3 percent for the earlier period.[36]

The measure of the severity and duration of a crisis was the extent to which the annual GDP growth rate deviated from the trend on its account and then recovered. Specifically, for each country, Bordo and Eichengreen calculated the growth rate in the crisis year relative to its trend over the five years preceding the crisis; crisis-year growth relative to its three-year trend preceding the crisis; the difference between crisis-year growth and the preceding year's growth rate; the difference between growth the year following the crisis and the crisis-year growth rate; the difference between the three-year-trend growth rate following the crisis and the crisis-year growth rate; and finally the difference between the five-year-trend growth rate following the crisis and the crisis-year growth rate.

Table 1.2, adapted from Bordo and Eichengreen (1999), presents summary statistics of cross-country averages of the growth rates calculated as

Table 1.2   Fluctuations in Annual Growth Rates around the Time of Crises (summary statistics 1880–1913, 1973–1998: emerging and advanced countries)

	Emerging Countries (15)	Emerging Countries (10)
All crises: mean (number of crises)	1880–1913 (22)	1973–1998 (30)
$g_{crisis} - g_{(-5)}$	–0.02	–0.03
$g_{crisis} - g_{(-3)}$	–0.01	–0.03
$g_{crisis} - g_{(-1)}$	–0.02	–0.03
$g_{(+1)} - g_{crisis}$	–0.02	0.02
$g_{(+3)} - g_{crisis}$	0.01	0.02
$g_{(+5)} - g_{crisis}$	0.03	0.03
Twin crises: mean (number of crises)	1880–1913 (9)	1973–1998 (14)
$g_{crisis} - g_{(-5)}$	–0.02	–0.05
$g_{crisis} - g_{(-3)}$	–0.02	–0.05
$g_{crisis} - g_{(-1)}$	–0.02	–0.05
$g_{(+1)} - g_{crisis}$	–0.00	0.03
$g_{(+3)} - g_{crisis}$	0.01	0.05
$g_{(+5)} - g_{crisis}$	0.02	0.05
Banking crises: means (number of crises)	1880–1913 (8)	1973–1998 (5)
$g_{crisis} - g_{(-5)}$	–0.02	–0.03
$g_{crisis} - g_{(-3)}$	–0.02	–0.03
$g_{crisis} - g_{(-1)}$	–0.03	–0.02
$g_{(+1)} - g_{crisis}$	–0.03	0.02
$g_{(+3)} - g_{crisis}$	0.00	0.02
$g_{(+5)} - g_{crisis}$	0.05	0.01
Currency crises: means (number of crises)	1880–1913 (5)	1973–1998 (11)
$g_{crisis} - g_{(-5)}$	0.00	–0.02
$g_{crisis} - g_{(-3)}$	0.03	–0.01
$g_{crisis} - g_{(-1)}$	–0.01	–0.00
$g_{(+1)} - g_{crisis}$	–0.03	0.01
$g_{(+3)} - g_{crisis}$	0.02	0.00
$g_{(+5)} - g_{crisis}$	0.00	0.01

SOURCES: Bordo and Schwartz (1996) database; IMF (1999).

NOTES: g_{crisis} is the annual growth rate of real GDP at the crisis year. $g_{(N)}$ is the average annual growth rate of real GDP N years before (–) or after (+) the crisis.

described above for the emerging market countries for the pre-1914 and post-1972 periods (see also fig. 1.7). A key fact is that the output effects of banking and financial crises in emerging market countries were somewhat more severe in the recent period compared to the pre-1914 period. Whereas growth declined by 3 percentage points relative to trend in the typical post-1972 crisis, the comparable number for emerging markets in the pre-1914 period was 2 percentage points. The contrast is sharpest for twin crises (combinations of both banking and currency crises), which have been exceptionally disruptive since 1972 (when the average decline

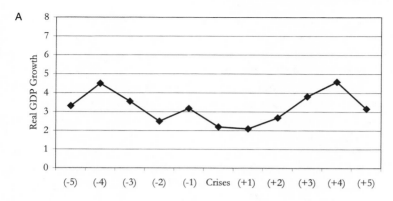

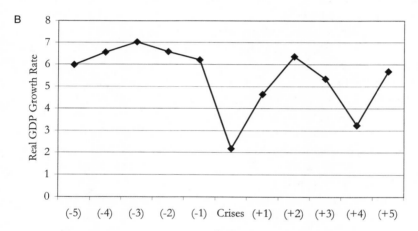

Fig. 1.7   Growth Rate of Real GDP, All Crises: Panel A: Emerging Countries, 1880–1913 (20); Panel B: Ten Emerging Countries, 1973–98 (22)
SOURCE:
See Bordo and Eichengreen (1999).

in the growth rate was 5 percent) but were less so prior to 1914 (when the average drop was again "only" 2 percent). Whatever the contrast, however, these differences are not large.[37]

By these measures, the fall in output in the recent Asian crisis was especially steep: Korea's growth rate declined 7 percentage points below its precrisis five-year-average growth rate, 8 percentage points below its three-year precrisis average, and 7 percentage points from the year preceding the crisis. Indonesia's performance was similar, while Thailand's was the worst (at minus 13, 13, and 11 percentage points, respectively).

The severity of these countries' crises in 1997–98 is well known; the point here is that their recessions were dramatic relative to the typical crisis in emerging markets prior to 1914.

How does recent Asian experience compare with the worst of the pre-1914 era? The two most infamous pre–World War I crises in emerging market countries, the United States in 1893 and Argentina in 1890, were even worse than Asian crises in recent years.[38] For the United States, growth during the crisis year declined by 9 percentage points relative to its previous five-year trend, 12 percentage points below its three-year precrisis trend, and 14 percentage points from the precrisis year. For Argentina the numbers are even more dramatic if the conventional statistics are to be believed: minus 17, 20, and 24 percent, with recovery in growth not complete after five years.[39]

The experience of the six advanced countries in the pre-1914 period in general was much more peaceful than that of the emerging market countries, with the exceptions of currency crises in Germany in 1903 and 1907 associated with large drops in growth relative to trend, and severe twin crises in France in 1889 (Bordo and Eichengreen 1999, table 1).

Table 1.2 also suggests that emerging market countries recovered more quickly from currency crises before 1914 than after 1972. Before 1914, the growth rate rose by 2 percentage points between the crisis year and the three years following; after 1972, the growth rate failed to rise at all. In contrast, the recovery from banking crises starts earlier in the modern period, in the first postcrisis year as opposed to the second or third. This is true regardless of whether banking crises were accompanied by currency crises.

Explanations for these contrasts between the pre-1914 and post-1972 eras refer to a number of factors. Faster recovery before 1914 could be attributable to adherence, or attempted adherence, to the gold-standard rule. Prior to 1914, countries driven off the gold standard generally intended to restore convertibility at the previously prevailing exchange rate once the crisis passed. While investors who held domestic-currency-denominated assets suffered losses when the exchange rate collapsed, they anticipated gains as the currency recovered to its traditional parity (Miller 1996, 1998). To put the point another way, insofar as the authorities were committed to reestablishing the previous rate of exchange, there was little reason to fear that abandoning the currency peg would unleash uncontrolled inflation. Hence, devaluation did not incite persistent capital flight; rather, gold and capital began flowing back in at a relatively early date, stabilizing the economy and stimulating recovery (see DeLargy and Goodhart 1999).

The slower recovery from banking crises in the early period may reflect the absence of effective lenders of last resort, capable of restoring depositor confidence, stabilizing supplies of money and credit, and sustaining the provision of financial services to the economy. The U.S. crises of 1893 and 1907, which were greatly aggravated by the absence of last-resort lending (leading in turn to the establishment of the Federal Reserve), make this point.[40]

One could also argue that regulatory forbearance and central bank bailouts have adverse long-term effects by weakening market discipline and leading to a less efficient allocation of capital. Indeed, there is some suggestion of this in the data: Although recovery from banking crises is initiated earlier in the post-1972 period, the subsequent expansion accelerates less dramatically and is sustained less successfully, as if market discipline and the efficiency with which credit is allocated are less pronounced (than in comparable episodes 100 years ago).

This comparison ignores the fact that profound banking problems in the recent crisis countries (e.g., Mexico, Korea, Thailand) had not been resolved when, according to the data, recovery began.

Finally, the fact that the decline in real growth was greater on average in today's crises may simply reflect the presence of the safety net provided by the IMF and other international financial institutions. The belief that emerging market countries would be bailed out may have encouraged more capital to flow in than would have been the case in the absence of the safety net. Hence the reversal of capital flows and their effects on the real economy became more serious.[41]

The interwar years, as is well known, were notoriously crisis prone: the incidence of crisis per country-year was 10 percent. The drop in output following crises was exceptionally sharp for both advanced and emerging market countries, exceeding that for emerging market countries today. The difference between the interwar and the two aforementioned periods (pre-1914 and post-1972) was the exceptional severity of the banking and twin crises of the 1930s. This was of course Friedman and Schwartz's (1963) explanation for the severity of the Great Depression in the United States, which they attributed to the failure of the Federal Reserve to act as a lender of last resort, in conjunction with the disappearance of the private lifeboat operations by the clearinghouse associations that were so important before the war. The twin-crises version is the explanation for the exceptional depth of the global slump elaborated by Bernanke and James (1991). The crises of the interwar period however were not crises associated with globalization-lending booms and busts. They were crises of global macro instability and a flawed exchange rate.

Under Bretton Woods, crises were mild. There were no banking crises in our sample, reflecting the restrictions imposed on banking systems in response to the disasters of the 1930s.

While currency crises continued to occur despite the adoption of restrictions on capital mobility, their output effects were mild by the standards of the pre-1914 and interwar periods. This plausibly reflects the more limited scope for capital flight in the controlled financial environment of the 1950s and 1960s, and the greater scope for central banks to continue pursuing policies to sustain output and demand behind the shelter of controls. Those recessionary effects were more pronounced in emerging market than advanced economies, but the contrast is less than in either of the preceding periods, plausibly reflecting the prevalence of capital controls and the quiescence of international financial markets.[42] Thus, like the interwar, crises in this period were not a product of the open capital markets of globalization but were related to the flaws of the adjustable peg regime.

International Rescues

Many of the currency crises of the past ended with a devaluation of the currency, on some occasions countries held sufficient reserves to successfully stave off the attack, while some crises were averted by international rescues.[43]

In the period before World War II, rescue loans to central banks and sovereign governments were often arranged by or intermediated by private investment banks, such as Rothschilds, Barings, and JPMorgan. Since World War II, all of the rescues have been arranged by official monetary authorities, or international agencies, the IMF, BIS, and the World Bank.

The Classical Gold Standard

In the century before World War I, frequent short-term loans were made to central banks and other monetary authorities to relieve pressure on their reserves during financial crises. The recipients of these loans were primarily the advanced countries of Western Europe; with rare exception, the emerging countries were not rescued. In virtually every case, rescue loans were made on commercial terms to central banks that had a record of solvency and of credible adherence to specie convertibility. The loans were regarded as a supplement to (or, in some cases, a substitute for) other remedial actions designed to replenish the monetary authorities' reserves, such as raising the discount rate and credit rationing. In many cases the loans were made on a reciprocal basis. Thus, in the period from 1825 to 1914, the Banque de France on many occasions established temporary credits to the Bank of England and vice versa.

Two episodes from the pre-1914 era with resonance for today are the Barings crisis of 1890 and the U.S. silver crisis of 1895. The Bank of England averted a panic following the failure of the House of Barings in November 1890 resulting from a debt default in Argentina, whose securities it had underwritten, by arranging a lifeboat operation whereby the government guaranteed loans by London banks to recapitalize Barings. The bank's share in the rescue would have depleted its gold reserves sufficiently to threaten convertibility. In addition to raising the discount rate, the bank protected its reserves by borrowing £2 million in gold from the Banque de France, with the Rothschilds acting as intermediaries. Subsequently, it borrowed a further £1 million. The Imperial Bank of Russia also agreed to provide £1.5 million in German gold coins. British Exchequer bonds served as collateral for each of the loans. The news of the loans as much as the fact of them restored confidence.

In the second episode, a U.S. budget deficit after 1890 and the issue of legal tender treasury notes of 1890, redeemable in silver coin and mandated by the Sherman Silver Purchase Act of 1890, created uncertainty about the convertibility of the U.S. dollar into gold. In January 1895, a run on gold in exchange for legal tender reduced the treasury's reserve to $45 million. In February 1895, the treasury secretary contracted with the Belmont-Morgan banking syndicate to market a 4 percent bond issue and provide the treasury with a six-month, short-term, interest-free gold credit to restore the gold reserve. During the five months after the contract was signed, no gold was withdrawn from the treasury.

The Interwar Period

The regime that was restored from 1924 to 1936 was a gold-exchange standard that differed profoundly from the pre-1914 gold standard. Flaws in the structure and inappropriate policies by its members meant that whatever attempts at rescues were made when crises struck in 1931 were doomed from that start.

A rescue package from the BIS was insufficient to stem the crisis facing Austria after its bailout of the insolvent Credit Anstalt in May 1931. A second rescue attempt by the Bank of England also followed. The crisis then spread to Germany, whose Reichsbank sought and obtained an international loan of $100 million ($24 million each from the Bank of England, Banque de France, Federal Reserve Bank of New York, and the BIS) on June 25. The loan proved insufficient to stem the speculative attack. A second loan for $1 billion foundered in the face of opposition by both the Banque de France and the Federal Reserve. The external drain was finally halted by the announcement of a standstill agreement on 20 July and the imposition of exchange controls.

The final act of the crisis was a speculative attack on sterling. The combination of the continental banking crisis, which froze debts payable to British banks, and a worsening current account deficit and growing budget deficit placed mounting pressure on the Bank of England's gold reserves. The bank rate was raised twice in July, from 2.5 percent to 4.5 percent. In the final week of July 1931, the Bank of England obtained matching credits of £25 million from the Banque de France and the Federal Reserve Bank of New York. The amount was inadequate to halt the run. Further loans to Britain of $200 million each from a syndicate formed by JPMorgan in New York and a syndicate in Paris also proved inadequate. With reserves dwindling, the government suspended convertibility on 19 September.

Bretton Woods

The framers of the Bretton Woods agreement in July 1944 established an international monetary framework that would overcome the perceived problems of the interwar period, especially the perceptions that capital flows (hot money movements) were a key source of the instability of the 1930s and that international cooperation had failed. Free capital mobility was not encouraged. The IMF was established to provide temporary assistance to countries with current account imbalances. A precedent to IMF lending was the U.S. Treasury's Exchange Stabilization Fund (ESF) established in 1934; ESF stabilization loans date from 1936, initially to Latin American countries (e.g., Mexico, 1936, 1938).[44]

The Bretton Woods era was marked by currency crises that affected countries with parities inconsistent with domestic policies and competitive trends. The crises were resolved either by devaluations, revaluations, or IMF or G10 rescue loans. In two instances (sterling, November 1967, and the dollar, August 1971), currencies that were under attack succumbed despite rescue loans for the former and varied devices to protect U.S. gold reserves. In several other instances (the Canadian dollar, June 1962; the lira, March 1964), the rescue loans were successful. As the resources required for rescues mounted, the Bretton Woods system fell apart, a dissolution that the policies of the United States, the center country, compelled (Bordo and Schwartz 1999).

Recent Rescues

Rescue loans before the 1990s were made in an attempt to prevent a devaluation or the abandonment of pegged exchange rates by the core advanced countries. They were temporary loans, at commercial market rates, limited in magnitude, but sufficient to offset a current account deficit.

Rescue loans in the 1990s were extended to emerging market countries (Mexico, 1994; Thailand, Indonesia, and Korea, 1997–98) and to Russia, a country in transition from a command economy.[45] The loans have been multiples of the amounts that were granted in the past (see Bordo and Schwartz 2000). The recent loans are intended to offset capital account outflows, the effect of which was to endanger repayment of the lenders. The sizes of the loans were enough to provide the wherewithal to repay foreign and domestic lenders of foreign currency, involving wealth transfers from the recipient taxpayers to wealthy investors. In this sense they represent bailouts and not simply rescue loans.

The chief indictment of the bailout model of international lending is that it promotes moral hazard. In the crisis countries, investors believed that there was an implicit government guarantee against failure of banks. If banks were threatened because depositors wanted foreign exchange for domestic deposits, governments would provide it until their foreign exchange reserves were exhausted. When foreign bank deposits were no longer guaranteed, investors decamped (Dooley 1997). International loans then replaced government guarantees. Lenders presumed that, regardless of whether the resources they provided were put to prudent use, they were not at risk. Borrowers presumed that, if there were a reversal of the conditions that invited the inflow of funds, their debts would be repaid by others or drastically discounted. Indeed, the rescues of the second golden age differed from those of the earlier one not primarily because the lenders changed from private banks to international financial institutions but because the underlying environment changed—from one in which insolvent borrows were allowed to default and insolvent banks to fail to one in which "too big to fail" is the norm.

Have the recent rescues been successful? Some argue the Mexican rescue (as well as Thai and Korean rescues) was successful because the IMF and other creditors are being repaid and growth is recovering quickly to precrisis levels. Yet the debt burdens to be serviced by the taxpayers of these countries are immense. Moreover, recent empirical evidence suggests that, on average over the 1973–98 period, countries receiving IMF assistance in financial crises fared no better in terms of real growth, the level of real per capita GDP, or real consumption, than did comparable countries that were not rescued (Bordo and Schwartz 2000). This comparison accounts for the self-selection bias that countries that turn to the IMF have special characteristics distinguishing them from those that do not.

The question then arises whether, with the resurgence of the international financial markets in recent years (described previously), why can the private capital markets not handle the rescues of emerging countries through, for example, advance lines of credit (Feldstein 1998)? Moreover, if countries knew that they were not to be rescued, or that the amounts forthcoming would be insufficient to cover both interest and principal, why would they not hold large reserves (as did Taiwan) or make other arrangements?

Globalization, Crises, and Backlash

The recent spate of financial crises has led to cries by some for capital controls and the slowing down of the integration process. Others argue that at the very least, the liberalization of countries that still have significant barriers to free capital mobility should not be encouraged until significant financial-sector reforms involving greater transparency and adequate supervision and regulation facilities are instituted. It is argued that liberalization's benefits to economic welfare and growth may not be worth the costs of the crises.

The recent case for reimposing controls to prevent crises is based on the argument that asymmetric information fosters lending booms that can suddenly collapse in the face of a sudden change in market sentiment, which may or may not reflect fundamentals (Rodrik 1998). Herding behavior creates a massive capital flow reversal. In turn, contagion effects lead to massive capital flows from neighboring countries facing similar economic problems and even from emerging countries that are not.

The case against imposing controls in general is that it prevents the optimal allocation of resources, it prevents optimal portfolio diversification, it encourages irresponsible macropolicy, and it leads to corruption (Cooper 1998).

The proposals for controls range from preventive controls on outflows to alleviate balance-of-payments pressure before a crisis; temporary controls on outflows (curative controls) imposed during a crisis (e.g., in Malaysia); and controls on capital inflows to prevent a crisis (e.g., in Chile; Edwards 1999).

What is the evidence on the effectiveness of capital controls? Edwards (1999) presents a convincing case based on the Latin American experience that preventive controls on capital outflows are largely ineffective because they are easily evaded and they lead to corruption and bad policies. Curative crisis controls also were associated with unsatisfactory GDP growth following the crisis (Edwards 1999, 9).

The most prominent recent example of controls on capital inflows is that of Chile which on two occasions in the past two decades has required foreigners wishing to invest in the country to hold non-interest-bearing deposits at the central bank. According to Edwards (1999), the controls were successful in lengthening the maturity structure of foreign indebtedness and hence reducing vulnerability to sudden reversals, but that this was achieved at the expense of a higher cost of capital, especially to small and medium sized firms. The controls also did give the monetary authorities extra independence to pursue policies that could help insulate the domestic economy from external shocks, but the evidence on how protected Chile's financial markets were from contagion during the recent Asian crisis is mixed: the volatility in stock prices declined but not the volatility of short-term interest rates.

What about the effects of the liberalization of capital controls on growth? According to Rodrick (1998), based on a panel regression for twenty-three countries from 1993 to 1996, "capital controls are essentially uncorrelated with long-term economic performance once we control for other determinants" (61).[46] The historical evidence is mixed. Bordo and Eichengreen (1998), based on a panel regression, found that the hypothetical removal of capital controls during the Bretton Woods period 1959–73 would have had negligible effects on the growth rates of industrial countries but weak positive effects on the growth of emerging countries.[47] Moreover, the historical pattern of growth rates and financial crisis incidence and the presence or absence of controls is also mixed. In the pre-1914 period, during which there were no capital controls, the incidence of currency crises in both advanced and emerging countries was considerably less than under Bretton Woods (a regime with capital controls and twice the growth rate; Bordo and Eichengreen 1999).

In summary, more research is needed to determine whether the incidence of crises affects long-term growth and whether using controls to suppress them really matters one way or the other. Indeed, the problem may not be the capital inflows to emerging countries at all but what is done with them—whether they are used to finance productive investment or conspicuous consumption, or something in between. This is related in turn to the structure of the financial system, including its regulation and supervision. Financial crises are more likely to happen in unsound financial environments. Whether this implies an orderly sequencing of reforms before capital markets are opened, or opening the capital markets and allowing the domestic financial system to be exposed to the light of day with a crisis as a wake-up call for reform, is another matter.

The argument over capital controls to prevent the crisis consequences of international financial market integration is part of a more general debate on globalization—whether its benefits to aggregate economic welfare may be outweighed by disruptive distributional effects. O'Rourke and Williamson (1999) provide comprehensive and convincing historical evidence on this issue from their analysis of the earlier golden age of globalization before World War I.

In that golden age, unprecedented mobility of goods, labor, and capital contributed to rapid real growth. The growth of international trade reflected a reduction in tariff barriers in the third quarter of the nineteenth century and declining transportation costs throughout the century. Labor moved freely in waves of mass migration from the Old World to the New to take advantage of higher real wages. Capital, as discussed above, moved from the capital-abundant regions of Western Europe to take advantage of the higher real returns in the resource-rich lands of new settlement.

The consequence of trade and factor mobility in the golden age was the convergence of real wages and per capita real incomes between the core countries of Western Europe and much of the periphery. According to O'Rourke and Williamson (1999) and Williamson (1996), this reflected the operation of classical trade theory. Both factor flows and goods flows fostered factor price equalization. Most of the convergence in real wages (70 percent) is explained by factor movements, especially by labor mobility (with mobile capital as a minor player); the rest (30 percent), according to the Hecksher-Ohlin theorem, by international trade.

These forces had important effects on the distribution of income. The massive migrations in the 1870–1914 period reduced the returns to land owners in the land-scarce, labor-abundant countries of Europe and at the same time worsened the income distribution in the countries of new settlement, as unskilled immigrants competed with more established workers for jobs.

A political backlash ensued in each region. In the Old World, landowners successfully lobbied for the increased tariff protection of agriculture in the last two decades of the nineteenth century. In the New World, in the United States, Canada, Australia, and Argentina, labor was ultimately successful in closing the doors to migrants by the second decade of the twentieth century. The backlash to globalization may in turn have fanned the flames of nationalism and been a key cause of World War I.

As detailed previously, the turbulent interwar period witnessed the virtual termination of capital mobility as nation states turned to protect their monetary sovereignty in the face of the Great Depression.[48]

Today is another golden age of globalization. Should we worry about a backlash like that which killed the first one? Compared to the earlier age, international labor mobility is not of great importance, whereas capital flows and trade are of significantly greater importance. Moreover, Williamson (1996) viewed capital flows in the pre-1914 period as partial substitutes for labor mobility in explaining the convergence of real wages. Thus there are some tendencies that could augur a back-to-the-future backlash scenario.

On the other hand, the growth of international trade is more widespread than in pre-1914 and hence the groups that may be harmed are outweighed by those that benefit from it. Moreover, today there are more escape valves in trade legislation to relieve trade pressure than there were earlier (Bordo, Eichengreen, and Irwin 1999). Also unlike in the pre-1914 era, trade disputes can be resolved by multinational agencies such as the WTO that were not present then (Irwin 1993). Finally, most countries in recent years have learned to pursue stable macroeconomic policies in sharp contrast to the unstable macro environment that led to the shutting down of the capital markets in the interwar period.

Conclusion

What are history's lessons from our survey of the record on the globalization of international financial markets?

First, financial market integration has followed a U-shaped pattern, declining in the middle years of the twentieth century from the high levels achieved before 1914 to similar or higher levels today. It took the restoration of macro stability by the advanced countries in the 1970s and 1980s, specifically the resolution of the policy trilemma with the advent of floating exchange rates, to allow the resurgence of capital mobility to take place. This record makes a strong case for a floating exchange rate regime for the advanced countries. This does not rule out regional exchange rate arrangements like the exchange rate mechanism (ERM), or emerging countries' adopting a currency board or dollarization to establish credibility. The historical record, however, as developed here and in Obstfeld and Taylor (1998), makes the case for intermediate arrangements harder to defend.

Second, financial market integration is broader and deeper today than it was before 1914. This largely reflects financial innovations to overcome barriers to asymmetric information. Also at work have been improvements in communications and government regulations to encourage transparency in financial markets.

Third, financial crises have always been part of the scene. They may be the product of asymmetric information, and they most likely reflect shocks and inconsistent fundamentals. The effects of crises are and were worse in emerging countries (with the exception of the interwar period). This is the case because they are financially underdeveloped and have thinner markets, less diversified portfolios, less effective supervision and regulation, less well defined property rights and bankruptcy codes, and a greater proclivity to follow unstable macro policies. All of these features make them more prone to asymmetric information problems, lending booms and busts, and banking crises.

This was the case in some emerging market countries before 1914. The United States is a stellar example. It was prone to periodic financial crises because of the unsound state unit banking system, which prevented interregional portfolio diversification, and because it did not have an effective lender of last resort (although private arrangements such as the clearinghouses in many cities did on occasion alleviate banking panics).

The lesson from the experience of emerging countries like the United States, Australia, Canada, and the Scandinavian countries that graduated to advanced status is to allow financial markets to develop and mature. This requires a set of rules including secure property rights, an effective lender of last resort, and a sound macro policy environment. Some of these attributes can be imported by allowing financial institutions from advanced countries to operate freely in the emerging countries. Others develop with time.

Finally, the case for an international lender of last resort to manage today's crises is not an obvious one. Today, with extensive open private capital markets, many countries in distress can borrow what they need at market interest rates. There is less need for international rescues.

In the past, the international lender-of-last-resort function was only a partial function, because then (as today) no international institution could issue high-powered money. Before 1914, international rescues involved temporary loans between central banks on the basis of sound collateral, on commercial terms (Bordo and Schwartz 1999). In the twentieth century, until the past two decades, rescues have been made by groups of countries (the IMF and the BIS) to countries facing temporary current account reversals. Today, in the face of capital account reversals, the size of the rescues has increased dramatically—as has the risk of moral hazard. In today's environment of open global capital markets the only role for an international crisis manager should be to provide liquidity to countries that cannot access the private capital markets, and then to lend short-term on the basis of sound collateral and at a penalty rate.

Notes

1. Much of this section and the following one is based on Bordo, Eichengreen, and Kim (1998) and Bordo, Eichengreen, and Irwin (1999).

2. Obstfeld and Taylor present two versions: the ratio of assets (liabilities) to world GDP and the ratio to sample GDP. The latter reflects an adjustment for the smaller sample of countries (seven) with foreign investment data than countries with GDP data. The adjusted ratio, which is an upper bound estimate, is greater than 50 percent in the years just before 1914, falls to a low of 12 percent in 1945, and then rises to 54 percent in 1995.

3. Extensive international financial market integration began well before 1880. Neal (1990) documents the integration that occurred in northwest Europe after 1700. Capital flows from Britain to the United States, Latin America, and the British colonies accelerated in the years after the Napoleonic wars (Zevin 1992).

4. This compares with the peaks in Japan's and Germany's current account surpluses in the mid- and late 1980s of 4–5 percent of GDP.

5. Although there was also significant foreign direct investment.

6. The countries in this sample that are labeled Group 1 are Argentina, Australia, Canada, Denmark, Finland, France, Germany, Italy, Japan, Norway, Sweden, the United Kingdom, and the United States. However, Finland was not included in figure 1.1. All of these countries except Argentina graduated from emerging-country status to advanced-country status. For explanations for Argentina's retardance see, e.g., Taylor (1997). Argentina was kept in the sample past World War II even though it clearly belongs with the Group 2 countries discussed below because of its major importance as a capital recipient before 1914.

7. Recently, the standard series on current account balances have been revised by Jones and Obstfeld (2000) to account for nonmonetary gold flows under the pre-1914 and the interwar gold standards. The problem with the standard sources, as Jones and Obstfeld explain, is that their designers did not distinguish monetary gold exports, which are capital account credits, from nonmonetary gold exports, which are properly included in the current account. Jones and Obstfeld adjust for these discrepancies, and these are the data presented in figures 1.1 and

1.2. See Bordo, Eichengreen, and Kim (1998), appendix figure 1, for the individual country data.

8. The United States exhibited current account deficits comparable to these countries earlier in the nineteenth century. Evidence for persistence is based on the Phillips-Perron z-statistic. See Bordo, Eichengreen, and Kim (1998).

9. The individual country data for this sample labeled Group 2 are in Bordo, Eichengreen, and Kim (1998), appendix figure 1. The countries are Algeria, Brazil, Chile, China, Colombia, Egypt, Hungary, India, Israel, Korea, Malaysia, Mexico, Morocco, Pakistan, Peru, the Philippines, Poland, Romania, South Africa, Thailand, Turkey, and Venezuela.

10. For a sample of only capital importers, the ratio was 4.4 percent. (See tables 1 and 2 in Bordo, Eichengreen, and Kim 1998 which show the mean and the standard deviation of the data for each country across four exchange rate regimes from 1880 to the present.)

11. Using data averaged for five-year periods.

12. A recent review of the literature is Coakley, Kulasi, and Smith (1998).

13. These conclusions have recently been affirmed by Jones and Obstfeld using their revised data.

14. Taylor (1994) presents supporting evidence explaining some of the anomalous coefficients by omitted demographic variables. Taylor (1996) also uses an error correction methodology to distinguish between short-run shocks and the long-run equilibrium.

15. Among other things, this comparison rules out pure country risk.

16. For supporting evidence on uncovered interest parity for the United States and United Kingdom in the gold-standard period 1879–1914, see Calomiris and Hubbard (1996). These studies test for arbitrage in short-term financial securities. Bordo and Rockoff (1996) focus on the yields on long-term securities for nine capital-importing countries in the period 1890–1914. They show marked convergence in the nominal yields of both gold and paper securities after 1900 to the yield on British consols. Before 1900 gold yields moved closely with the consols yield.

17. Argentina was omitted from the calculation because its experience of high and variable inflation since World War II made its real interest rate considerably more volatile than that typical of countries in Group 1.

18. For an explanation of how this series was calculated, see Bordo, Eichengreen, and Kim (1998).

19. These estimates, from Royal Institute for International Affairs (1937), are based on the earlier work of Herbert Feis. Davis and Gallman (2000), focusing on the "19th century emerging markets," find that nine of every ten pounds of British investment in Argentina, Australia, Canada, and the United States between 1865 and 1890 went into railroads and government bonds. According to their estimates, the fraction ranges from 86 percent in Australia to 92 percent in Canada (Davis and Gallman, 7). Davis and Huttenback (1986) provide comparisons with domestic investment in quoted securities. Their chart 2.8 confirms the picture of a pattern of overseas portfolio investment concentrated in agricultural and extractive activities (especially in the British Empire), in transportation, and in public utilities. Domestic portfolio investment, in contrast, was disproportionately concentrated in manufacturing and in the commercial and financial sectors.

20. Note that even for the United States, the most industrialized of the regions of recent overseas European settlement, commodity exports (gold, silver, and agricultural commodities, and later petroleum) were the dominant source of export revenues throughout this period (Wright 1990).

21. According to Wilkins, "classic" multinational enterprises in which firms maintained operations in many countries became an increasingly important conduit for FDI over the period being discussed here.

22. It is not possible to put together a complete record of the global composition of foreign investment between portfolio and foreign direct investment for the world for our century of experience. Twomey (1998) and Kregel (1994), however, have assembled some of the data. Twomey presents a breakdown into portfolio and direct investment for the world from 1900 to 1938, which shows a significant increase in the total share of FDI from 31 percent to 48 percent between 1914 and 1938. For developing countries FDI represented two-thirds of foreign investment until World War II. Since then, FDI to less developed countries has declined significantly relative to the industrialized nations. According to Kregel, FDI increased relative to portfolio investment during the post-WWII Bretton Woods period, but since the 1980s there has been a resurgence of portfolio investment.

23. Also see O'Rourke and Williamson (1999). They emphasize three factors as key determinants of the high degree of financial integration before 1914: technology, financial institutions (especially the gold standard), and favorable political factors.

24. This view has been expressed by several prominent economists. Zevin (1992, 43), for example, believes that "while financial markets have certainly tended toward greater openness since the end of the Second World War, they have reached a degree of integration that is neither dramatic nor unprecedented in the larger historical context of several centuries." Sachs and Warner (1995, 5) argue that "the reemergence of a global, capitalist market economy since 1950, and especially since the mid-1980s, in an important sense reestablishes the global market economy that had existed one hundred years earlier." Rodrik (1998, 2) concludes that "in many ways, today's world falls far short of the level of economic integration reached at the height of the gold standard."

25. The cable reached Buenos Aires in 1878 and Tokyo in 1900.

26. The 1997 issue of the World Bank's *Global Development Finance* suggests that stocks and bonds are now of roughly equal importance in international portfolio capital flows to emerging markets, after a long period in which debt instruments (bonds and bank loans) dominated purchases of equities.

27. See Wilkins (1998). Free-standing companies became increasingly important as British investors gradually diversified beyond investments in railroads and government bonds into farming, ranching, mining, and brewing and sought to surmount the agency problems associated with the attempt to control far-distant American management.

28. As also emphasized by Davis and Gallman (2000).

29. This phenomenon will be familiar to observers of the Asian crisis. There, banks that were prohibited from maintaining open foreign positions and that therefore offset their foreign currency liabilities by making foreign currency loans to domestic corporations simply substituted credit risk for currency risk.

30. Much of this section is based on Bordo and Eichengreen (1999).

31. See Bordo and Murshid (2001) for evidence on the international transmission of financial crises and contagion effects from 1880 to the present.

32. The countries, which include many of today's advanced countries, are Argentina, Australia, Brazil, Canada, Chile, Denmark, Finland, Greece, Italy, Japan, Norway, Portugal, Spain, Sweden, and Switzerland.

33. The countries are Argentina, Brazil, Chile, Indonesia, Korea, Malaysia, Mexico, the Philippines, Singapore, and Thailand.

34. For an episode to qualify as a banking crisis, there had to be either bank runs, bank failures, and the suspension of convertibility of deposits into currency (a banking panic); or else significant banking-sector problems (including failures) that are resolved by a fiscally underwritten bank restructuring.

This allowed Bordo and Eichengreen (1999) to distinguish between liquidity crises before 1914, in which lender-of-last-resort intervention was either absent or unsuccessful, and events (like those typical of more recent years), in which a lender of last resort or deposit insurance was in place and the main problem was bank insolvency. In fact, however, a number of banking crises that occurred in Europe before 1914 did not involve panics and in this respect were not dissimilar from episodes occurring more recently. For an episode to qualify as a currency crisis, there had to be a forced change in parity, the abandonment of a pegged exchange rate, or an international rescue.

35. It is calculated as a weighted average of the percentage change in the exchange rate with respect to the core country (the United Kingdom before 1914, the United States thereafter), the change in the short-term interest rate differential with respect to the core country, and the difference in the percentage change in reserves of a given country and the percentage change in reserves of the core country.

This builds on the exchange-market-pressure model of Girton and Roper (1977), following the methodology of Eichengreen, Rose, and Wyplosz (1995, 1996). An episode is counted as a currency crisis when it shows up according to either of these indicators.

36. Note, however, that the post-1972 sample was not selected randomly; the ten countries considered were selected as the subjects of well-known crises. Using a similar chronology (that underlying chapter 4 of the *World Economic Outlook* [WEO], May 1998) for a larger sample of thirty emerging countries, the incidence is somewhat higher than ours. This reflects a larger number of crises in the WEO sample. However, the incidence of twin crises in our sample greatly exceeds that in the larger WEO sample.

37. While crises may have been somewhat less severe on average before 1914 than today, *t*-tests of the differences of means do not permit us to reject the null that the severity of downturns was the same across periods.

38. Categorizing the United States as an emerging market is likely to be controversial. Our categorization follows Eichengreen (1992), which classes the United States as a "peripheral" country prior to 1913 on the grounds that it was dependent on capital imports for much of the period, lacked a lender of last resort to backstop domestic financial markets, and was not fully committed to the maintenance of gold convertibility (and thus was not the recipient of stabilizing capital flows). For a contrasting interpretation, see Bordo and Schwartz (1996).

39. Two other famous emerging financial crises associated with serious real effects were those in Australia in 1893 and the United States in 1907–08. The exceptional severity of these episodes should serve as a warning that generalizations about the pre-1914 period must be drawn cautiously, since that period appears to have featured a small number of extraordinarily severe crises along with numerous milder episodes. This is another way of understanding why it is difficult to reject the null that the severity of crises was the same across periods; the standard deviation of the fall in output was large, reflecting the aforementioned heterogeneity, relative to the mean, both before 1914 and after 1972.

40. So does the fact that recovery from banking crises and twin crises was on average initiated earlier in the advanced countries than in the prewar emerging-market countries, given the fact that lender-of-last-resort capacity was more highly developed in the center.

41. Indeed, Bordo and Eichengreen (1999) show that the swings in capital flows were larger in the recent compared to the earlier crises.

42. Bordo and Eichengreen (1999) also examine the behavior of a number of ancillary variables: net exports, money growth, and real interest rates across the four regimes. In general the evidence for these variables supports that of De-Largy and Goodhart (1999) that adherence to the resumption role of the classical gold standard did make a difference for countries facing a currency crisis—the current account reversed more quickly and real interest rates spiked more quickly compared to the recent spate of crises.

43. Much of this section is adapted from Bordo and Schwartz (1999).

44. According to Gold (1988), the IMF is an offshoot of the ESF. Many of its procedures were developed there.

45. The debt crisis of the 1980s is not a precursor to the bailout loans of the 1990s. In the 1980s, U.S. money center banks were saved from closures by the actions of the IMF and the U.S. monetary authorities but were not bailed out in the sense that they were not saved from major losses on their loans to the emerging-market countries.

46. Edwards (1999) criticizes the IMF index of capital controls used in the study as too general to pick up country-specific restrictions.

47. Also see Klein and Olivei (1999), who present evidence for a panel of advanced and emerging countries for the past two decades showing that capital account liberalization raised growth rates via a financial deepening effect for the advanced countries but not for the emerging countries.

48. See James (2001), who argues that the backlash against the pre-1914 era of globalization was the primary factor leading to the Great Depression.

References

Bairoch, Paul, and Richard Kozul-Wright. 1998. Globalization myths: Some reflections on integration, industrialization, and growth in the world economy. In *Transnational corporations and the global economy,* ed. Richard Kozul-Wright and Robert Rowthorn, 3–27. New York: St. Martin's.

Bank for International Settlements (BIS). 1997. *Central bank survey of foreign exchange market activity.* Basel, Switzerland: BIS.

Baskin, Jonathan B. 1988. The development of corporate financial markets in Britain and the United States, 1600–1914: Overcoming asymmetric information. *Business History Review* 62 (Summer): 197–237.

Bayoumi, Tamim. 1990. Saving-investment correlations: Immobile capital, government policy, or endogenous behavior? *IMF Staff Papers* 37 (2):360–87.

Bayoumi, Tamim, and Barry Eichengreen. 1996. The stability of the gold standard and the evolution of the international monetary system. In *Modern perspectives on the gold standard,* ed. Tamim Bayoumi, Barry Eichengreen, and Mark Taylor, 165–88. Cambridge: Cambridge University Press.

Bernanke, Ben, and Harold James. 1991. The gold standard, deflation, and financial crisis in the Great Depression: An international comparison. In *Financial markets and financial crises,* ed. R. Glenn Hubbard, 36–68. Chicago: University of Chicago Press.

Bloomfield, Arthur I. 1963. Short-term capital movements under the pre-1914 gold standard. Princeton Studies in International Finance no. 11. Princeton University, Department of Economics, International Economics Section.

———. 1968. Patterns of fluctuation in international finance before 1914. Princeton Studies in International Finance no. 21. Princeton University, Department of Economics, International Economics Section.

Bordo, Michael D., and Barry Eichengreen. 1998. Implications of the Great Depression for the development of the international marketing system. In *The defining moment: The Great Depression and the American economy in the twentieth century,* ed. Michael D. Bordo, Claudia Goldin, and Eugene N. White, 403–54. Chicago: University of Chicago Press.

———. 1999. Is our current international economic environment unusually crisis prone? In *Capital flows and the international financial system,* ed. David Gruen and Luke Gower, 18–74. Sydney: Reserve Bank of Australia.

Bordo, Michael, Barry Eichengreen, and Douglas A. Irwin. 1999. Is globalization today really different than globalization a hundred years ago? In *Brookings trade forum,* ed. Susan M. Collins and Robert Z. Lawrence, 1–50. Washington, D.C.: Brookings Institution.

Bordo, Michael D., Barry Eichengreen, and Jongwoo Kim. 1998. Was there really an earlier era of financial globalization comparable to today? In *The implications of the globalization of world financial markets,* Bank of Korea, 27–83. Seoul: Bank of Korea.

Bordo, Michael, and Finn Kydland. 1996. The gold standard as a commitment mechanism. In *Modern perspectives on the gold standard,* ed. Tamim Bayoumi, Barry Eichengreen, and Mark Taylor, 55–100. Cambridge: Cambridge University Press.

Bordo, Michael D., Michael Edelstein, and Hugh Rockoff. 2002. Was adherence to the gold standard a "Good Housekeeping Seal of Approval" during the inter-war period? In *Finance, intermediaries, and economic development,* ed. Stanley Engerman, Philip Hoffman, Jean L. Rosenthal and Kenneth Sokoloff. New York: Cambridge University Press, forthcoming.

Bordo, Michael D., and Anna J. Schwartz. 1996. The operation of the specie standard: Evidence for core and peripheral countries, 1880–1990. In *Currency convertibility: The gold standard and beyond,* ed. Jorge Braga de Macedo, Barry Eichengreen, and Jaime Reis, 11–83. New York: Routledge.

———. 1999. Under what circumstances, past and present, have international rescues of countries in financial distress been successful? *Journal of International Money and Finance* 18:683–708.

———. 2000. Measuring real economic effects of bailouts: Historical perspectives on how countries in financial distress have failed with and without bailouts. *Carnegie Rochester Conference Series on Public Policy* 53:81–167.

Bordo, Michael D., and Antu Murshid. 2001. The international transmission of financial crises before World War II: Was there contagion? Chap. 14 in *International financial contagion,* ed. Stijn Claessens and Kristin Forbes, 367–403. Boston: Kluwer Academic Publishers.

Bordo, Michael D., and Hugh Rockoff. 1996. The gold standard as a Good House-keeping Seal of Approval. *Journal of Economic History* 56 (June): 389–428.

Calomiris, Charles, and R. Glenn Hubbard. 1996. International adjustment under the classical gold standard: Evidence for the U.S. and Britain, 1879–1914. In *Modern perspectives on the gold standard,* ed. Tamim Bayoumi, Barry Eichengreen, and Mark P. Taylor, 189–217. Cambridge: Cambridge University Press.

Coakley, J., F. Kulasi, and R. Smith. 1998. The Feldstein-Horioka puzzle and capital mobility: A review. *International Journal of Finance and Economics* 3:169–94.

Cole, Harold L., James Dow, and William B. English. 1995. Default, settlement, and signaling: Lending resumption in a reputational model of sovereign debt. *International Economic Review* 36:365–85.

Cooper, Richard N. 1998. Should capital-account convertibility be a world objective? In *Should the IMF pursue capital-account convertibility?* Essays in International Finance no. 207, 11–19. Princeton University, Department of Economics, International Finance Section.

Davis, Lance E., and Robert Gallman. 2000. *Waves, tides, and sandcastles: The impact of foreign capital flows on evolving financial markets in the New World, 1865–1914.* New York: Cambridge University Press.

Davis, Lance E., and Robert A. Huttenback. 1986. *Mammon and the pursuit of empire.* Cambridge: Cambridge University Press.

DeLargy, P. J. R., and Charles Goodhart. 1999. Financial crises: Plus ça change, plus c'est la meme chose. LSE Financial Markets Group Special Paper no. 108.

DeLong, J. Bradford. 1999. Financial crises in the 1890s and the 1990s: Must history repeat? *Brookings Papers on Economic Activity,* Issue no. 2: 253–94.

Dooley, Michael P. 2000. A model of crises in emerging markets. *Economic Journal* 110 (460): 256–72.

Edwards, Sebastian. 1999. How effective are capital contracts? NBER Working Paper no. 7413. Cambridge, Mass.: National Bureau of Economic Research, November.

Eichengreen, Barry. 1992. *Golden fetters.* Oxford: Oxford University Press.

Eichengreen, Barry, and Ashoka Mody. 1998. What explains the changing spreads on emerging-market debt: Fundamentals or market sentiment? NBER Working Paper no. 6408. Cambridge, Mass.: National Bureau of Economic Research, February.

Eichengreen, Barry, Andrew Rose, and Charles Wyplosz. 1995. Exchange market mayhem: The antecedents and aftermath of speculative attacks. *Economic Policy* 21:249–312.

———. 1996. Speculative attacks on pegged exchange rates: An empirical exploration with special reference to the European Monetary System. In *The new transatlantic economy,* ed. Matthew Canzoneri, Wilfred Ethier, and Vittorio Grilli, New York: Cambridge University Press.

Feldstein, Martin. 1998. Self-protection for emerging market economies. Harvard University, Department of Economics. Mimeograph.

Feldstein, Martin, and Charles Horioka. 1980. Domestic saving and international capital flows. *Economic Journal* 90 (June): 314–29.

Fishlow, Albert. 1985. Lessons from the past: Capital markets during the nineteenth century and the interwar period. In *The politics of international debt,* ed. Miles Kahler, 37–94. Ithaca, N.Y.: Cornell University Press.

Flandreau, Marc. 1998. Caveat emptor: Dealing with sovereign risk in the age of globalization, 1871–1913. Ecole des Hautes Etudes en Sciences Sociale, Paris. Mimeograph, April.

Flandreau, Marc, Jacque Le Cacheux, and Frederic Zumer. 1998. Stability without a pact? Lessons from the European gold standard, 1880–1914. *Economic Policy* 26 (April): 115–62.

Friedman, Milton, and Anna J. Schwartz. 1963. *A monetary history of the United States, 1867–1960.* Princeton: Princeton University Press.

Friedman, Thomas L. 1999. *The Lexus and the olive tree.* New York: Farrar, Straus, and Giroux.

Garbade, Kenneth D., and William L. Silber. Technology, communication, and the performance of financial markets: 1840–1975. *Journal of Finance* 33 (1): 819–32.

Girton, Lance, and Donald Roper. 1997. A monetary model of exchange market pressure applied to postwar Canadian experience. *American Economic Review* 67:537–48.

Gold, J. 1988. Mexico and the development of the practice of the International Monetary Fund. *World Development* 16:127–42.

Hatton, Timothy J., and Jeffrey G. Williamson. 1992. International migration and world development: A historical perspective. Harvard Institute of Economic Research Discussion Paper no. 1606. August.

———. 1998. *The age of mass migration: Causes and economic impact.* New York: Oxford University Press.

International Monetary Fund (IMF). 1999. *International financial statistics* [CD-ROM]. Washington, D.C.: IMF.

Irwin, Douglas A. 1993. Multilateral and bilateral trade policies in the world banking system: An historical perspective. In *New dimensions in regional integration,* ed. J. De Melo and A. Panngariya, 9–119. New York: Cambridge University Press.

James, Harold. 2001. *The end of globalization.* Cambridge, Mass.: Harvard University Press.

Jones, Matthew T., and Maurice Obstfeld. 2000. Saving, investment, and gold: A reassessment of historical current account data. In *Money, capital mobility, and trade: Essays in honor of Robert Mundell,* ed. Guillermo Calvo, Rudi Dornbusch, and Maurice Obstfeld, 313–64. Cambridge: MIT Press.

Klein, Michael, and Giovannino Olivei. 1999. Capital account liberalization, financial depth, and economic growth. NBER Working Paper no. 7384. Cambridge, Mass.: National Bureau of Economic Research, October.

Kregel, Jan. 1994. Capital flows: Globalization in production and financing development. *UNCTAD Review 1994:* 1–38.

Lothian, James R. 1995. Capital market integration and exchange-rate regimes in historical perspective. Fordham University, Graduate School of Business. Mimeograph.

Madden, John J. 1985. *British investment in the United States, 1860–1880.* New York: Garland.

Marichal, Carlos. 1989. *A century of Latin American debt crises.* Princeton: Princeton University Press.

Marston, Richard C. 1993. Interest differentials under Bretton Woods and the post–Bretton Woods float: The effects of capital controls and exchange risk. In *A retrospective on the Bretton Woods System: Lessons for international monetary reform,* ed. Michael D. Bordo and Barry Eichengreen, 515–38. Chicago: University of Chicago Press.

———. 1995. *International financial integration: A study of interest differentials between the major industrial countries.* Cambridge: Cambridge University Press.

Miller, Victoria. 1996. Exchange rate crises with domestic bank runs: Evidence from the 1890s. *Journal of International Money and Finance* 15:4.

———. 1998. Domestic bank runs and speculative attacks on foreign currencies. *Journal of International Money and Finance* 17:2.

Neal, Larry. 1990. *The rise of financial capitalism: International capital markets in the Age of Reason.* Cambridge: Cambridge University Press.

———. 1998. The Bank of England's first return to gold and the stock market crisis of 1825. Federal Reserve Bank of St. Louis *Review* 80 (3): 53–76.

Nurkse, Ragnar. 1944. *International currency experience.* Geneva: League of Nations.

O'Rourke, Kevin H., and Jeffrey G. Williamson. 1999. *Globalization and history: The evolution of a nineteenth century Atlantic economy.* Cambridge: MIT Press.

Obstfeld, Maurice. 1995. International capital mobility in the 1990s. In *Understanding interdependence: The macroeconomics of the open economy,* ed. Peter B. Kenen, 201–61. Princeton: Princeton University Press.

Obstfeld, Maurice, and Alan Taylor. 1998. The Great Depression as a watershed: International capital mobility over the long-run. In *The defining moment: The Great Depression and the American economy in the twentieth century,* ed. Michael D. Bordo, Claudia Goldin, and Eugene N. White, 353–402. Chicago: University of Chicago Press.

———. 2001. Globalization and capital markets. NBER Working Paper no. 8846. Cambridge, Mass.: National Bureau of Economic Research, March.

Rodrik, Dani. 1998. The debate over globalization: How to move forward by looking backward. In *Should the IMF pursue capital account convertibility?* Essays in International Finance no. 207, 55–65. Princeton University, Department of Economics, International Finance Section.

Royal Institute of International Affairs. 1937. *The problem of international investment.* London: Oxford University Press.

Sachs, Jeffrey, and Andrew Warner. 1995. Economic reform and the process of global integration. *Brookings Papers on Economic Activity,* Issue no. 1: 1–118.

Snowden, Kenneth A. 1995. The evolution of interregional mortgage lending channels, 1870–1940: The life insurance–mortgage company connection. In *Coordination and information: Historical perspectives on the organization of enterprise,* ed. Naomi R. Lamoreaux and Daniel M. G. Raff, 209–46. Chicago: University of Chicago Press.

Soros, George. 1998. *The crisis of global capitalism.* New York: Public Affairs Books.

Sussman, Nathan, and Yishay Yateh. 2000. Institutions, economic growth, and country risk: Evidence from Japanese government debt in the Meiji period. *Journal of Economic History* 60 (2): 442–67.

Taylor, Alan M. 1994. Domestic saving and international capital flows reconsidered. NBER Working Paper no. 4892. Cambridge, Mass.: National Bureau of Economic Research, October.

———. 1996. International capital mobility in history: The saving-investment relationship. NBER Working Paper no. 5743. Cambridge, Mass.: National Bureau of Economic Research, September.

———. 1997. Argentina and the world capital market: Saving, investment, and international capital mobility in the twentieth century. NBER Working Paper no. 6302. Cambridge, Mass.: National Bureau of Economic Research, December.

Twomey, Michael J. 2000. *A century of foreign investment in the third world.* London: Routledge.

United Nations (U.N.). 1949. *International capital movements during the inter-war period.* Lake Success, N.Y.: United Nations.

Wilkins, Mira. 1998. Conduits for long-term investment in the gold standard era. Florida International University, Department of Economics. Mimeograph, March.

Williamson, Jeffrey G. 1996. Globalization, convergence, and history. *Journal of Economic History* 56 (June): 277–306.

Wright, Gavin. 1990. The origins of American industrial success. *American Economic Review* 80:651–68.

Zevin, Robert. 1992. Are world financial markets more open? If so, why and with what effects? In *Financial openness and national autonomy,* ed. Tariq Banuri and Juliet B. Schor, 43–83. Oxford, U.K.: Clarendon Press.

Chapter Two

Capital Movements: Curse or Blessing?

Michael P. Dooley and Carl E. Walsh

Interest in capital controls has been a highly cyclical industry. As Tobin (1996) observed, "The interest that occasionally arose [for his transactions tax proposal] came from journalists and financial pundits. It was usually triggered by currency crises and died out when the crisis passed from the headlines" (ix–xviii). Financial crises have certainly been a frequent and painful feature of the international monetary system in recent years. The obvious welfare costs of crises have led to a general reevaluation of strategies for opening repressed financial systems to international competition.

The limitations and fragility of private credit markets in developing countries should not have been a surprise. Financial markets in industrial countries are highly regulated and there is a very large and sophisticated literature on the market failures that make this regulation necessary. The primary objective for supervision and regulation in industrial countries remains the maintenance of financial stability. In this paper we note that the regulatory framework in industrial countries has evolved away from crude controls over insured banks' ability to compete for liabilities. Nevertheless, capital controls designed to limit insured residents' ability to sell liabilities to nonresidents may be the best available prudential control in emerging markets today.

We argue below that controls over bank liabilities, such as regulation-Q ceilings on deposit interest rates in the United States, were effective prudential controls when the United States was an emerging market. Limita-

Michael P. Dooley is professor of economics at the University of California, Santa Cruz, currently on academic leave at the Deutsche Bank's Global economic research department, and a research associate of the National Bureau of Economic Research. Carl E. Walsh is professor of economics at the University of California, Santa Cruz.

tions on capital inflows to banks were designed to limit banks' ability to compete for deposits in order to exploit government-provided deposit insurance. Because such controls are costly, the United States and other industrial countries have moved to a regulatory environment based on complex assessments of capital adequacy and risk. While financial liberalization in emerging markets has generally relaxed constraints on liability management of insured institutions, however, it is almost certain that the authorities cannot jump overnight into a modern regulatory framework. For a newly liberalized emerging market, an appropriate entry tax on capital inflows may be an effective transitional measure. If the authorities cannot regulate the risk-taking activities of domestic financial firms, it might still succeed in limiting their ability to compete for foreign funds.

Should governments of developing countries introduce controls on international financial transactions if controls could mitigate this loss? We should be careful to do the accounting correctly. If controlled capital markets generate a lower growth in tranquil times, the present value costs of this policy are potentially enormous. The complexity of intertemporal resource allocation gives market mechanisms the decisive edge over planning, but we have ample evidence that badly structured and poorly regulated private financial markets can also misallocate resources. Certainly the empirical literature provides conflicting answers. Edwards (1999) suggests that countries with more open capital accounts have benefited in terms of economic growth, although this positive effect may operate only after a country has reached a threshold level of development. Glick and Hutchison (2000) find evidence that capital controls may actually make a country more vulnerable to currency crises. To begin to answer these important questions we have to better understand the relationship between capital controls and financial crises.

Net or Gross Capital Flows?

What is at stake in choosing to participate in international capital markets? Is it the net resource transfer that alters the time path for consumption or capital formation? Or is it the more efficient intermediation of foreign *and* domestic savings that results in a more productive capital stock? If we assume that the productivity of the domestic capital stock is independent of the process of financial intermediation, controls on capital inflows or outflows can be evaluated according to their effect on the marginal real cost of domestic capital formation. An effective capital control program is defined as one that distorts yields faced by nonresidents and, in turn, alters net private capital inflows.

A very large traditional literature reviewed in Dooley (1996a) examines initial conditions that might make such a government intervention a second best welfare-improving policy. An empirical study of the Chilean control program (Edwards 1999) estimates the cost of distorting *net* capital flows in recent years and finds it substantial.

In our view there is a good possibility that such exercises miss the essential issue in evaluating capital controls because they do not focus on the economic costs and benefits of international financial intermediation. That is, for a given trajectory for the current account—or its mirror image, the net capital account balance—does two-way trade in financial assets improve the efficiency of the savings and investment process in the participating countries? As Rogoff (1999) points out, the United States has done quite well with a low domestic savings rate; a small increment of foreign savings; and a stable, competitive, and efficient financial market.

Proponents of controls point out that financial structures that work in the industrial countries often do not work in developing countries. They emphasize moral hazard, asymmetric information and a variety of other potential market failures that require sophisticated management of financial markets. Although there are a variety of welfare costs associated with these market failures, the dominant cost seems to be associated with financial crises. Since sophisticated management is in short supply in emerging markets, unsophisticated management in the form of capital controls may be the next (third) best alternative.

Models of distortions in financial markets imply that an effective capital control program can be defined as one that alters the scale or the composition of two-way trade in financial assets. Industrial countries chose just such a system of very restricted domestic financial markets following the economic chaos of the Great Depression and World War II. The Bretton Woods system of international financial arrangements was built on the foundation of capital account restrictions.

There is no natural correlation between the welfare implications of gross and net capital flows. For example, an effective welfare-improving capital control program might reduce the volume of gross capital flows and, if the remaining flows are more efficient, increase the net capital inflow to a country. Alternatively, an effective program might decrease net inflows but increase gross flows. By increasing the efficiency of intermediation this might increase the productivity of the capital stock and improve welfare. We can think of circumstances in which the two effects are related. Suppose, for example, that a net capital inflow swamps the ability of domestic financial intermediaries to make sensible investment decisions. In this case large inflows are also poorly intermediated.

With this in mind we turn to a series of models of crises the better to understand the rationale, if any, for capital controls associated with each. Our main organizing principle is that alternative models have very different behavioral assumptions for governments and private investors. Alternative analytic frameworks place the blame for crises on governments, all private investors, some private investors, or some combination of private and government market participants.

Sources of Financial Crises

The important message from first-generation models of crises is that inconsistent macro-policy regimes will end in spectacular but predictable and anticipated crashes. The timing of crises does not appear to be related to fundamental macroeconomic policies, but it is. The policy advice that flows from this framework is straightforward: get the fundamentals right and there is nothing to fear.

An important part of the appeal of first-generation models is that private investors are rational and competitive and that capital mobility is perfect. At every point in time before and after the crisis, private creditors earn a return on domestic securities and money that is consistent with an exogenous world rate of interest. Governments, in contrast, are quite myopic. They insist on trying to monetize a fiscal deficit but succeed only in financing the deficit by selling off a stock of reserves that was somewhat mysteriously there in the beginning.

The assumption of perfect capital mobility keeps net and gross private capital flows in the background. With no violence to the logic of these models, we could add the assumption that expected returns on foreign and domestic real capital are the same and that time preference is the same so there is no reason for net intertemporal trade. The assumption that the government cannot borrow is equivalent to the assumption of Ricardian equivalence; that is, the optimal current account balance is zero and is independent of government financial decisions.

In an important extension of the basic model, Calvo (1987) demonstrates that, even if the private capital account were completely closed, the inconsistent government behavior posited in this model would eventually generate a crisis. If members of the private sector are prevented from adjusting their money balances through the capital account, they will do so through net trade in goods and services. In particular, residents will rearrange their intertemporal consumption so that the government's reserves are exhausted in financing a trade deficit, and eventually there will be a crisis that forces a change in the regime. Clearly, in this important class of first-generation models, capital controls are not a promising policy tool. Governments obviously are to blame for crises, and capital control programs are simply incapable of righting this wrong.

Government Behavior and Multiple Equilibria

The first-generation models discussed above assume that private speculators are rational and competitive but that governments are very simple-minded. The apparent absence of such government behavior prior to the European Monetary System (EMS) crisis suggested that a more sophisticated model of government behavior might be needed to understand crises. Once a more complex assumption concerning government behavior is introduced, the same rational and competitive private investors are obliged to form expectations about government behavior in addition to the other fundamentals. We will refer to models in which multiple equilibria can arise due to the government's behavior as *MEG models*, because they rely on quite specific assumptions about government behavior. In the next section we discuss multiple-equilibrium models based on financial intermediation.

In MEG models, arbitrary shifts in private expectations about government behavior can generate crises. It has long been recognized that expected changes in policy can generate a successful speculative attack even if the government follows fully consistent policies preceding the attack (Krugman 1996; Garber 1996), but this is not the story behind this literature.

A much more stringent condition for a self-fulfilling attack is that a shift in private expectations about government behavior generates a change in the *optimal* policy regime. Calvo (1988, 648) summarizes the implications of the argument as follows: "The implications for policy could be staggering: for our results suggest that postponing taxes (i.e., falling into debt) may generate the seeds of indeterminacy; it may, in other words, generate a situation in which the effects of policy are at the mercy of people's expectations—gone would be the hopes of leading the economy along an optimal path." Flood and Garber (1984) and Obstfeld (1986) show that if a government is expected to follow more expansionary monetary policies following a successful speculative attack on the fixed exchange rate regime, policy regimes that would otherwise be viable can be forced to collapse by self-fulfilling private expectations.

Obstfeld (1994) refines the argument by specifying the political economy that might account for the government's behavior before and after an attack. The analysis sets out a rational government that seeks to maximize a plausible objective function. Since the government's objectives are the same in any exchange rate regime, it follows that policy setting under different regimes must reflect changes in the economic environment rather than arbitrary assumptions concerning the government's behavior.

Several papers have examined crises in emerging markets and concluded that shifts in private expectations are important elements in an attack sequence. Calvo and Mendoza (1996) argue that the crisis in Mexico in 1994 is consistent with the idea that the government's short-term debt and the anticipation of a bailout for a weak banking system made it vulnerable to a shift in private expectations. Cole and Kehoe (1996) also argue that events in Mexico are consistent with the definition of a self-fulfilling crisis. Sachs, Tornell, and Velasco (1996) examine characteristics of twenty countries that seem to contribute to their vulnerability to speculative attacks following the Mexican crisis in 1994. They find that prior lending booms, overvalued exchange rates, and low levels of reserves relative to M2 explain a large part of this experience. They also find that fiscal and current account deficits seem to be unrelated to a country's vulnerability to attack.

Capital Controls and Multiple Equilibria

In MEG models, crises can be blamed on the government because the government decides to incur debt and to issue a debt structure that is vulnerable to shifts in private expectations about future government policy. Investors are also partly to blame, however, because it is the arbitrary shifts in private expectations that trigger the swing from a good to a bad equilibrium.

Capital controls are surprisingly difficult to evaluate in this class of crisis models. If only a subset of investors were prone to shifting expectations, it would follow that a control program that prevented such investors from acquiring claims on the debtor country would be effective in preventing crises. The argument is even more attractive if it is possible to limit investors with volatile expectations while at the same time interfering less, or not at all, with investors that base their expectations on fundamentals. This is the basic logic behind the well-known Tobin tax proposal. The key feature of this government intervention is that it is designed to tax relatively heavily capital inflows that are held for short periods of time. This presumes such flows are dominated by traders that move in and out of the market more frequently than could be reasonably associated with changes in expectations about the fundamentals:

> The hope that transactions taxes will diminish excess volatility depends on the likelihood that Keynes's speculators have shorter time horizons and holding periods than market participants engaged in long-term foreign investment and otherwise oriented toward fundamentals. If so, it is speculators who are the more deterred by the tax. (Eichengreen, Tobin, and Wyplosz 1995, 165)

This is a sensible conjecture but does not stand up to empirical evaluation. Dooley (1996b) argues that there is no evidence that high transactions costs tend to deter noise traders relative to investors who evaluate fundamentals, and there is some weak evidence to the contrary. Perhaps more importantly, there is considerable doubt that reducing the variability of prices can generate increases in welfare because the turnover tax tends to increase the volatility of expected yields.

The more conventional assumption is that expectations are uniform across private speculators but subject to arbitrary shifts. In this case an effective ex post restriction on capital outflows would prevent the move to a bad equilibrium. Self-fulfilling attacks can go the opposite direction, however. For example, a spontaneous decline in private inflationary expectations could set in motion a sequence of falling interest rates and fiscal deficits that generate a good equilibrium. It is perhaps informative that there seem to be few examples of changes in private expectations generating self-fulfilling virtuous responses by governments. Countries that start from a bad equilibrium should shun capital controls since they would delay adjustment to the new more optimistic private expectations.

A number of papers have exploited the idea that controls themselves might be powerful signals concerning the government's future policies. If private-sector investors know that the system is protected by controls, they would be less impressed by observed stability. Lane and Rojas-Suarez (1992), for example, argue that the use of controls has ambiguous implications for the credibility of a monetary policy regime.

Dellas and Stockman (1993) show that a speculative attack might be generated by the expectation that capital controls will be introduced. If the government can commit not to introduce controls, the fixed rate regime is sustainable. In this model a regime that is otherwise viable becomes vulnerable to expectations that controls will be imposed in response to the attack. This increases interest rates before the attack and generates the conditions for a self-fulfilling devaluation.

Bartolini and Drazen (1997) develop the idea that controls themselves are a signal that affects private-sector expectations concerning the government's future treatment of investors. In their model the removal of controls signals to investors that the government is less likely to tax foreign capital income, or reimpose controls once the capital inflow is in place.

Finally, Obstfeld (1986) shows that capital controls can generate multiple equilibria where none exist with capital mobility. In this model multiple equilibria are a feature of a maximizing model with effective capital controls. Residents of the controlled economy maximize the utility of real money holdings and consumption over time subject to their balance sheet constraint. Owing to effective capital controls, residents can accumulate real money balances only through current account surpluses, which have as a mirror image increases in the central bank's net foreign assets. Because the net foreign asset position of the central bank earns the world interest rate, a current account surplus generates an increase in the expected permanent income of residents. An unstable equilibrium occurs if the increase in real money balances, and the associated increase in expected income, is not more than matched with an increase in current consumption. If not, the current account surplus increases and money balances and income continue to rise until a stable equilibrium is reached. This is not an argument for or against capital controls. It only demonstrates that when the domestic interest rate is distorted through a capital control program the usual assumptions that generate convergence to unique steady state equilibrium are not sufficient.

This literature presents a genuine problem for the policy implications of capital controls. On the one hand, an effective capital control program might buy enough time for the government to move the fundamentals to a region where self-fulfilling speculative attacks are less likely. The implication seems to be that controls might be a temporary measure to buy time for a virtuous government to establish its reputation. On the other hand, it is easy to show that the fact that controls might be introduced in the future can generate attacks where none would occur otherwise. Finally, the market might interpret the removal of controls on capital outflows as a commitment not to penalize foreign investors. If so, the removal of controls would generate capital inflows.

On the surface it appears that controls might delay or even prevent a speculative attack and the associated costs—but the typical policy of imposing controls as the attack occurs, probably because the authorities believe that the controls are not effective for long, can also be a powerful force to trigger speculative attacks. Finally, a careful treatment of expectations can suggest that policies designed to limit net capital inflows might have just the opposite effect.

Capital Controls and Third-Generation Models of Speculative Attack

Third-generation models of speculative attacks also predict that good and bad equilibria are possible but in these models shifts in private expectations interact with private financial intermediaries rather than with the government. In our view, multiple-equilibrium financial structure (MEF) models offer the most interesting and potentially useful framework for evaluating capital controls.

There is a range of closed-economy models that provide insights into the structure of financial markets, the sources of financial fragility, and the role that policies might have on both the efficiency of financial markets and their stability. By and large, these models have not been designed to address directly the issues associated with international capital flows. Typically, theory deals with broad classes of agents—lenders versus borrowers, consumers versus firms, entrepreneurs versus savers. These categories do not necessarily correspond to whether the market participants are foreign or domestic residents. However, economic theory does highlight important sources of credit market imperfections and their implications for financial instability.

In this section, some key models of financial market structure are reviewed. We begin with a discussion of bank runs, situations in which a bank is unable to meet the withdrawal demands of its depositors. Bank runs represent one possible equilibrium, a bad one, in models in which the absence of a run, the good equilibrium, is also possible. The role of the sequential service constraint, herd-like behavior, and information cascades that might generate bank runs are discussed in the next section. We then turn to the asset side of the bank or country balance sheet. Here, moral hazard problems and asymmetric information affect the nature of financial contracts.

Depositor-Investor Runs

A useful starting point for an analysis of financial fragility is the classic Diamond-Dybvig (1983) model of bank runs. This model provides a well-defined environment in which there is a demand for liquidity, and banks can perform a maturity transformation function that, in equilibrium, is welfare improving. However, there is a second equilibrium in which a bank run occurs. In this second equilibrium, all depositors attempt to withdraw their funds from the bank. Losses are suffered as the bank liquidates its assets to meet these withdrawals.

The basic Diamond-Dybvig model focuses on two key factors. First, investments normally require that funds be committed for some period of time. This can be thought of as reflecting higher expected returns on long-term investments, or simply that there are costs of liquidating asset holdings. Assets held to maturity offer higher returns than assets sold before maturity. Second, individuals are uncertain as to when they will need their funds. There is a positive probability that an investor will need to liquidate before maturity.[1]

In the absence of aggregate uncertainty, a predictable fraction of all individuals will discover they need their funds early. In this environment, a bank can provide liquidity risk insurance to individual agents, accepting deposits and investing in the long-term asset. The deposit contract specifies the amount a depositor may withdraw prior to the asset's maturity. Because there is no aggregate uncertainty, banks can always hold exactly the level of reserves necessary to meet withdrawals by impatient consumers. Patient consumers will be better off if they leave their funds in the bank and receive a higher payout when the investment asset matures.

A bank run can take place, however, if patient depositors believe other patient depositors will draw their deposits. If all patient depositors attempt to withdraw their funds from the bank, the bank will, even after liquidating its assets, have insufficient funds to meet withdrawals—the bank fails. So if a patient depositor expects others to withdraw early, it is individually rational to try to withdraw early as well.

Bank Runs and Country Runs

The idea that there are patient and impatient international investors has been a prominent feature of informal discussions of international capital flows. The traditional analysis of hot money flows assumes that the nature of the financial instrument traded reveals something about the behavior of the investor. In particular, investors that are likely to become impatient and start a run on a country are assumed to prefer short-term debt instruments.

Chang and Velasco (2001) use the Diamond-Dybvig structure to analyze international capital flows. They focus on the problem of illiquidity, defined as a situation in which the domestic financial sectors' short-term potential liabilities exceed the liquidation value of its assets. Access to foreign borrowing can reduce the chances of a bank run by providing the domestic bank with an additional source of short-term funds. However, failure of foreign lenders to extend lending when domestic banks experience a run has the effect of making banks more vulnerable to runs. The belief on the part of domestic depositors that foreign lenders will refuse to extend short-term credit can trigger a bank run and force the closure of domestic banks. The presence of short-term foreign borrowing makes the domestic financial sector more vulnerable to a decision by foreign lenders not to roll over the existing stock of debt. In that sense, short-term foreign debt increases financial-sector fragility.

The basic insights of this model have focused attention on two issues. First, what might cause panic runs on the bank or country? This is essentially a question about equilibrium selection. What determines whether the good (no-run) equilibrium or the bad (run) equilibrium occurs? Second, can the deposit–external debt contract offered by the bank or country be restructured to eliminate the possibility of a run? This question is of particular relevance for an analysis of capital controls. Can the nature of domestic liabilities held by foreign investors be altered via regulations in ways that reduce the possibility of a panic?

Narrow Banking

Four basic solutions that focus on the nature of the deposit contract have been examined. The first is narrow banking. A bank could be required to hold a level of reserves sufficient to meet withdrawals in all possible circumstances. Although narrow banking eliminates the possibility of a run, it does so by essentially eliminating the ability of banks to offer maturity transformation services. Since this was the benefit to be derived from banks in the first place, narrow banking essentially returns the economy to the autarkic equilibrium.

The capital control regime that is the counterpart to narrow banking is one that would require that the maturity structure of a country's external liabilities match the maturity structure of the country's assets. Although this solution to runs is a nonstarter for banks, it makes more sense in the context of international financial markets. Emerging markets have typically borrowed short and invested in a portfolio of assets including international reserves, private claims on foreigners, and the domestic capital stock. However, it is not clear that liquidity transformation is a necessary or welfare-improving aspect of international lending to developing countries.

If nonresident investors were forced to accept long-term debt or equity claims on the debtor country this could be viewed as a useful way for them to coordinate on the good (patient) equilibrium. Moreover, if the problem was self-fulfilling runs, foreign investors would presumably recognize this as a superior structure of debt and lend on better terms.

Suspension

Diamond and Dybvig offer a second solution—suspension of convertibility. If the bank can perfectly predict the number of impatient consumers, it can hold reserves sufficient to meet the withdrawals of impatient consumers. If additional depositors attempt to withdraw funds, the bank simply suspends convertibility. All the impatient consumers are able to withdraw their funds, and the patient consumers have no incentive to withdraw early since they know the bank will always have adequate funds in the future. The bank will have adequate funds because it suspends convertibility if deposit withdrawals threaten its reserves.

Allowing for a suspension of convertibility does not affect the fundamental maturity-transformation service banks provide. It acts more as an equilibrium-selection device, ensuring that the economy achieves the good equilibrium without runs. Prior to the founding of the Federal Reserve System, U.S. banks normally suspended convertibility during banking crises.

This model offers a relatively clear and convincing reason for seriously considering capital controls as a policy to minimize crises. Diamond and Dybvig advocated suspension of convertibility as a cure for bank runs that allowed banks to continue to provide liquidity services. The obvious parallel in international financial markets would be the controls on capital outflows from Malaysia following the 1999 crisis. Such controls make nonresident claims temporarily inconvertible into cash, much like the suspension of bank deposits into cash. There is, of course, the problem that nonresidents may doubt the temporary nature of this policy and may also doubt that they will ever receive the fair market value of their investments following the crisis. However, if the policy actually is temporary and prevents fire sales, nonresident investors should welcome such a policy as being in their collective interests. The fact that they did not welcome this initiative may have more to do with the perceived intentions of the Malaysians than with the economic logic behind the policy.

Proposals for International Monetary Fund– (IMF-) sanctioned suspension of debt service payment are also in the same spirit. The problem, of course, is in deciding when the problem is only impatient investors and when there is a real loss to be allocated. Nevertheless the logic is compelling. If the fault for the crisis lies with the incomplete contracts, in this case with the fact that the contracts are not state contingent, then a natural solution to the problem is to make the contracts state contingent ex post.

Deposit Insurance or Lender of Last Resort

A third class of solutions to the bank run problem, deposit insurance or a lender of last resort, is the most commonly observed. Under a deposit insurance scheme, patient depositors have no incentive to withdraw their deposits. Of course the presence of deposit insurance can lead to a moral hazard problem because banks have an incentive to hold riskier assets. (We discuss the role of government insurance in creating the conditions for a crisis later in this chapter.)

The interesting application to international crisis management is that an international lender of last resort is an *alternative* to capital controls in preventing runs. As discussed below, however, the moral hazard generated by insurance can also provide a powerful rationale for controls.

Equity or Direct Investment Only

A fourth solution, due to Jacklin (1987), alters the nature of the deposit contract, essentially replacing it with an equity stake in the bank. Depositors who discover they are impatient can sell their shares at a market-determined price. Depositors who discover they are patient will wish to buy additional shares in the bank. While eliminating the possibility of a run, equity contracts may do worse than deposit contracts as a means of providing liquidity insurance.

The potential inefficiency with equity contracts is of less concern when applied to international capital flows. There, the stability of the domestic financial sector, rather than the provision of liquidity to international investors, would be of primary concern. While equity contracts do solve the problem of runs, the attractiveness of equity contracts is diminished as soon as additional credit market imperfections are recognized. Imperfect information about investment projects, for example, can lead to agency costs that, in turn, give rise to a role for collateral. In such an environment, fluctuations in the share price of the bank may affect the bank's ability to raise funds.

Effectiveness and Derivatives

An important problem with these and similar arguments for capital controls is the assumption that different types of capital flows can be differentially taxed. This is an empirical issue, since it depends on the authority's ability to monitor the behavior of private investors and to tax only some types of activities. In our view, recent experience is not encouraging. While capital control programs have been able to change the description of capital flows, it is not clear that this also changes the economic behavior of the investors. It is quite easy to modify the economic nature of an international investment by combining the balance sheet entry subject to regulation with a derivative position that is very difficult to monitor. Professionals in this area claim they can "undo anything better than you can."

Sequential Service Constraints, Herding, and Financial Fragility

The first-come-first-served nature of deposit contracts creates an incentive for even patient depositors to withdraw funds immediately if they fear others may withdraw their deposits. The same problem is obvious in the international context. Investors that get to the central bank before its reserves are exhausted are paid in full while latecomers suffer losses. In this environment investors' beliefs about what other investors will do become critically important, and multiple self-fulfilling expectational equilibria can exist. A set of financial institutions and regulations may support an efficient and welfare-enhancing equilibrium, but the same set of institutions may also be vulnerable to shifts in expectations that push it into a bad equilibrium.

The fragility of financial markets to runs and investor panics has always provided a primary rationale for regulation. Regulations typically are designed to reduce the incentive for runs by such means as deposit insurance and to limit the riskiness of the underlying asset portfolio held by the bank through prudential regulation. Capital controls can be viewed as one mechanism for changing the incentives to run, but to evaluate their possible role requires some consideration of the underlying reasons for investor panics.

One approach has emphasized the problems that may arise when investors have little information themselves, and so base their actions to a large extent on what they see others doing. Seeing others invest in emerging markets, for example, some investors draw the conclusion that such investments are promising, leading to a large flow of capital to emerging markets. Seeing others pull their funds out, some investors follow suit. This highlights the potentially important role of herd behavior and informational cascades. Investors may base their actions on what they see others doing, rather than on their own information about underlying fundamental conditions.[2] The distinction between observing the information of others and simply observing what others have done is critical, but it is also quite realistic. Particularly in the environment of a crisis, actions speak louder than words.

If enough individuals are observed having made one choice (say, withdrawing deposits), subsequent agents will disregard their own private information and mimic the actions of others. The weight of the evidence (the choices others have made) outweighs the individual's own information. Agents may behave in ways that are inconsistent with their own private information if others have made a different choice. At some point, herd behavior results. Everyone ignores their own information and follows the behavior of the earlier movers.

In this environment, the decisions by the earlier movers can be critical. For example, if a few investors liquidate holdings in a country, others may assume that they must have had good reason to do so (whether in fact they did or not). Making such an inference, they also liquidate positions, and a run occurs. This can happen even if the later movers all had private information that indicated they should not liquidate.

Three important points are worth emphasizing. First, the quality of the individual agent's own information will be important. If an individual believes he or she has very good information, that individual may ignore the actions taken by others, deciding instead to act on his or her own private information. Second, beliefs about the quality of the information others possess are also important. If investors think that the first to liquidate are likely to be better informed on average, it becomes more likely that herd behavior will result. Third, herding behavior can result in the wrong choice being made.

When multiple equilibria based on nonfundamental factors are possible, it may also be possible for government policies to serve a coordinating role that focuses expectations, and therefore the actual outcomes, on the good equilibrium. When capital outflows result from herding behavior, can capital controls help select the correct equilibrium? If capital flows are particularly sensitive to herd behavior, does a role for controls emerge?

The heart of the problem is information, or rather the lack of accurate information. Public information might help, but two difficulties present themselves. First, it is not clear that anyone knows the true state. Second, a government might attempt to provide information on the state of the economy, but clearly a domestic government faced with a financial crisis has an incentive to release only information that would stem the panic. Credibility becomes a critical issue.

Herd behavior arises when agents infer beliefs from observed actions—but it is also the ability to react to the observed actions of others that generates the information cascade. Capital controls would make it more difficult, or more expensive, to withdraw funds. This by itself would not affect the argument that information cascades can generate panic outflows unrelated to underlying values. However, controls could serve to stem outflows in a crisis simply by limiting the actions available to foreign investors. If shorter term funds are restricted, uninformed agents no longer have the actions of others to guide their own decisions.

Pure information cascades may have implications for contagion effects as well. The inferences investors make based on the observed actions of others are key. The information provided by observing actions is very coarse—in the case of a currency crisis, for example, the general conclusion drawn might simply be that expected returns have fallen, but it will matter greatly whether international investors assume this is due to country-specific factors or more general factors. In the case of the latter, they will conclude that expected returns are now lower not just in the country under attack, but in all countries viewed as similar.

This type of contagion might be expected to be the norm. Herding behavior is most likely to arise when individual agents have relatively poor private information. This is why they may ignore their own information and follow the herd. In such situations, it is unlikely that investors will be able to draw a clear inference about whether a crisis results from country-specific factors or whether it results from factors affecting all countries in a similar risk class. Any signs of a crisis spreading may lead quickly to attacks on other countries.

Because information cascades can lead to runs that, ex post, are based on incorrect information, they generate inefficient outcomes. As noted earlier, the solution is to provide better information, but this may not be possible. Governments might have little credibility because they clearly have no incentive to provide accurate information unless it is good news. International agencies might have greater credibility, but again the likelihood is that they too would be viewed as unlikely to provide truthful information unless it is good news.

Rational Information-Based Runs

Both the Diamond-Dybvig model of runs and the herd behavior that results from information cascades are essentially reflections of bubble phenomena—there is no fundamental reason for the runs. An alternative view of bank runs is that they are based on fundamentals and, in particular, that they can be information based (Gorton 1985).

The basic idea is that bank portfolios are subject to risk, and depositors have only imperfect information about the value of these underlying portfolios. As in any model of the pricing of risky assets, current portfolio choices and asset prices will depend critically on the perceived comovements among asset returns. Thus, any new information about returns on one class of assets will also affect prices of other assets with correlated returns (see Kaminsky and Reinhart 1999). In particular, bad news about returns in one country will lead investors to sell off holdings in other countries viewed as similar. Contagion arises as the rational response to new information.

Gorton (1985) shows how suspension of convertibility can be an efficient response to information-based bank runs. Healthy banks need to signal to their depositors that they are healthy. One means of doing so is to suspend convertibility. Such actions were beneficial to depositors because they prevented solvent banks from collapsing.

A rational, information-based financial panic bears some resemblance to inefficient information cascades. Imperfect information plays a key role in each case. A key distinction is that information cascades can lead to inefficient equilibria in which agents ignore valuable information. Information-based runs of the type Gorton analyzes reflect rational reassessments of risk on the basis of new information. Since agents cannot distinguish solvent from insolvent borrowers, any inefficiencies are ex post, not ex ante, in nature.

As in any information-based crisis, there may be a role for policy that either provides information or that limits the ability of investors to run. The first type of policy emphasizes the role of prudential regulation. Countries with adequate systems of financial supervision and regulation are unlikely to suffer contagion effects. When runs are based on a reassessment of risks, standard recommendations to limit short-term capital flows may also play a role in limiting a crisis. Again, however, this is only the case if the underlying system is actually solvent.

Insurance Attacks

The distortion in the model outlined in this section is generated by a lender-of-last-resort solution to financial panics caused by runs. This policy regime generates incentives for investors to acquire insured claims on residents and to then acquire the government's assets when yield differentials make this optimal. The credit constraint faced by governments of developing countries is important in determining the incentives faced by private investors and the timing of their international investment decisions.

A key feature of the insurance model (Dooley 2000b) is that free insurance raises the market yield on a set of liabilities issued by residents *for a predictable time period.* This yield differential generates a private gross capital inflow (a sale of domestic liabilities to nonresidents) that continues until the day of attack. The private inflow is necessarily associated with some combination of an increase in the government's international reserve assets, a current account deficit, and a gross private capital outflow. When the government's reserves are exactly matched by its contingent insurance liabilities, the expected yield on domestic liabilities falls below market rates and investors sell the insured assets to the government, exhausting its reserves. The speculative attack is fully anticipated and at the time of the attack nothing special happens to the fundamentals or expectations about the fundamentals.

This sequence of events is illustrated in figure 2.1. The positive vertical axis in the top panel measures the stock of assets the government, including the central bank, is expected to liquidate during a crisis in order to redeem liabilities to the private sector. The negative vertical axis measures the government's total stock of contingent and noncontingent liabilities. We start from a situation in which the value of assets, A_0, is growing but is less than L_0, the value of debt. A fall in international interest rates at t_1 reduces the value of government's long-term liabilities from L_0 to L_1, but it does not affect the contractual value of short-term assets. A part of the government's assets can now support additional liabilities.

The critical difference between industrial and developing countries is not the nature of the insurance distortion but the conditions under which the insurance is credible. For industrial countries it is reasonable to assume that the government can always borrow in order to honor implicit or explicit insurance commitments. Thus, governments of industrial countries must always monitor and discourage efforts by the private sector to exploit the insurance.

For governments of developing countries it is reasonable to assume that they will face market interest rates in the midst of a crisis that make borrowing unattractive or infeasible. It follows that their insurance commitments are credible only if they have assets, or lines of credit with predetermined interest rates, that can be liquidated to support the insurance. The interesting problem is that insurance and ineffective monitoring of the private sector do not generate a distortion all the time but only when

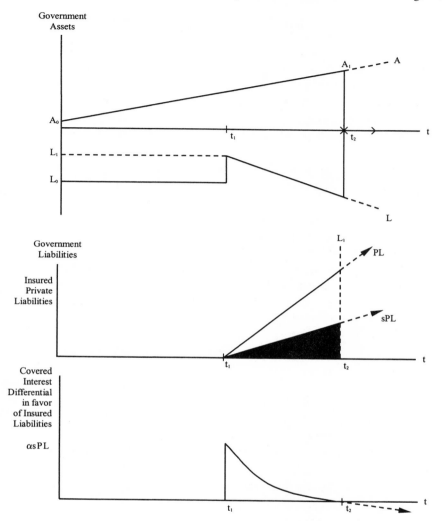

Fig. 2.1 Sequence of Events in the Insurance Model

the government has acquired assets. Moreover, the distortion will not last for a long time because the private sector will immediately set out to capture assets acquired by the government.

In the middle panel we illustrate this process. At t_1 a capital gain on existing government liabilities or assets generates a net liquid asset position for the government. Residents who can issue insured liabilities will now offer to do so in order to appropriate some share s of the proceeds.[3] Sellers of such liabilities are residents simply because only residents' liabilities are eligible for insurance. The government's contingent liability is the same fraction of new insured liabilities (the shaded area in the middle panel).

The value of s is specific to the country and is small in a well-regulated market and large in a poorly regulated market. The time derivative of the flow of new issues (the slope of PL) is also specific to each country and is a function of the supervisory system in place. Relatively poorly regulated financial markets will see a relatively rapid increase in insured liabilities.[4]

Investors are willing to buy residents' liabilities because they are insured and because competition among (resident) sellers will force them to share a part of their appropriation with (nonresident) creditors. This will take the form of above-market expected yields on residents' liabilities.[5] Yields will be the same for both domestic currency and foreign currency liabilities of residents as long as the insurance is expected to cover both types of domestic liabilities.

As long as the foreign investors earn above-market yields there is a disincentive for an attack on the government's assets. Investors will prefer to hold the growing stock of high-yield insured liabilities of residents and allow the government to hold reserves that earn the risk-free rate.[6] Private profits are realized before the attack, which is generated by competition to avoid losses. When the contingent liabilities of the government are just equal to liquid assets ($A_2 = L_2$), competition among investors will insure that all will call the insurance option.

The bottom panel of figure 2.1 reflects the assumption that nonresidents demand a constant premium in order to accumulate insured deposits. On the day of the attack the expected value of this premium becomes negative because each depositor's share of the insurance pool will begin to shrink. Resident borrowers will continue to appropriate a part of new loans and this will depress expected yields on deposits that after t_1 are only partially insured.

Following an attack the regime returns to its initial equilibrium in which the government's net international reserves have returned to zero.

The insurance model provides a clear rationale for taxing distorted capital flows. The appropriate tax can limit the access of banks and other insured firms to international capital flows and in turn reduce their ability to exploit insurance profitably. This was a central feature of the U.S. banking system after the Federal Deposit Insurance Corporation (FDIC) was established in 1933 to insure deposits. The authorities recognized that individual banks would have strong incentives to offer high deposit rates and reach for risk in order to take advantage of insurance. The ceilings on deposit rates were understood as a device to discourage competition among banks and thereby reduce the incentives to exploit insurance. This type of liability restraint has been largely abandoned in the industrial countries but there is no reason to believe that it cannot play a role in emerging markets today.

The insurance model outlined above does suggest that welfare-reducing capital flows might be taxed more heavily by a transaction tax—or its close relative, an entry tax—on capital flows to a developing country. Moreover, an entry tax is much less subject to evasion because a comprehensive tax on capital inflows cannot be easily avoided through derivative transactions. Capital inflows motivated by an insurance policy have a known—and probably short—expected holding period.

The model also suggests that the capital inflow–crisis sequence depends on the condition that the resident can appropriate more than must be paid to the nonresident investor to increase his or her claims on residents of the developing country. Other things equal, an increase in the spread demanded by nonresidents to hold domestic deposits reduces the profitability of exploiting insurance for the resident bank or firm. There is an interesting interaction here in that the entry tax necessary to stop an inflow crisis sequence is higher if the profitability of appropriation is high but is lower if the inflow crisis sequence is short. This is because investors enjoy unusual returns only during the inflow phase of the sequence.

In summary, the insurance model suggests that controls can be a useful policy option. The simple argument is that regulation of capital inflows might be an effective way to starve an insurance crisis of the fuel that sustains it. The key is that the insurance model provides a good reason to believe that holding periods of investors exploiting insurance are different, and probably shorter, as compared to those of normal (honest) investors. The capital inflow–crisis sequence has an expected duration. If this is relatively short a transactions tax might fall disproportionately on this type of capital flow. The right tax would eliminate the incentive to exploit the insurance. Moreover, the usual finding that controls effect the structure of the capital account but not of total private flows is exactly the result that might reduce the probability of an insurance inflow/attack sequence.

Conclusion

There is an interesting relationship between domestic liberalization and the liberalization of international capital flows. The first offers obvious advantages in terms of resource allocation. However, domestic financial liberalization also means that so-called good policies include a number of additional and stringent constraints on governments' behavior. In the short run it may prove difficult to get all of these conditions right. In these circumstances international capital flows might feed the growth of welfare-reducing financial intermediation. In fact, a good summary of the historical record is that any very rapid growth in financial intermediation is likely to turn out badly. In a fully liberalized economy prudential controls will sort this out, but in the early phase of domestic liberalization some residual control on international capital mobility might be a useful component of the government's array of prudential controls.

Notes

1. In autarky, each individual would self-insure by investing less than his or her whole wealth in the productive asset, holding some wealth in liquid form. If a bond market opens, an agent who discovers that he or she needs liquidity can finance early consumption by issuing a bond rather than liquidating (at a cost) the long-term asset. This improves over autarky but still fails to provide liquidity insurance efficiently.

2. Banerjee (1992) and Bikhchandani, Hirshleifer, and Welch (1992) provide models of herd behavior. The common structure of these models involves a discrete choice (e.g., leave funds in the bank or withdraw them) that must be made sequentially by agents on the basis of limited information. Agents are assumed to have two sources of information. First, they have a private but noisy signal about which choice is the correct one. Second, they can observe what others before them have done. A key assumption is that although agents can observe the choices made by those who have gone before them, they cannot observe the private signals the earlier movers received.

3. A more realistic form of appropriation is state contingent. That is, insured residents exploit insurance by reaching for risk. They share returns earned in good states of the world and default in bad states of the world.

4. We assume in this example that the growth in liabilities is greater than the growth in assets, but this is clearly an empirical issue.

5. The accounting is straightforward if we abstract from financial intermediation. Suppose a resident household can issue a $10.00 liability to a foreign investor. The household plans on repaying $5.00. The household shares its gain by paying the investor $2.50 and keeping $2.50. The investor expects the government to purchase the liability for $10.00 in one year. The government's contingent liability is $5.00. More realistic examples will involve one or more financial intermediaries in this process. The distribution of the rents among the participants will depend on their relative bargaining power. If investors' demand for claims on residents is very elastic, residents will capture most of the rents. This seems to us the most likely outcome. It is difficult to interpret historical evidence for deposit rates. As insurance became credible after 1989, deposit rates should

have fallen as the government absorbed default risk. In Mexico real ex post rates on domestic deposits (adjusted for actual changes in dollar exchange rates) fell from about 15 percent above U.S. rates in 1990 to equality with U.S. rates in late 1994. Although this pattern in returns is consistent with our model, Mexico's stabilization program may have had important implications for this history of yield differentials.

6. In most emerging markets the capital inflows have been partially sterilized so that gross reserve assets also begin to grow more rapidly at t_1. However, the government must issue domestic currency debt to finance the purchase of reserves. In this simple example we assume that sterilized intervention does not add to the net stock of liquid assets expected to be exhausted at the time of attack. A more realistic treatment of the relative seniority of alternative government liabilities and expected capital gains and losses on gross positions would not change the qualitative results of the model.

References

Banerjee, A. V. 1992. A simple model of herd behavior. *Quarterly Journal of Economics* 107 (3): 797–817.

Bartolini, Leonardo, and Allan Drazen. 1997. Capital account liberalization as a signal. *American Economic Review* 87 (1): 138–54.

Bernanke, B., and M. Gertler. 1989. Agency costs, net worth, and business fluctuations. *American Economic Review* 79 (1): 14–31.

———. 1990. Financial fragility and economic performance. *Quarterly Journal of Economics* 105 (1): 87–114.

Bikhchandani, S., D. Hirshleifer, and I. Welch. 1992. A theory of fads, fashion, custom, and cultural changes as informational cascades. *Journal of Political Economy* 100 (5): 992–1026.

Calvo, G. 1987. Balance of payments crises in a cash-in-advance economy. *Journal of Money, Credit, and Banking* 19 (1): 19–32.

———. 1988. Servicing the public debt: The role of expectations. *American Economic Review* 78 (4): 647–61.

———. 1996. Capital flows and macroeconomic management: Tequila lessons. *International Journal of Finance and Economics* 1 (3): 207–23.

———. 1997. Varieties of capital-market crises. In *The debt burden and its consequences for monetary policy,* ed. G. Calvo and M. King, 181–202. London: MacMillan.

Calvo, Guillermo, and Enrique Mendoza. 1996. Mexico's balance of payments crisis: Chronicle of a death foretold. *Journal of International Economics* 41 (November): 235–64.

Chang, R., and A. Velasco. 2001. A model of financial crises in emerging markets: A canonical model. *Quarterly Journal of Economics* 116 (2): 489–517.

Cole, H., and T. Kehoe. 1996. A self-fulfilling model of Mexico's 1994–95 debt crisis. *Journal of International Economics* 41:309–30.

Dellas, H., and A. Stockman. 1993. Self-fulfilling expectations, speculative attack, and capital controls. *Journal of Money, Credit, and Banking* 25 (4): 721–30.

Diamond, D. W., and P. H. Dybvig. 1983. Bank runs, deposit insurance, and liquidity. *Journal of Political Economy* 91:401–19.

Dooley, M. P. 1996a. A survey of literature on controls over international capital transactions. *IMF Staff Papers* 43 (4): 639–87.

———. 1996b. The Tobin Tax: Good theory, weak evidence, questionable policy. In *The Tobin Tax: Coping with financial volatility,* ed. M Ul Haq, I. Kaul, and I. Grunberg, 83–108. Oxford: Oxford University Press.

———. 2000a. Debt management and crises in developing countries. *Journal of Development Economics* 63:45–58.

———. 2000b. A model of crises in emerging markets. *The Economic Journal* 110 (460): 256–72.

Edwards, S. 1999. How effective are capital controls? *Journal of Economic Perspectives* 13 (4): 65–84.

Eichengreen, B., J. Tobin, and C. Wyplosz. 1995. Two cases for sand in the wheels of international finance. *The Economic Journal* 105:162–72.

Flood, R. P., and P. M. Garber. 1984. Gold monetization and gold discipline. *Journal of Political Economy* 92:90–107.

Garber, P. 1996. Comment. *NBER Macroeconomics Annual 1996* 11: 403–06.

Glick, R., and M. Hutchison. 2000. Capital controls and exchange rate instability in developing countries. FRBSF Center for Pacific Basin Monetary and Economic Research Working Paper no. PB-005. San Francisco: FRBSF, December.

Gorton, G. 1985. Bank suspension of convertibility. *Journal of Monetary Economics* 15:177–93.

Jacklin, C. J. 1987. Demand deposits, trading restrictions, and risk sharing. In *Contractual arrangements for intertemporal trade,* ed. E. Prescott and N. Wallace, 26–47. Minneapolis: University of Minnesota Press.

Kaminsky, G., and C. Reinhart. 1999. The twin crises: The causes of banking and balance-of-payments problems. *American Economic Review* 89:473–500.

Krugman, P. 1996. Are currency crises self-fulfilling? *NBER Macroeconomics Annual* 11:345–78.

Lane, T., and L. Rojas-Suarez. 1992. Credibility, capital controls, and the EMS. *Journal of International Economics* 2:321–37.

Obstfeld, M. 1986. Rational and self-fulfilling balance-of-payments crises. *American Economic Review* 76:72–81.

———. 1994. The logic of currency crises. *Cahiers Economiques et Monetaires* 43:189–213.

Rogoff, K. 1999. International institutions for reducing global financial instability. *Journal of Economic Perspectives* 13:21–42.

Sachs, J., A. Tornell, and A. Velasco. 1996. Financial crises in emerging markets: The lessons from 1995. *Brookings Papers on Economic Activity,* Issue no. 1: 147–98.

Tobin, J. 1996. Prologue. In *The Tobin Tax: Coping with financial volatility,* ed. M Ul Haq, I. Kaul, and I. Grunberg. Oxford: Oxford University Press.

Chapter Three

Should We Fear Capital Flows?

René M. Stulz

Over the last fifty years, barriers to international investment have crumbled for developed economies and have fallen dramatically for many emerging markets. As a result of this evolution, U.S. investors can buy the securities of a large number of foreign companies with almost no restrictions and U.S. firms can make direct investments in a large number of countries without difficulties. Corporations in many countries can list their shares abroad and can choose where to raise funds. Gross flows of financial securities have become extremely large among major industrial countries. As an example, in 1975, gross cross-border transactions in bonds and equities for the United States were equivalent to 4 percent of gross domestic product (GDP). These transactions exceeded GDP for the first time in 1991 and by 1997 they had grown to 213 percent of GDP (see Adams et al. 1998, 187). Figure 3.1 shows the evolution of cross-border transactions in bonds and equities for the United States since the 1970s.

Emerging markets benefited substantially from financial liberalization, but they also discovered that net capital flows can change in a hurry. Table 3.1 provides some data on how capital flows to developing countries have changed over time. It is clear that the size of net capital flows to developing countries increased dramatically in the 1990s compared to earlier

René M. Stulz is the Reese Chair of Banking and Monetary Economics at the Ohio State University and a research associate of the National Bureau of Economic Research.

The author is grateful for comments from participants at the Bush School Conference on International Financial Markets, Leonardo Auernheimer, and two anonymous referees, and to the New York Stock Exchange for financial support. *103*

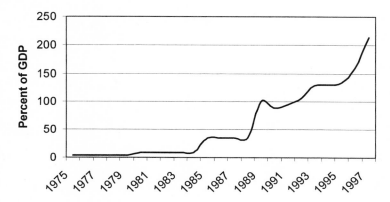

Fig. 3.1 Cross-Border Transactions in Bonds and Equity as a Percentage of
GDP for the United States.

NOTES:

The data are available each year from 1989. For the earlier years, the data are available for
1975, 1980, and 1985. It is assumed that the cross-border transactions in bonds and equity
as a percentage of GDP stay constant when no new data are available.

years. Furthermore, the growth in net portfolio investment in the early
1990s was spectacular. At the same time, however, flows decreased dramatically after 1996, so that net private capital flows in 1998 were less than
one third what they were in 1996. The East Asian crisis countries went
from net private capital flows of $62.4 billion in 1996 to net private capital
flows of −$46.2 billion in 1998.

The dramatic change in net private capital flows that takes place in crisis periods, as evidenced by the statistics for East Asia in table 3.1, has led
many policymakers to question whether the financial liberalization process has gone too far and whether controls on capital flows should be rein-
troduced. The recent upheavals in Asia and Russia have led to the reimposition of some barriers to international investment in some countries.
Prominent economists have argued that, although trade liberalization
should be encouraged, financial liberalization should not. For instance,
Stiglitz (1998, 32) called for greater regulation of capital flows, arguing
that "developing countries are more vulnerable to vacillations in international flows than ever before." Krugman (1998, 76) argued as follows:

> What turned a bad financial situation into a catastrophe was the way
> a loss of confidence turned into self-reinforcing panic. In 1996 capi-
> tal was flowing into emerging Asia at the rate of about $100 billion a
> year; by the second half of 1997 it was flowing out at about the same
> rate. Inevitably, with that kind of reversal Asia's asset markets

Table 3.1   Capital Flows to Developing Countries (US$ billions)

Net Capital Flows to Developing Countries (yearly averages)

	1977–82	1983–89	1990–94
Total net capital flows	30.5	8.8	104.9
Net direct investment	11.2	13.3	39.1
Net portfolio investment	−10.5	6.5	43.6
Other	29.8	−11.0	22.2

Net Private Capital Flows to Emerging Markets

	1995	1996	1997	1998	1999	2000
Net private capital flows	189.0	224.1	126.2	45.2	71.5	32.2
Net direct investment	96.9	120.4	144.9	148.7	153.4	146.0
Net portfolio investment	42.6	85.0	43.3	23.8	53.7	58.3
Bank loans and other	49.5	18.7	−62.1	−127.2	−135.6	−172.1

Net Private Capital Flows to East Asian Crisis Countries

	1994	1995	1996	1997	1998
Net private capital flows	33.2	62.5	62.4	−19.7	−46.2
Net direct investment	6.0	13.9	13.4	16.6	18.2
Net portfolio investment	8.3	17.0	20.0	12.6	−6.5
Other net investment	18.4	36.9	32.9	−44.5	−47.8

SOURCES: Net capital flows to developing countries, Folkerts-Landau and Ito (1995); net private capital flows to emerging markets, Mathieson and Schinasi (2001); net private capital flows to East Asian crisis countries, IMF (1999).

plunged, its economies went into recession, and it only got worse from there.

He then went on to argue that the solution is to impose currency controls, finishing with an apocalyptic description of what would happen without them: "But if Asia does not act quickly, we could be looking at a true Depression scenario—the kind of slump that 60 years ago devastated societies, destabilized governments, and eventually led to war" (80). Bhagwati (1998) states that "this is a seductive idea: freeing up trade is good, why not also let capital move freely across borders? But the claims of enormous benefits from free capital mobility are not persuasive. . . . It is time to shift the burden of proof from those who oppose to those who favor liberated capital."

In this paper, we consider whether the benefits of free capital mobility are large enough to offset the so-called costs of free capital mobility. Although the benefits are clear, the costs are more difficult to identify and evaluate. The arguments against free capital mobility cited in the previous paragraph are that a country incurs large costs when foreigners withdraw capital they invested in that country. Many argue that, because of contagion, foreigners withdraw capital even when there are no valid reasons for them to do so. If indeed "animal spirits" guide foreign investors, leading them to withdraw funds from countries and wreck economies without rhyme or reason, the case against capital mobility is strong. As the quotation from Krugman points out, the withdrawal of funds from Southeast Asia in 1997 was dramatic. There is no question that such withdrawals of funds are extremely painful for the countries that experience them. This does not mean, however, that a world where such withdrawals could not happen would be a more prosperous world in the long run. The flip side of withdrawals is the existence of large capital inflows that enable countries to grow faster than they would otherwise and help to allocate capital efficiently throughout the world.

We argue that the benefits from capital mobility overwhelm its costs in the long run. Therefore, the question countries should focus on is not how to limit capital mobility but how to make capital mobility work for them. They should focus on how to make sudden withdrawals less likely and to reduce the costs of these withdrawals when they occur.

The paper is organized as follows. The first section discusses three key benefits of capital mobility: First, capital mobility makes it possible for a country's savings to differ from its investments. Second, capital mobility enables greater risk-sharing and therefore reduces the cost of capital. Third, capital mobility improves corporate governance. Since the first benefit of capital mobility we discuss is the one that has received the most attention over time, we focus on the other two benefits. The next section considers the issue of whether the costs of sudden withdrawals of capital by foreign investors are large enough to offset the benefits of capital mobility discussed in the first section. The final section addresses the problem of how to reduce the costs of sudden withdrawals of capital by foreign investors, and provides concluding remarks.

Some Benefits of Capital Mobility

In the first part of this section, I examine the role of capital mobility in a simple world with one good and no risk. In this world, capital mobility separates savings from investment at the country level. In the second part of this section, I show how capital mobility increases the efficiency of investment in the presence of risk. Finally, in the last part of this section, I turn to the impact of capital mobility on how firms raise and invest funds. In discussing the benefits of capital mobility, there is no loss of generality in assuming that there is only one currency and therefore in ignoring exchange rates altogether.[1]

The Benefits and Costs of Cross-Country Borrowing and Lending

Consider a world without risk and without capital mobility. There is a single good that can be consumed or used in production. All countries produce the same good and have the same aggregate production function. There are no transportation costs. The production function exhibits decreasing returns to scale. To maximize world output, the good should be used in production across countries so that the marginal return for putting the good into production should be the same in each country. Without capital mobility, this is unlikely to take place. To see this, suppose that each country maximizes a logarithmic utility function of wealth with the same rate-of-time preference. This means that each country consumes the same fraction of its wealth. As a result, wealthier countries invest more and the marginal product of investment is lower in these countries.

In the simple world considered here, there is no reason for trade in the good if trade in capital is not allowed. Since each country consumes a constant fraction of its wealth, it does not need to import or export. Furthermore, the rate of interest will differ across countries. Wealthier countries will have lower rates of interest than poorer countries because their marginal product of investment is lower.

Consider now what happens in this simple world if we allow trade in capital. Since the interest rate is higher in poorer countries, investors in richer countries invest in poorer countries. The poorer countries increase their investment by using the funds borrowed to purchase the good in richer countries. Now, there is both trade in goods and trade in capital. Trade in capital makes it possible for production to be more efficient than it would be otherwise. The source of the benefit from trade in capital is the same as the source of the benefit from trade in goods: Capital is invested where it is most productive.

Adding uncertainty to our simple world can help understand the problem that arises with capital withdrawals. Suppose now that production takes time, but it is financed with loans that have a shorter maturity than the production lag. For instance, producing the good could take one year but loans would have a six-month maturity. In this case, nonrenewal of loans creates a problem.[2] Three solutions are possible. First, the country could choose to consume less to repay the loans without disrupting production. Second, the country might have to interrupt the production process, which would be costly. Third, the country might choose not to repay the loans and default. All three possible solutions are costly to the country. Nevertheless, one has to be careful in evaluating the cost of these solutions. After all, the country borrowed. If it had correctly assessed the probability of nonrenewal of loans, ex ante the country was better off borrowing. This means that if nonrenewals occur it is because borrowers believe that they are better off borrowing and taking the risk of nonrenewals than they would be by not borrowing. Hence, with this reasoning, it immediately follows that there is a prima facie case for capital mobility, which is that whenever borrowers believe that the cost of nonrenewals is too high, they can simply choose not to borrow. In the world just described, trade in capital can adversely affect welfare ex ante only in the presence of market imperfections that make it possible to improve on the equilibrium resulting from the actions of individuals. In other words, it would have to be that it is optimal for individuals to trade capital but not for countries. Assuming that individuals are rational and have the same information as policymakers, this would require a situation in which the choices of individuals have externalities that they do not take into account in making their decisions.

The Benefits of International Trade in Risky Securities

In the previous part of this section, we saw how capital mobility equalizes interest rates across countries. I now extend the analysis to investigate risk sharing. To do so, I assume that markets for assets safe in nominal terms are completely integrated, so that interest rates are the same across countries, but markets for risky assets are completely segmented.[3] Without loss of generality, I assume that markets for risky assets are equity markets. In a world where barriers to international investment are such that equity markets are completely segmented from each other, investors in each country have to bear all the risk of the economic activities of that country. Investors in a country require a risk premium on equity to bear that risk. Suppose that investors in each country are risk averse and care only about the expected return of their invested wealth and the variance of that return. They therefore measure risk by the variance of the returns of their portfolios. Furthermore, to simplify the exposition, I assume that all investors are the same within each country. In that case, as the return volatility of a country's market portfolio (defined as the value-weighted portfolio of all risky assets in the country) increases, the risk premium of the market portfolio (defined as the expected return on the market portfolio minus the risk-free rate) increases. For instance, if investors have the same constant coefficient of relative risk aversion, the risk premium on the market is the coefficient of relative risk aversion times the variance of the return on the market portfolio. As a result, if the return variance of the market portfolio in country A is twice that of country B, country A's risk premium is twice the risk premium of country B.

We now consider how a country's risk premium is affected when that country and others decide to open up their equity markets to each other. To do that, we take the economic activities of the various countries as given. As a country opens up its capital market to foreign investors and lets its residents invest abroad, the residents of the country no longer have to bear all the risks associated with the economic activities of the country. Foreign investors, by investing in the country, bear some of these risks. In exchange, domestic investors, by buying foreign securities, bear some foreign risks. For domestic investors, the benefit from bearing both domestic and foreign risks rather than only domestic risks is that some of these risks offset each other through the process of diversification. A country might have bad news on one day, but another country might have good news. Because of diversification resulting from access to global capital markets, domestic investors can construct a portfolio of equities that has less risk for the same expected return.

It is useful to think of equity markets that are integrated with each other as forming essentially one market, which I call the *global equity market*. I call the value-weighted portfolio of all equities in the global equity market the *world market portfolio*. In integrated markets, investors hold an internationally diversified portfolio of risky securities and measure the risk of individual risky securities by how they contribute to the variance of the returns of their internationally diversified portfolios. Since all investors are assumed to be the same, they invest their wealth in the same way and the country they come from is irrelevant. If all investors hold the same portfolio of risky assets, they have to hold the world market portfolio. As a result, the capital asset pricing model (CAPM) holds for the global equity market.[4] In the global equity market, the expected return of a risky security is therefore equal to the risk-free rate plus beta times the risk premium on the world market portfolio, where beta is equal to the covariance of the return of the security with the return of the world market portfolio divided by the variance of the world market portfolio. Beta measures the risk of the security. If a security covaries more with the world market portfolio, its risk is more similar to the risk of the world market portfolio and therefore it must have an expected return more similar to the expected return of the world market portfolio.

Consider now a small country whose equity markets are completely segmented from the equity markets abroad. Remember that investors measure risk by the return variance of their portfolios. The price per unit of risk for these investors is the risk premium divided by the variance of the return. To eliminate the impact of differences in risk aversion across countries, I assume that all investors in the world have the same constant relative risk aversion. With that assumption, the price of risk in that country before its market opens up is a constant, which I denote by T. Consequently, the risk premium on the small country before integration is

(1)   Risk premium before globalization = $\sigma^2_{\text{Small country}} T$

where $\sigma^2_{\text{Small country}}$ is the small country's market portfolio return variance.

I now consider the risk premium after liberalization. Remember that after liberalization, the small country's equity market becomes part of the global equity market. Since the country is small, adding that country to the world equity markets does not increase the risk premium on the world market portfolio. Denote the expected return of the world market portfolio by $E(R_{\text{World}})$. If R is the risk-free rate, the risk premium on the world market portfolio is $E(R_{\text{World}}) - R$. The CAPM holds for the global equity market, so that the risk premium on a risky asset depends on its beta coefficient with respect to the world market portfolio:

(2)   Risk premium after globalization = $\beta_{\text{Small country}}[E(R_{\text{World}}) - R]$
$$= \rho\sigma_{\text{Small country}}\sigma_{\text{World}} T$$

where σ_{World} is the return volatility of the world market portfolio, $\sigma_{\text{Small country}}$ is the return volatility of the small country's market portfolio, and ρ is the correlation coefficient between the return of the small country portfolio and the return of the world market portfolio. The beta of the small country market portfolio with respect to the world market portfolio, $\beta_{\text{Small country}}$, is defined as $(\rho\sigma_{\text{World}}\sigma_{\text{Small country}} / \sigma^2_{\text{World}})$. The second line in equation (2) follows from the fact that the price of risk in the world equity markets is T as well because all investors in the world are the same. It follows from a comparison of the risk premium before and after globalization that a necessary and sufficient condition for globalization to reduce the risk premium of the small country is that

(3) $\left(\dfrac{\sigma_{\text{Small country}}}{\sigma_{\text{World}}} \right) > \rho$

Equation (3) holds whenever an investor in the small country who has invested all his or her wealth in that country's market portfolio can construct

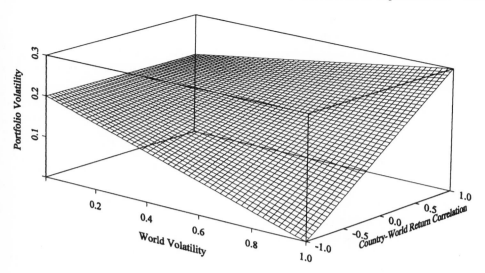

Fig. 3.2   Volatility of the Portfolio of the Investor from the Small Country with a Small Investment in the Global Equity Markets

NOTES:

This figure shows the volatility of the return of the portfolio of the small-country investor, $\sigma_{\text{Portfolio}}$, when the portfolio share of the global market is 0.10. The volatility of the return of the market portfolio of the small country is assumed to be 25 percent. $\sigma_{\text{Portfolio}}$ is shown as a function of the volatility of the world market portfolio, σ_{World}, and the correlation between the return of the small-country market portfolio and the world market portfolio, $\rho_{\text{Small country,World}}$, where the world market portfolio does not include the small-country market portfolio.

a portfolio that has a lower variance of return than the market portfolio of the small country by selling some of his or her holdings of the small country market portfolio and investing in the world market portfolio. Figure 3.2 shows the impact on the volatility of the return of the portfolio of an investor in the small country of adding an investment in the world market portfolio to the portfolio. It assumes that the country market return has a volatility of 25 percent. It considers the volatility of the portfolio of an investor who reduces the portfolio share of his or her country in the portfolio from 1.0 to 0.9 and who increases the portfolio share of the world market portfolio (which does not include the small country) from 0 to 0.1. The figure shows that the volatility of the return of the investor's portfolio falls below 25 percent unless the volatility of the world market portfolio is high and the world market portfolio has a high correlation with the market portfolio of the investor's country. Other than in the exceptional case in which a country's market portfolio is very similar to the world market portfolio, liberalization decreases the risk borne by investors in the country that liberalizes.

I now consider whether a large country that belongs to the global equity market has a smaller risk premium than it would have if it did not belong to that market. To answer that question, one must take into account the fact that the risk premium of the global equity market depends on whether the country belongs to that market. With our assumption that all investors are the same and have constant relative risk aversion, the larger country has a lower risk premium when it belongs to the global market than when it is segmented, provided that investors in the large country can construct a lower variance portfolio by taking a long position in the equity of the other countries that belong to the global market portfolio. In that case, both the larger country and the other countries in the global market portfolio benefit from belonging to the global equity market.

The analysis here shows that globalization decreases a country's risk premium. We may consider some empirical evidence that is supportive of this analysis. First, there is considerable evidence that for liberalized countries, risks become priced globally rather than locally. For instance, Harvey (1991) provides evidence generally supportive of the view that the CAPM holds across countries. Second, equation (3) provides a condition that must be satisfied for globalization to decrease the risk premium. In Stulz (1999b), I checked whether this condition holds for thirty-seven countries for a ten-year period ending on 28 October 1998. The results are shown in table 3.2. The condition is satisfied for every country in the sample. Admittedly, this test is simplistic because it assumes that each country had the same volatility of returns throughout the sample period even if its integration in global markets changed. However, as we shall see, there is no clear evidence that globalization increases volatility. Third, remember that stock prices are, all else being equal, negatively related to the risk premium. Consequently, an unexpected decrease in barriers to international investment in a country should lead to an unexpected increase in stock prices. This suggests that one might be able to estimate the impact of globalization on the risk premium by investigating the impact of the opening of countries on stock markets. Henry (2000b) investigates the stock market impact of capital market liberalizations. He uses a sample of twelve countries that liberalize. In his first test, he considers the impact of liberalization on a period that starts four months before the announcement and ends three months after the announcement. Over that period, stock returns are higher by 4.6 percent per month on average, for a total cumulative abnormal return of 36.8 percent. He then investigates whether this impact of globalization still holds when he controls for variables that influence stock returns, in particular macroeconomic variables. The im-

Table 3.2   Estimates of the Discount Rate Reduction Due to Globalization

	Weekly Return Standard Deviation	Weekly Average Return	Correlation with World Market Portfolio	Condition
Argentina	0.1635	0.0188	0.0460	0.0266024
Australia	0.0254	0.0018	0.5160	0.0003978
Austria	0.0305	0.0021	0.4800	0.0006532
Belgium	0.0219	0.0028	0.6250	0.0002213
Canada	0.0186	0.0016	−0.0170	0.0003523
Chile	0.0319	0.0039	0.2530	0.0008672
China	0.1189	0.0101	−0.0870	0.0143338
Denmark	0.0249	0.0029	0.4750	0.0003951
Finland	0.0337	0.0224	0.4570	0.0008429
France	0.0257	0.0028	0.6540	0.0003437
Germany	0.0268	0.0028	0.6450	0.0003897
Greece	0.0464	0.0032	0.0280	0.0021245
Hong Kong	0.0432	0.0038	0.5050	0.0014521
Indonesia	0.0765	−0.0015	0.2990	0.0054153
Ireland	0.0259	0.0032	0.5700	0.0003927
Italy	0.0351	0.0024	0.4760	0.0009151
Japan	0.0372	−0.0004	0.7610	0.0008465
Korea	0.0515	−0.0005	0.2780	0.002383
Malaysia	0.0552	0.0017	0.4340	0.0025918
Mexico	0.0476	0.0061	−0.0220	0.0022895
The Netherlands	0.0213	0.0034	0.7300	0.0001595
New Zealand	0.0283	0.0013	0.4460	0.0005645
Norway	0.0338	0.0026	0.5430	0.0007978
The Philippines	0.0477	0.0021	0.3140	0.0019917
Poland	0.0648	−0.0023	0.3830	0.0037289
Portugal	0.0279	0.0018	0.4730	0.0005308
Singapore	0.0343	0.0018	0.5660	0.0008092
South Africa	0.0338	0.0012	0.4500	0.0008539
Spain	0.0293	0.0027	0.6640	0.0004913
Sweden	0.0309	0.0028	0.6180	0.0005945
Switzerland	0.0252	0.0034	0.6320	0.0003348
Taiwan	0.0535	0.0027	−0.0750	0.0029377
Thailand	0.0589	0.0020	0.3500	0.0030768
Turkey	0.0727	0.0051	−0.0450	0.0053411
United Kingdom	0.0226	0.0029	0.6780	0.0002228
United States	0.0194	0.0033	0.6940	0.0001223
Venezuela	0.0775	0.0045	0.0610	0.0059175
World	0.0189	0.0019	1.0000	

NOTES: The table uses the Datastream weekly indexes in dollars from 30 September 1988 to 28 October 1998, or since they became available. We denote by condition the difference between the variance of the return of the country portfolio minus its covariance with the world market portfolio. Condition must be positive from the analysis in "Some Benefits of Capital Mobility" for the country to have a lower cost of capital in world markets rather than in autarky.

pact of liberalization falls somewhat, to about 30 percent, but the impact is still statistically and economically significant. His evidence therefore indicates that liberalization increases wealth substantially. Using a standard stock market valuation model, Henry's evidence implies that if the discount rate before liberalization is 20.0 percent and the expected growth rate of dividends is 5.0 percent, the discount rate falls to 16.5 percent if the percentage change in the equity capitalization is 30.0 percent. Bekaert and Harvey (2000) use a sample of twenty emerging markets to estimate the impact of liberalization on the risk premium. They find that liberalization decreases the risk premium by 5 to 90 basis points.

The decrease in the risk premium associated with liberalization estimated in Bekaert and Harvey (2000) and Henry (2000b) seems small. To make sense of it, it is important to understand that the extent of financial globalization has been limited. For risks to be shared internationally, investors have to hold foreign securities. They have done so increasingly over time, but the extent to which they do so is still limited. Table 3.3

Table 3.3   Estimates of U.S. Ownership for Selected Markets in 1997

	Share of Country in U.S. Stock Portfolio (%)	**Share of Country in World Market Portfolio (%)**
Developed economies		
Australia	0.10	0.26
Canada	0.54	2.49
France	0.65	2.96
Germany	0.49	3.62
Japan	1.04	9.72
The Netherlands	0.81	2.05
Spain	0.19	1.27
Sweden	0.30	1.20
Switzerland	0.47	2.53
United Kingdom	1.66	8.76
Emerging markets		
Argentina	0.10	0.26
Brazil	0.24	1.12
Chile	0.03	0.32
China	0.02	0.91
India	0.05	0.56
Indonesia	0.02	0.13
Malaysia	0.04	0.41
Mexico	0.27	0.69
Peru	0.02	0.08
Thailand	0.02	0.10
Venezuela	0.02	0.06

SOURCE: These data come from Pinkowitz, Stulz, and Williamson (2001).

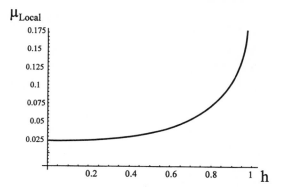

Fig. 3.3   Home Bias and the Risk Premium

NOTES:

This figure shows the relation between the risk premium of the local market, μ_{Local}, and the fraction of investors who invest at home only, h, assuming that the volatility of the local market is 30 percent, that the local market is uncorrelated with the world market, that the local market is 10 percent of the world equity capitalization, and that the coefficient of relative risk tolerance is 2.

shows that U.S. investors do not come close to holding the world market portfolio. This preference of investors for domestic securities, called the home bias, has been widely documented for U.S. investors as well as for foreign investors.[5] As an example, in 1996, U.S. investors held 90 percent of the value of their stock portfolio in U.S. stocks.[6] At that time, however, U.S. stocks represented less than half of the world market capitalization of stocks. Consequently, if U.S. investors had been holding the world market portfolio of stocks, their holdings of U.S. stocks would have represented less than 50 percent of their holdings of stocks. In 1987, U.S. investors held 96.2 percent of their stock holdings in U.S. stocks, so that the home bias of the United States fell from the mid-1980s to the mid-1990s. However, the home bias of U.S. investors did not fall after the mid-1990s (see Karolyi and Stulz 2001). The home bias exists in all foreign countries for which statistics on ownership are available. Table 3.3 provides further evidence on the home bias of U.S. investors by comparing the weight of stocks from various countries in the portfolio of U.S. investors and the weight of these countries in the world market portfolio. The appendix provides a simple model showing that there is a direct relation between the extent of the home bias and the risk premium of a country. Figure 3.3 plots the main result of that model. As the home bias gets stronger, globalization decreases the risk premium less. Recent empirical evidence by Bekaert, Harvey, and Lumsdaine (2002) shows that equity inflows decrease a country's risk premium, which is consistent with the prediction of figure 3.3.

The second factor that limits the decrease in the risk premium measured with the tests described here is that liberalization has a complicated impact on a country. As the risk premium falls, investment increases. Henry (2000a) shows that liberalization increases investment. Everything else equal, the increase in investment has to lead to a worsening of the current account and to an increase in the price of non-tradable goods. As a result, expected future cash flows for equity can fall because of an increase in the price of production inputs. If this effect is important, it means that the studies discussed above understate the impact of liberalization on the risk premium.

In my analysis, I have focused on the impact of globalization on the risk premium. It is important to remember that globalization affects welfare as well as the risk premium. Although the impact of globalization on the risk premium is theoretically ambiguous, its impact on welfare is less so.[7] Consider again our small country. As that country joins the global equity market, its risk premium increases or decreases. If the risk premium of that country increases, the value of its market portfolio falls so that globalization makes investors in that country financially worse off. We saw that this outcome is unlikely; suppose, however, that it did occur. In this case, investors in the small country get to invest their wealth in the world market portfolio. Because of the benefits from international diversification, these investors can invest in a portfolio that has the same variance as that of the small country market portfolio but has a higher expected return. It turns out that for reasonable utility functions, investors in the small country with a choice between having that country remain segmented or become part of the global equity market will choose globalization because the risk-sharing that globalization enables them to achieve increases their expected utility sufficiently to overcome the adverse effect on their wealth.

We have emphasized the benefits of financial globalization in reducing the cost of capital of firms because of better sharing of risks. The reduction in the cost of capital is only one of the benefits associated with the increased sharing of risks that results from globalization. As a result of better sharing of risks, domestic residents become less affected by adverse shocks to domestic industries. This decreased dependence on domestic industries means that countries can become more specialized in production and that consumption does not have to be tied to the production of domestic industries.[8] For a country whose financial markets are segmented from the rest of the world, some industries may face a low cost of capital because they provide diversification at the country level. This diversification becomes less useful when the country opens its financial markets to the world because local investors can get the diversification by investing abroad. As a result of liberalization, industries that were profitable in closed markets may no longer be profitable when markets are open. With open financial markets, a country is better able to grow industries in which it has a comparative advantage. Objecting to free capital mobility therefore amounts to arguing for policies that limit a country's ability to maximize its benefits from international trade in goods.

Globalization, Governance, and Financial Services

John D. Rockefeller used to explain that his main problem in business was to raise capital. He generally found this to be an extremely difficult and costly process that prevented him from investing as much as he felt was worthwhile.[9] There are two important reasons for this. First, managers are typically better informed about expected future cash flows than are investors. The fact that managers have better information than shareholders creates what we call the *information asymmetry problem*. Second, management has its own objectives, which may differ from those of investors. We call the problem created by management's pursuit of its own objectives the *agency costs of managerial discretion problem*. These two problems interact in important ways. Typically, management wants the firm to grow. As a result, managers and investors often disagree about expected cash flows. Because managers usually want to raise as much capital as they can, it will almost always be the case that investors do not believe that expected cash flows are as high as management forecasts (see Stulz 1990). As a result, management cannot raise as much capital as it wants for new projects. Also, for existing firms, management may have to give up too much of the value of the firm to raise as much capital as it wants. Viewed from this perspective, a firm's cost of capital depends crucially on the firm's governance, which we define broadly as the set of mechanisms that affect how the information and agency-cost problems impact firm value. Firms with poor governance are then firms for which the information asymmetry and agency-cost problems are important. Such firms find it more expensive to raise funds.

An example can help clarify this argument. Suppose that investors agree with management about the distribution of the cash flows from investment, but believe that there is a good chance management will waste these cash flows because the firm is not expected to have valuable investment opportunities in the future. If the firm issues equity to finance investment instead of debt, management is better able to waste the cash flows because with debt it must use the cash flows for debt service.[10] As a result, an equity issue will result in a fall in firm value, which will be a dead-weight cost of equity finance. However, if the firm has a board that monitors management actively and prevents it from wasting cash flows, firm value will fall less with an equity issue and the deadweight cost of equity issues is lower. External finance has deadweight costs for the firm. These deadweight costs increase as agency costs of managerial discretion and information asymmetries increase, but they decrease as governance improves, so that management is better monitored. In most countries, deadweight costs associated with external finance are higher than in the United States because the providers of capital are less well protected than in the United States.[11]

Globalization reduces the deadweight costs associated with external finance in five ways, as follows.

Increases monitoring efficiency. As a country liberalizes its capital markets, its firms become monitored more effectively. First, firms that can access global markets have a lower cost of capital. As a result, they become stronger competitors to firms that cannot access global markets. Firms that can access global markets are those that convince investors that they will not be expropriated quickly because management and large shareholders maximize private benefits from control at the expense of the investors in the firm. To convince investors of this, firms must put in place mechanisms that insure that management and large shareholders are monitored at least to some degree. Such mechanisms might be a commitment to greater disclosure that comes from listing abroad, the issuance of securities where the firm becomes subject to laws stricter than domestic laws, the use of investment-banking firms that have some degree of independence, and so on. By committing to greater monitoring, however, the firms that seek to access global markets put pressure on all firms in their country to commit to more monitoring. Second, cross-border takeovers become possible as a disciplining mechanism. Third, foreign analysts can start following domestic firms. Fourth, international rating agencies can start evaluating the securities issued by local firms. Fifth, foreign investors can take large stakes in some firms because they approve of their management or want to influence their actions. Sixth, the foreign press starts following local firms more actively in response to the interest of foreign shareholders. As a result of the liberalization of its capital markets, a country therefore exposes its firms to more monitoring, which increases equity values and decreases the cost of external funding.

An example of this increased monitoring resulting from globalization is the case of Olivetti, which was the fourth largest public company in Italy in 1995. It was sustaining huge losses in its personal computer (PC) division. Its chairman, Carlo de Benedetti, had to raise funds from international institutional investors in December 1995, giving them a 70 percent stake in the company. He promised then to solve the problems of the PC division. By September 1996, the new investors thought he was floundering. The share price was then at 726 lire and Benedetti was forced out. Eventually, the company divested its losing assets. By the time of the announcement of the last major divestiture at the beginning of 1998, the share price was at 1,958 lire (*New York Times,* 3 March 1998).

Increases access to financial expertise. Deadweight costs associated with external finance can often be reduced or eliminated by the appropriate choice of financing instruments and deal structures. For these solutions to be implemented, considerable expertise can be required. Often, this expertise will not be available within a country but will be available in global financial markets. For instance, it could be that the optimal method of financing for a firm involves an unusual security that has been used in similar cases in other countries. By accessing the global markets, the firm would have access to investors who are already familiar with this type of security, so that issuing the security would be cheaper because of investor familiarity. By issuing the security on global markets, the firm can also take advantage of the technology already developed for similar securities. For instance, it might be able to use similar legal documents. Often, the optimal way to structure a deal will be to provide financial experts with an ownership claim. For instance, investment bankers will often receive options as compensation. Such transactions would not be possible with foreign investment bankers if they could not hold investments in the country.

Fosters competition in the financial industry. In a closed capital market, firms can only sell securities locally and borrow from local financial institutions. With liberalized capital markets, firms buy financial services from foreign institutions, sell securities abroad, and borrow from foreign banks. They can therefore avoid being hostages to local financial institutions and can use competition among these institutions to reduce costs of financial services. A clear example of such an evolution is the case of bond issues in Japan. Early in the 1980s, the issuance of bonds in Japan was highly restricted and extremely expensive. Japanese firms began to issue on the Euro markets, where competition enabled them to issue at a lower cost. Eventually, to keep business in Japan, Japanese banks reduced issuance costs and made it easier for firms to issue bonds in Japan (see Kang et al. 1995). Interestingly, the ability of firms to raise funds abroad was not all positive for Japanese companies, because globalization weakened existing relationships between firms and Japanese banks and decreased the ability of Japanese banks to monitor firms.

Increases access to foreign institutions. In a closed economy, a firm has no choice but to list its shares on the local stock market. If listing shares on that market is difficult or expensive, firms will often choose to forgo a public listing. If the market has low listing standards, the firms may have no means to commit to disclosure and protection of minority shareholder rights. Coffee (1999) develops a bonding hypothesis: firms can bond themselves through U.S. listings to protect minority shareholder rights. The U.S. legal and regulatory systems protect minority investors well; firms that list in the United States are subject to the rules of that system. With liberalized capital markets, firms can choose where to list. They can choose to list on exchanges that have high listing requirements to increase the value of their shares and decrease their cost of raising funds.[12] Listing on foreign exchanges can also enable them to use these exchanges to raise funds and gain access to other shareholder clienteles.

An example of access to foreign institutions is provided by American depository receipt (ADR) programs. These programs enable foreign firms to list on U.S. exchanges. Foerster and Karolyi (1999) and Miller (1999) investigate both the return around the announcement of an ADR program and the return around the day when the actual listing takes place. They find positive returns both around the announcement date and around the listing date. Foerster and Karolyi (1999) examine 153 ADR listings on Nasdaq, American Stock Exchange (Amex), and New York Stock Exchange (NYSE) from 1976 to 1992. They find an abnormal return during the listing week of 1.2 percent. Miller (1999) finds an average announcement abnormal return of 1.04 percent for a sample of 125 announcements from 1985 to 1995. Miller's sample includes all ADRs, including Level I and Rule 144(a). In his study, the average announcement abnormal return for the 53 ADRs listed on NYSE or Nasdaq is 2.63 percent. He differentiates between firms from emerging markets and firms from developed markets. To the extent that emerging markets have more barriers to international investment than developed markets, we would expect a greater abnormal return for firms from emerging markets. He finds an announcement return of 1.54 percent for firms from emerging markets and of 0.87 percent for firms from developed markets. However, the difference between the two is not significant.

Even though Miller (1999) interprets his evidence from the perspective that listing shares on a foreign market relaxes barriers to international investment, it is important to note that his evidence is fully supportive of models such as those of Cantale (1998) and Fuerst (1998) that demonstrate that management signals its quality by listing on stricter exchanges and that listing on stricter exchanges increases shareholder wealth because it reduces private benefits from control. From this perspective, we would expect a larger stock-price reaction for listings on stricter exchanges and a larger stock-price reaction for firms coming from environments with looser disclosure standards and less protection of minority shareholders. We would therefore expect higher abnormal returns for firms listing on the NYSE or Nasdaq than for Level I over-the-counter listings or 144(a) issues, and higher abnormal returns for firms listing from emerging markets where protection of minority shareholders is weaker than in other markets. This is exactly what Miller finds. Cantale investigates the stock-price reaction to the announcement that a firm from continental Europe or the United Kingdom intends to list on the NYSE, the London Stock Exchange, or the Paris Stock Exchange. He argues that the disclosure requirements are strictest on the NYSE, followed by those on the London Stock Exchange and the Paris Stock Exchange. He finds that thirty-four continental European firms listing on the NYSE experience an average abnormal return of 3.7 percent; forty-six continental European firms listing on the London Stock Exchange have an average abnormal return of 2.14 percent; finally, twenty-two continental European firms listing on the Paris Stock Exchange experience an abnormal return of 1.15 percent. All abnormal returns are significant and are significantly different from each other.

Two recent papers provide supportive evidence for the view that listing in the United States provides greater protection of minority shareholders. First, Reese and Weibach (forthcoming) show that firms from civil-law countries (which are notoriously poor at protecting the rights of minority shareholders) that list in the United States issue more equity after the listing, both in the United States and in their home markets. This is consistent with the view that listing in the United States reduces the deadweight costs of external finance associated with poor minority shareholder protection. Second, Doidge, Karolyi, and Stulz (2001) show that foreign firms listed in the United States have significantly higher valuations than foreign firms not listed in the United States. This valuation difference is highest for firms that list on the NYSE or Nasdaq. A listing on the NYSE or Nasdaq provides more protection to minority shareholders than if the firm makes ADRs available over the counter. Their evidence is consistent with the argument that listing in the United States bonds managers and large shareholders to respecting the rights of minority shareholders more carefully.

Provides access to different legal and regulatory systems. The legal system plays two roles (see Shleifer and Vishny 1997b). First, it limits the rights of management: with a poor legal system, managers can steal from shareholders. As the legal system improves, such theft becomes more difficult.

Second, the legal system provides a mechanism for investors to monitor management and exercise their rights. As shareholders discover actions by management that hurt them, they can use the legal system to force management to rescind such actions. With globalization of financial markets, firms coming from countries with poor protection of minority shareholders that raise funds and have their shares listed in countries with better protection of minority shareholders expose themselves to legal actions from investors in these countries. As a result, minority shareholders are better protected. An example of this is the case of Velcro Industries (La Porta et al. 2000a), which was incorporated in the Netherlands Antilles and listed on the Montreal Stock Exchange. Two-thirds of the shares were in the hands of the Cripps family, which tried to reduce the share price by slashing earnings with the hope of buying out minority shareholders cheaply. The stock price fell from $30 in 1988 to $12 within a year, but rebounded to $20 in 1990 when the Cripps family made an offer to repurchase minority shares at $21. An American minority shareholder sued in New York. According to *Forbes* (23 May 1994), "When a New York judge ruled that the U.S. was the proper jurisdiction, secretive Sir Humphrey Cripps decided to call off his offer rather than go under the light of U.S. court of law." By 1994, the shares were trading at $57. Besides leading to greater monitoring of firms that participate in the international markets, globalization also puts pressure on politicians to improve their countries' legal system so they can better participate in the global markets.

How Costly Is Financial Globalization?

We saw in the previous section that financial globalization permits countries to invest more than they save when they have good investment opportunities; that it permits risk sharing, which leads to more efficient production; and that it decreases agency costs and costs of information asymmetries in firms. We now turn to the question of whether the costs of financial globalization are large enough to offset these benefits. The main concern about financial globalization is that capital flows can destabilize economies. It is best to first consider whether capital flows can be destabilizing and why. I divide this analysis into two parts: first, the subject of equity flows, then that of other flows, and finally the question of contagion.

Are Equity Flows Destabilizing?

The first obvious question to ask is whether allowing free capital mobility increases equity volatility.[13] The mainstream view among economists is the one expressed by Dornbusch and Park (1995), that "there is ample evidence that financial market opening is likely to increase the volatility of asset prices" (39). Figure 3.4 provides one perspective on this issue. In that figure, I compute the monthly volatility of the Standard and Poor's (S&P) 500 and of the Datastream World Index from 1973 to 1999. Note that the World Index incorporates more and more emerging countries over time as these countries become part of the world market. In that figure, by far the biggest volatility event is the crash of 1987. Another interesting point in that figure is that most volatility spikes for the S&P 500 are accompa-

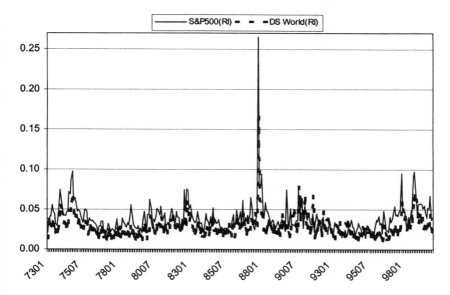

Fig. 3.4   World and S&P 500 Return Volatility

NOTES:

Monthly volatility of S&P 500 and World Portfolio (January 1973–December 1999). The volatility is computed monthly from daily returns of the Datastream world portfolio using the method proposed by Schwert (1989).

nied by smaller spikes for the World Index. In other words, diversification worked when U.S. volatility spiked upward. There is no evidence in the graph that volatility becomes systematically higher as financial globalization moves forward. Finally, the volatility impact of the Mexican and East Asian crises on the volatility of the world market portfolio is difficult to discern.

A number of studies have examined how liberalization affects stock return volatility at the country level. Kim and Singal (2000) consider changes in volatility around liberalizations for a sample of sixteen emerging markets. In their study, they find that the volatility for the first twelve months following a liberalization is not significantly different from the volatility for the previous twelve months. However, they also find that after the first twelve months, volatility falls significantly on average. They provide other evidence that is consistent with an increase in volatility for some countries and with no effect for most countries. Interestingly, the countries for which they find large significant increases are Argentina, Chile, and Mexico. Richards (1996) estimates volatility for emerging markets using weekly data and concludes that "the period 1992–1995, which saw foreign institutional investors playing a more significant role in emerging markets has been characterized by volatility that is marginally lower than the remainder of the sample period (1975 to 1992)" (473). His result is surprising in that it covers the period of the Mexican crisis. Bekaert and Harvey (1997) consider twenty emerging markets and examine stock return volatility before and after liberalization. Using a variety of approaches, they find in all cases that, on average, liberalization decreases volatility. In another paper, Bekaert and Harvey (2000) use a longer sample period and a different method. Again, they find little evidence of an economically significant increase in volatility. Depending on the other determinants of volatility they control for, they find that a slight increase or decrease in volatility is associated with liberalization. The bottom line from these studies is that the claim that liberalization increases volatility is not supported by empirical evidence.

It could well be that volatility does not increase following liberalization but that flows can still move prices in a dangerous way. Before considering the evidence on whether flows move prices, it is important to ask *why* flows would move prices. There is a long tradition in financial economics that argues that demand and supply shocks that do not convey information about fundamentals are unimportant. The evidence supporting this view builds on Scholes (1972), who shows sales of large blocks of stocks have a negligible impact on the stock price when these trades are made purely for liquidity reasons. The reason is straightforward. If the equity of an individual firm becomes underpriced, investors can make money by buying it. Similarly, if equity is overpriced, those who own that equity can make money by selling it. Trades undertaken purely for liquidity reasons provide no information about the value of the equity for investors and hence do not change investors' assessment of the value of equity. If the investors suspect that a large trade is undertaken because investors have information about the firm, then the large trade will naturally have an impact on the value of equity because buyers will buy only at a price that protects them from the adverse information the seller has. With this view, the demand for securities is perfectly elastic at given prices as long as information about the securities does not change. This view implies that capital inflows or outflows have an impact on valuations only if they are undertaken because of information that foreign investors have that is not yet incorporated in prices.

Are there any reasons to suspect that foreign investors at times are better informed than domestic investors? Until recently, financial economists have viewed this possibility as unlikely. As already mentioned, it is well known that investors do not take advantage of international diversification as much as simple models would suggest. There are many possible explanations for this phenomenon, but a leading one is that investors are less well informed about foreign securities than about securities of their own country. They are therefore concerned that when they buy equity from foreign investors, they buy the equity that foreign investors believe to be overvalued. Recent evidence casts some doubt on the view that resident investors are better informed, but the evidence is mixed. Grinblatt and Keloharju (2000) show that foreign investors performed better on the Finnish market than domestic investors, but Shukla and Van Inwegen (1995) provide evidence that U.S. mutual fund managers outperform U.K. mutual fund managers for portfolios of U.S. stocks. Seasholes (2000) shows that in Taiwan foreign investors accumulate shares of firms before they have positive earnings surprises and sell shares of firms before they have negative earnings surprises. He argues—as do Grinblatt and Keloharju—that investment professionals of global firms have better skills and can draw on more expertise from the institutions they belong to. Hau (2001) finds, however, that traders closer to Frankfurt perform better in trading on the automated German exchange, and Choe, Kho, and Stulz (2001) find that foreigners pay more for the shares they purchase in Korea than do resident investors.

None of the evidence we reviewed is evidence corresponding to a period associated with large capital outflows. The Mexican crisis offers evidence consistent with foreign investors' being at an informational disadvantage in crisis periods. Capital outflows from residents took place throughout 1994 following the assassination of the presidential candidate Colosio on 23 March. In contrast, foreign investors were net buyers of Mexican equity even in December 1994. Frankel and Schmukler (1996) investigate the returns of Mexican closed-end funds that trade in the United States. A closed-end fund typically trades at a price that differs from the value of the portfolio that it represents. The value of the underlying portfolio is called the net asset value (NAV) of the fund. Frankel and Schmukler reason that the price of a fund moves because of its U.S. investors whereas the NAV moves because of Mexican investors since the underlying portfolio is a portfolio of Mexican stocks that trade in Mexico City. They find that the NAV moves before the price of the fund and causes changes in the price of the fund. Their interpretation is that Mexico City moves Wall Street's assessment of Mexican stocks rather than the reverse.

If foreign investors are less well informed than domestic investors, they will be more sensitive than domestic investors to public announcements. First, public announcements are less likely to be news for domestic investors, who are more likely to be insiders. Second, since foreign investors are less well informed, their assessment of a country is less precise and hence can be altered more by public information. This makes capital flows sensitive to news. Brennan and Cao (1997) model this phenomenon and provide supporting evidence.

Foreign investors could buy following positive returns and sell following negative returns for perfectly rational reasons. However, by doing so, they could be pushing prices up when they are increasing and pushing them down when they are falling. As a result, they could also, as Dornbusch and Park (1995) argue, be creating bubbles and bursting bubbles. Investors who buy following price increases and sell following price decreases are called *positive feedback traders*. Several recent studies examine whether foreign investors are positive feedback traders, namely whether they buy following positive returns and sell following negative returns. Bohn and Tesar (1996) find evidence of positive feedback trading using monthly data for a large number of countries. Using daily data on trades from the investors who use State Street Bank & Trust as their custodian, Froot, O'Connell, and Seasholes (2001) conclude that "there is very strong trend following in international inflows. The majority of the co-movement of flows and returns at quarterly intervals is actually due to returns predicting future flows" (18). Using data from Korea, Choe, Kho, and Stulz (1999) find evidence of positive feedback trading for foreign investors in that country in 1997. Surprisingly, however, the evidence of positive feedback trading is weak for the last three months of 1997, when the Asian crisis hit Korea. Griffin, Nardari, and Stulz (2001) find evidence of positive feedback trading for a sample of nine countries using daily data.

One might argue that the existing evidence is ill suited to addressing the question of whether flows can make markets crash. It could be that flows keep increasing prices up to the point at which, suddenly, they abruptly fall as foreign investors withdraw. On theoretical grounds, positive feedback trading need not be destabilizing. For instance, if markets are slow to incorporate information into stock prices, positive returns can be expected to be followed by positive returns. Consequently, positive feedback trading is profitable, but investors who trade that way make markets more efficient rather than destabilize them because they accelerate the incorporation of information into prices. If domestic investors are better informed than foreign investors, they will hold more domestic shares on average. The reason for this is that foreign investors discount share prices relative to domestic investors, who tend to sell if they have adverse information that is not incorporated in asset prices. This means that foreign investors do not take as much advantage of international diversification as they would if all investors had the same information. This home bias resulting from information asymmetries implies that the cost of capital in the domestic country is higher than it would be in the absence of these asymmetries because domestic investors bear more risk. As flows leave the country because of bad news, equity prices fall because domestic investors have to hold more domestic shares. Inflows have the opposite effect. This means that, in such a model, flows have an impact on the risk premium. It is also the case that information asymmetries between domestic and foreign investors increase equity returns volatility. There is no reason for flows induced by new information to be destabilizing, however. As information is revealed, investors change their holdings, which has a permanent effect on prices.

When shares are sold from domestic to foreign investors, the shares become held by investors who are internationally diversified and who do not view domestic shares to be as risky as domestic investors. Unexpected changes in investor composition affect equity prices for two reasons, one permanent and one transitory. The permanent reason is the one discussed in the previous paragraph, namely, that investors requiring a lower risk premium bought the shares. Support for this effect is provided by Bekaert,

Harvey, and Lumsdaine (2002). As foreign investors come to the domestic country, however, there might also be a transitory effect: Because they seek to buy the securities, they have to offer domestic investors an inducement to sell. This compensation affects prices only in the short run and its size depends on the liquidity of the markets. In very liquid markets, the compensation is trivial; as markets become less liquid, it might be substantial. This liquidity compensation must be paid by investors who seek to buy, as well as by investors who seek to sell. If an investor wants to get out of a country quickly, that investor must offer a discount on the shares he or she wishes to sell. As shown by Campbell, Grossman, and Wang (1993), this liquidity compensation creates reversals in stock prices. When a large group of investors want to get out of stocks in a market, they have to provide compensation to buyers of their shares in the form of a larger short-term return. Buyers can obtain this return only by buying the shares at a temporarily low price. There is evidence for the United States that such an effect exists, but there is also evidence that it becomes much weaker over time as markets become more efficient.[14]

This liquidity compensation is a cost that investors pay to trade and it affects their trading strategies. In particular, it sharply reduces the ability of foreign investors to move quickly out of an equity market as a group. In the extreme case, an illiquid market has a lock-in effect: The discount to be paid to get out is too high and therefore investors do not sell and ride out the bad times. Illiquidity can also keep investors out, however. Not surprisingly, international investors tend to hold securities for which this liquidity compensation is small, namely, securities of large firms. Although some have argued that liquid markets promote short-term horizons on the part of investors, which in turn hurts economies, it is important to remember that liquid markets facilitate purchases by investors.[15] Investors who cannot sell in a country have no incentives to invest in that country.

We now look at the evidence of the impact of flows on returns. Before turning to the international evidence, we first consider some evidence for the United States. An inflow of mutual fund money is mostly money that was not invested in the stock market. In an interesting recent study, Warther (1995) argues that the impact of an unexpected flow of mutual fund money in the U.S. stock market is rather considerable. He estimates that a 1.0 percent increase in mutual fund stock assets, which for his sample period corresponds to an inflow in the stock market of $4.57 billion, brings about an increase in stock prices of 5.7 percent. His concern is naturally whether this is a reversible price impact due to liquidity or a permanent price impact. Although he looks closely to find reversals, he is unsuccessful. It appears that this effect is a permanent effect. A plausible explanation for this is that a broadening of the shareholder base lowers the risk premium as risks are spread across more investors.

There is some evidence that flows move prices. One would expect this to be the case if the risk of stocks is spread across more investors. The alternative explanation is that flows move prices because they drive stock prices away from fundamentals. As investors flow into a market, they push prices up without regard for fundamentals, as if driven by some feeding frenzy. Eventually, prices collapse. Clark and Berko (1996) attempt to distinguish between these two views in the case of Mexico, which saw a dramatic increase in foreign ownership during their sample period. From 1989 to the end of 1993, foreign ownership of Mexican equities increased from a trivial amount to more than one-fourth of the Mexican market capitalization. Like Warther (1995), they find a strong effect of flows on returns. Their estimate is that an unexpected inflow equal to 1 percent of the capital of the market leads to a contemporaneous increase in prices of 13 percent. This estimate is actually smaller than Warther's. They find no evidence of price reversals, suggesting that the impact of flows is permanent rather than transitory and cannot be explained by price pressure. They also find no support for the hypothesis of positive feedback trading. Therefore, their evidence is fully supportive of the investor-base-broadening hypothesis.

Froot, O'Connell, and Seasholes (2001) provide an extensive analysis of daily equity flows using data made available to them by State Street Bank & Trust. The data they use correspond to the equity flows of the institutional investors who use State Street as their custodian. They analyze equity flows for forty-four countries and estimate that a 1.0 basis point shock to equity flows has a contemporaneous impact of 0.6 basis points on prices. Bekaert, Harvey, and Lumsdaine (2002) find evidence of such a price-pressure effect using monthly data. Griffin, Nardari, and Stulz (2002) show that there is a strong contemporaneous association between flows and returns using daily data. A striking result of Froot, O'Connell, and Seasholes is that flows forecast returns, which would be consistent with foreign investors' having better information.

Some studies relate flows directly to volatility. Hamao and Mei (2001) do this for the case of Japan using monthly data on equity purchases and sales by foreign investors. Foreign portfolio equity investment in Japan was small over the last twenty years, peaking in 1984 at 10.31 percent, but falling back to less than 5.00 percent in 1990. This means that evidence for

Japan must be viewed with caution. Nevertheless, they find that the trades by foreign investors do not differ in impact on volatility from the trades by other investors.

Folkerts-Landau and Ito (1995) provide some data resulting from their computation of the volatility of emerging markets for periods that differ in the intensity of portfolio flows. They also show evidence on the issue of whether a day of high volatility for the Dow Jones predicts a high volatility the next day on an emerging market for periods in which the nature of flows differ. Overall, their evidence is rather mixed. Mexican stock prices appear to be the least volatile when flows are most volatile. In contrast, however, Hong Kong stock return volatility is higher when flows are most volatile. There seems to be evidence that the local volatility is more strongly linked to the volatility of the Dow Jones in periods of more volatile flows. Models in which foreign investors are less well informed than local investors and alter their holdings when they receive new information produce a positive relation between stock return volatility and flow volatility. However, in this case, the relation results mostly from flows and stock prices being driven by the same factors. The relation between flows and volatility may be a source of concern if it is due to temporary increases and decreases in stock prices. Such a concern is often expressed as a concern about herding by institutional investors. The idea is that institutional investors behave alike, pouring in and out of stocks as a group. In the most detailed and careful study to date, Wermers (1999) studies whether U.S. institutional investors herd and whether this behavior leads to temporary changes in stock prices. He finds strong evidence of herding behavior, especially for smaller stocks. However, at the same time, he fails to find evidence that herding leads to temporary changes in stock prices. An increase in institutional ownership is associated with an increase in stock prices, but this increase appears to be permanent.

In a detailed investigation of the behavior of foreign investors in Korea in 1997, Choe, Kho, and Stulz (1999) find evidence of herding among foreign investors. Their data include all trades on the Korea Stock Exchange for 1997. For each trade, they have information on whether a party to the trade is a foreign investor and the country of origin of that investor. They show that there is herding among investors from different countries. Furthermore, herding measures for investors from the United States, although upwardly biased because of the nature of the data, seem extremely high. Surprisingly, however, they find that herding measures are smaller during the last three months of 1997, when the Asian crisis hit Korea, than

before. To investigate whether foreign investors have a destabilizing impact on prices, they estimate the impact on prices of large purchases and
large sales by foreign investors. They argue that if foreign investors destabilize prices, they should start a run on prices. Instead, most of the price
impact of trades by foreign investors is incorporated in prices within the
first ten minutes after those trades are made; nothing else happens following trades by foreign investors. In other words, there is no evidence
that foreign investors start a run on prices. Roughly, the impact of large
trades by foreign investors in Korea is no different from the impact of
large trades by institutional investors on the NYSE.

Are Debt Flows Destabilizing?

Table 3.1 shows a dramatic reversion in bank loans to East Asia during the
crisis period. This dramatic reversion contrasts with the experience for
equity and direct investment. Direct investment in East Asia actually increased during the crisis years. Portfolio investment fell, but it was still
positive in 1997. While portfolio investment was negative in East Asian
countries in 1998, it remained positive across all emerging markets. There
is no evidence in this of dramatic equity flows swirling around the globe.
The story is different for bank debt and short-term debt. Furman and
Stiglitz (1998, 51) state that "the ability of this variable [short-term debt],
by itself, to predict the crises of 1997, is remarkable." From 1988 to 1997,
foreign debt to emerging markets went from $1 trillion to $2 trillion. Much
of the increase was in short-term debt. As a result of the role of short-term
debt in crises, many have argued that short-term debt should somehow be
regulated or limited. I argue here that regulating short-term debt is not
the appropriate solution, but before doing so, it is important to understand why short-term debt can be a cause of instability.

There is a fundamental difference between a reversal of equity flows
and a reversal of debt flows. When foreign investors sell shares in a country, the firms whose shares are sold do not have to give the money back.
To the extent that the departure of foreign investors decreases share prices
because it increases the risk premium in a country, firms experience a cost-
of-capital increase that reduces their investment in the future and increases the cost of funds they raise. In contrast, when lenders leave a country, they take with them the money paid to them by the borrowing firms
and these firms then have to find funds to replace what they lost. Equity
outflows do not lead to default and bankruptcy; debt outflows do. When

debt has to be repaid, a company might be in a situation where it cannot borrow because it would not be able to pay the interest that lenders require (see Stiglitz and Weiss 1981). In emerging markets, this situation could occur because the company is facing difficulties or because the country has become more risky. When a company has a large amount of debt maturing, being unable to borrow new money can force the company into default. To avoid such situations, a firm will limit its leverage and choose the maturity of its debt to coincide with times when it expects its financial situation to be such that it can raise funds to repay the debt or to have the internal funds to do so. For instance, a firm with a new project that will not generate cash in the near future will generally choose debt that matures after the project starts generating cash.[16] A firm that expects its situation to improve will choose short-term debt that can be refinanced on better terms when the situation does improve.

It is possible, however, for a firm to find long-term debt to be too expensive because of information asymmetries and agency costs. Shareholders and managers can take advantage of bondholders in many ways. In particular, they can issue long-term debt when they expect the situation of the firm to worsen; large shareholders and managers can extract private benefits from control that limits cash flows available for bondholders; shareholders can increase the value of equity at the expense of the bondholders by making the firm more risky. When bondholders expect that they will be taken advantage of, they will require a higher coupon on debt to compensate for the fact that, as a result of actions by shareholders and managers, the promised coupon is not paid. In the extreme case in which bondholders expect not to receive the promised payments because managers or large shareholders can remove corporate assets from the firm before maturity of the debt, there is no promised coupon payment that would enable the firm to issue debt. To issue fixed rate debt with a lower coupon, shareholders and managers can attach covenants to the debt that restrict their ability to expropriate bondholders.[17] However, covenants are valuable only if they can be enforced. In countries in which covenants cannot be enforced easily, they cannot be used to reduce debt coupons. If covenants cannot be used to reduce the cost of long-term debt, firms can issue equity or borrow over the short term. Unfortunately, if a country is such that debt covenants cannot be enforced, it is likely to be a country where the rights of minority shareholders are poorly enforced and where, consequently, equity is expensive. This means that countries with poor legal systems will be countries where neither equity financing nor long-term debt is a low-cost source of funds. Such a situation forces firms to fund themselves with short-term loans. Shorter maturity debt makes it more difficult for shareholders and managers to take advantage of bondholders. If it takes time to expropriate lenders, short-term debt enables lenders to stop lending if they observe that the shareholders and managers are trying to expropriate them. In addition, if shareholders try to increase the risk of the firm to decrease the value of the debt, the lenders can adjust the terms of the debt to reflect the greater risk or can refuse to roll the debt over.

The problem with shorter maturity debt is that the firm has to raise funds to pay back debt more often than if it finances itself with long-term debt. In firms where information asymmetries or agency costs are not important, refinancing of short-term debt is not a problem. As long as the value of the firm exceeds the face value of the debt, the firm can refinance the debt. Unfortunately, in the presence of agency costs and information asymmetries, it is perfectly possible for the true value of the firm to exceed the value of the debt and yet for the firm to be unable to find funds to refinance the debt. This could be because the firm cannot credibly communicate its true value or because agency conflicts make it impossible to restructure the claims against the firm in such a way that all parties agree to raise new funds.

In emerging economies, short-term debt is a crucial financing tool because the financial structure often does not support long-term debt for corporations. Unfortunately, a country with short-term debt is one where runs can take place when the country has limited foreign exchange reserves and a fixed exchange rate. To see this, consider the situation of a lender to a corporation. Suppose that suddenly there is a nontrivial probability of a devaluation of the local currency. Even if the lender is hedged, such a devaluation can be costly for the lender if it affects the creditworthiness of the borrower. As a result, it becomes optimal for the short-term lenders with loans coming due not to renew those loans. If the country's reserves are limited, any lender who gets his money back does so at the expense of other lenders. This creates a run on the reserves from the short-term lenders. Since all short-term lenders benefit from demanding their own money first, this leads to a creditors' panic in which all short-term lenders want their money back. The firms in the country are drained of liquidity as a result of this panic. This forces them to contract, or even leads to default. Faced with a short-term debt run, firms will find it difficult to raise funds to replace short-term debt after a devaluation. Consider a firm that lost its short-term debt. It is left with senior debt that has become more risky. Any new money will increase the value of the senior debt. To be able to compensate the providers of new money, the value of equity held by old shareholders must fall. The old shareholders may therefore conclude that they are better off not to raise funds (see Myers 1977).

It is immediately clear from this that a crisis can develop quickly if banks conclude that they have to withdraw funds from a particular country. One could argue that a simple solution would be for local firms to borrow over the long term, thereby preventing liquidity crises of the sort discussed here. Many have argued that firms borrowed excessively using foreign short-term debt and that such practices should be regulated.[18] It is clear that high short-term borrowing has substantial externalities. A country with high short-term borrowing is one where a drop in reserves can create a run on firms, which feeds back into a run on the currency. Unfortunately, shifting from short-term to long-term borrowing is not easy. Countries differ vastly in their financial structures, where financial structure is defined to consist of the institutions, financial technology, and rules of the game that specify how financial activity is organized at a given time (Stulz 2000). Countries with weak financial structures do not support long-term debt contracts for most firms. The reason is that long-term debt holders have limited ability to influence the actions of management. Therefore, they have to rely on the monitoring of management by others who have different incentives. When this monitoring is poor and firm insiders have large benefits from control, long-term debt is highly risky and therefore too expensive. Short-term debt holders can monitor the firm more effectively because they can withdraw their money quickly. It is therefore not surprising that firms would use large amounts of short-term debt when a country's financial structure is weak. Preventing firms from using short-term foreign debt amounts to limiting their growth and hence reducing the growth of the country that imposes these limitations.

To avoid having crises triggered through nonrenewal of short-term loans, it would seem obvious that an important element of the solution has to be an exchange rate regime under which private parties do not find it optimal to trigger a run. Possible solutions to this problem are either a floating exchange rate or a fixed exchange rate that cannot be adjusted. However, even if foreign exchange reserves do not lead to runs, it is still the case that countries should improve their financial structures so they can support longer term contracting. There is clear evidence that long-term debt is more prevalent in countries that score high on a legal efficiency index (see Demirgüç-Kunt and Maksimovic 1998). If a firm is financed only with long-term debt, there is no opportunity for creditors to withdraw their funds quickly. As a result, these creditors might even be willing to restructure the debt if by doing so they increase their chances of receiving the promised payments. For creditors to be willing to make long-term loans, they have to be comfortable that bankruptcy rules lead to efficient resolutions of bankruptcies, that large shareholders cannot expropriate them, that inflation is under control, that political risk is minor, and so on.

At this point, there exists empirical evidence showing that financial structure variables are helpful in predicting how countries fared during the crises of 1997 and 1998. Johnson et al. (2000) relate the performance of emerging market economies to financial structure variables. They find that rule of law and lower corruption are good predictors of the devaluation of a currency during the crisis period, whereas macroeconomic variables do not seem as useful.

Contagion

We now turn to the contagion issue. It applies to both equity and debt flows. It is important to distinguish between contagion that rationally takes place as the price mechanism works its way to digest shocks to fundamentals, and contagion that cannot be justified based on shocks to fundamentals. To clarify this distinction, consider a country whose main industry suddenly becomes less competitive. It cannot sell as much of its products as it used to. As a result, it lays off workers and buys fewer goods from firms and shops within the country. In such a situation, the competitive shock that affects the industry ends up having an impact on other businesses because it reduces the demand for their products. In this scenario, the other businesses in the country were perfectly healthy before the industry experienced its competitive shock. Yet, afterward, they will be economically weaker as a direct consequence of the competitive shock affecting the industry. As a result, investors will invest less in these businesses. This is a case of healthy businesses' becoming weaker because of contagion. This contagion is just the price mechanism at work: If the industry shrinks, the country cannot support as many businesses as it did before. Bailing out the affected businesses would make little sense. The businesses have to shrink and bailing them out would prevent this shrinkage. Obviously, if something could be done about the competitive shock, this might solve the problem. For instance, if the industry became less competitive because of an exchange rate kept artificially high, letting the exchange rate float could help things. However, a bailout of the country would not seem to be the right solution because it would only hinder the workings of the price mechanism.

Suppose now that foreign investors invest less in the country that was affected by the competitive shock because they believe that businesses in that country have worse prospects than before the shock. This would be perfectly rational. One would expect these investors to behave that way to insure that capital flows to the countries that can make the best use of it. However, consider now another country that is isolated from the one with the industry that has a competitive shock, so that the economic fortunes of the former are truly independent from those of the latter. There would be no reason for investors to invest significantly less in the second country. If they did so, this would not seem rational. The investments made in the second country would seem to be as good after the competitive shock as before. Nonfundamental contagion occurs if the second country experiences less foreign investment as a result of the difficulties of the first (totally unrelated) country.[19] If nonfundamental contagion occurs, a good case can be made to help the countries hit by that nonfundamental contagion. Remember that there is a good chance that the victimized country is one with a great deal of short-term debt. As a result, the immediate impact of contagion is to create a liquidity crisis for firms, which leads to contraction. Providing liquidity reduces the problem and prevents the country from being hurt too much by the nonfundamental contagion.

Whereas observers seem convinced that nonfundamental contagion is of crucial importance, the empirical evidence is not definitive. It often relies on views of financial markets that are incomplete. For instance, commentators and economists make vast use of stories showing that some investors do not know what they are doing and fundamentally misunderstand the economies in which they invest. There is no question that most investors in emerging markets would fail simple tests on the economic conditions of the markets they invest in. However, for financial markets to be efficient and function well, it does not have to be that all investors are smart. What is required is that when there are profit opportunities, some investor will find them and take advantage of them. By the same token, evidence that institutional constraints, information asymmetries, or agency problems lead some classes of investors to make decisions consistent with nonfundamental contagion is not sufficient to show that there is nonfundamental contagion. The reason is that trading patterns by one group of investors can always be offset by trading patterns of other investors. The critical question, therefore, is whether there is enough "arbitrage capital" or "smart money" to take advantage of mispricings in markets resulting from the actions of less well informed investors or investors constrained in their actions by institutional or other considerations. The problem is that to assemble pools of money that can be used to take advantage of apparent arbitrage opportunities is often difficult.[20] The individuals who invest in such pools often have limited knowledge of the strategies pursued by these pools. As a result, they must rely on rules of thumb rather than on quantitative analysis. These individuals will often use performance as a measure of the ability of the fund managers to find and exploit arbitrage opportunities. Unfortunately, managers can have great ability in finding arbitrage opportunities but can still lose money over periods of time as arbitrage spreads widen. A manager who has discovered an arbitrage strategy but finds that the widening of the arbitrage spreads creates temporary losses may have a hard time explaining what is going on to investors. The investors have to decide whether to trust the manager or pull out their money because they think the manager is not competent. These types of problems limit the extent to which there are pools of money that can counteract nonfundamental contagion. As a result, nonfundamental contagion can exist when potential arbitrageurs are capital constrained. It will be especially important when arbitrageurs are less active, perhaps because they have sustained losses that depleted their capital or because of other reasons.

It is useful to illustrate these points in the context of existing analyses of contagion. Several papers have focused on a bank channel for contagion, which works as follows (see Kaminsky and Reinhart 2000; Rijckeghem and Weder 1999). As a bank makes losses in a country, it has a smaller amount of funds to lend because its capital has fallen. This leads the bank to lend less to other countries. Hence, these other countries could suffer from nonfundamental contagion. However, the fact that banks are withdrawing from a country for nonfundamental reasons means that there are profit opportunities in that country for other banks and investors. For the bank channel to lead to nonfundamental contagion, therefore, it has to be that other banks or institutions do not try to offset the actions of the banks that decrease their lending for nonfundamental reasons.

Numerous studies have attempted to estimate contagion by evaluating changes in correlations across countries between noncrisis and crisis periods. It is generally the case that correlations increase during crisis periods. One could therefore easily conclude that because crises make markets move more together, there must be contagion. Unfortunately, that sort of analysis suffers from many problems. The main problem is that crisis periods are periods of high absolute returns.[21] Suppose that, in computing the correlation of returns between two countries, one splits the sample period so that one period has higher absolute-value returns than the other. The period with higher absolute-value returns will be the crisis period. If the two countries' returns share a common factor as well as each having a country-specific factor, it must be the case that when one of the countries has a large absolute value return the probability that the common factor has a large absolute value return is higher than the unconditional probability. Consequently, the correlation conditioned on the presence of large absolute returns must be higher than the unconditional correlation even if the unconditional correlation is constant. As a result, one could be misled into believing that there is contagion when there is none because returns conditioned on crisis periods will mechanically give the appearance of contagion. Empirical research that accounts for the statistical difficulties in isolating contagion effects has not been very successful in showing that there is contagion. For instance, Baig and Goldfajn (1998) have trouble finding clear evidence of increases in correlations in equity markets during the East Asian crisis after controlling for a number of economic variables (see also Forbes and Rigobon 2001). They argue that correlations of sovereign spreads increase significantly after accounting for fundamentals, but they do not include second moments in their fundamentals. Since we know that second moments are crucial determinants of credit spreads, it is not clear what one can conclude from their study with respect to sovereign spreads.

Bae, Karolyi, and Stulz (forthcoming) take the view that irrational contagion must correspond to a nonlinearity in the transmission process of shocks. If there is irrational contagion, it has to be that large shocks propagate differently from small ones. Using a database of daily returns for emerging markets, they provide evidence that there is such a nonlinearity in the transmission process of shocks. Large negative returns in Asia make it more likely that Latin America will have large negative returns. This contagion effect cannot be predicted based on correlations alone. At the same time, however, this contagion effect turns out to be small, so that its economic importance is a matter of debate.

Conclusion

We saw in this paper that there are compelling arguments that there are significant benefits to financial globalization. There have been a large number of painful crises. These crises were partly caused by exchange rate regimes that require periodic crises for countries to change to more appropriate exchange rates. More fundamentally, however, economies in countries with poor financial structures are naturally fragile because they do not support long-term contracting as well as those with more advanced financial structures do. What are the changes that need to be implemented to make emerging market economies less fragile? It seems difficult to find good arguments for the preservation of adjustable exchange rate pegs. Adjustable pegs come with embedded crises because, at some point, a peg becomes a money machine for hedge funds and other speculators. If inflation cannot be controlled without pegging a currency to another, a currency board would seem a better approach. However, central bank independence should make it possible to control inflation in a flexible exchange rate system. If the exchange rate regime does not generate crises, it is important to make it possible for economic agents to engage in long-term contracting. Low inflation uncertainty is critical for that to be the case. It is also important for bankruptcy mechanisms to function well, for creditors to be protected, and for renegotiation to be possible. Absent shareholder protection, firms can finance themselves mostly through debt, ending up with too much debt relative to a situation in which shareholders' rights would be enforced. High leverage is a source of instability, but often this is a risk worth taking for firms because they have no other choice. The appropriate policies to eliminate the fragility of emerging economies are policies that foster better financial structures, so that long-term contracting can be supported. Such better financial structures can neither be developed nor can they survive in countries that choose to close their financial markets off from the rest of the world.

Notes

1. A vast literature discusses the implications of capital mobility for fixed or pegged exchange rates. In this literature, capital mobility is generally viewed as an obstacle that prevents countries from pursuing particular exchange rate policies. We therefore postpone discussion of exchange rates to the next section, in which we discuss the costs of capital mobility.

2. This type of setup is familiar from the literature on bank runs. See Diamond and Dybvig (1983).

3. Stulz (1999a) provides a nontechnical summary of this section.

4. See Stulz (1999c) for a review of how and when the CAPM applies to global markets.

5. See Cooper and Kaplanis (1994), French and Poterba (1991), Kang and Stulz (1997), and Tesar and Werner (1995).

6. See Tesar and Werner (1998) for these numbers.

7. See Subrahmanyam (1975). However, Basak (1996) shows that the interest

rate increase associated with globalization can decrease a country's welfare. This happens only if the country that liberalizes is large in the sense that its actions have a significant impact on the world interest rate and if this country borrows for current consumption.

8. See Obstfeld (1994) for an analysis of the impact of financial globalization on production.

9. "The hardest problem all through my business career was to obtain enough capital to do all the business I wanted to do and could do, given the necessary amount of money." John D. Rockefeller, cited in Chernow (1998, 68).

10. See Jung, Kim, and Stulz (1996) for this argument and for supportive evidence.

11. See La Porta et al. (2000b) for a review of the evidence on investor protection.

12. Cantale (1998) and Fuerst (1998) develop theoretical models in which firms reveal their good prospects by listing abroad. See also Huddart, Hughes, and Brunnermeister (1998) for an analysis that focuses on how the competition among exchanges for trading volume affects disclosure requirements. They argue that this competition leads to a race to the top rather than to the bottom in terms of disclosure requirements.

13. Stulz (1999c) provides a review of the literature on flows. This section pays more attention to work written since that paper was published and less attention to contagion mechanisms.

14. Froot and Perold (1995) document that the short-term behavior of stock prices is different in recent years from what it has been historically. Yesterday's stock returns have much less information about tomorrow's stock returns than they used to. Gagnon and Karolyi (1997) show that the volume-returns relation is much weaker after the crash of 1987 than before.

15. For instance, Thurow (1992) argues that "the United States has organized a system that is the exact opposite of that of Germany and Japan. Those countries have organized a system (business groups) to minimize the influence of impatient shareholders, while the United States has organized a system (fund dominance) to maximize the influence of impatient shareholders."

16. See Barclay and Smith (1995) for evidence on how U.S. corporations choose the maturity of their debt.

17. See Smith and Warner (1979) for an analysis of the role of covenants.

18. See Rodrik and Velasco (1999) for a discussion of this debate.

19. See Claessens, Dornbush, and Park (2001) for a discussion of various types of contagion.

20. See Shleifer and Vishny (1997a) for an analysis of these issues.

21. See Rigobon (2002) for an analysis of the statistical difficulties in estimating changes in correlations between crisis and non-crisis periods.

References

Adams, C., D. Mathieson, G. Schinasi, and B. Chadha. 1998. *International capital markets: Developments, prospects, and key policy issues.* Washington, D.C.: International Monetary Fund.

Bae, K. H., G. A. Karolyi, and R. M. Stulz. (Forthcoming). A new approach to measuring financial contagion. *Review of Financial Studies.*

Barclay, M. J., and C. W. Smith. 1995. The maturity structure of corporate debt. *Journal of Finance* 50:609–31.

Basak, S. 1996. An intertemporal model of international capital market segmentation. *Journal of Financial and Quantitative Analysis* 31:161–88.

Bekaert, G., and C. R. Harvey. 1997. Emerging equity market volatility. *Journal of Financial Economics* 43:29–77.

———. 2000. Foreign speculators and emerging equity markets. *Journal of Finance* 55:565–613.

Bekaert, G., C. R. Harvey, and R. L. Lumsdaine. 2002. The dynamics of emerging market equity flows. *Journal of Financial Economics* (forthcoming).

Bhagwati, J. 1998. The capital myth. *Foreign Affairs* 77 (3): 7–12.

Bohn, H., and L. Tesar. 1996. U.S. equity investment in foreign markets: Portfolio rebalancing or return chasing? *American Economic Review* 86:77–81.

Brennan, M. J., and H. H. Cao. 1997. International portfolio investment flows. *Journal of Finance* 52:1851–80.

Campbell, J. Y., S. J. Grossman, and J. Wang. 1993. Trading volume and serial correlation in stock returns. *Quarterly Journal of Economics* 10:407–32.

Cantale, S. 1998. The choice of a foreign market as a signal. Tulane University, A. B. Freeman School of Business, New Orleans, La.

Chernow, R. 1998. *Titan: The life of John D. Rockefeller, Sr.* New York: Random House.

Choe, H., B.-C. Kho, and R. M. Stulz. 1999. Do foreign investors destabilize stock markets? The Korean experience in 1997. *Journal of Financial Economics* 54:227–64.

———. 2001. Do domestic investors have more valuable information about individual stocks than foreign investors? NBER Working Paper no. 8073. Cambridge, Mass.: National Bureau of Economic Research, December.

Claessens, S., R. Dornbusch, and Y. C. Park. 2001. Contagion: Why crises spread and how this can be stopped. In *International financial contagion*, ed. S. Claessens and K. J. Forbes, Boston: Kluwer Academic Publishers.

Clark, J., and E. Berko. 1996. Foreign investment fluctuations and emerging market stock returns: The case of Mexico. Federal Reserve Bank of New York. Unpublished Working Paper.

Coffee, J. 1999. The future as history: The prospects for global convergence in corporate governance and its implications. *Northwestern University Law Review* 93:641–708.

Cooper, I. A., and E. Kaplanis. 1994. Home bias in equity portfolios, inflation hedging, and international capital market equilibrium. *Review of Financial Studies* 7:45–60.

Demirgüç-Kunt, A., and V. Maksimovic. 1998. Law, finance, and firm growth. *Journal of Finance* 53:2017–138.

Diamond, D. W., and P. H. Dybvig. 1983. Bank runs, deposit insurance, and liquidity. *Journal of Political Economy* 91:401–19.

Doidge, C., A. Karolyi, and R. Stulz. 2001. Why are foreign firms listed in the U.S. worth more? Ohio State University, Department of Finance. Working Paper.

Dornbusch, R., and Y. C. Park. 1995. Financial integration in a second best world: Are we still sure about our classical prejudices? In *Financial opening: Policy lessons for Korea,* ed. R. Dornbusch and Y. C. Park, Seoul: Korea Institute of Finance.

Foerster, S. R., and G. A. Karolyi. 1999. The effects of market segmentation and investor recognition on asset prices: Evidence from foreign stocks listing in the U.S. *Journal of Finance* 54:981–1013.

Folkerts-Landau, D., and T. Ito. 1995. *International capital markets: Developments, prospects, and policy issues.* Washington, D.C.: International Monetary Fund.

Forbes, K., and R. Rigobon. 2001. No contagion, only interdependence: Measuring stock market co-movements. *Journal of Finance* (forthcoming).

Frankel, J. A., and S. L. Schmukler. 1996. Country fund discounts, asymmetric information, and the Mexican crisis of 1994: Did local residents turn pessimistic before international investors? NBER Working Paper no. 5714. Cambridge, Mass.: National Bureau of Economic Research.

French, K., and J. Poterba. 1991. International diversification and international equity markets. *American Economic Review* 81:222–26.

Froot, K. A., P. G. O'Connell, and M. S. Seasholes. 2001. The portfolio flows of international investors. *Journal of Financial Economics* 59:151–93.

Froot, K. A., and A. F. Perold. 1995. New trading practices and short-run market efficiency. *Journal of Futures Markets* 15:731–65.

Fuerst, O. 1998. A theoretical analysis of the investor protection regulations: Argument for global listing of stocks. Yale School of Management. Working Paper.

Furman, J., and J. E. Stiglitz. 1998. Economic crises: Evidence and insights from East Asia. *Brookings Papers on Economic Activity,* Issue no. 2: 1–135.

Gagnon, L., and G. A. Karolyi. 1997. Information, trading volume, and international stock market comovements. Working Paper no. 97–19. London, Ontario: University of Western Ontario, Richard Ivey School of Business.

Griffin, J., F. Nardari, and R. M. Stulz. 2002. Daily cross-border equity flows: Pushed or pulled? Ohio State University, Department of Finance. Working Paper.

Grinblatt, M., and M. Keloharju. 2000. The investment behavior and performance of various investor-types: A study of Finland's unique data set. *Journal of Financial Economics* 55:43–67.

Hamao, Y., and J. Mei. 2001. Living with the "enemy": An analysis of investment in the Japanese equity market. *Journal of International Money and Finance* 20 (5): 715–35.

Harvey, C. R. 1991. The world price of covariance risk. *Journal of Finance* 46:111–58.

Hau, H. 2001. Location matters. *Journal of Finance* 56:1959–83.

Henry, P. B. 2000a. Do stock market liberalizations cause investment booms? *Journal of Financial Economics* 58:301–30.

———. 2000b. Stock market liberalization, economic reform, and emerging market equity prices. *Journal of Finance* 55:529–64.

Huddart, S., J. S. Hughes, and M. Brunnermeister. 1998. Disclosure requirements and stock exchange listing choice in an international context. *Journal of Accounting and Economics* 26:237–69.

Johnson, S., P. Boone, A. Breach, and E. Friedman. 2000. Corporate governance in the Asian financial crisis. *Journal of Financial Economics* 58:141–86.

Jung, K., Y.-C. Kim, and R. M. Stulz. 1996. Timing, investment opportunities, managerial discretion, and the security issue decision. *Journal of Financial Economics* 42:159–85.

Kaminsky, G. L., and C. M. Reinhart. 2000. On crises, contagion, and confusion. *Journal of International Economics* 51:145–68.

Kang, J.-K., Y.-C. Kim, K. Park, and R. M. Stulz. 1995. An analysis of the wealth effects of Japanese offshore dollar-denominated convertible and warrant bond issues. *Journal of Financial and Quantitative Analysis* 30:257–70.

Kang, J.-K., and R. Stulz. 1997. Why is there a home bias? An analysis of foreign portfolio equity ownership in Japan. *Journal of Financial Economics* 46:3–28.

Karolyi, G. A., and R. M. Stulz. 2001. Are assets priced locally or globally? In *Handbook of the economics of finance,* ed. G. Constantinides, M. Harris, and R. M. Stulz. Amsterdam: North-Holland (forthcoming).

Kim, E. H., and V. Singal. 2000. Stock market openings: Experience of emerging economies. *Journal of Business* 73:25–66.

Krugman, P. 1998. Saving Asia: It's time to get radical. *Fortune,* September 7, pp. 74–80.

La Porta, R., F. Lopez-de-Silanes, and A. Shleifer. 1999. Corporate ownership around the world. *Journal of Finance* 54:471–517.

La Porta, R., F. Lopez-de-Silanes, A. Shleifer, and R. Vishny. 2000a. Agency problems and dividend policies around the world. *Journal of Finance* 55:1–33.

———. 2000b. Investor protection and corporate governance. *Journal of Financial Economics* 58:3–27.

Mathieson, D. J., and G. J. Schinasi. 2001. *International capital markets: Developments, prospects, and key policy issues.* Washington, D.C.: International Monetary Fund.

Miller, D. P. 1999. The market reaction to international cross-listings: Evidence from depositary receipts. *Journal of Financial Economics* 51:103–23.

Myers, S. C. 1977. Determinants of corporate borrowing. *Journal of Financial Economics* 5:147–75.

Obstfeld, M. 1994. Risk-taking, global diversification, and growth. *American Economic Review* 84:1310–29.

Pinkowitz, L., R. Stulz, and R. Williamson. 2001. Corporate governance and the home bias. Dice Center Working Paper no. 2001–19. Columbus, Ohio: Ohio State University.

Pomerleano, M. 1998. The East Asia crisis and corporate finances: The untold micro story. World Bank Policy Research Working Paper. Washington, D.C.: World Bank, October.

Reese, W., and M. Weisbach. (Forthcoming). Protection of minority shareholder interests, cross-listings in the United States, and subsequent equity offerings. *Journal of Financial Economics.*

Richards, A. J. 1996. Volatility and predictability in national stock markets: How do emerging and mature markets differ? *IMF Staff Papers* 43:461–501.

Rigobon, R. 2002. Contagion: How to measure it? In *Preventing currency crises in emerging markets,* ed. S. Edwards and J. Frankel. Chicago: University of Chicago Press (forthcoming).

Rijckeghem, C. V., and B. Weder. 1999. Spillovers through banking centers: A panel data analysis. IMF Working Paper no. 00/88. Washington, D.C.: International Monetary Fund.

Rodrik, D., and A. Velasco. 1999. Short-term capital flows. NBER Working Paper no. 7364. Cambridge, Mass.: National Bureau of Economic Research, September.

Scholes, M. 1972. The market for securities: Substitution versus price pressure and the effects of information on share prices. *Journal of Business* 45:179–211.

Schwert, G. William. 1989. Why does stock market volatility change over time? *Journal of Finance* 44:1115–53.

Seasholes, M. S. 2000. Smart foreign traders in emerging markets. University of California at Berkeley, Haas School of Business. Working Paper.

Shleifer, A., and R. W. Vishny. 1997a. The limits of arbitrage. *Journal of Finance* 52:25–55.

———. 1997b. A survey of corporate governance. *Journal of Finance* 52:737–84.

Shukla, R. K., and G. B. Van Inwegen. 1995. Do locals perform better than foreigners? An analysis of U.K. and U.S. mutual fund managers. *Journal of Economics and Business* 47:241–54.

Smith, C. W., Jr., and J. B. Warner. 1979. On financial contracting: An analysis of bond covenants. *Journal of Financial Economics* 7:117–62.

Stiglitz, J. 1998. Boats, planes, and capital flows. *Financial Times,* March 25, p. 32.

Stiglitz, J., and A. Weiss. 1981. Credit rationing in markets with imperfect information. *American Economic Review* 71:393–410.

Stulz, R. M. 1990. Managerial discretion and optimal financing policies. *Journal of Financial Economics* 26:3–27.

———. 1999a. Globalization, corporate finance, and the cost of capital. *Journal of Applied Corporate Finance* (Fall): 8–25.

———. 1999b. Globalization of equity markets and the cost of capital. NBER Working Paper no. 7021. Cambridge, Mass.: National Bureau of Economic Research, March.

———. 1999c. International portfolio flows and security markets. In *International capital flows,* ed. M. Feldstein, 257–93. Chicago: University of Chicago Press.

———. 2000. Financial structure, corporate finance, and economic growth. *International Review of Finance* 11:1–28.

Subrahmanyam, M. 1975. On the optimality of international capital market integration. *Journal of Financial Economics* 2:3–28.

Tesar, L., and I. Werner. 1995. Home bias and high turnover. *Journal of International Money and Finance* 14:467–93.

———. 1998. The internationalization of global securities markets since the 1987 crash. *Brookings-Wharton Papers on Financial Services,* ed. R. E. Litan and A. M. Santomero, 281–372. Washington, D.C.: Brookings Institution.

Thurow, L. 1992. *Head to head: The coming economic battle among Japan, Europe, and America.* New York: William Morrow.

Warther, V. A. 1995. Aggregate mutual fund flows and security returns. *Journal of Financial Economics* 39:209–35.

Wermers, R. 1999. Mutual fund herding and the impact on stock prices. *Journal of Finance* 54:581–622.

Appendix

1. Let σ_H be the return volatility of the small country market portfolio, σ_W be the volatility of the return of the market portfolio for the rest of the world, and ρ be the correlation coefficient between the two portfolios. Consider a portfolio with an investment of w in the rest of the world and $(1 - w)$ in the small country. The portfolio has a volatility σ_P given by

$$\sigma_P^2 = w^2\sigma_W^2 + 2(1 - w)w\rho\sigma_W\sigma_H + (1 - w)^2\sigma_H^2.$$

Taking the derivative with respect to w and setting $w = 0$ yields

$$\frac{d\sigma_P^2}{dw} = 2\sigma_H^2 - 2\rho\sigma_H\sigma_W$$

A necessary condition for an increase in w from the position of no foreign investment to decrease the volatility of the portfolio is that the above expression is positive, which is the condition given by equation (3).

2. Let T be the relative risk tolerance, h the fraction of investors that invest in their home country only, σ_H be the volatility of return of the small country, σ_w be the volatility of the rest of the world (which is viewed as one country), δ the capitalization of the small country as a fraction of the world capitalization, μ_D the risk premium of the small country, and μ_w the risk premium of the rest of the world. We assume zero correlation between the small country and the rest of the world. With constant relative risk tolerance and zero correlation, we have the following demands for the market portfolio of the small country:

$$w_I^H W_I^H = T\left(\frac{\mu_H}{\sigma_H^2}\right)\delta hW$$

$$w_H^H W_I^H = T\left(\frac{\mu_H}{\sigma_H^2}\right)\delta(1 - h)W$$

$$w_I^W W_I^W = T\left(\frac{\mu_H}{\sigma_H^2}\right)(1 - \delta)hW$$

where the demands for the small country market portfolio are, respectively, the demand from the small country investors without home bias, the demand from the small country investors with home bias, and the demand from the rest of the world without home bias. In equilibrium, these demands have to sum up to the market capitalization of the small country market:

$$w_I^H W_I^H \ + \ w_H^H W_I^H \ + \ w_I^W W_I^W \ =$$

$$T\left(\frac{\mu_H}{\sigma_H^2}\right)\delta h W \ + \ T\left(\frac{\mu_H}{\sigma_H^2}\right)\delta(1 \ - \ h)W \ + \ T\left(\frac{\mu_H}{\sigma_H^2}\right)(1 \ - \ \delta)h W$$

$$= \ M_H$$

where M_H is the capitalization of the small country market portfolio.

Chapter Four

Capital Flows or Capital Flaws?

Guillermo A. Calvo

The difficulty lies, not in the new ideas, but in escaping from the old ones, which ramify, for those brought up as most of us have been, into every corner of our minds. *Keynes (1961, p. viii)*

Introduction

This paper presents an overview of recent crises in emerging market economies (EMs), aiming to assess their nature, find effective cures, and prevent their future occurrence. A hypothesis maintained in the discussion will be that EMs suffer from serious credibility problems, in addition to exhibiting highly incomplete financial structures—two issues that are not necessarily unrelated. This makes them significantly different from advanced economies. Thus, for instance, whereas a devaluation spells expansion in the latter, it is a mixed blessing in EMs. The degrees of freedom enjoyed by policymakers in advanced countries are luxuries that most EMs cannot afford.

The paper is organized as follows. A discussion of crisis diagnosis is covered in the next three sections. The section on "Recent Crises: A Heavy Blow to the Conventional Wisdom" notes that, independently of one's interpretation of the causes, crises themselves have brought about a radical revision of the conventional wisdom. This contributed to the intellectual confusion that has prevailed since 1995, and may have resulted in bad policy advice. "Recent Crises: A Closer Look" discusses some of the

Guillermo A. Calvo is Distinguished Professor of Economics at the University of Maryland and an associate of the National Bureau of Economic Research. He is currently chief economist at the Inter-American Development Bank, on leave from the University of Maryland.

key stylized facts that preceded crises, as well as those in the aftermath. Emphasis is put on financial and balance-sheet issues, including the destabilizing behavior of central banks. "Explaining Capital Flows" attempts to shed some light on these issues and focuses on the role of U.S. short-term interest rates, and the development of the market for Brady bonds.

The fifth section, titled "Crisis Management," deals with what to do when a crisis strikes. Special attention is paid to rescue packages and tight monetary and fiscal policies. "The New Financial Architecture: Domestic Policy" shifts the focus to the medium term, and discusses policies that can unilaterally be taken by individual countries to lower capital-flow volatility and the depth of financial crises. It examines the role of the banking system, maturity of public-sector debt, exchange rates, and controls on capital mobility. The final section closes the paper with some conclusions on flows and flaws.

Recent Crises: A Heavy Blow to the Conventional Wisdom

The central features of recent financial crises are as follows: (a) On some dimension, they all contain a large unanticipated component; (b) short-maturity bonds are at the center of the action; (c) victims include countries with bad and good fundamentals, as conventionally defined (i.e., in terms of current account deficit, real currency appreciation, fiscal deficit, inflation); and (d) they spread to other countries (contagion). The last characteristic is particularly confusing and alarming. Since crises arose after a period of large capital inflows, this has led some observers to conjecture that the capital market suffers from fundamental flaws and needs further regulation. High on the list is control on capital mobility—à la Chile, for instance—but there are also proposals for a complete overhaul of the international financial architecture. In my opinion, this is a result of panic-driven overreaction, due partly to the surprise element highlighted in point (a), but perhaps even more to the shock of seeing economies crash for no clear reason (i.e., reasons that fall outside the precrisis conventional wisdom, such as short debt maturities).

When the tequila crisis hit Mexico in 1994–95, most observers quickly reached the conclusion that Mexico's key problem was a bloated current account deficit (it was around 8 percent of gross domestic product [GDP] in 1994, and expected to reach 9 percent in 1995). In addition, as Argentina also ran into crisis, many people saw a replay of 1982. The verdict was quickly reached, and it was: *low savings*. This conclusion was reached despite the facts that fiscal deficits in the region had shown a sharp decline (see Calvo, Leiderman, and Reinhart 1993) and that Argentina's current account deficit was around 4 percent of GDP, substantially lower than its average annual growth rate in the 1991–94 period (which starts with the implementation of the Currency Board)—making it difficult to argue that Argentina was running *unsustainable* current account deficits. However, hardly any time elapsed between these conventional explanations' reaching the printing press and the crash in Thailand, toppling in its wake mighty Korea and others in the region. This dealt a heavy blow to the conventional wisdom because, on the whole, these countries had exhibited a very solid fiscal position, sky-high saving rates, no major current account imbalance, and so on.

However, old ideas die hard. Thus, some saw Japan's devaluation against the dollar as the likely culprit (bringing back to the table real exchange rate considerations), whereas others believed to have found it in crony capitalism and other perversions, despite the high praise conferred on East Asia in a World Bank opus published not long before crises struck (see World Bank 1993).[1]

Then, Russia happened. The Russian default in August 1998 dealt a fatal blow to the conventional wisdom. Russia represents less than 1 percent of world GDP, and its trade with EMs is very limited. However, country risk premiums in EMs skyrocketed and never came back to their previous levels (see figure 4.1). The malfunctioning of standard fundamentals was nowhere to be seen and, nevertheless, EMs fell to their knees.[2] Thus, the Russian crisis left an air of eery helplessness: "A serious accident happened and no one knows why!" Not surprisingly, since capital flows were at the center of the action, one panic-driven reaction was, "Stop 'em!"—and since soft exchange-rate pegs were a common feature in crisis episodes, calls for "Float!" and "Dollarize!" also pierced the air in raucous dissonance.

Recent Crises: A Closer Look

Figure 4.2 summarizes a central aspect of capital markets in EMs, and highlights the key role played by portfolio capital. Although capital inflows take different forms, it is clear from the figure that a large source of financing stemmed from bonds and stocks. This is shown in the clear break in the data beginning in 1989 as a result of a strong upsurge of net portfolio flows. The surge, however, is sharply reversed in 1995 by the tequila crisis. Although it resumed in 1996, full recovery was aborted by Asia in 1997, and totally trounced by Russia in 1998. As a result, portfolio flows in 1999 were back at their negligible pre-1990 levels.

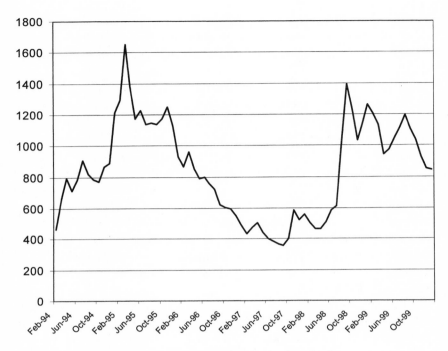

Fig. 4.1   Emerging Markets Bond Index (EMBI basis points)
SOURCE:
JPMorgan

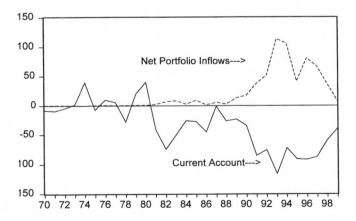

Fig. 4.2   Emerging Markets: Portfolio Flows and Current Account (US$ billions)
SOURCE:
IMF (1999)

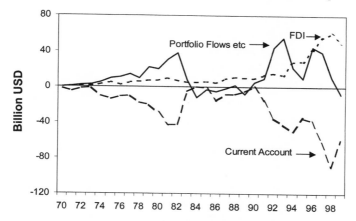

Fig. 4.3   Latin America: Capital Flows and Current Account
SOURCE:
IMF (1999)

The picture in Latin America is very similar, except for the advent of a new form of capital inflow, namely, foreign direct investment (FDI). Figure 4.3 shows what is denoted as "portfolio flows etc." which is the sum of "net portfolio flows" and "other investments." Bank loans are a major share of "other investments" and played a key role in the 1982 debt crisis (but not in the most recent one). The reason for adding the two is that in this fashion one can get a one-shot view of all the relevant capital flow items in Latin America since 1970. Thus, one can see the surge and sudden collapse of "portfolio flows etc." around 1980, and the later surge and collapse in the 1990s. In contrast with the aggregate for all the EMs, figure 4.3 shows that in Latin America the current account deficit grew larger after the tequila crisis, and started to display signs of adjustment only in 1999.[3] Clearly, this high-wire balancing act could be achieved by the help of a large surge of FDI. (A question for future study is, will FDI suffer a fate similar to that of "portfolio flows etc."?)

Another key characteristic of financial crises is the large contraction of capital flows that takes place in a short span of time around crises (or *sudden stops;* see Calvo 1998a and Calvo and Reinhart 2000). These are very large changes that, if international reserves were to remain constant, would call for equivalent contractions in aggregate demand. As a result, all afflicted countries have chosen to smooth out the collapse in capital inflows by running down their international reserves. However, there is no clear indication that this policy worked as expected. Reserves are typically held at the central bank and, as a general rule, have been run down through an expansion of domestic credit in a hopeless attempt to keep domestic interest rates from skyrocketing while defending the exchange rate. This opens the door for speculators to reap sizable profits from "peso" shorting (i.e., borrowing in domestic currency and, for instance, repaying dollar debts), without necessarily relieving, and possibly worsening, the required adjustment in the current account. Mexico is a case in point. Figure 4.4 shows Bank of Mexico's balance sheet. The crisis comes to fruition in December 1994. The monetary base is surprisingly stable, so much so that the term *currency crisis* would seem inappropriate.[4] Apparently, this policy was prompted by central bank officials thinking they were facing a temporary rise in interest rates that, if allowed to materialize, could have seriously deteriorated the already shaky banking system. Interestingly, however, this phenomenon can be observed in almost all recent crisis episodes, which suggests there could be common underlying factors. A leading suspect is shaky banking and financial systems. This is a plausible conjecture given the high incidence of *twin crises*—that is the almost simultaneous occurrence of currency and banking crises (see Calvo and Reinhart 2000; Kaminsky and Reinhart 1999).

Finally, as a general rule, sudden stops have far exceeded available international reserves (partly, I suspect, due to gross monetary mismanage-

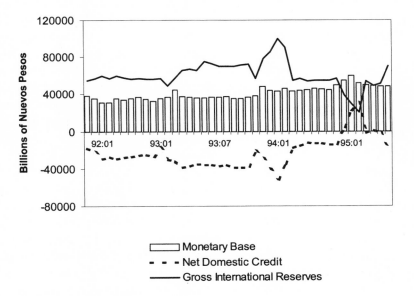

Fig. 4.4 Mexico: Central Bank Balance Sheet

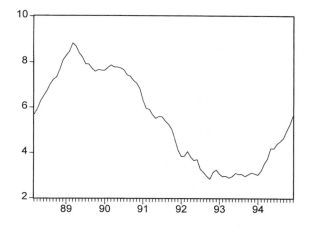

Fig. 4.5   Interest Rate on U.S. Treasury Bills

ment). Therefore, most crises have been accompanied by a large collapse in aggregate demand, resulting in large output losses (see Calvo and Reinhart 2000). This is the most serious consequence of recent crises.

Explaining Capital Flows

I will focus on the capital inflow episode that began around 1990. Two major developments took place at the beginning of the nineties: (a) a decline in U.S. interest rates (see figure 4.5) and (b) the development of the Brady bond market.[5] Interest rates on U.S. treasury bills are a particularly important factor in Latin America (Calvo, Leiderman, and Reinhart 1993).

Lower U.S. Interest Rates

United States treasury bills are short-term maturity instruments. Therefore, a change in their interest rates should, in principle, have no sizable impact on investment and consumption. The implication is quite different, however, if for some reason lower U.S. short-term interest rates result in a relaxation of liquidity constraints in EMs. A leading conjecture in this respect (first put forward by Rodriguez 1993) is that lower U.S. interest rates lead depositors to shift their funds from U.S.-based to EM-based banks; the latter, in turn, lend these funds to liquidity-constrained EM agents (typically, consumers and small- and medium-sized firms), expanding aggregate demand in EMs. Depositors are initially EM residents and the operation is equivalent to repatriation of flight capital.[6] Moreover, the associated increase in aggregate demand puts pressure on the price of nontradables, appreciating the currency in real terms. If low U.S. interest rates are expected to last for a while, the expected return on investment in the nontradables sector goes up, bringing about a further expansion in aggregate demand and real currency appreciation. However, this type of expansion has feet of clay. The moment U.S. interest rates reverse their course—as happened in 1994 (see figure 4.5)—depositors take their money out, and the situation begins to unravel. Upswing and downswing phases, however, need not be symmetric. Typically, banks borrow short and lend long.[7] Thus, an unexpected deposit withdrawal could create serious liquidity difficulties for the banking system. Banks first react to a liquidity crunch by raising interest rates, but if high interest rates persist over time, they run the risk of becoming insolvent. Thus, the central bank is likely to intervene by increasing domestic credit. This policy results in a loss of international reserves or currency devaluation. Policymakers shy away from currency devaluation under these circumstances because capital inflows have financed investment in the nontradables sector. Thus, a devaluation may result in massive bankruptcies.[8] The alternative is to run down international reserves, a road that most countries end up taking (illustrated in figure 4.4).

The analysis shows an example of twin crisis. If the reserve drainage is sustained over time, the initial bank liquidity squeeze gives rise to a balance-of-payments crisis and, possibly, a large devaluation. In addition, as depositors anticipate the latter, deposit interest rates rise or there is a shift in composition from "peso"- to dollar-denominated deposits. Both circumstances tend to lower credit to the nontradables sector because the latter becomes more vulnerable. This is so because, on the one hand, if the sector borrows at the high nominal interest rate and devaluation does not take place, ex post real interest rates rise, making some investment projects infeasible. On the other hand, if the sector takes dollar loans and devaluation does take place, the higher nominal debt service may make projects infeasible, except in the unlikely case in which a nominal devaluation has no effect on the real exchange rate. Lower credit, in turn, results in lower output (especially in liquidity-constrained firms).

Why would *nominal* lead to *real* devaluation? One possibility is that, as lenders anticipate that a real devaluation may take place and generate financial turmoil, they raise interest rates, lowering aggregate demand and actually causing real depreciation. Actual nominal devaluation will not cure this impasse if, again, lenders believe that the real devaluation will not go away.[9] The damage caused by expected and actual devaluation is highly country specific. It depends, among other things, on the ability of the domestic banking system (including the central bank) to generate additional credit when faced with a bank run. Thus, for example, local banks with no close ties to the international capital market are less likely to generate that kind of funding than large multinational banks.[10]

Brady Bonds and the Bond Market

Brady bonds were the result of securitizing banks' nonperforming loans to sovereign states, which, in turn, is equivalent to taking entries from the asset side of banks' balance sheets, sprucing them up with enhancements (collaterals), and placing them in the capital market to be traded under the label of Brady bonds. As shown in figure 4.6, market capitalization of those bonds went from around US$20 billion in 1990 to more than US$100 billion in 1997. Recent repurchases by the sovereign states and the increase in country risk premia (see figure 4.1) brought down their market value to less than US$80 billion in September 1999, which, nevertheless, is still considerably larger than the market value at their inception.

Trading sovereign bonds requires information about macroeconomic and political variables.[11] The cost of acquiring that kind of information is independent of the sums being traded and, to a large extent, of the size of the sovereign states. Fixed costs are sizable because this kind of informa-

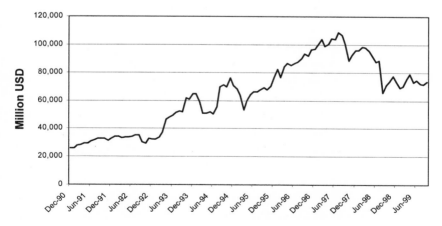

Fig. 4.6   Brady Bonds: Market Value
SOURCE:
JPMorgan

tion has a very short shelf life. This is particularly true in EMs where new economic structures have been put into place and politics is in a state of flux. Thus, in order to have effective information, frequent updating is necessary. These economies-of-scale conditions, if coupled with realistic constraints on short positions (i.e., leveraging or margin constraints), lead to the formation of *specialist clusters*—teams of highly qualified macroeconomists and financial analysts—surrounded by a sea of uninformed investors who are clients of the specialists and who mimic their behavior, or just diversify risk, changing direction like tumbleweeds at the touch of the slightest wind (see Calvo 1998c; Calvo and Mendoza 2000a,b).[12]

These observations lead to the conjecture that the development of the Brady bond market contributed to better information about a variety of sovereign states that up to that point had been excluded from the capital market. The phenomenon is equivalent to the creation of a market for EMs' bonds, because once country-specific knowledge is acquired, it can be applied to the trading of other bonds issued by either sovereign states or their residents. True, lending to the private sector in EMs entails learning about the borrowers' specific characteristics. However, macroeconomic and political considerations are always crucial for the evaluation of private-sector projects. The net return from investing in EMs must take into account policy and political issues such as controls on capital outflows, expectations of wealth taxes, and downright nationalization. Moreover, to the extent that investment projects involve nontradable goods, country-specific macroeconomic information is also very valuable. It is thus plausible to conjecture that Brady bonds could be a key factor behind the surge in portfolio flows shown in figures 4.2 and 4.3.[13]

The development of the EM bond market was not an unmitigated blessing.[14] The above-average information enjoyed by informed investors makes it attractive for them to finance their long positions in EM instruments by short-selling safe assets (e.g., U.S. treasury bills)—in other words, leveraging. Thus, an exogenous and unexpected negative shock, such as Russia's debt repudiation, lowers informed investors' portfolio values and, in turn, triggers margin calls (i.e., instant debt-repayment obligations on leveraged positions). In an ideal perfect-information world, deleveraging associated with the collapse of a very small share of the world's financial portfolio (as Russian debt was) should not result in an across-the-board implosion of EM markets. This implication, however, is not valid if informed investors were liquidity constrained. Under those circumstances, new EM debt instruments, for example, would have to be acquired by uninformed investors. This may bring about a major disturbance in the capital market, as I will explain. For the sake of exposition, I will analyze each of the following increasingly realistic situations: (a) Initially, the uninformed hold no EM paper; (b) they do hold EM paper, and (c) the uninformed keep track of informed investors' strategies (this is the most interesting and, I believe, relevant case).

1. *The uninformed hold no EM paper.* In this case, uninformed investors' reservation price would be below the market's, implying that for them to be willing to take EM debt, its price must take a dip. This extreme case helps illustrate how prices can plunge beyond what would be called for by (conventional) fundamentals. However, the example is not realistic because there are, for example, open-end EM mutual funds designed especially for the uninformed small investor. Therefore, one should pay attention to the case in which, initially, holders of EM securities include both informed and uninformed investors.

2. *Both the informed and uninformed hold EM paper.* The informed investors' sellout brings about a fall in the price of EM debt. This is so because the uninformed end up holding a larger share of EM paper. However, for the fall to be significantly large, one would have to argue that initially the uninformed held a tiny fraction of EM securities, or that their risk assessment or risk aversion was much larger than that of informed investors. This may very well be the case, but I will now offer what seems to me a more relevant explanation.

3. *The information set of the uninformed includes the informed investors' actions.* Uninformed investors are not completely in the dark. They read Barron's and the *Wall Street Journal,* and thus follow the informed investors' opinions and actions (albeit at a distance and with a lag). In particular, the uninformed will not be indifferent to the fact that (for example) liquidity-constrained informed investors stay out of the market for new EM debt.[15] Thus, the uninformed face what is sometimes called a *signal-extraction problem:* "Do informed investors stay out because they are liquidity-constrained, or because they know something bad about these countries that I don't know?" It seems plausible to me that, upon observing that the informed stay out of the market for new EM issues, the uninformed will attach some probability that the EMs have been hit by a negative—albeit unobserved—across-the-board shock. This would lead them to lower their assessments for all EMs, causing a sudden market value loss for all EM debt. Furthermore, as informed investors realize that their actions are closely watched by the uninformed (bringing about a sudden across-the-board fall in prices),

they will have a strong incentive to dump their EM securities holdings before the uninformed have time to react. However, in order for the informed to be able to sell as a group, they must find buyers among the uninformed. In the realistic case in which the uninformed take this dumping by the informed as a strong signal that there are fundamental problems with all the EMs, the sellout will increase further. This is so because the informed investors' dumping would go far beyond what is necessary to meet the margin calls associated with the Russian shock.[16] Thus, depending on how the uninformed revise their expectations in light of these developments, one might even conceive of situations in which the market for new EM debt obligations freezes up completely.[17]

In short, although the development of the Brady-bond market may have induced a large surge of capital inflows in EMs, it also generated a situation in which "errors" in the capital market give rise to sudden and basically unjustified runs against EM securities. This market-creation factor associated with Brady bonds had a likely counterpart in the 1970s in *syndicated bank loans*. This was a device to improve risk-sharing among banks, and was associated with the surge of bank loans in the 1970s. The main difference, however, is that syndicated bank loans do not automatically create instruments that can be traded in the market. Thus, after international banks left the scene in 1982, there were no obvious candidates to fill the vacuum and continue lending to EMs. The present situation may be different because a larger number of institutions have been involved in lending to EMs.

Crisis Management

The above discussion highlighted the relevance of financial markets and, especially, the role of information. External factors, such as interest rates and crises in other countries, which raise the possibility that crises will spread to similar countries, cannot be discounted, and may have played a central role. However, the discussion also pointed out that the effects of those factors depend very much on domestic vulnerabilities, especially the strength of the domestic financial sector. Although those vulnerabilities may not directly be the cause of crises, crises are likely deepened by the existence of domestic vulnerabilities, and may not have occurred without them (see Calvo and Goldstein 1996 for a discussion of this issue in the context of Latin America). Therefore, any discussion on how to cope with crises should focus on informational and vulnerability issues.

I will highlight two issues that have figured prominently in the crisis management discussion: bailout packages and tight monetary and fiscal policy.

Bailout Packages

Bailout packages have been a feature of many recent crises. Mexico received a US$50 billion package in 1995, which was mostly used to repay *tesobonos* (i.e., short-term Mexican treasury bonds denominated in U.S. dollars) and negotiable banks' U.S.-dollar debts. Critics say this package unfairly favored fixed-income foreign-exchange denominated financial instruments and that, in addition, it may have encouraged reckless lending to Thailand and other Asian countries that were later struck by crisis in 1997 (i.e., the moral hazard argument; see Meltzer et al. 2000).

In my view, bailout packages for EMs are similar to bailout packages in response to domestic crises such as the savings and loan scandal or the stock market meltdown of October 1987. The theory behind them is also the same: existence of multiple equilibria, or just the fear of multiple equilibria, which may lead the economy astray and into a morass of bankruptcy and breaching of implicit contracts from which it may take years to recover. Besides, in 1995 the alternative no-bailout route did not look very promising. It had been tried in the 1980s (under the "muddle-through" label) and failed.

Bailout packages steered by the International Monetary Fund (IMF) make a lot of sense. The informational asymmetries mentioned above and the sudden stop effect could give rise to multiple equilibria. Thus, the IMF could help to coordinate expectations on the "good" equilibrium. In addition, the imposition of strong conditionality, involving occasionally excessively tight monetary and fiscal policy, acts as a deterrent for repeat offenders (and may lower the incidence of moral hazard).

Let me briefly discuss the issue of moral hazard in the present context, starting with a question: If Mexico's package induced moral-hazard problems in Asia, how did this phenomenon happen? It would be hard to argue that, as a result of Mexico's package, governments in Asia were tempted to issue more fixed-income instruments. Mexico's output fell more than 6 percent in 1995, and the ruling political party saw its popularity weaken to dangerously low levels. However, the picture is quite different for fixed-income lenders. They came out whole. So it could be argued that their willingness to lend to Asia increased, encouraging more risk-taking by the private sector. This argument is especially forceful if crony capitalism led powerful individuals to expect public-sector bailout. One can certainly find elements of that kind in Thailand, Korea and Indonesia. Therefore, to lower the incidence of moral hazard, tight fiscal and monetary policy may not be enough. IMF conditionality should cut the incestuous ties between the government and the private sector, and stop the socialization of private debts that takes place during crises (for an early and insightful discussion of the case of Chile in the 1980s, see Diaz-Alejandro 1981). To make this effective, however, it is mandatory to have good bankruptcy laws and procedures. Otherwise, preventing the government from bailing out the private sector could halt the economy in its tracks (very much like what the muddle-through strategy did for highly indebted countries in the 1980s). This shows, incidentally, why the IMF could (and sometimes should) drive into terrains that lie far and away from its central mandate (this implication, incidentally, runs counter to one of the main policy recommendations in the Meltzer Report, which calls for a narrowly focused IMF).

Bailout packages are good not only for the recipient countries. They may benefit the rest of the EMs as well. As argued in the previous section, the negative impact of the Russian crisis on EMs could be traced back to margin calls on Wall Street institutions. Actually, Russia was the first and only large country for which a bailout was not set in place, which reasserts my view that imperfect-information-cum-liquidity-crunch can generate systemic effects over all EMs.

Tight Monetary and Fiscal Policy

The IMF was taken to task for imposing tight monetary and fiscal policy in Asia, which critics argue was inappropriate because Asia was very far from insolvency. Some critics go further and claim that the fund's fiscal programs were actually responsible for the depth of the recession. This really makes little sense to me. Take the case of Thailand, where the crisis started—even a large 4 percent fiscal adjustment looks small in comparison to the 26 percent sudden stop there (see table 4.1).[18]

A more subtle issue is monetary policy. I will conduct the discussion under the assumption that when a crisis strikes, EMs lose access to the capital market in the sense that external borrowing is impossible. However, I will assume, realistically, that lending abroad (i.e., capital outflows) is unrestricted. Therefore, when a crisis strikes the exchange rate shows a strong tendency toward depreciation. In this context, the monetary authority has the following polar options: on the one hand, to set low interest rates and let the exchange go through the roof; or, on the other, to raise interest rates to keep the exchange rate near its precrisis level. The second option is very difficult to implement because, once the central bank stops intervening, the exchange rate shows a strong tendency to overshoot. However, the IMF keeps advising countries to set high interest rates in the aftermath of a crisis, and in the medium term the policy appears to have worked in several instances (e.g., Brazil in 1999, Mexico in 1995, and Korea in 1997). So, prima facie, the second option seems to have something to recommend it. Critics, however, claim that the high-interest policy is unnecessarily contractionary, and that having the exchange rate bear the full brunt of the adjustment would be preferable. Some claim that after the exchange rate overshoots, interest rates will fall because no further devaluation would be expected. The latter, in turn, will be expansionary or, in any case, less contractionary than its polar-opposite alternative.

Unfortunately, this debate has not benefitted from rigorous modeling. Issues such as which interest rate is controlled by the central bank are barely discussed. Central banks do not control the whole spectrum of interest rates. Typically, they can set price or interest rates on a very narrow range of assets. For instance, some specific government short-maturity bond (e.g., CETES in Mexico) or central bank obligation (e.g., central bank bonds in Peru, LETES in Venezuela).[19] Holders of those bonds are usually banks. In a credit-constrained situation, marginal bank funding stems mostly from deposits. Thus, within certain limits, raising or lowering a policy interest rate tends to be reflected in larger or smaller deposit and bank loan short-term interest rates. For reasons that will not be discussed in this paper, EMs' bank deposits and loans are either of short maturity or their interest rates are indexed to some short-maturity rate. Therefore, within certain limits, changes in the policy interest rate are reflected in parallel changes in most bank loans and deposits. Notice that the situation would be quite different if the country were not credit constrained. For example, if there were perfect capital mobility, the policy interest rate would have negligible or no impact on the other rates.

What are the "certain limits" referred to above? A lower limit is determined by devaluation and default (DD) expectations. A policy rate that is below what is called for by those expectations would stimulate banks' demand for central bank credit, generating an expansion of net domestic assets (NDA) at the central bank.[20] The latter, in turn, would trigger capital outflows or currency devaluation (or both), giving rise to expectations of further DD. This is a vicious cycle that is likely to end up in a large DD and high, not low, interest rates.[21] On the other hand, the policy interest rate is also subject to upper bounds. For instance, once the interest rate calls into question the solvency of the public sector, higher policy interest rates become ineffective or counterproductive.[22]

Let us now focus on the monetary policy debate. Consider the first option mentioned earlier: a lax monetary policy. A major problem faced by an economy that has been hit by a crisis is reestablishing credibility. When a crisis hits, even experts are at a loss to explain what happened (especially if they rely on precrisis conventional wisdom; recall the section on "Recent Crises: A Heavy Blow"). Therefore, it is likely that DD are expected to be high. As a result, the lower bound on the policy interest rate will be high and thus a low-interest policy would be counterproductive. Moreover, many EMs display liability dollarization (i.e., foreign-denominated debts, implying that a large devaluation may bring about serious financial disruption and bankruptcies).[23] On the other hand, high interest rates (the second policy option) may also provoke bankruptcies because, as pointed out above, under credit constraint a policy rate hike could bring about a general rise in interest rates.[24] Thus, these considerations reveal the tight corset within which monetary policy must operate in the aftermath of a financial crisis.

The appropriate monetary stance depends on credibility—its present state and strategies to improve it. Given that the biggest blow comes from sudden stops, policies should focus on how to reverse them. In my view, a rescue package is one of the few effective policies that are available in the aftermath of financial crises, because it helps to reduce the expectations-determined lower bound on the policy interest rate. As noted, however, an aggressive low-interest-rate policy spearheaded by the central bank could be quite risky. It may set the economy on a vicious cycle, which can only get worse under liability dollarization. Thus, it seems that a prudent crisis-management strategy would be to start with high policy interest rates and gradually lower them until their lower bound is reached. Interestingly, this is the kind of strategy that has been advocated by the IMF in several recent crisis episodes.

The New Financial Architecture: Domestic Policy

This section will discuss policies that can be implemented by individual EMs in normal times, and that are aimed at reducing capital-flow volatility and the depth of financial crises. I will focus on the following issues: (a) the banking sector, (b) public debt, and (c) exchange rate and controls on capital mobility.

Banking Sector

As shown in Kaminsky and Reinhart (1999), banking crises are a common feature of currency crises, and tend to occur first. This fact is in line with the view that EMs suffer, first and foremost, from capital market crises (recall "Explaining Capital Flows"). Why banks? McKinnon and Pill (1999) have argued, for example, that banks are especially susceptible to crises because the protection they receive from the central bank leads them to take unduly risky strategies. This is a persuasive argument for advanced countries, but somewhat less so for EMs, because in order to protect the banking system the government has to be able to *tax* or *borrow*. Borrowing is essential because, otherwise, the whole rescue operation would have to be financed by setting higher present taxes—which is not feasible given the celerity and sums usually required by bank bailouts. Thus, given the incidence of capital market crises in EMs, bank protection by their governments appears to be less likely than in advanced countries.

Of course, the bank bailout could be financed by issuing domestic money resulting in a large devaluation. The public is aware of this possibility and, hence, financial contracts in EMs are usually indexed to some price level (e.g., in Chile) or, most commonly, to some foreign currency (the U.S. dollar being the currency of choice in EMs; see IMF 1999a).[25] Indexation, however, impairs even more the effectiveness of the central bank as lender of last resort. Since financial contracts are expressed in real terms, money printing may risk generating hyperinflation. Notice that, in most cases, the monetary base is less than 10 percent of GDP, whereas bank bailout packages in EMs (Mexico, Venezuela, Chile) have exceeded that percentage. Actually, the money-printing remedy could be worse than the disease because, under these circumstances, large devaluation could bring about massive bankruptcies in sectors (typically, services and other home goods) that are less than fully dollarized—creating a real banking problem.

A common mechanism behind banking and currency crises has been outlined in "Explaining Capital Flows," but it is worth discussing it here. Agents expect a currency crisis and, as a result, go short on domestic currency (i.e., borrow in "pesos") and long on foreign exchange (buy foreign exchange or repay foreign-exchange denominated debt). This raises peso interest rates. The central bank increases NDA and a crisis unfolds. NDA expansion is a consequence of not letting the policy interest rate rise with the other rates (reflecting the higher expected devaluation). Why? Because of the damage caused by high interest rates, given the maturity mismatch in the banking sector.[26] The alternative of allowing for high interest rates is not very promising, either, and can get the monetary authority in a catch-22 situation: "If the crisis does not occur, ex post interest rates are high, and a crisis unfolds for real reasons. Otherwise, a crisis occurs." Therefore, the central bank will be tempted to keep relatively low interest rates and "gamble for redemption." This sets the stage for rational players (mostly large and internationally well-connected firms) to generate a ferocious run on banks and currency (because the run stems from peso-shorting at low policy interest rates, not from a decline in domestic-money demand).

Therefore, a key policy objective should be to deactivate the ticking bomb at the central bank. This is not easy. Just saying no to NDA is not enough because of the time-inconsistency problem highlighted above. Thus, central bank independence is not enough (the central bank of Mexico was independent when crisis unfolded during 1994 but, as shown in figure 4.4, it did not prevent the bank from expanding NDA). Independence will have to be complemented with other regulations that shield the central bank from incentives to fight back high interest rates. One suggestion is to put explicit limits on the expansion of NDA, which could only be circumvented by an act of Congress (the Argentinean central bank is subject to such limits). Another complementary policy is the internationalization of the domestic banking system, so that the lender-of-last-resort services are provided by the rest of the world.

Recent experience, however, sheds some doubts on the role of international banks in providing stable credit. A complaint often heard in Latin America, for example, is that those banks have operated in a highly procyclical manner: Lending when the chips are up, and sharply cutting credit when the chips are down, their behavior is quite similar to that of bond holders (recall the discussion in the "Crisis Management" section), and possibly deepening the sudden stop problem.[27] This behavior is in sharp contrast to that of state-owned banks and leads some policymakers to want to keep a public foothold in the banking sector. Presumably, state-owned banks could help to coordinate the "good" equilibrium and eliminate or drastically soften the sudden stop effect. However, it is hard to imagine that a local bank will help to improve expectations about the country by lending into what private-sector banks see as risky investments. Actually, the countercyclical policy of state-owned banks is likely to be perceived as hidden subsidies, which will eventually be reflected in larger fiscal deficits. This certainly will not help reduce the size of sudden stops, and might very well make them bigger.

Public Debt

Since crises in EMs are essentially capital market crises, debt instruments—particularly, short-term debt—have been at center stage. Following the dictum "once burned, twice shy," several EMs have made a strong effort to lengthen the maturity of public debt. Argentina and Mexico have been quite successful in that respect. In addition, the Greenspan-Guidotti rule (see Guidotti 1999; Greenspan 1999) would have EMs accumulate international reserves so as to cover most debt obligations coming due within the next twelve months. These policies are not without cost, so the question arises, "What principles should guide the maturity structure of government debt?"

Debt-maturity structure and credibility are intimately linked. With full credibility maturity structure is irrelevant, except as an insurance device against fluctuations in the rate of interest. In this case, long-maturity debt would be attractive for a small country facing risk-neutral investors (see Barro 1998). However, as pointed out above, credibility is a key issue to EMs and lies behind the occasional capital market crisis. Does this kind of situation weaken the case for long-maturity debt? For foreign exchange–denominated debt, the answer is, in principle, no if both government and investors have similar assessments of the country's risks. However, if the government believes that the risks are more favorable than investors do, then it might be optimal to choose a short-maturity debt structure (see Calvo 1997).[28]

In contrast, optimal domestic currency–denominated debt has a short-term bias. The reason is that long-term debt is a "sitting duck," the real value of which can easily be whittled down by inflation. However, since investors are likely to be aware of this mechanism, they will require high interest rates, and equilibrium inflation would be inefficiently high. This tilts the maturity structure toward the short end of the spectrum. A possibly better alternative would be to index debt to a price level or exchange rate, keeping a long-maturity structure.[29]

In a nonstochastic environment, (credible) debt indexation is superior to nominal debt (in terms of domestic currency) because it lowers incentives to generate inflation. In fact, it may even be optimal for the government to have a negative stock of nominal debt—that is, to be a net borrower in nominal terms. In this fashion, temptation to liquidate (the real value of) the monetary base and private-sector nominal debt through inflation would diminish. This strong conclusion is modified if there are real shocks (e.g., shocks to the terms of trade). Nominal debt allows the government to use inflation as an insurance device against those real shocks. For example, prices could be jacked up in response to a negative shock on the terms of trade, thus partly offsetting the effect of the negative shock. This is a second best response to the existence of real shocks. A first best solution would be to issue state-contingent, fully indexed debt. However, this solution may not be available for low-probability events (due to transactions costs) or moral hazard considerations. Conceivably, this market failure could be remedied by contingent credit lines from the World Bank or the IMF. Without this kind of facility, EMs could be tempted to engage in open debt repudiation. This would impair the credibility of debt indexation and possibly lead to inferior solutions.

In short, a strong case could be made in favor of long-term-maturity-indexed public debt. However, the credibility of this debt should be enhanced by means of contingent credit lines. In this respect, there is possibly a role for international financial institutions. Short-term debt could be attractive if investors have a more negative opinion of the economy's prospects than the government. However, I would expect this to be a phenomenon that occurs sporadically (perhaps during global financial crises). Hence, on average, the economy should aim for long-maturity debt.

Exchange Rate and Controls on Capital Mobility

The previous section shows the advantage of expressing debt contracts in units different from domestic money. Thus the question arises, "What is the advantage for EMs to have their own money?" The short answer is "insurance against *real* shocks." The previous section highlighted this type of insurance in the context of debt obligations. In addition, under incomplete markets or sticky wages and prices, changes in the rate of exchange can help to soften the adjustment called for by real shocks (for a longer answer, see Calvo 2001). However, this objective of monetary policy can also be fulfilled by fiscal policy. True, fiscal policy moves at a snail's pace compared to monetary policy, but given that it normally requires congressional approval, it may be more predictable and less discretionary.

Nevertheless, perhaps the main reservation that most people have against dollarization (i.e., total abandonment of a national currency) is that the economy will be deprived of a lender of last resort. More specifically, the concern is that the central bank would be unable to print money (i.e., to expand NDA) to bail out the banking system if it is hit by a systemic shock (e.g., a systemic run on bank deposits). First, it should be noted that advanced countries do not print money, they *borrow* to finance their lender-of-last-resort operation (Ricardo Hausmann, quite appropriately, suggests changing "*lender* of last resort" to "*borrower* of last resort"). Second, as pointed out in "Crisis Management," merely printing money without additional government borrowing (or running down international reserves) results in large devaluation, which, in many circumstances, brings about serious financial difficulties of its own (recall liability dollarization). Therefore, it is highly questionable whether EMs will lose much by being deprived of issuing their own money.

A system that has recently acquired great popularity is *inflation targeting* (IT; see Bernanke et al. 1999; Mishkin 2000; Svensson 2000). Instead of pegging to a foreign currency, IT calls for pegging to a basket of goods that contains a sizable domestic (i.e., home goods) component.[30] How credible is IT in EMs? Empirical evidence in Mexico, for example, shows that inflation could be way off target when a crisis strikes (as in 1998). In addition, if liability dollarization is a relevant feature, large fluctuations in the exchange rate would be costly, probably leading the monetary authority to exchange rate pegging and departing from IT.[31] I have no doubt that IT dominates soft exchange-rate pegging because the monetary authority is less committed to using international reserves in order to comply with the policy commitment. However, because the IT price level is an average, it may be difficult to keep it on course under crisis conditions. I think this is a potentially serious drawback of IT. Emerging markets are not much different from advanced economies under normal conditions; it is under crises that they appear to be subject to different laws. Therefore, the design of monetary policy should place considerable weight on crisis scenarios. In this respect, I am inclined to recommend dollarization as a better system.[32]

Let me now turn to capital controls. The available empirical evidence suggests that they are ineffective in putting a leash on total capital inflows or outflows. However, controls could be effective for changing the maturity structure of private-sector capital inflows toward the long end of the spectrum (Edison and Reinhart 2001). This evidence must be taken with a grain of salt, however, because a clever use of derivatives allows the private sector to make short-term look like long-term debt.[33] Even if controls on capital inflows were effective, they do not prevent the existence of sudden stops, or even net capital outflows. This is so because a large potential for capital flight is in the banking system where, as a general rule, deposits have short-term maturity. Moreover, tilting the balance toward long-term maturity inflows could actually drive the private sector toward shortening the maturity of domestic financial assets and liabilities. These financial-engineering operations are more widely available for large and internationally well-connected firms than for the credit-constrained sectors referred to in "Explaining Capital Flows." This provides an unfair edge to the former.[34]

Chilean monetary authorities have occasionally claimed that controls on capital inflows have allowed them to conduct an independent and effective monetary policy. Although this is empirically debatable (see Calvo and Mendoza 1999), it illustrates the possibility that EMs that attempt to conduct an independent monetary policy may be led to impose controls on capital mobility.

Capital controls could be justified if the flows are driven by "exuberant expectations," or the flows are so large that investors may mistake a bubble for a fundamental. Unfortunately, this is very difficult for the policymaker to assess in a timely manner (witness the enormous and sustained rally in the U.S. stock market). Emerging markets must, almost by definition, provide sizable investment opportunities. If those opportunities have not been fully exploited yet it must be because of historical reasons, bad policy, or (perhaps) the parochial nature of the pre-1989 capital market environment. Thus, relative prices and income distributions could show radical changes without necessarily implying irrationality.

Controls on capital outflows (Krugman's Plan B) belong to another chapter. They are very difficult to implement (although Malaysia claims to have succeeded). They are a natural response to sudden stops and could, in principle, avoid the subsidiary financial problems (e.g., sharp changes in relatives prices) caused by this phenomenon. In any case, this is at best a crisis-management policy, and thus it does not pertain to this section's discussion.

Flows or Flaws?

The paper has given several examples in which capital flows could lead to socially costly crises. Some of the flaws stem from the world capital market due to imperfect information and incomplete markets. There is nothing that EMs can do in that respect. Dealing with those flaws requires global decisions that fall outside the realm of any single country (even the mighty United States), and will have to rely on international cooperation.

A central flaw of EMs is imperfect credibility and infant capital markets (justifying the word *emerging*). There is also little that EMs can do in the short run to improve that state of affairs. However, taking these global and local flaws as a given, the paper identified policies that EMs could unilaterally take to mitigate their negative effects. Will these policies avoid the repetition of recent financial crises? I hope so, but it is too early to tell. The strategies underscored in this chapter are highly pro-market and pro-openness of financial markets (e.g., internationalization of the banking sector, lengthening of the maturity of public debt, and dollarization). Capital controls were not ruled out but they were deemed, at best, as transitory policies.

In closing, I would like to say that if EMs must rely on capital mobility controls on a more permanent basis, these controls are likely to eventually permeate the whole economy with highly detrimental effects. Actually, if the kinds of policies discussed in this chapter fail to prevent a replay of recent financial crises, EMs should seriously consider regional or international unions to make them part of more robust economic systems. The era of nation states may be coming to an end, and the recent financial crises could be the first chords of its funeral march.

Notes

1. Joe Stiglitz, one of the authors behind this report, continued to blow the clarion in praise of the old Asian system, and blamed crises partly on the liberalization of financial systems.

2. High-quality U.S. corporates also saw their premiums rising.

3. Figures for 1999 are IMF estimates (dated May 1999).

4. It should be noted, however, that the stability of the monetary base could itself be a result of the expansion in domestic credit.

5. See Calvo, Leiderman, and Reinhart (1993), in which the effects of factor (a) and other factors (but not factor [b]) are subject to statistical analysis. Another development in that period is the relaxation of U.S. regulations involving institutional investors.

6. This is difficult to verify because to cover their tracks domestic residents usually mask the operation as a bank loan, which they can easily obtain by placing their offshore deposits as collateral.

7. A leading explanation for this maturity mismatch is that banks expect a bailout from the central bank if they undergo a systemic liquidity shock, such as a systemic deposit withdrawal. McKinnon and Pill (1999) argue that this phenomenon leads to EMs' overborrowing.

8. This is but one example of fear of floating that is studied in greater detail in Calvo and Reinhart (2000).

9. Notice that this argument would be fully consistent with rational expectations if the associated financial turmoil implied existence of multiple equilibria.

10. However, private banks could be more destabilizing than state-owned banks if conditions of the type that will be discussed in what follows trigger capital outflows.

11. If the existence of a market for a country's bonds gives incentives to acquire country-specific information, then one should find that, if for some reason the bond market shrivels in size, incentives to learn about the country in question should also wane. I had a chance to test this view at a recent meeting with otherwise savvy specialists, a few weeks after Ecuador stopped servicing its Brady bonds. No one in the room appeared to have followed recent events in Ecuador; even basic data seemed news to them. Moreover, the air of indolence that pervaded the room as they politely listened to the Washington bureaucrats in charge of monitoring Ecuador left no doubt in my mind that they would forget the new information as soon as they stepped out of the room, if not sooner.

12. This high sensitivity of uninformed investors to "news and rumors" can be rationalized in a context in which uninformed investors have several not-perfectly-correlated projects to choose from, and display mean-variance utility functions (see Calvo 1998c; Calvo and Mendoza 2000b).

13. Michael P. Dooley reports that in 1989 a very distinguished group of international economists was assembled by the Federal Reserve Board. They were asked how they saw the chances of highly indebted countries to regain access to the capital market. The unanimous answer was "never, in our lifetimes." Hence, according to the present interpretation of the facts, they badly missed (a) predicting the ensuing fall in U.S. interest rates, (b) anticipating the strong impact that short-term rates have on several EMs, or (c) the market-creation effect entailed by the appearance of Brady bonds. My guess is that even if this group had been right in predicting the downward trend in U.S. interest rates, they would have missed (b) and (c), which in my view represent two key lessons that the profession was not sufficiently aware of at the turn of the 1990s.

14. The following discussion is extracted from Calvo (1998b).

15. The new debt market is likely to be active as long as some EMs run current account deficits.

16. A sophisticated uninformed investor would realize that the sellout is partly motivated by the informed's attempt to avoid capital losses. However, because the uninformed face a signal-extraction problem, they are still likely to attach some probability to the existence of a negative shock to fundamentals for the entire EM.

17. The situation is reminiscent of the celebrated "lemon" problem that arises in the market for used cars. For a recent exposition, see Kreps (1990). For a formal discussion and reference to related literature in finance, where similar issues arose in connection with the October 1987 stock market meltdown, see Calvo (1999).

18. The fund has, with unusual candidness, acknowledged excessive fiscal adjustment in Asia. They could be right. However, my point is that the error looks too small relative to sudden stops to have possibly caused the large output losses that were experienced throughout the region.

19. In what follows, I will refer to the interest rate controlled by the monetary authority as the *policy interest rate*.

20. Let i^*, ε, and δ denote the international (pure) rate of interest, the rate of devaluation, and the rate of default, respectively. Then, demand for central bank credit is likely to be triggered if the policy rate is significantly less than $i^* + \varepsilon + \delta$.

21. These are nominal interest rates, which, however, would become high ex post real interest rates if the policy is successful and actual DD is kept low—but this would be a contradiction, because the higher ex post real interest rates are likely to generate high DD. Recall the related discussion in the "Explaining Capital Flows" section.

22. Critics of high interest rate also point out that there exists an upper bound beyond which inefficient bankruptcy in the private sector would arise.

23. This factor played an important role in the context of the tequila crisis, and tilted the balance in favor of a tight monetary policy.

24. Joe Stiglitz has been one of the most vocal advocates of this view.

25. The indexation phenomenon was discussed in "Explaining Capital Flows" but only in the context of an impending crisis. These arguments show that there are grounds for expecting it to be a more permanent feature of EMs that risk the chance of being excluded from the capital market.

26. Central banks are scared stiff of banking crises, primarily for the devastating effect that they have on the domestic payments system.

27. It is worth pointing out, however, that international banks appear to have behaved countercyclically in Panama; see Moreno-Villalaz (1999).

28. By definition, a long-maturity debt structure is one in which the debtor plans to repay most of the debt coming due in any particular period and, hence, refinancing needs are minimal. In contrast, a short-maturity structure would call for significant refinancing.

29. These issues are discussed in terms of a formal model in Calvo and Guidotti (1990).

30. However, it should be pointed out that under a high pass-through coefficient the difference between IT and exchange rate pegging becomes considerably blurred.

If IT is credible, incidentally, the discussion in previous section would call for indexing debt to the price of the IT basket of goods. Interestingly, that is exactly what Chile has done.

31. In a recent press interview, Nicolas Eyzaguirre, the current finance minister of Chile, openly recognized that liability dollarization was a major roadblock for monetary policy in that country. Moreover, it is worth recalling that Chile narrowed its exchange rate band during the Russian crisis in 1998, instead of allowing the exchange rate to depreciate.

32. Several EMs have opted for IT. Thus, we should eventually have a better statistical basis to evaluate their performance in EMs.

33. Chilean authorities have acknowledged that they learned about these tricks when they dismantled capital inflow controls, and the private sector no longer had the incentives to hide those transactions.

34. The policy's unfairness was fully appreciated in the debate about the desirability of maintaining these controls in Chile.

References

Barro, Robert J. 1998. Optimal funding policy. In *The debt burden and its consequences for monetary policy,* ed. G. Calvo and M. King, 69–80. IEA Conference vol. 118. New York: Macmillan.

Bernanke, Ben S., Thomas Laubach, Frederic S. Mishkin, and Adam S. Posen. 1999. *Inflation targeting: Lesson from the international experience.* Princeton, N.J.: Princeton University Press.

Calvo, Guillermo A. 1997. Optimal maturity of government debt. Center for International Economics, University of Maryland, College Park. Manuscript, 19 July.

———. 1998a. Capital flows and capital-market crises: The simple economics of sudden stops. *Journal of Applied Economics* 1 (1): 35–54.

———. 1998b. Understanding the Russian virus: With special reference to Latin America. Paper presented at Deutsche Bank Conference, Emerging Markets: Can They Be Crisis Free? Washington, D.C. 3 October.

———. 1998c. Varieties of capital-market crises. In *The debt burden and its consequences for monetary policy,* ed. G. A. Calvo and M. King, 181–202. London: Macmillan.

———. 1999. Contagion in emerging markets: When Wall Street is the carrier. University of Maryland, Center for International Economics. Manuscript, February.

———. 2001. Capital markets and the exchange rate, with special reference to the dollarization debate in Latin America. *Journal of Money, Credit, and Banking* 33 (May, pt. 2): 312–34.

Calvo, Guillermo A., and M. Goldstein. 1996. What role for the official sector. In *Private capital flows to emerging markets after the Mexican crisis,* ed. G. A. Calvo, M. Goldstein, and E. Hochreiter, 233–82. Washington, D.C.: Institute for International Economics.

Calvo, Guillermo A., and Pablo Guidotti. 1990. Indexation and maturity of government bonds: An exploratory model. In *Capital markets and debt management,* ed. R. Dornbusch and M. Draghi, 52–82. New York: Cambridge University Press.

Calvo, Guillermo, Leonardo Leiderman, and Carmen M. Reinhart. 1993. Capital inflows to Latin America: The role of external factors. *IMF Staff Papers* 40 (March): 108–51.

Calvo, Guillermo A., and Enrique G. Mendoza. 1999. Empirical puzzles of Chilean stabilization policy. In *Chile: Recent policy lessons and emerging challenges,* ed. G. Perry and D. Leipziger, 25–54. Washington, D.C.: World Bank.

———. 2000a. Capital-market crises and economic collapse in emerging markets: An informational-frictions approach. Papers and Proceedings of the American Economic Association, *American Economic Review* 90 (2): 59–64.

———. 2000b. Rational contagion and the globalization of securities markets. *Journal of International Economics* 51 (1): 79–113.

Calvo, Guillermo A., and Carmen M. Reinhart. 2000. When capital flows come to a sudden stop: Consequences and policy. In *Reforming the international monetary and financial system,* ed. Peter B. Kenen and Alexander K. Swoboda. Washington, D.C.: International Monetary Fund.

———. 2002. Fear of floating. *Quarterly Journal of Economics* 117 (2): 379–408.

Diáz-Alejandro, Carlos F. 1981. Southern-cone stabilization plans. In *Economic stabilization in developing countries,* ed. W. R. Cline and S. Weintraub, 119–41. Washington, D.C.: Brookings Institution.

Edison, Hali, and Carmen M. Reinhart. 2001. Stopping hot money: On the use of capital controls during financial crises. *Journal of Development Economics* 66 (2): 533–53.

Guidotti, Pablo. 1999. Private sector involvement in crisis prevention and resolution: A comment. Universidad Torcuato Di Tella. Mimeograph.

Greenspan, Alan. 1999. Currency reserves and debt. Paper prepared for the World Bank Conference on Recent Trends in Reserves Management. 29 April, Washington, D.C.

International Monetary Fund (IMF). 1999a. Monetary policy in dollarized economies. Occasional Paper no. 171. Washington, D.C.: IMF.

———. 1999b. *World economic outlook.* Washington, D.C.: IMF.

Kaminsky, Graciela L., and Carmen M. Reinhart. 1999. The twin crises: The causes of banking and balance-of-payments problems. *American Economic Review* 89 (3): 473–500.

Keynes, John M. 1961. *The general theory of employment, interest, and money.* London: Macmillan.

Kreps, David M. 1990. *A course in microeconomic theory.* Princeton, N.J.: Princeton University Press.

McKinnon, Ronald I., and Huw Pill. 1999. Exchange-rate regimes for emerging markets: Moral hazard and international borrowing. *Oxford Review of Economic Policy* 15 (3): 19–38.

Meltzer, Alan H. 2000. Report of the International Financial Institution Advisory Commission. U.S. Senate Committee on Banking, Housing, and Urban Affairs.

Mishkin, Frederic. 2000. Inflation targeting in emerging countries. *American Economic Review* 90 (2): 105–09.

Moreno-Villalaz, Juan Luis. 1999. Lessons from the monetary experience of Panama: A dollarized economy with financial integration. *CATO Journal* 18 (3): 421–39.

Rodriguez, Carlos A. 1993. Money and credit under currency substitution. *IMF Staff Papers* 40:414–26.

Svensson, Lars. 2000. Open economy inflation targeting. *Journal of International Economics* 50 (1): 155–83.

World Bank. 1993. *The Asian miracle.* Oxford: Oxford University Press.

Chapter Five

The Dollarization Debate in Argentina and Latin America

Pablo E. Guidotti and Andrew Powell

Introduction

For emerging markets, and for Latin America in particular, the 1990s represented the decade of globalization. For Latin America, globalization meant the return to international capital markets on a significant scale after a long period of inward orientation, especially marked by the protracted resolution of the debt crisis of the 1980s.

Globalization translated rapidly into higher economic growth, increased trade flows, and strong and increasing foreign direct investment (FDI) to emerging market economies. The largely rosy picture that characterized the world economy during the first half of the decade was a reinforcing combination of a relatively benign policy environment in industrial countries coupled with the implementation of significant structural reforms in developing countries.

Nevertheless, the decade's second half showed suddenly a face of globalization that had not been fully anticipated: that of volatility and contagion. This new environment prompted a wide and multilateral discussion on what became known as the *international financial architecture*. This discussion was motivated by the perception that crises in international capital markets might become recurring events. The Russian debt moratorium showed that crises in emerging markets could affect the functioning of liquid markets in industrial countries and that emerging market economies

Pablo E. Guidotti is director of the School of Government at the Universidad Torcuato Di Tella. Andrew Powell is professor of economics at the Universidad Torcuato Di Tella. The views expressed are exclusively those of the authors. We wish to thank in particular Verónica Cohen Sabban and Elena Grubisic for excellent research assistance. Any mistakes naturally remain our own.

were becoming very sensitive to events occurring in places with which there was no significant apparent real or financial connection. Consequently, there was a focus on measures to strengthen domestic policies and to reduce contagion through increased transparency and through redefining the role of multilateral organizations—in particular, the International Monetary Fund (IMF).

Furthermore, the discussions on the international financial architecture also renewed the debate regarding exchange rate policy. On the one hand, many in the official community appeared to be quickly seduced by a simple solution: that emerging market economies would be more easily shielded from capital market volatility by the adoption of flexible exchange rates. On the other hand, based on the apparent resilience of Argentina's convertibility system and Hong Kong's currency board in the recent crises, some praised countries that adopted very strong commitments to exchange rate stability. Thus the bipolar theory on exchange rate regimes was born.

The experience of the financial crises of the 1990s, however, did not provide hard evidence to settle the debate on the optimal choice of exchange rate regime. Through the 1990s, it is interesting to note that, although virtuously all so-called crises involved the abandonment of weak currency pegs, in some cases countries with professed monetary independence have appeared to suffer more (through higher interest rates or reserve losses) than countries with less monetary independence (e.g., Hong Kong and, in the 1990s, Argentina[1]). Moreover, emerging market countries with stated independence tended not to use that independence to significantly counteract the negative shocks but have rather had to maintain higher interest rates in pro- rather than countercyclical fashion.[2] It seems that stated independence does not necessarily correlate with countercyclical policy, probably due to the twin problems of highly dollarized liabilities and maintaining credibility in the policy regime itself.

In this context, some have argued that a preferable option to reduce global volatility is in fact to reduce the number of currencies in world circulation (see, e.g., Guidotti 1999; Pou 1999; Calvo 1999). In this way, one would reduce the risk implicit in countries' adopting unsustainable pegs, the abandonment of which would lead to contagion and at the same time would capture the benefits that come with greater credibility in monetary institutions.

A clear example of this line of thought is provided by the debate that originated in Argentina in response to the sequel of capital market crises that characterized the second half of the 1990s. During that decade, the convertibility plan (designed to open and deregulate the economy while implementing a currency board to attain price stability) was a significant economic success. Growth averaged 4.7 percent (1991–99, inclusive) and the economy proved itself able to surpass a series of sharp shocks. Financial shocks (including the tequila crisis and the Russian debt moratorium) had a greater negative impact on the economy, but did not blur the view that the currency-board mechanism had served Argentina well. Indeed, at that time, a result of these shocks was to promote a debate on how to deepen the currency-board mechanism to dispel any perception of devaluation risk and hence reduce the country risk-spread. As a result, in 1999, the Argentine government argued publicly in favor of the adoption of the U.S. dollar as a regional currency, stating that if such a move would receive congressional approval from the concerned countries, then risk in the region could be greatly diminished. Interest in this proposal sparked a debate on dollarization across the American region.[3]

This debate was influenced strongly by the ongoing process of the European Monetary Union (EMU). European convergence brought about significant benefits to the peripheral countries in terms of lower inflation and lower nominal and real interest rates. Although the EMU may have been motivated largely by political reasons, the economic gain—especially in peripheral countries—is a striking case study for emerging market economies.

This paper discusses the origins and nature of the dollarization debate in Argentina, reviewing the arguments concerning deepening convertibility and discussing how, through a monetary agreement with the United States, such a deepening might be effected. In this paper we review the main costs and benefits of dollarization, understood as a substantive institutional step that requires a decision of both government and Congress and, hence, involves political as well as economic trade-offs. In this respect, recent events in Argentina have cast a shadow of doubt over the future of convertibility and over whether dollarization might be considered a desirable policy option. In the present context, the dollarization debate has evolved from a discussion regarding deepening institutions into a discussion more concerned with emergency measures to contain an unraveling crisis.[4] This paper focuses on the 1998–99 institutional dollarization debate that, in our view, remains central when one is thinking about monetary institutions in Latin America.

This chapter is organized as follows. The next section focuses on "The

Origins of the Dollarization Debate" and on how the experience of the Argentine economy with the convertibility system in the 1990s led to the dollarization proposal. We examine the main benefits achieved by the system as well as the economy's response to the sequence of external shocks it faced during the second half of the 1990s. This analysis explains the genesis of the dollarization proposal. The section also examines the lessons that can be drawn from the EMU for the dollarization debate. In particular, we examine the issue of convergence of inflation and nominal and real interest rates.

In "Exploring the Options," we review the main arguments of the ongoing debate on the choice of the exchange rate regime in the emerging market economies' context. Such debate, as well as the experience of emerging market economies with various exchange rate regimes, constituted the background for the dollarization proposal.

"A U.S.-Argentine Monetary Agreement" examines in detail a specific proposal put forward by the Argentine government in 1999.[5] In particular we analyze the consequences of full dollarization of the Argentine economy subject to a monetary agreement with the United States, and its potential benefits and costs. We also compare the proposal with an easier-to-implement but (in our view) a less desirable alternative: that of unilateral dollarization. Although we analyze conceptually the 1999 proposal, in doing so we take into account recent events in Argentina when obtaining updated estimates of seigniorage revenues and when considering other relevant aspects of its potential implementation.

The monetary agreement examined in this paper assumes that Argentine seigniorage revenues are preserved. It also proposes the construction of a liquidity facility, using these potential seigniorage flows as collateral. The latter would at least substitute for the current liquidity lender-of-last-resort capabilities of the Argentine central bank. It leaves open the matter of whether this facility is set up with the United States authorities or with commercial banks.

The principal benefit envisaged is the reduction in country risk that would ensue after dollarization. Other benefits include the reduction in the volatility of country risk, the improvement in terms of public and private financing, and the resultant more stable economic environment. Indeed, it is argued that the monetary agreement would result in a consolidation of Argentina's position regarding trade and capital account openness, hence fostering greater trade with and investment to and from the United States.

The final section contains some concluding remarks.

The Origins of the Dollarization Debate
The Argentine Context

The economic turbulence of the 1980s, which culminated in hyperinflation, represented a watershed in Argentine economic history. Inflation had become so endemic that normal economic transactions broke down and the use of domestic currency was reduced so significantly that M3/gross domestic product (GDP) dropped to about 5 percent, and a significant part of the Argentine financial system moved offshore. At the same time the use of the U.S. dollar in Argentina as both a store of value and a means of payment rose significantly. The costs associated with high inflation remain firmly etched in the hearts and minds of the Argentine public, politicians, and policymakers of all persuasions.

The presidential elections in 1989 resulted in a new economic program that commenced with a policy that led to the opening of both the capital and the current accounts, and a strong fiscal reform that rapidly transferred a large number of public-sector companies to the private sector. During 1989–91, exchange rate instability remained. Hence, in April 1991 the Convertibility Law was passed, introducing a currency-board mechanism to bring stability and to provide a nominal anchor to abate inflation. This law fixed the exchange rate to the U.S. dollar (initially at 10,000 australes per dollar and then at 1 peso per dollar), compelled the Central Bank to hold international reserves to fully back the monetary base, and explicitly prohibited all forms of indexation.[6] In contrast to a "pure" currency board, convertibility allows for a significant spectrum of central banking functions. However, in the spirit of currency boards, these activities are subject to specified legal limitations.

Convertibility allows the use of the U.S. dollar and other currencies for both transactions and contracts. The Convertibility Law stipulates that the only legal tender in Argentina is the Argentine peso, meaning that payments in dollar bills or other currency can be refused. Yet it also stipulates that contracts written in dollars or any other foreign currency are legal, and payment on such contracts in the contracted currency can be enforced under the law.

In 1992 Congress approved a new charter for the Central Bank, an essential complement to the Convertibility Law. The new legislation made the Central Bank independent, recreated the Banking Superintendence as a semiautonomous unit within the Central Bank, and provided the Central Bank with specific powers, including a limited lender-of-last-resort function.[7] In particular, the Central Bank is allowed to conduct repurchase agreements and rediscount operations with banks subject to suitable collateral and restrictions on the solvency of the institutions concerned. The charter also provided a list of prohibited activities, including issuing debt and lending to government (at any level—federal, provincial, or municipal) or to nonfinancial private- or public-sector companies. The convertibility system stipulates that the Central Bank can back as much as one-third of the monetary base with government bonds purchased and valued at market prices. In addition, the charter of the Central Bank introduced the restriction that the institution's bond holdings can increase only up to 10 percent in any fiscal year (in nominal terms).

Since 1992 there have been considerable efforts to strengthen the financial system. International capital standards were brought in and increased gradually over the 1992–94 period to reach a basic minimum of 11.5 percent of assets at risk at the end of 1994. However, the credit risk capital requirements are significantly increased by the inclusion of bank-specific multiplicative factors related to CAMEL ratings and loan-specific multiplicative factors related to loan interest rates. Additionally, market-risk and interest-rate-risk capital requirements have also been introduced, bringing minimum capital requirements to some 14 percent of assets at risk, with actual capital at 21 percent of assets at risk. At the same time, liquidity was also strengthened through high and remunerated reserve requirements.

Economic performance under convertibility improved markedly relative to the previous decade. Inflation fell rapidly during 1992, and investment and growth rose significantly (see table 5.1).

In addition, the Argentine currency board surpassed various exogenous shocks during the second half of the 1990s. Real shocks included a

Table 5.1   Economic Results Pre- and Postconvertibility (annual average growth rates, %)

	1985–91	**1992–98**	**1999**
GDP	−1.4	5.1	−3.0
Fiscal deficit (% of GDP)	5.8	0.9	2.6
Investment	−6.3	10.9	−7.6
Total factor productivity	−1.3	2.7	n.a.
Employment	2.0	1.8	1.7
Inflation	564	4.3	−1.8

SOURCES: Ministry of the Economy and authors' own calculations.

period of boom and contraction in Brazil—a period of exceptionally high and then exceptionally low commodity prices and periods of high and low valuations of the U.S. dollar versus other major currencies. These real shocks all have naturally had their effects on Argentina, affecting growth and employment in particular.

At the same time the currency board also surpassed a number of financial shocks. These include the tequila period, the Asian devaluations, a speculative attack on Hong Kong, the Russian debt moratorium, and the Brazilian devaluation. (We classify the Brazilian devaluation as a financial shock rather than a real shock because we contend that the increase in the sovereign risk premium due to the devaluation had a greater effect on Argentina than did the trade effect.) In contrast to the real shocks, financial shocks have had a much more serious effect on Argentine growth. We discuss each in turn.

The deepest financial shock of the 1990s for Argentina was the tequila crisis following immediately after the Mexican devaluation at the end of 1994. The tequila crisis had a tremendous impact on the financial system as some 18 percent of bank deposits left Argentina. It also provoked a sharp credit crunch in the economy that ultimately induced a 2.8 percent recession for that year.[8] The lender-of-last-resort powers of the Central Bank were used at that time virtually to their legal maximum.[9] This was done to offset the effect on credit, and it is estimated that of the $8 billion that left the system, the Central Bank offset some $3 billion with the reduction in reserve requirements and $2 billion through repurchase agreements and rediscount operations. Hence it significantly dampened the negative impact on credit and economic activity (a further $2 billion was financed by the increase in foreign credit lines to the banking system, and the residual $1 billion was the reduction in credit).

The tequila shock was then controlled in part by the Argentine authorities' actions. These measures, along with the fiscal and other reforms that were introduced in the context of a significant IMF financial assistance package in March 1995, considerably dampened the tequila shock. Deposits and other financial-sector variables turned around very quickly after the May 1995 presidential election. As noted, the economy suffered a recession, but the recovery was also rapid with only three quarters of negative, seasonally adjusted, quarter-on-quarter growth (that cumulated to −5.8 percent) and a recovery of 1 percent in quarter-on-quarter seasonally adjusted GDP growth in the fourth quarter of 1995. Moreover, many were surprised by the shift in the current account deficit, which had reached 4.3 percent of GDP in 1994 and declined to 1.9 percent of GDP in 1995.

Helped by the effects of the real plan in Brazil, merchandise exports grew by an incredible 32.4 percent between 1994 and 1995 while merchandise imports fell by 6.8 percent. These figures are important not only because they implied a rapid about-turn in the current account, but also because they reflected the competitiveness and flexibility of the Argentine economy.

The other financial shocks that the currency board has withstood include the international shocks stemming from the Asian devaluations, the speculative attack on Hong Kong in October 1997, the Russian debt moratorium, and finally the Brazilian devaluation of January 1999. The Asian devaluations had little impact on Argentina, with the so-called Asian flu arriving only with the speculative attack on Hong Kong. As can be seen in figure 5.1, this caused a significant spike in prices such as Argentine peso-dollar yield differentials, country risk spreads, and a short-lived spike in domestic interest rates. However, financial aggregates such as reserves and bank deposits showed little reaction. Domestic peso interest rates quickly fell along with peso-dollar spreads, and sovereign spreads declined more slowly and to higher than pre-October levels.

A significantly more serious financial shock in terms of world financial markets was the Russian debt moratorium in August 1998. Argentine peso-dollar spreads and country risk spreads, together with those of other emerging markets spiked very high (broadly to the same level as during the tequila crisis) and again there was a sharp spike in domestic interest

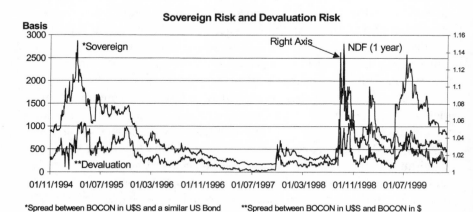

Fig. 5.1   Peso-Dollar and Country Risk Spreads
SOURCE:
IMF, International Financial Statistics.

rates. Although these spikes were shorter lived than those following the October Hong Kong attack, sovereign risk spreads once again fell back to higher than previous levels. Despite the fact that there was no capital outflow from Argentina, August 1998 was a point of inflection in the rate of the growth of reserves and deposits in the financial system with the rate of growth slowing markedly in the second half of that year. In turn, investment began to fall off during the second quarter in 1998 in seasonally adjusted terms, anticipating the ensuing contraction of the economy. At first the Russian financial shock appeared to have provoked a very sharp and indiscriminate sell-off in Argentine assets. Then, as discrimination prevailed, sovereign spreads receded, but a lasting effect remained that translated into lower investment and growth.

Finally, the Brazilian devaluation in January 1999 caused another spike in sovereign yields. However, in common with the previous trend, this spike was shorter lived than either the Hong Kong or Russian shocks, and indeed the government returned to the international bond market more quickly than after either of the previous events.[10] After accounting for falls in international reserves due to seasonal changes in money demand, there is no evidence whatsoever of outflows from Argentina during the Brazilian event, although the deposits' and reserves' growth rates fell (see figure 5.2). These multiple financial shocks produced negative growth in Argentina for 1998's fourth quarter and for the first three quarters of 1999. The end of 1999 saw a fall in reserves and, in December, a fall in deposits. However, this was largely a seasonal effect compounded possibly by political uncertainty (presidential elections were held in October 1999 and the new government took office in December) and Y2K fears. Since then deposits and reserves have rebounded. Moreover, although the 1999 recession was deeper than first anticipated, the fourth quarter of 1999 showed a strong economic recovery.[11]

This experience suggests that it is difficult to reconcile the effects of financial shocks on the Argentine economy, especially when other fundamentals are sound. Moreover, the spikes in the peso-dollar yield spreads that accompany each international shock suggest that the currency board system, while giving economic and price stability to Argentina, was unable to gain 100 percent credibility in the eyes of international investors. Thus, in 1998 the question arose in the mind of policymakers whether Argentina would benefit by the adoption of the U.S. dollar as its national currency, given the high degree of dollarization of financial contracts prevalent de facto in the economy.[12]

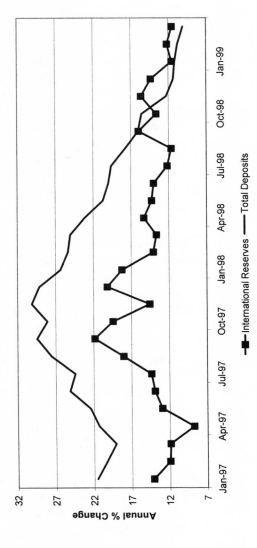

Fig. 5.2 Deposit and Reserves Growth Rates

SOURCE:

Central Bank of Argentina.

Lessons from the European Monetary Union

The recent history of European exchange rate management reflects well the debate among floating, fixed-but-adjustable, and truly fixed exchange rates. The fact that eleven European nations finally decided, after trying many other different systems, to form a monetary union constitutes an important case study and provides useful insights to any country wishing to fix exchange rates permanently or to adopt another country's currency as its own. In this section we attempt to draw out some of the most relevant aspects.

Although many argue that the soft exchange rate mechanism (ERM) period of, say, 1979 to 1986 (when realignments were frequent) was a success in terms of economic performance, the system gradually changed into a harder exchange rate system. This happened between 1986 and 1990 with fewer realignments and greater calls for discipline among its members. This process of a gradual hardening of the ERM gives some ammunition to those who argue that soft regimes of fixed but adjustable rates are inherently unstable.

The 1990 devaluation of the lira, and the sterling and lira crisis of 1992, showed that not even the hard version of the ERM could survive. For some countries the political incentives generated by a harder fixed exchange rate—toward greater discipline in terms of domestic inflation and fiscal probity—could not keep opposing forces in check. The 1992 crisis resulted in a significant widening of the ERM bands, although for many currencies implicit narrower bands remained.

This is not the place for a detailed discussion of the origins of the EMU, which clearly reflect political as well as economic aims. However, the decision to press ahead with the monetary union after a somewhat inauspicious ERM period clearly reflects a view that although the hard exchange rate mechanism proved to be unstable, a full monetary union would force the discipline necessary to maintain the stability of the pact for those countries that qualified.

The Maastricht Treaty consisted of a set of convergence criteria, essentially fiscal, for countries to qualify for EMU membership. It might be argued that the role of these convergence criteria was to ensure that monetary union, unlike a hard ERM, was dynamically stable (i.e., to ensure that only those countries that had demonstrated the discipline necessary to maintain the pact—in particular, in terms of inflation and fiscal results—would enter).

At the time the conditions were set, it was unclear how many countries would qualify. Indeed, many commentators suggested that if the criteria were interpreted strictly there would be several countries that might not qualify. Attention was mostly focused on the 3 percent budget deficit. It was well known that the 60 percent debt-to-GDP ratio would be breached, and indeed the Maastricht Treaty allowed for countries to be above this limit if their figures were moving in the right direction. However, our main point is that the convergence criteria provided a focus for market expectations, and the critical question in bond and currency markets became which countries would qualify (which for many observers simply meant convergence to German interest rates and an exchange rate close to the central parity in the post-1992 ERM) and which would not. The implications of nonqualification were higher interest rates and potentially weaker currencies with levels subject to significant uncertainty. This market focus provided further impetus for policymakers as qualification became the yardstick by which their political success would be judged. It might be argued that this process led to a virtuous circle with countries eager to qualify, and markets anticipating qualification by lowering borrowing costs and thus adding further momentum to policymakers' decisions.[13]

Success in terms of European convergence can be readily appreciated from figure 5.3, which plots the movement in fiscal deficits, inflation, and nominal and real interest rates in selected European countries. Fiscal deficits and inflation improved rapidly in many of the countries considered and, in large part as a result, nominal interest rates fell sharply. As can be seen by comparing the graphs of nominal and real interest rate declines, and as detailed in table 5.2, most of the decline in nominal interest rates can be accounted for by the fall in inflation. However, in some countries real rates also fell significantly, representing an additional benefit through reputation effects.

Various authors have estimated the benefits of the single currency. The European Community (EC) has estimated that the benefit of eliminating intra-European currency transactions ranges from 0.25 to 0.50 percent of EC GDP, whereas the elimination of currency risk has been estimated— perhaps somewhat generously—as 2 percent of GDP. Moreover, the estimates of the reduction in the nominal financing cost of public debt range from an average 1 percent of GDP across the eleven EMU countries to as much as 2 percent of GDP for Italy.

The fundamental benefits of EMU are surely the higher investment stemming from lower interest rates and the adjustment to a higher capital stock, which then implies further multiplier effects to give permanent gains to growth. These effects will be particularly evident in the peripheral countries where interest rate reductions have been concentrated. A slightly different view is expressed in Currie (1992), who considers explicitly the difference between Germany, which is characterized as a high-reputation country, and the other EMU members. The gain in reputation for the other members allows them to achieve, in a Barro-inspired framework, a permanently lower inflation rate at little cost in terms of output (see also Giavazzi and Giavannini 1989). Depending on the assumed social welfare function, this calculation may yield further significant benefits.

To conclude, it might be argued that the EMU arose out of the somewhat inauspicious background of the ERM experience that proved to be dynamically unstable. Europe then opted for monetary union and significantly greater institutional development. The setting of the convergence criteria had an important effect on markets and it can be conjectured that market behavior then fed back to tightened policy objectives, thus creating a virtuous circle. Convergence was extremely impressive with respect to the substantial fall of inflation rates, fiscal deficits, and nominal interest rates in peripheral countries. Moreover, in some countries real interest rates also fell significantly, reflecting gains in reputation due to the institutional changes.

Exploring the Options

In this section we briefly review a more academic debate regarding floating versus fixed exchange rates versus currency boards versus currency unions, drawing out selected salient points. This debate provided the background for the dollarization proposal. We will use the term *currency union* because it is the term generally applied in the academic literature. However, our focus is on a small country considering monetary union with a larger partner such that it would have no significant say in subsequent monetary policy decisions.

On Floating versus Fixed Exchange Rates

The traditional literature on the choice between floating and fixed exchange rates focuses on the effects of different types of shocks. Broadly speaking, fixed rates are preferred when shocks are mostly monetary whereas floating rates are superior when shocks are mostly exogenous and real in nature.

In practice, however, many countries have adopted intermediate solutions rather than pure floats or truly fixed exchange rates. These include

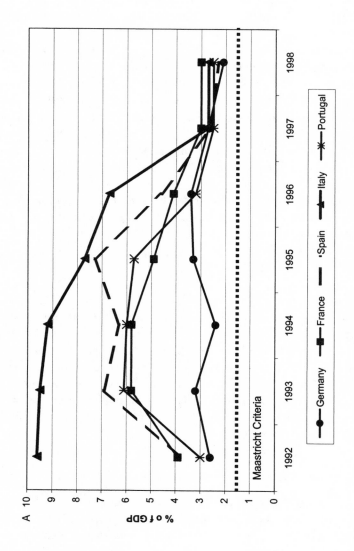

A 10

% of GDP

9

8

7

6

5

4

3

2

1

0

1992   1993   1994   1995   1996   1997   1998

Maastricht Criteria

—●— Germany   —■— France   ·✳· Spain

—▲— Italy   —✳— Portugal

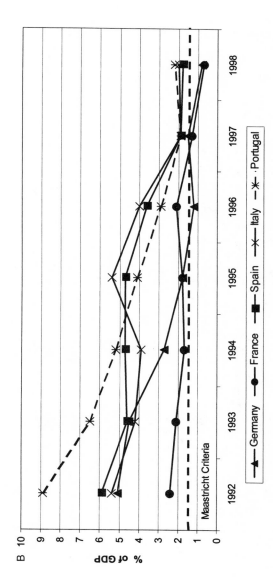

Fig. 5.3 European Convergence: Panel A, Fiscal Deficit; Panel B, Inflation; Panel C, Long-Term Interest Rates
SOURCES:
Ministry of Economics, JPMorgan, and authors' own calculations.

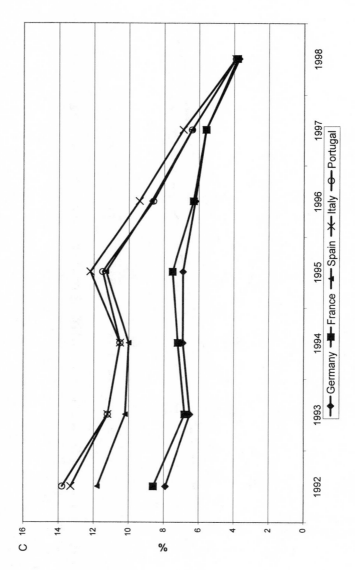

Fig. 5.3 (cont.)

Table 5.2   European Convergence (%)

Country	Fiscal Deficit (as % of GDP)		Inflation		Long-Term Interest Rates		Long-Term Real Interest Rates	
	1992	1998	1992	1998	1992	1998	1992	1998
Germany	2.6	2.1	5.1	0.8	7.9	3.7	2.8	2.9
France	3.9	3	2.4	0.7	8.6	3.8	6.2	3.1
Spain	3.8	2.3	5.9	1.8	11.8	3.9	5.9	2.1
Italy	9.6	2.7	5.4	2	13.3	3.9	7.9	1.9
Portugal	3.0	2.5	8.9	2.2	13.8	3.9	4.9	1.7

SOURCE: IMF, *International Financial Statistics.*

dirty floats, or floats subject to bands that might crawl, or crawling rates subject to some managed flexibility. On the one hand, proponents of intermediate regimes argue that these systems combine the advantages of a flexible exchange rate (in terms of responding to exogenous real shocks) while limiting the costs (by avoiding an excessive reaction to monetary shocks). On the other hand, the literature on speculative attacks has highlighted problems that may arise in these intermediate solutions or indeed in any fixed exchange rate not supported by appropriate monetary or other policies. In particular, it is well established that under certain conditions the market may provoke a fully rational attack on the system, forcing the authorities to change the regime. The 1992 ERM crisis and more recent failures of fixed but adjustable pegs have led many to conclude that given the levels of global capital flows, these intermediate solutions are increasingly difficult to maintain over time; hence, to prevent currency crises, countries may need to choose between fairly pure floats (where perhaps some intervention can be used for short-term objectives) and truly fixed exchange rates backed by firm commitment (e.g., either a currency-board mechanism or a full-fledged currency union). In this respect the debate has come full circle and is once again more clearly a debate between two extremes: to fix or to float.

However, the terms of the debate have also changed based on the realization that neither a pure float nor a pure fix will follow the perfect textbook model. On the one hand, Calvo and Reinhart (1999) have documented that many emerging market countries with flexible exchange rate regimes have displayed a fear of floating, characterized by relatively stable exchange rates (at last in comparison to their Group of Seven [G7] counterparts), with proactive interest rate policies and higher levels of reserve volatility implying foreign exchange intervention. Hence it appears that, despite exchange rate flexibility, policymakers have often preferred to maintain relatively stable rates but at the cost of substantially higher interest rates, as also described by Hausmann et al. (1999). On the other hand, as we document in this paper, Argentina's pure fix backed by a currency board has also suffered from a lack of full credibility and hence from perceived devaluation risk.

Thus, although the choice facing countries today may appear to be cast in terms of the extremes of floating versus fixed as depicted in the traditional literature, in our view, the real choice facing policymakers in emerging markets is often a different one: the choice between an imperfect floating regime in which monetary policy may not be employed to react optimally to real shocks, and an imperfect fixed exchange rate regime in which devaluation risk remains present.

The issue of credibility is critical to understanding these imperfections, and credibility itself is a dynamic concept. In a floating rate regime, it might be argued that as credibility is gained it becomes more possible to use countercyclical monetary policy. It might also be argued, however, that in the context of a fixed exchange rate regime, perceived devaluation risk may fall over time as the system becomes more credible.

A fear of floating, as advanced by Calvo and Reinhart, is often tied to the presence of dollarized liabilities. In a highly dollarized economy, exchange rate fluctuations may be very costly and hence optimal monetary policy decisions may be significantly constrained by balance-sheet considerations (see Baliño, Bennet, and Borensztein 1999). In turn, de facto dollarization may itself be a result of a lack of credibility because the option of issuing debt in local currency may be much more expensive than that of issuing in dollars if the monetary regime itself is not credible.[14] Indeed, as argued by Calvo and Guidotti (1990), dollarization of liabilities may itself be a powerful instrument to strengthen the credibility of the exchange-rate or monetary policy. In turn, as an independent monetary policy becomes more credible, or as a fixed exchange rate becomes more credible, it is to be expected that the economy may de-dollarize over time.

On Floating Exchange Rates versus a Currency Union or Currency Board

The literature on optimal currency areas (OCAs) closely follows the traditional literature on fixed versus floating exchange rates. Thus, advocates of flexible rates tend to use the arguments from the OCA literature to stress that currency unions are costly when real shocks affect countries asymmetrically. On the other hand, a currency union may seem desirable to the advocates of truly fixed rates as a mechanism to solve the credibility problem mentioned above. If a truly fixed rate is preferred, then a currency-board mechanism or a currency union may be required, first, to ensure the monetary policy is consistent with the fixed rate (a political-economy argument may suggest that this is necessary or desirable); and second, to ensure that the market considers the rate fully credible, reducing the possibility of a speculative attack. Alesina and Barro (2000) model the trade-off between, on the one hand, the benefit of a currency union as the solution of a Barro-Gordon type of credibility problem and, on the other hand, the associated cost of losing an instrument to respond to asymmetric shocks. Hence they develop alternative rules for deciding under which conditions it is optimal for a small country to adopt the currency of another country as its own.

An important consideration relates to the endogeneity of the OCA conditions. It was suggested above that the Maastricht conditions for EMU set in place a virtuous circle that influenced policymakers. Hence it might be argued that the conditions for EMU were, to a significant extent, endogenous to the decision to join the union. In a similar vein, many argue that a prerequisite for a fixed exchange rate or monetary union is price flexibility. However, it might be contested that price flexibility is also, to a significant extent, endogenous to the monetary regime in place. Moreover, a common criticism of currency boards or currency unions is that countries may have different economic cycles. A counterargument is that economic cycles are also endogenous to the regime and that, through a currency board or currency union, trade will increase and economic cycles will become much more symmetric.[15]

Traditional OCA theory stresses the role of asymmetric real shocks and many have in mind shocks to the price of oil or other basic commodities, or, indeed, productivity shocks. This analysis was especially relevant for a world of low capital mobility, but in a world of high capital mobility certain shocks to financial variables may also constitute shocks that affect aggregate wealth and are then equally valid "real" shocks. The correlations of financial indicators (e.g., bond and stock prices) are high for a wide range of emerging markets and especially within the Americas. Moreover, taking into account regime changes, they are also high between emerging countries and the United States. This evidence suggests that although traditional real shocks may be asymmetric, real shocks stemming from financial variables may be more highly correlated. Thus, rethinking what we mean by *real shocks* in a world of high capital mobility may also have implications for traditional OCA theory.[16]

At times, financial shocks may be highly asymmetric, as when an increase in risk aversion makes capital flow out of emerging market economies and into safe havens. The traditional argument for flexible exchange rates would hold in a case such as this in exactly the same way as when there are widespread asymmetric terms-of-trade, demand, or productivity shocks (to name a few examples). However, the counterargument related to the benefits of gaining credibility also applies. Especially in the case of countries with a history of high inflation, gaining credibility through a very fixed exchange rate or a monetary union may significantly outweigh the potential cost arising from asymmetric real or financial shocks between the countries involved.

This suggests that although, according to traditional theory, emerging countries and the United States may not form an OCA because of the existence of asymmetric real and financial shocks, if the gain in credibility is considered this result may be overturned. Indeed, a monetary union may contribute to the elimination or significant reduction of (asymmetric) financial shocks.

On Currency Boards versus Currency Unions

In terms of the traditional economic theory, the only significant difference between a pure currency board and a currency union is the issue of seigniorage revenue. Under the assumption that a sharing rule could be found that would leave Argentina with no net loss in terms of seigniorage, we do not discuss this matter further here.[17] However, there is a set of issues that traditional theory does not take into account.

A pure currency board is a construct of economic theory and, in practice, currency boards tend to have some flexibility built within them. In the Argentine case, the Central Bank has the flexibility of reducing international reserves to two-thirds of the monetary base. This is subject to the additional restriction that total reserves (including Argentine government dollar-denominated bond holdings) must cover 100 percent of the monetary base. However, to the extent that a liquidity facility is agreed upon within the context of the monetary agreement that effectively replaces this flexibility of the Argentine Central Bank, there may once again be little difference between a currency board and currency union.[18]

The credibility of the institutional arrangement is an important issue. A currency board might be thought of as the hardest form of fixed exchange rate that maintains the real existence of a domestic currency.[19] Given that the domestic currency remains in circulation, an advantage of the currency board is then that it leaves open the possibility that at some future date the currency might float. However, leaving open that option gives rise precisely to the cost of imperfect credibility of the fixed peg. It might be argued that a currency union removes virtually any possibility of reintroducing a domestic currency, thus increasing the credibility of the monetary arrangement. In our view, to the extent that the currency union is enshrined in a bilateral treaty or agreement with seigniorage-sharing and other features, this credibility will be heightened.[20] It is then the option value (and its cost in terms of residual imperfect credibility) of the currency board that makes it different from dollarization.[21] Naturally, there may be other dimensions to this difference. As mentioned earlier, Frankel and Rose (2000) find a significant effect of a currency union (or use of another's currency) to trade that is not present when considering currency-board countries.

Conclusions

This section suggests that, in today's world of global capital, the traditional debates among floating and fixed rates, currency boards, and monetary unions may need significant revision. First, the feasibility and benefits of an independent monetary policy may be lower than previously thought. Second, a fixed but adjustable exchange rate may be subject to destabilizing speculative attacks. A currency board is a mechanism to subjugate monetary policy more directly for the defense of the currency peg, and hence buys credibility, arguably, at the cost of monetary flexibility. However, as credibility becomes more and more important, the desirability of a currency union over a currency board increases. Yet if real shocks are very large or very costly, then the option value of the currency board increases, as does the potential gain from floating. In the next section, we consider what form of currency union might be applicable to the Argentine case. We discuss, in particular, the structure that a U.S.-Argentine monetary agreement might eventually take.

A U.S.-Argentine Monetary Agreement

As described in previous sections, the dollarization debate emerged from a combination of factors. First, convertibility had set the basis for a wide range of reforms and, as a consequence, in the 1991–98 period macroeconomic performance had improved significantly. Thus, convertibility enjoyed widespread popular and political support. Second, especially after Brazil devalued in January 1999, there was a perception that although convertibility had gained credibility over time it was certainly less than 100 percent credible, implying a perceived and significant devaluation risk—as evidenced, for example, in the peso forward rates against the dollar. Furthermore, it appeared that Argentina was subject to significant contagion effects through world financial markets. These effects were very costly in terms of the adverse effect that higher interest rates had on investment, growth, and employment.

In this section we examine how the implementation of a U.S.-Argentine monetary agreement could constitute an effective strategy to reduce such perceived risk, to reduce contagion, and to promote economic stability within Argentina (and hence to reduce sovereign spreads and interest rates), and to increase investment and growth. As we argued above, if successful such a strategy might also jump-start a regional trend toward monetary unification. The discussion that follows is about the implementation of dollarization in an institutional context such as that prevailing at the time of the 1998–99 debate, and not as a response to a crisis scenario.

What Would a Monetary Agreement Consist Of?

A monetary agreement between Argentina and the United States might be considered the framework under which Argentina would adopt the U.S. dollar as legal tender, phasing out the use of the peso.[22] It could consist of a set of bilateral agreements. Those that we consider here are (a) an agreement on the sharing of seigniorage revenues and (b) an agreement by which Argentina would establish or gain access to a liquidity facility.

As we discuss further below, our assessment is that an institutional arrangement containing agreements on these issues is necessary in order for Argentina to reap the full benefits of dollarization. In particular, our view is that a unilateral dollarization would not provide the maximum benefits in terms of the elimination of devaluation risk, as a greater incentive to reintroduce a domestic currency would remain than under a monetary agreement. Also, unilateral dollarization could potentially increase risk because of the resulting reduction in the lender-of-last-resort powers of the Central Bank without a corresponding liquidity facility taking its place. Moreover, a full loss of the seigniorage revenue with no corresponding compensation would place a significant obstacle in the required process of reaching a broad social and political consensus needed to ensure the success of dollarization.[23]

A critical issue is whether a monetary agreement with the United States would imply any additional contingent liabilities for the U.S. authorities other than those included in the specific agreements. Certainly, the agreements examined here contain no explicit wider responsibility in terms of banking supervision or access to the Federal Reserve discount window. However, a concern might be raised in the sense that given the official use of the dollar in Argentina, the United States might feel committed to assist Argentina in the wake of any arising problems. There are several responses to this. First, our view is that the initial conditions should be such as to make very slim the probability of any future financial problem in Argentina. We are not thinking here of dollarization as a response to the current crisis but rather as a reform to be implemented during better times. Second, our view is that the elimination of devaluation risk (and hence the impossibility of any future currency crisis), the lowering of country risk, and the resulting economic stability would significantly reduce the probability of needing to access extraordinary IMF, other international financial institutions, or bilateral support in the future. Third, even if a crisis occurred after dollarizing it is not at all obvious that the United States would be expected to provide more assistance to Argentina simply because of the existence of a monetary agreement. Indeed, the most recent rescue packages, including that for Argentina, have revealed the United States to be a major contributor through its significant support to the IMF and other international financial institutions—and in some cases even directly. Hence, an institutional arrangement that significantly reduces the probability of Argentina's needing such funding in the future could be thought of as reducing any possible U.S. contingent liability rather than increasing it.

Seigniorage   *Seigniorage* is the revenue earned by issuing notes and coins that the public holds willingly without receiving interest. The Central Bank, which typically has the monopoly on issuing the national currency, can exchange currency for interest-bearing securities. In Argentina there are currently $10.4 billion pesos in circulation (including those held by the public and by banks). As discussed above, these are fully backed by hard currency reserves at the Central Bank along with some $2.9 billion held by banks in the form of liquidity requirements.[24] A very simple estimate of the current flow of seigniorage revenue is obtained by multiplying this $10.4 billion stock by a relevant interest rate (e.g., thirty-day London Interbank Offered Rate [LIBOR], which on 31 October 2001 stood at 2.3 percent), a calculation providing a flow of about $240 million per annum. However, this estimate may underestimate the potential long-run seigniorage revenue because LIBOR is currently at a very low rate. For instance, if we took the level of LIBOR one year before, which stood at 6.6 percent, then the estimate rises to $680 million per annum. Moreover, one might consider that the monetary base could grow over time, given the currently low level of monetization of the economy. Currently, notes and coins in pesos stand at about 3.6 percent of GDP.

From the yearly flow estimate, and making some assumption about the future behavior of GDP and monetization, one can obtain a useful stock concept expressing the present discounted value of future seigniorage revenues. Assuming a growth rate of 4 percent per annum, and that the monetary base declines over time (using a simple hyperbolic function) but then stabilizes at 2.5 percent of GDP forever if LIBOR remains at 2.3 percent, then the present discounted value of future seigniorage considering the next fifty years (discounted changes in stocks and interest earnings) is about $57 billion. If LIBOR were to rise back to 6.6 percent, the figure would be lower: $20 billion in present-value terms (because of the higher discount rate). These figures may appear large but represent only about 0.25 percent of the discounted Argentine GDP flows over the same 50 years in each case.[25] In the discussion that follows, we will consider the issue of seigniorage-sharing in general terms but bearing these estimates in mind.

One way of considering how the monetary agreement might deal with this issue is to think that Argentina is selling the Federal Reserve System the right to be the monopoly note issuer in Argentina. At current levels of monetization, the present value of this "license" is $10.4 billion (or $280 million per annum forever at an interest rate of 2.3 percent).[26]

The Argentine Central Bank would then cancel its peso liabilities with Argentine residents by drawing down its international reserves, mostly in U.S. financial assets. The public and the banks in Argentina would complete their currency substitution with this new stock of U.S. dollars, which would be legal tender and would be used to meet all functions of currency: unit of account, means of payment, and reserve of value.[27] Other monetary and financial assets and liabilities in pesos would automatically be converted to dollars at par.

In the United States the financial institutions that manage the international reserves of the Argentine Central Bank would have to sell assets (say, U.S. treasury bonds) in order to cancel their debt to the Argentine Central Bank. On the other hand, the U.S. Federal Reserve would issue

$10.4 billion new dollars by purchasing the same amount in U.S. treasury bonds. Since this supply of new dollars would satisfy a new and equivalent demand (by Argentines), it would have no inflationary effect.

However, by withdrawing from the market $10.4 billion in U.S. treasury bonds, the U.S. government would be saving the interest on this stock of securities. In principle, this net seigniorage gain could then be passed on to the Argentine government on an annual basis. Thus, neither the government nor the country as a whole would lose or gain from the change. Whereas the Argentine Central Bank would basically be selling the dollars it receives by drawing down on its foreign investments (as in any exchange market intervention), the U.S. Federal Reserve would basically be purchasing U.S. government securities. An agreement of this sort would then represent a zero-cost transaction for both the U.S. and the Argentine authorities.

Alternatively, seigniorage revenues could be shared between the U.S. treasury and the Argentine government. In this alternative only a portion of the net seigniorage gain would be passed on to the Argentine government. In 1999, Senator Connie Mack attempted to introduce legislation to the U.S. Congress proposing a rebate of a specified percentage of the seigniorage gain to dollarizing countries.[28]

Another issue is the treatment of the additional seigniorage income from a potential increase in the demand for dollars in Argentina, as discussed in our estimate of seigniorage in Argentina (above). There are several possibilities in this case.

A first alternative is to establish a monitoring system such that dollar bills exported from the United States to Argentina and reexported from Argentina to other countries can be estimated. The U.S. authorities do have a controlling system of dollar bills exported to Argentina, but currently there is no attempt to directly measure those exported from Argentina to other countries. Such a monitoring system has its problems. These problems are both practical, in that it may be difficult to obtain a complete picture, and impractical, in that there is a danger that the establishment of such a procedure might increase perceived convertibility risk (and one objective of full dollarization may be precisely to reduce such risks). An alternative monitoring system would be for the Federal Reserve to print new dollar bills with the thirteenth letter M—the first twelve letters currently correspond to the twelve Federal Reserve districts—and then to export these dollars to Argentina and subsequently monitor their flows.[29]

A second alternative is to establish a simple sharing rule for future seigniorage flows in a somewhat similar vein to the currently proposed rules for sharing seigniorage within the eleven EMU countries. A simple formula employing population and GDP estimates has been agreed upon, to share seigniorage from euro-note issuance in the different EMU countries. A similar rule could be established for the future flow of dollar bills to Argentina depending on Argentine population and GDP growth.

A third alternative is that proposed by the paper circulated by the Joint Economic Committee Staff Report (Office of the Chairman, Senator Connie Mack) of the U.S. Congress.[30] According to this proposal Argentina would receive a yearly proportion of the total demand for dollars in the world. This proportion would be determined by the amount of peso notes converted into dollars at the time of dollarization divided by the total demand for dollars at that time. Thus Argentina would gain from any future increase in total dollar demand, and lose from any future decline in total dollar demand. In fact, under this scheme, Argentina would become a shareholder in the dollar.

A fourth alternative is simply to ignore the flow income. This could probably represent a significant net gain to the U.S. authorities but would depend on the future use of cash in Argentina. The bill submitted to the U.S. Congress by Senator Mack essentially takes that line.

We remain somewhat agnostic with respect to these alternatives. However, an issue that is highly relevant both politically as well as for building a reliable liquidity facility is that the rebate of seigniorage should take the form of a nondiscretionary, multiyear commitment.

Access to a Liquidity Facility   Adopting the full use of the dollar in Argentina implies that Argentina would lose the hard currency reserves that currently back the peso notes and coins in circulation. This would effectively leave the backing of the liquidity requirements that the Central Bank currently imposes on banks as the first line of defense against liquidity problems. Thus, compared to the present situation it could be argued that dollarization would significantly reduce the Central Bank's limited capacity as a lender of last resort. To compensate for this loss, the monetary agreement might include specified access to a liquidity facility.

To a large extent, the Contingent Repo Facility set up in 1996 by the Central Bank of Argentina with fourteen private banks may provide a model for how this could be arranged. This innovative contract gave the Central Bank of Argentina the right to sell Argentine assets to international banks subject to a repurchase clause. The *repo* is subject to standard haircut and margining rules, and if used attracts an implicit cost of funds by which the arrangement is currently significantly out of the money. The collateral under the contract essentially consists of Argentine government paper. There is no trigger for the facility and it is activated solely on the decision of the Central Bank. Each bank has a separate contract and all of these are similar except for the economic conditions. These conditions were determined through a bidding process at the commencement of the contract in December 1996. At that time, the minimum contract length was two years, and the idea was to roll this forward every three months (subject to an evergreen clause), and the average cost of funds if the facility were used is LIBOR + 200 basis points. In 2001, the facility was drawn down for some $1.2 billion.

One possibility would be to establish an agreement between the Central Bank of Argentina and the U.S. government that would allow the Central Bank of Argentina to draw down a specified amount subject to a set of economic conditions (an agreed maximum, an interest rate, a minimum payback period, etc.). An obvious maximum is the present value of the seigniorage revenue that would be shared with Argentina. Then, the future seigniorage flows could provide the collateral behind any advance made under this arrangement, assuming that seigniorage would be payable annually. This arrangement would imply very low risks for the U.S. authorities.

Alternatively, the seigniorage flow income from the U.S. authorities might be used as collateral for a private facility to be set up by the Central Bank of Argentina. This might closely follow the current private Contingent Repo Facility but using the dedicated flow income from the U.S. authorities rather than principally Argentine government bonds as collateral.

The Option Value of the Currency Board

It is typically argued that a cost to currency union is the loss of an independent monetary policy. However, the Convertibility Law of April 1991 implies that Argentina had already given up any independent monetary policy. Hence, comparing the monetary agreement to today's situation, there is in principle no further cost in this regard, other than (as discussed above) the loss of the option value of floating in the future. The value of this option depends crucially on assumptions regarding the potential benefit of floating, the rate-of-time preference, and the estimated time it would take to gain the relevant credibility.

One view is that the current crisis was a direct consequence of the combination of a fixed exchange rate and a set of very strong exogenous shocks such as the fall in commodity prices, the increase in risk aversion in capital markets, and the Brazilian devaluation. Those believing that these are the fundamental factors behind the current crisis may think that while it was relevant to consider dollarizing when the volatility of shocks was lower, it may not be relevant today because the option value of the currency board and the potential value of floating have increased.

However, another view is that, given the imperfect credibility of the current arrangement, the effect especially of higher risk aversion in capital markets on devaluation risk and country risk spreads has been much larger than otherwise has been the case, developing a vicious cycle of high interest rates, growth, and fiscal balance. For those believing that the latter explanation is the fundamental explanation of the current crisis, the dollarization alternative is still an attractive policy. The cost-benefit equation is then critically related to the importance (and feasibility) of a floating exchange rate to adjust to real shocks versus the effect of nominal shocks in a world of imperfect credibility. In this section we discuss various themes that relate to this fundamental trade-off.

Real Shocks and OCA Conditions   It is often argued that Argentina and the United States do not constitute an OCA. The more recent literature on this topic asserts that countries are ideal partners for a monetary union when they satisfy a number of conditions:

1. They have very substantial trade relations so that they show a high degree of positive correlation along the trade cycle.
2. Their economic structures are quite similar so that shocks will affect them in a relatively homogeneous way (not requiring large bilateral exchange rate corrections).
3. There is a high degree of labor and capital mobility between them.
4. They have integrated fiscal systems.

It is clear that Argentina and the United States do not satisfy these conditions. However, as reviewed above, Argentina has already adopted U.S. monetary policy since 1991. These costs, then, apply to the currency board as well as to a full currency union. The only difference in terms of these two systems relates to the value of losing the option to float in the future.

As argued in previous sections, the traditional OCA literature needs enhancement in an emerging country context. In the case of Argentina, the effect of financial shocks has been very significant, and indeed the current recession can be traced back to the decline in investment that began after the Russian default in 1998. As reviewed above, financial asset prices are highly correlated with those in the United States; hence, including these variables, shocks appear more symmetric. However, the argument is also that given a monetary agreement with the United States, the amplitude of these kinds of shocks may also decline.

Finally, as also discussed previously, the initial conditions emphasized by the traditional OCA literature are endogenous and are likely to be affected by the currency union. For instance, a monetary agreement with the United States is likely to increase trade between the two countries and would then align the cycles of the two economies more closely.

Costs in Terms of Other Objectives   A monetary agreement with the United States also rules out other alternatives, such as a monetary union with Europe. Considering current trade links, Europe may appear to be a more natural candidate than the United States because Argentina trades more with the European Union than with the United States.[31] Nevertheless, virtually all foreign currency financial contracts in Argentina are expressed in U.S. dollars and not in euros. However, adding the possibility of "euroizing" in the future increases the option value of the current currency board arrangements and, in terms of Craine's (2001) analysis, would reduce the attractiveness of stopping today via a currency union with the United States.

Moreover, according to current Argentine legislation, when the euro reaches parity with the U.S. dollar the present currency board will switch to a fifty-fifty euro-dollar peg. In our view, although this change could bring the benefit of allowing the nominal exchange rate to fluctuate more in line with the real shocks affecting Argentina from commodity and currency movements, it has also clearly increased the perception that Argentina might float in the future, hence reducing the credibility of the present currency board.[32]

Also, many have raised the issue of how a monetary agreement might affect Mercosur. Mercosur has been a very important strategic objective for Argentina during the past nine years as a free-trade area as well as a custom union. Moreover, the strategy has been to begin with Mercosur and progressively expand the free-trade area (e.g., Chile and Bolivia have recently joined the free-trade area). It is clear that a monetary agreement with the United States, while not changing the current Argentine monetary policy (which implies a fixed exchange rate to the dollar anyway), would rule out a single independent currency for Mercosur and may have deeper consequences as well.

Indeed, the issue of a single Mercosur currency is a complex one and is perhaps more a political issue than a monetary one. Viewing the issue first in strictly economic terms, one might hypothesize that a single Mercosur currency may not reduce the problem of imperfect credibility to the same degree as a currency union with the United States (in the language of Alesina and Barro, a Mercosur anchor may not be one that solves a Barro-Gordon imperfect credibility problem whereas a U.S. anchor may do exactly that), but may allow Argentina to have an exchange rate that adjusts better to real shocks affecting the economy, in particular to shocks that emanate from Brazil. However, wider issues clearly are also at stake. One argument in favor of Mercosur is that as a bargaining unit for a Free Trade Area of the Americas (FTAA), Mercosur may have more weight than individual countries bargaining bilaterally with the United States. How the deepening of Mercosur through the adoption of a single currency affects that bargaining game is a complex issue. Moreover, if the final objective is an FTAA with a single currency, then this may also change the nature of the bargaining game.

Potential Benefits

In this section we review a set of specific benefits of the full dollarization of the Argentine economy under the auspices of a monetary agreement as described in the following section.

Elimination of the Perceived Risk of Devaluation   There has clearly remained a market perception of a risk of currency depreciation in Argentina. Market measures of this risk manifest themselves in the spread between yields on peso and dollar denominated public securities, and in the peso-dollar forward rate. These indicators have been positive virtually throughout the currency-board period and have also been highly volatile, rising every time there is a shock to the economy. At the time of this writing the perceived devaluation risk is extremely high by any historical standard.

Arguably, it might be the case that convertibility could eventually gain full credibility. However, experience suggests that this would be a long process and with fluctuating and potentially significant devaluation risk on the way. Thus, a currency union with a monetary agreement with the United States would essentially eliminate the currency risk during the whole intermediate period between the moment it is implemented and the point in the (distant) future when a process of increasing credibility had eliminated all lingering perceptions of currency risk within the currency board.

Elimination of the risk of currency depreciation during this significant period of time may have substantial net benefits for the Argentine economy. These benefits spring from the generally more certain environment for investment and economic activity that would be brought about. Argentina has a very open capital account and capital flows are extremely important for continued growth. Disruptions to these flows have had very significant negative effects on growth. To the extent that eliminating currency risk reduces the probability of such disruptions, full dollarization could have substantial benefits.

Moreover, significant exchange rate changes generate sudden changes in relative prices that disrupt normal economic activity. Even with a credible fixed exchange rate, a remote possibility of maxidevaluation creates the risk of there being large and sudden redistributions of income and wealth with very adverse effects on the economic environment in which plans are formulated. Thus, all economic agents must take this source of uncertainty into account when formulating their plans, which means that investment demand will be lower, planning horizons will be shorter, and growth and incomes will be lower.

Reduction in the Perceived Country Risk   There is also a relationship between currency and country risks, and simple correlations between different measures of these two concepts are very high. However, it is very difficult to distinguish the causality and quantify the potential benefit in terms of a reduced country risk premium from eliminating devaluation risk. In this section we discuss the theoretical arguments and then briefly review the empirical relationships.

1. Whenever perceptions of exchange rate risk increase, government solvency is reduced. Because most Argentine government debt is dollar denominated (and as much as 93 percent is foreign currency denominated) whereas revenues are almost exclusively peso denominated (and foreign currency–denominated debt by far exceeds international reserves in the Central Bank), a depreciation of the peso would reduce the government's solvency, increasing the perceived risk of government default. Consequently, the cost of financing government deficits and refinancing amortization of government debt would increase. In table 5.3 we give some summary statistics of balance-sheet foreign currency mismatches in Argentina.

2. Increases in exchange rate risk perceptions also increase the perception of solvency risk in the financial system. This in turn implies a potential risk to the Central Bank's and the government's balance sheets, if

Table 5.3   Balance-Sheet Effects in Argentina (mismatches in US$ billions, November 1999)

	Assets	Liabilities	Position
Public sector	2.7	111.0	−108.3
Central Bank[a]	25.8	8.9	16.9
Nonfinancial private sector[b]	191.9	144.2	47.7
Financial sector	119.1	98.9	20.2
Total			−23.5

[a]Assets include international reserves + Argentine US$ government bonds

[b]Assets include external assets + dollar-denominated deposits in the financial system + AFJP (Argentine pension fund) assets + US$ cash holdings. Liabilities include external liabilities + dollar-denominated loans of the financial system.

SOURCES: Ministry of the Economy, Central Bank of Argentina, and authors' own calculations.

assistance to the financial sector is required. This may then increase the risk premium of government debt. The solvency risk of the financial system is affected by currency depreciation through various channels, including currency-flow mismatches between assets and liabilities (even if the stocks are currency matched) and increases in the credit risk of clients who have peso incomes and revenues. Hence, the funding costs of banks increase whenever there is an increase in currency risk even if they are dollar denominated.

3. Currency depreciation would without a doubt cause a very serious upheaval in the domestic economy and would most likely foster a very serious recession. For a country with a recent hyperinflationary experience and that has been under a currency board for seven years, it would be very unlikely that there would be a soft landing from the fixed exchange rate. The market perception of a devaluation scenario is one of a major devaluation; hence, any increase in the exchange rate risk increases the probability of the worst case scenario and makes interest rates generally rise. Moreover, any currency depreciation would reduce borrowers' solvency in dollars. So whenever there is an increase in the perceived exchange rate risk, the cost of funding to firms with dollar debts rises.

4. The increase in exchange rate risk perceptions may result in an outflow of capital and, through the currency-board mechanism, an increase in interest rates which then depresses economic activity. This in turn worsens the government's fiscal position and hence increases the risk of default.

5. There is also a set of very different arguments that the elimination of currency risk may reduce country risk. The above four arguments are based on the assumption that financial markets evaluate country risk per-

fectly and that there are no contagion effects, no herd instincts, and no multiple equilibria that might justify different valuations of country risks even in a model of purely rational investors. However, a great deal of recent literature has suggested that these types of market imperfections are indeed important in country risk valuations. If eliminating currency risk shifts the valuation of Argentine country risk from one equilibrium to another or reduces herd-type behavior by differentiating Argentina from other emerging markets where currency risk remains important, then this may have a very significant effect on country risk spreads. Naturally, almost by definition these effects are extremely difficult to quantify; however, to the extent that such market imperfections are important, they may be very significant.

6. There may also be feedback from country risk to devaluation risk. Although, as we have noted, due to the structure of assets and liabilities a devaluation would actually worsen the government's accounts in Argentina, many perceive that if the government were placed in a position of having to default it might provoke a devaluation following the experience of other countries where devaluations have been used to reduce the (dollar) value of domestic debt. Moreover, an increase in country risk may induce greater hedging of currency risks of (particularly) foreign financial and nonfinancial institutions in Argentina. Indeed, there is evidence that when country risk spreads rise, it is foreign companies that generally seek protection in the somewhat shallow market for peso forwards, perhaps due to head-office directives to balance currency positions.

Having argued that there are theoretical reasons to believe there is a link between devaluation risk and credit risk and hence that eliminating devaluation risk should reduce even local dollar interest rates, the question is whether this is likely to be significant in practice. It turns out that this is actually a very difficult question to answer empirically because of causality problems. Although we have argued above that it is quite reasonable to think that devaluation risk may cause default risk, it is also the case that default risk could cause devaluation risk. Hence any simple correlation between the two clearly is not necessarily evidence of a causal relationship in either direction in particular. In this section, we discuss three potential methodologies that might be employed, and give some preliminary results for the case of Argentina. Then we propose an alternative methodology to obtain a market measure of the potential reduction in country risk that would follow dollarization.

VECTOR AUTOREGRESSION ANALYSIS. The first method is simply to run a vector autoregression with the two series—devaluation risk and default risk—as endogenous variables. Vector autoregression analysis is frequently employed to analyze causal relationships between potentially endogenous variables where the causal relationships are unclear or where there may be complex causal relationships between different variables; hence, it is a natural choice in this context. In the example we provide below, we measure default risk as Argentina's subindex spread against U.S. treasuries of JPMorgan's Emerging Markets Bond Index Plus (EMBI+). We measure devaluation risk as the annual discount on the Argentine peso forward contract traded over the counter in New York (known as the nondeliverable forward; figures also supplied by JPMorgan). For both we use daily closing prices. We also include, as exogenous variables, the ratio of the reserves of the Central Bank to the money base, the EMBI+ index (excluding Argentina), and the U.S. treasury thirty-year bond yield to control for other factors that may affect default or devaluation risk.

The results are shown in table 5.4. In this specification, it turns out that devaluation risk is significant in explaining default risk but not vice versa. The point coefficient estimate, however, is not quantitatively very large. Using that estimate gives a benefit to eliminating devaluation risk of some 120 basis points (in this and all results to follow we use as a base the average Argentine EMBI+ subindex spread over the period June 1997 to February 1999, which was 594 basis points)—that is, a 20 percent reduction in the default spread. However, this methodology has two very significant drawbacks. The first is that, empirically, the specification reported here (as was the case with other alternative regressions that were estimated) was not robust to alternative specifications that gave different results. A rea-

Table 5.4   Vector Autoregression Results

	Default Risk	**Devaluation Risk**
Default risk $(t-1)$	0.709 (0.024)	0.014 (0.029)
Devaluation risk $(t-1)$	0.048 (0.017)	0.884 (0.020)
Reserves/monetary base (t)	0.017 (0.006)	0.005 (0.007)
EMBIWARG (t)	0.224 (0.017)	0.037 (0.021)
US30YRS (t)	0.224 (0.052)	0.020 (0.062)
Constant	0.001	0.007

NOTE: Standard errors in parentheses.

sonably robust result, confirmed by bilateral Granger causality tests, was that there is a dual causality between the two variables. However, coefficient estimates in different vector-autoregression specifications were frequently nonsignificant. Moreover, there is an even more serious conceptual drawback regarding this methodology. Both spreads that are being used here are derived from market instruments. Hence, given an assumption that these markets are perfectly efficient, any news should be picked up immediately by both. It would then not be particularly surprising to find no lagged relationship between these variables. Of course in practice these markets may not be perfectly efficient. In particular, the nondeliverable-forward market and peso markets in general are probably less liquid and less efficient than the market for dollar Argentine assets. Thus it would not be surprising to find country risk causing devaluation risk, simply because of this potential difference in market liquidity or efficiency.

AN EVENT-STUDY APPROACH.   An alternative approach is to consider particular events and to analyze how devaluation and default risk changed over those periods. The idea here would be to select events in which it could be argued that the news incorporated into the market spreads reflected news regarding currency risk rather than default risk. In the case of Argentina there are a number of such events, including, for example, the devaluation of the Mexican peso in December 1994; the speculative attack against Hong Kong in October 1997; the devaluation of the Brazilian real in January 1999; and a *Financial Times* interview with then–presidential candidate Domingo Cavallo, who was interpreted as being in support of floating the peso. In table 5.5 we give the results. In particular we detail the changes in devaluation risk and default risk from ten days before these events to the end of the business day of the event itself. We also give the change in both variables from the day of the event to ten days later.

As can be seen from the table, each event produces a very significant rise in both devaluation and default risk. The movement patterns after the events differ such that in some cases subsequent to the event (Mexican devaluation and Cavallo interview), although devaluation risk falls, default risk rises, reflecting changes in default risk not associated with devaluation risk. However, on the announcement effect (day of the event versus ten days before), all show a positive relation. Powell and Sturzenegger (2001) extend this analysis for Argentina, for other Latin American countries, and for European countries in the run-up to the EMU and perform the relevant statistical tests for significance. These authors find that for countries in the region with high de facto dollarization (such that one would expect the balance-sheet effects to be strong), events identified as

Table 5.5   Event Study Results

Event	Δ Devaluation Risk	Δ Default Risk
Tequila (20 Dec. 1994)		
10 days before	107	110
10 days after	−52	221
Hong Kong (27 Oct. 1997)		
10 days before	872	287
10 days after	−500	−50
Brazil (14 Jan. 1999)		
10 days before	650	526
10 days after	−350	−129
Cavallo's *Financial Times* interview		
10 days before	465	176
10 days after	−60	111

increasing (decreasing) currency risk lead to increases (decreases) in default risks. Interestingly, they find insignificant effects or even coefficients going in the opposite direction for countries that have less de facto dollarization. For Europe they find that events that are judged to be positive news in favor of going ahead with the EMU reduced default risk in those countries that eventually joined EMU but increased default risk for those countries that did not (with Portugal being an exception to this rule).[33]

A SIMULATION ANALYSIS BASED ON BERG AND BORENSZTEIN (2000).   The final methodology that we report here uses a simulation analysis based on a simple model of probabilities as outlined in Berg and Borensztein (2000). The idea is as follows: The probability of default on government debt can be disaggregated into the probability of default given no currency crisis and the probability of default given a currency crisis, with these probabilities weighted by the appropriate probability of whether a currency crisis will occur. Using the spreads on government debt and an assumption on the recovery ratio given default, a total probability of default over the next twelve months can be estimated. Using the spreads on peso forward contracts and assumptions on the size of a devaluation given a currency crisis, the probability of a currency crisis can also be estimated. These probabilities are derived from simple no-arbitrage equations. Hence, if we assume the probability of default given a currency crisis, then we can solve for the probability of default given no currency crisis. This can then yield an estimate of what the default spread would be if there were no currency crisis risk at all (i.e., if devaluation risk were eliminated).

To see this argument mathematically, we begin from a decomposition of the probability of default,

(1) $P(d) = P(d/cc)P(cc) + P(d/ncc)P(ncc)$,

where $P(d)$ is the total probability of default, $P(d/cc)$ is the probability of default given a currency crisis, $P(d/ncc)$ is the probability of default given no currency crisis, and $P(cc) = [1 - P(ncc)]$ is the probability of a currency crisis occurring. Rearranging this equation, we have

(2) $P(d/ncc) = [P(d) - P(d/cc)P(cc)]/[1 - P(cc)]$.

As we discussed above we can estimate $P(d)$ from the sovereign bond spreads and an assumption of the recovery ratio, and $P(cc)$ from the spreads on peso forwards and an assumption on the size of devaluation if there is a currency crisis. Hence, with an assumption on $P(d/cc)$, we can calculate $P(d/ncc)$, from which we can calculate the default spread that would be appropriate if currency crisis risk were eliminated.

Once again, we use data on the EMBI+ Argentine subindex spreads to calculate $P(d)$ and the nondeliverable-forward spreads from the New York over-the-counter market to calculate $P(cc)$. In order to complete this calculation, we essentially use the covered interest parity condition and an assumption on the extent of the devaluation if there is a currency crisis. Moreover, as mentioned above, we also need to assume a probability of default if this devaluation actually occurred.

As Berg and Borensztein (2000), in table 5.6 we illustrate the results with different quantitative assumptions on these two variables. The different columns of the table represent different assumptions regarding the extent of devaluation, given a currency crisis. The different rows represent different assumed default probabilities if such devaluation occurred. The figures in the body of the table, then, represent the calculated reduction in the spread given a particular set of assumptions and using the average spreads of the EMBI+ Argentine subindex and the average twelve-month yields on the peso forward market. We include default probabilities (of 35, 42, and 50 percent) in the case of a currency crisis, $P(d/cc)$, given that, for the assumptions on the extent of the devaluation detailed, these values yield a reduction in default spreads of 100 percent (i.e., the full 594 basis points, which is the average of the EMBI+ series). We view this diagonal of the table as determining an extreme set of assumptions and that the meaningful values are above these. Moreover, for higher values of $P(d/cc)$,

Table 5.6   Results of a Simulation Exercise

EMBI+	Devaluation in Event of Currency Crisis		
	30%	40%	50%
Probability of default in the event of a currency crisis			
10	65.1	50.2	41.8
20	286.8	221.9	185.6
30	499.7	388.4	325.6
35	594.4	461.7	387.4
42		594.4	498.2
50			594.4

NOTE: Reduction in dollar spread on eliminating currency risk. Results using average data, June 1997–February 1999. See text for further details.

we find negative calculated probabilities of default given that there is no currency crisis $P(d/ncc)$ for the devaluation assumptions employed. We leave these combinations blank in the table.

The results show significant potential reductions. For example, in the case of a 40 percent devaluation in a currency crisis and a 20 percent probability of default (a case highlighted in Berg and Borensztein 2000), there is a reduction in the average spread of 220 basis points. In our view, given the extent of currency mismatches in Argentina and Argentine monetary history, the figures to the right and perhaps further down in the table may be more relevant. For example, in the case of a 50 percent devaluation and a 30 percent risk of default, the reduction is some 325 basis points.

Escudé, Grubisic, and Sabban (2000) note that a critical ingredient in the Berg and Borensztein (2000) methodology is the assumption of risk neutrality by investors, although there is considerable evidence that investors in bond markets tend to be risk averse. For example, the arbitrage equation from which $P(d)$ is calculated is

$$(3) \qquad [1 - P(d)](1 + i_A) + P(d)(1 + i_A)\alpha = 1 + i_{US},$$

so the expected return on an Argentine dollar bond should equal the expected return on U.S. treasury bonds (i_{US}) of similar duration. Alpha is the recovery value in case of default expressed as a percentage of the total contractual payment (principal plus interest). If there is risk aversion this equation should be modified to

(4) $[1 - P(d)](1 + i_A) + P(d)(1 + i_A)\alpha = 1 + i_{US} + \rho_d,$

where ρ_d is the market default risk premium. Similarly, the no-arbitrage equation for peso-denominated Argentine bonds versus dollar-denominated Argentine bonds needs to be modified in the same way, to

(5) $$\frac{[1 - P(cc)](1 + i_P) + P(d)(1 + i_P)}{1 + \delta} = 1 + i_A + \rho_{cc},$$

where ρ_{cc} is the currency risk premium.

Using data on Argentine Republic 2007 peso-denominated notes and Argentine Republic 2006 dollar-denominated unsubordinated bonds, as well as data from Merrill Lynch's High Yield Master II bond index and from Carty and Lieberman (1996) on average default and recovery rates for Ba (or, equivalently, BB in the S&P classification), they obtain reductions in default spreads that are lower than those shown in table 5.6 in the case of risk neutrality but that are nevertheless high. For example, assumptions on $P(d/cc)$ and δ of 40 percent (both) give way to a reduction of 310 basis points in the default spread.

When risk aversion is assumed, and using the same risk premium for default risk and for currency risk, the reduction in the default spread achieved as a consequence of full dollarization diminishes by about 25 percent with respect to the risk neutrality case. For example, assumptions on $P(d/cc)$ and δ of 40 percent (both) give way to a reduction of 234 basis points in the default spread.

Therefore, even correcting for risk aversion, the reduction in the default spread that could be achieved by full dollarization is quite significant.

AN ALTERNATIVE METHODOLOGY.   The methodologies presented above suggest that dollarization not only eliminates pure devaluation risk but also is likely to reduce default risk significantly. However, given the relatively small set of information on which the tests are performed, the results should be interpreted with caution. In particular, although it is encouraging that the three methodologies used point in the same direction, the quantitative estimate of the effect of dollarization on the default risk lies within a fairly large range.

Thus, it is useful to consider alternative practical means of obtaining a market estimate of the potential effect of dollarization on the risk of default. One way to obtain such an estimate involves an AAA-rated institution (for instance, the World Bank) in a financial transaction designed to extract from sovereign bond prices the necessary information to separate effectively default risk from currency risk. Such a transaction would imply the World Bank's issuing a AAA bond denominated in Argentine pesos (of course, the World Bank would be expected to hedge the corresponding foreign exchange risk).[34] The market price of such bond would then reflect the pure devaluation risk associated with the Argentine peso. Hence, by comparing the spread over U.S. treasuries of a bond (of the same duration) denominated in pesos issued by the Argentine Republic with the World Bank bond, a market measure of the pure default risk is obtained.

Finally, by comparing the measure of pure default risk with the spread over U.S. treasuries of a bond (of the same duration) denominated in U.S. dollars issued by the Argentine Republic, a market estimate of how much dollar spreads would fall following dollarization would be obtained.

Reduction in the Volatility of Country Risk   It should be noted that the elimination of the exchange rate risk would not only cause a reduction in the level of country risk but also in the volatility of this risk, further diminishing the uncertainty that the economy faces. This reduction in the volatility of country risk would have an impact on the level of investment and thus also on the level of growth. It would also diminish the amplitudes of economic cycles in Argentina.

More Stable Economic Environment and More Openness   Besides the benefits of the reduction in uncertainty (already discussed), the elimination of currency risk would have several indirect effects due to the creation of a more stable economic environment.

First, a more stable economic environment would lead to a larger financial system. Although the Argentine financial system has grown substantially, it remains small for a country of Argentina's level of development. In turn this reduces the availability of credit (especially to small and medium-sized companies that cannot access international credit markets) and increases banking-sector costs (because economies of scale cannot be fully exploited). A larger financial system would then result in lower costs and greater efficiency and hence lower interest rates and a greater availability of credit.

Second, a more stable economic environment would increase the attractiveness of Argentina as a recipient of foreign investment. Indeed, given dollarization it might be conjectured that particularly for U.S. investors the elimination of currency risk and the creation of a more stable economic environment would enhance investor interest in Argentina. Naturally, this would also lead to greater efficiency gains and improvements in management capabilities and systems and to greater technology transfer, and hence to greater growth.

Third, the presence of a more stable economic environment, the elimination of exchange rate risk, and the lowering of government default risk would also increase legal security for investments in Argentina.

Fourth, it is our view that these effects would also increase openness and foreign trade with their multifaceted benefits to the Argentine economy. Indeed, Frankel and Rose (2000) find that there is a very significant effect of a common currency on trade and that this has subsequent positive effects for growth.

Conclusion

In this chapter, we have attempted to give an account of the events, through the late 1990s, that prompted the then-Argentine government to consider a full dollarization of the economy subject to a monetary agreement with the United States. The emerging economy financial crises of the 1990s, and the contagion in international markets, highlighted the problem of less-than-perfect credibility of the currency-board regime and hence increased the cost of maintaining the option value of floating. Moreover, given the experience of those countries that had floated, the value of that option did not appear to be very high. Furthermore, estimates of the potential gain of eliminating currency risk, especially in terms of a reduction in country risk, appeared to be significant. This view was reinforced by the experience of the peripheral countries in Europe and the perceived convergence gains through the process leading up to EMU.

Nevertheless, although it might be argued that there were compelling economic arguments for a country such as Argentina to explore the dollarization proposal discussed in this paper, the successful implementation of this proposal requires a degree of political and social consensus that was clearly not present in Argentina at that time. This consensus is critical to the political processes required to implement such a project and to reap the rewards in terms of lower interest rates and higher growth.

It was not our objective in this paper to discuss more recent events in Argentina that have led to the current economic crisis, although it is interesting to note that the dollarization debate has recently resurfaced. In the current context, however, dollarization is seen more as an emergency measure than a positive step toward a deepening of the institutional ties across the region. Although the project may, depending on how the current crisis evolves, gain greater consensus as an emergency measure, it is not clear that all of the benefits to this project as outlined above remain available.

Notes

1. In this paper we do not discuss in detail the origins of Argentina's current (2001) economic crisis, but suffice to say that in our view it is not a simple case of exchange rate misalignment.

2. Hausmann et al. (1999) have argued convincingly this point.

3. Interest in dollarization can be found from Argentina to Canada; see Levy Yeyati and Sturzenegger (forthcoming) and Alesina and Barro (2000) for two interesting collections of papers, and Harris and Courchene (1999) specifically on Canada.

4. In this respect there are now more parallels with the dollarization debate in Ecuador, although we note that Argentina in 2001 remains a very different case. See De La Torre, García-Saltos, and Mascaró (2001) for an excellent review of the Ecuadorian case.

5. Previous versions of this paper served as the basis for informal discussions of the Argentine government with the U.S. treasury and the Federal Reserve while Pablo Guidotti was the Argentine treasury secretary and deputy minister of finance, and Andrew Powell was chief economist of the Argentine Central Bank.

6. The Convertibility Law was later modified in 2001 such that the peso will be fixed to a basket composed of the U.S. dollar (50 percent) and the euro (50 percent) beginning at the moment the euro–U.S. dollar exchange rate reaches 1 to 1.

7. However, the legal independence of the Central Bank did not prevent the removal of the Central Bank president by decree of the Argentine president. This is a vivid example of the difference between legal independence and actual independence as frequently noted in the literature on the topic.

8. A second financial crisis characterized by a sharp deposit outflow and credit contraction occurred in 2001.

9. The Central Bank was at that time more constrained than at present because 80 percent of the monetary base had to be backed by international reserves, excluding Argentine–U.S. dollar government bond holdings.

10. In the tequila crisis, the Argentine treasury had to wait for 150 days before being able to return to the market. In the Asian crisis it had to stay out of the capital market for 55 days, while after the Russian moratorium and after the Brazilian devaluation it suspended borrowing for 70 and 19 days, respectively.

11. Later, in 2000, with a new government in place that introduced a significant hike in taxes, the Argentine economy entered a new recession, which deepened in 2001.

12. Initial internal discussions on dollarization within the Argentine govern-

ment, and with the U.S. treasury and Federal Reserve, began in 1998. The first official public proposal by the Argentine government was, however, put forward in 1999 after the Brazilian devaluation.

13. Indeed, some have even suggested that without the market's response, qualification would not have been possible for several countries because the lower cost of borrowing made the difference in some cases to obtain a fiscal deficit of less than 3 percent of GDP.

14. Pedro Pou, the ex-president of the Central Bank of Argentina, has referred to the choice between issuing long term in dollars or short term in local currencies to reduce the costs of debt as the "devil's choice."

15. Frankel and Rose (2000) find very substantial trade effects for monetary unions.

16. Eichengreen (1997) argues that highly correlated stock prices in twenty-two industrialized countries represent evidence of highly correlated expectations of the effect of real shocks.

17. We do discuss below how such a sharing rule might be implemented.

18. Again, we discuss the implementation of such a liquidity facility below.

19. We use the phrase *real existence* because, even in dollarized countries such as Panama, Ecuador, and El Salvador, the national currency remains both as an accounting unit and in the form of coins.

20. Indeed, apart from the financial and political consequences of losing seigniorage revenue, it is the argument of heightening the credibility of the arrangements that is, in our view, the main attraction of dollarization with a monetary agreement versus simply unilateral dollarization.

21. In an interesting paper, Craine (2001) models a currency board's option value precisely in this way and the decision either to float or to dollarize (forever) as two ways of stopping in the context of an optimal stopping problem with stochastic disturbances. In this framework, the imperfect credibility of the currency board is also modeled in that there is an endogenous probability that the optimal policy would be to float, which then affects interest rates in the currency-board regime. He finds that as the size of real shocks rises, the option value of the currency board increases as does the potential benefit of floating; hence, the region where the optimal policy of stopping via a dollarization shrinks. Stopping via dollarization is optimal when the expected volatility of future real shocks is relatively small.

22. As in other dollarized countries, it might be efficient to keep the peso circulating for fractional units, in the form of coins.

23. In Hausmann and Powell (1999), initial conditions for dollarization are divided into (a) feasibility conditions, (b) conditions that ensure that dollarization is a "best option," and (c) conditions to ensure success. The authors argue that it is the third most stringent set of conditions that are the relevant ones and that broad social and political consensuses are required for this condition to be met.

24. Also, there is a significant quantity of dollar notes in Argentina. There are no Central Bank estimates of the dollar notes in circulation, although the Ministry of the Economy does employ an estimate in the balance of payments, and the estimate is over $20 billion. The U.S. authorities also have estimates based on dollar notes exported to Argentina. However, there is no hard information on

dollar bills reexported. We consider these estimates to be very high. If we take the ratio of dollar notes to peso notes held by banks, it is about 40.5 percent. This reflects roughly the ratio of sight deposits (checking and savings) in pesos to dollars (about 41.0 percent). The 41.0 percent figure implies an additional $5.8 billion in dollar notes currently in circulation, plus $892 million in dollar notes held by banks. This is likely to be an underestimate, but adding in estimates of the informal economy operating with dollar bills, it is difficult to obtain the estimates suggested above. This lower calculation would yield total notes (peso and dollar) in circulation or held by banks and then sum to just over $19 billion (about 7 percent of GDP).

25. Levy Yeyati and Sturzenegger (forthcoming) makes the assumption that the monetary base will grow at the same rate as long-term growth (4 percent in his base-case scenario). We view this as unrealistic in view of the dramatic decline in notes and coins in circulation in the last couple of years. We also consider his emphasis on a large nominal stock figure inappropriate. With the optimistic assumption of 4 percent GDP growth forever, it is surely more appropriate to compare the benefit of seigniorage in comparison to cumulative GDP.

26. This view of the seigniorage-sharing rule makes clear that there would have to be restrictions on Argentina's issuing a new currency (or if it did, it would be grounds to reduce or eliminate seigniorage payments from the United States). It is interesting to note that in the current context several Argentine provinces, most notably the province of Buenos Aires, has issued a type of bond, which—to the extent that this becomes a close money substitute—surely reduces the demand for pesos. The monetary agreement may have to restrict such actions on the part of Argentine provinces or adjust seigniorage sharing appropriately.

27. Banks' liquidity requirements in the Central Bank, the other part of the monetary base, were already dollarized shortly after the tequila crisis.

28. The bill was defeated in committee by a narrow majority. The then-Democrat executive voted largely against. However, amendments to the bill changed its nature severely, and, for example, included a clause that seigniorage would not be shared for the first ten years after official dollarization. A great deal of discretionary power for the U.S. secretary of the treasury was also built into the proposed legislation. It is not clear whether the bill was defeated because dissenters decided against the principle of seigniorage sharing or (more likely, in our view) because it was felt that this approach was not the right one or that the timing was inappropriate.

29. We are indebted to George McCandles for this suggestion.

30. See "Encouraging Official Dollarization in Emerging Markets," April 1999, Joint Economic Committee Staff Report (Office of the Chairman, Senator Connie Mack), U.S. Congress.

31. It is difficult to separate the eleven EMU countries in the trade statistics due to the importance of Rotterdam as a European (and not only as a Dutch or EMU-eleven) port.

32. The announcement of this policy led to a rise in Argentine risk spreads, bringing forward to some extent the cost in terms of a higher endogenous probability of future floating. The Argentine authorities also attempted to bring for-

ward the benefits by introducing a variable subsidy and tariff system for exports and imports as a function of the movement of the U.S. dollar–euro exchange rate.

33. Although we note that Portugal was arguably the country that entered the EMU with the other ten, there was uncertainty ex ante about whether its entry would be deemed to have complied with the Maastricht criteria.

34. It is to be noted that this proposal may not imply a significant departure from current practice, since the World Bank normally issues bonds denominated in some emerging market currencies as part of its financing policy.

References

Alesina, A., and R. Barro. 2000. Currency unions. NBER Working Paper no. 7927. Cambridge, Mass.: National Bureau of Economic Research.

Baliño, T., A. Bennet, and E. Borensztein. 1999. Monetary policy in dollarized economies. IMF Occasional Paper no. 171. Washington, D.C.: International Monetary Fund, March.

Berg, A., and E. Borensztein. 2000. The pros and cons of full dollarization. IMF Working Paper no. 00/50. Washington, D.C.: International Monetary Fund.

Calvo, G. 1999. On dollarization. University of Maryland, Center for International Economics. Mimeograph, April.

Calvo, G., and P. Guidotti. 1990. Indexation and maturity of government bonds: A simple model. In *Public debt management: Theory and history,* ed. R. Dornbusch and M. Draghi, 52–82. Cambridge: MIT Press.

Calvo, G., and C. Reinhart. 1999. Fear of floating: Theory and evidence. University of Maryland, Center for International Economics. Mimeograph.

Craine, R. 2001. Dollarization: An irreversible decision. Department of Economics, University of California, Berkeley. Mimeograph.

Currie, D. 1992. EMU: Institutional structure and economic performance. *Economic Journal* 102 (411): 248–64.

De La Torre, A., R. García-Saltos, and Y. Mascaró. 2001. Banking, currency, and debt meltdown: Ecuador crisis in the late 1990s. Washington, D.C.: World Bank. Mimeograph.

Eichengreen, B. 1997. One money for Europe? In *European monetary unification: Theory, practice, analysis,* ed. B. Eichengreen. Reprinted from *Economic Policy* (1992). Cambridge: MIT Press.

Escudé, G. J., M. E. Grubisic, and V. C. Sabban. 2000. The effect of risk aversion in the evaluation of the default risk reduction due to full dollarization: Comments on "The pros and cons of full dollarization" (technical note no. 7), by A. Berg and E. Borensztein. Buenos Aires: Central Bank of Argentina.

Frankel, F., and A. Rose. 2000. Estimating the effect of currency unions on trade and output. NBER Working Paper no. 7857. Cambridge, Mass.: National Bureau of Economic Research, August.

Giavazzi, F., and A. Giovannini. 1989. Monetary policy under managed exchange rates. *Economica* 56 (May): 199–213.

Guidotti, P. 1999. From floating exchange rates to full dollarization: What works for Latin America. In *IABD Annual Meetings Conference Proceedings*, 35–37. New York: Deutsche Bank Research.

———. 2000. On debt management and collective action clauses. In *Reforming the international monetary and financial system*, ed. P. Kenen and A. Swoboda, 265–76. Washington, D.C.: IMF.

Harris, R., and T. Courchene. 1999. Towards a North American common currency: An optimal currency area analysis. Mimeograph.

Hausmann, R., M. Gavin, C. Pages-Serra, and E. Stein. 1999. Financial turmoil and the choice of exchange rate regime. Inter-American Development Bank. Mimeograph.

Hausmann, R., and A. Powell. 1999. Dollarization: Issues of implementation. Paper presented at Inter-American Development Bank Conference on Dollarization. July, Panama.

Levy Yeyati, E., and F. Sturzenegger, eds. Forthcoming. *Dollarization*. Cambridge, Mass.: MIT Press.

Pou, P. 1999. Presentation to the national cabinet, Olivos, Provincia de Buenos Aires, Argentina, September 1.

Powell, A., and F. Sturzenegger. 2000. Dollarization: The link between devaluation and default risk. Universidad Torcuato Di Tella. Unpublished manuscript. Available at [http://www.utdt.edu].

Chapter Six

The Experience with a Floating Exchange Rate Regime: The Case of Mexico

Agustín Carstens and Guillermo Ortiz Martinez

Introduction

The unusual sequence of financial crises during the second half of the 1990s has spurred a great interest in trying to identify the potential causes of such disruptive events, giving way to a crusade to redefine the architecture of the international financial markets. According to many statesmen, analysts, market participants, and economists, one of the pillars of the new architecture should be the development of clear criteria to choose the appropriate exchange regime for each country.

This should not come as a surprise, because in all the financial crises of the last decade one of the common elements among them was the presence of an intermediate exchange rate regime—i.e., one that fell in between what Sebastian Edwards (2000) calls a *super-fix* (currency board or dollarization) and a floating exchange rate regime. This factor has invited very strong opinions against intermediate regimes. For example, the report of the Meltzer Commission (Meltzer 2000, 8) established in November 1998 by the U.S. Congress to recommend future U.S. policy toward international financial institutions, stated: "The [International Monetary Fund] IMF should use its policy consultations to recommend either firmly fixed exchange rates (currency board, dollarization) or fluctuating rates."

The empirical evidence shows that since the first "modern" financial crisis of the 1990s (Mexico's in 1994) an overwhelming majority of emerging economies have opted in favor of a floating exchange rate regime (in

Agustín Carstens is Mexico's undersecretary of finance. Guillermo Ortiz is governor of the Bank of Mexico. The views expressed here are those of the authors and do not necessarily reflect those of the Banco de México or the Ministry of Finance.

Asia, Thailand, Indonesia, Korea, and the Philippines, with—in the Middle East—Israel; in North and South America, Mexico, Colombia, Brazil, and Chile; and in Europe, Russia, Poland, and Hungary). In the case of super-fixes, in addition to Hong Kong and Panama (which have been under some form of super-fix for more than a decade), Argentina in early 1991 and Ecuador in January 2000 have been the only two major emerging economies that have decided to go in that direction. The overwhelming dominance of floating exchange rates among the emerging economies that during the last decade decided to (or were forced to) switch regimes could be a result of one of two factors: that at a particular point in time, it might not be optimal for a given country to adopt a super-fix exchange rate regime; or that, even if a given country wished to adopt a super-fix regime, it might not meet all the essential preconditions to go ahead in a credible fashion. Precisely one of the objectives of this paper is to address this set of issues for the case of Mexico.

After more than four years with a floating exchange rate regime, Mexico probably is the only country in Latin America—and for that matter, among the emerging markets—that has maintained such a regime for a relatively long period of time, not merely as the single feasible alternative after the 1994 crisis, but, as time has passed, as the preferred one.

The paper is organized as follows: in the next section, we briefly review Mexico's problematic transition to the floating exchange rate regime during 1994–95; we then go on, in the third section, to describe how monetary and exchange rate policy have been conducted under this regime. In the fourth section we take a close look at the behavior of inflation, exchange rates, and other financial and real variables during the float, concluding that in the case of Mexico such a regime has performed better than conventional wisdom would have led us to believe; and in the fifth we address squarely the issue of whether Mexico should and could adopt a super-fix regime. Finally, we present some concluding remarks.

1994–95: A Forced Transition to a Floating Exchange Rate Regime

The frailties accumulated during the early 1990s—the years of large capital inflows and financial liberalization—plus the negative external and domestic shocks faced by the Mexican economy during 1994, gave way to the balance-of-payments and financial crisis of December 1994, when, under severe pressure in the foreign exchange market, the central bank was no longer able to defend the predetermined parity and the authorities decided to let the peso float.[1]

As the weeks went by, it became clear that the crisis had four conceptually different aspects. The first was that the overspending in the economy had generated a current account deficit of significant proportions. This deficit was being financed by short-run capital inflows, which turned out to be unstable. The second aspect was precisely the eruption of the equivalent of a run on Mexican external liabilities, both public and private. Although debt and budget indicators highlighted the solvency of the Mexican government, the short maturity of the stock of government debt (in particular, of the dollar-indexed *tesobonos*) exposed the country to a financial panic. Even when investors recognized Mexico's solvency, they realized that if everyone else stopped the rollover of Mexican debt (especially the one that was dollar denominated or dollar indexed), the country would be unable to fulfill its coming financial obligations. Thus, the illiquidity of the Mexican government generated a run on its debt. The third aspect was the unfolding of a banking crisis, which required immediate attention, both to avoid a run on the banks (including one by their foreign creditors) and to bring consistency to the macroframework. Finally, the monetary authorities had lost all credibility and were urged to establish a new, reliable nominal anchor for the economy.

As the nature of the crisis became clear, the policy reaction evolved from a package designed primarily to adjust the overspending in the economy to one that, in addition to taking such an issue into consideration, generated enough confidence to stop the panic and restore confidence in Mexican assets, both external and internal. To achieve this, Mexico had to convince the markets of the feasibility of its fully complying with all its future financial obligations without relying on inflationary finance, but by applying a consistent set of policies.

In order to overcome these challenges, several measures were implemented in early 1995:

1. To contain the inflationary effects of the devaluation, a tight monetary policy was adopted. To make this policy credible, it became essential to spell out very clearly that this policy was going to be oriented exclusively toward stabilizing the nominal variables of the economy, consistent with Banco de México's autonomy. The banking-sector problems were going to be dealt with by specific programs (to be explained later), whose costs eventually were going to be absorbed through fiscal adjustments spread over many years. Therefore, monetary policy had only one objective—to reduce inflation—a condition that was essential under a floating exchange rate regime because, under such an arrangement, the policy should be the nominal anchor of the economy. To demon-

strate the resolve of the monetary authorities in preserving this separation, domestic interest rates were completely freed, a factor that, together with other actions, allowed the interest rates to rise from 16 percent in December 1994 to 86 percent in March 1995 (see figure 6.1).

2. In order to accomplish an orderly adjustment of the current account, fiscal policy was tightened considerably as the primary balance went from a surplus of 2.1 percent of gross domestic product [GDP] in 1994 to a surplus of 4.7 percent of GDP in 1995, a year in which GDP contracted by more than 6 percent. The fiscal effort was also necessary to begin absorbing the costs of the banking-sector restructuring program. Tight monetary and fiscal policies, together with the expenditure-switching effects caused by the devaluation, were essential to stabilize the currency and to achieve the current account correction in a relatively orderly fashion (see figure 6.2).

3. To honor the financial commitments of the country, and more important, to induce creditors to roll over their maturing loans to Mexico, the government negotiated and obtained a $52 billion emergency support

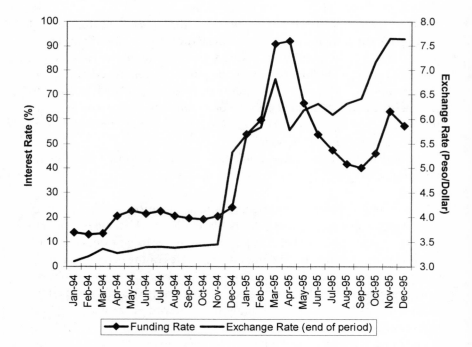

Fig. 6.1   Interest Rate and Exchange Rate (1994–95)

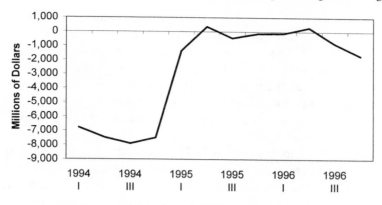

Fig. 6.2   Current Account (1994–96; $ millions)

package from the international financial community, with the U.S. government (i.e., the Exchange Stabilization Fund) and the IMF as the main suppliers of assistance.

4. To deal with the banking-sector problem, a comprehensive strategy was put in place. The frailties accumulated by the domestic financial system, the overindebtedness of firms and households, and the damaging effects of the crisis seriously threatened the health of the Mexican financial system. To preserve its integrity, the authorities implemented a series of programs, with the following objectives in mind:

a. To prevent a systemic run on the banking system;[2]

b. To combat moral hazard and minimize distortions;

c. To minimize the cost of the banking-sector restructuring, and consider it a fiscal issue;

d. To reduce as much as possible the need for the central bank to act as the lender of last resort; and

e. To strengthen financial-sector regulation and supervision.

It should be highlighted that the fiscal authority, by recognizing the fiscal costs of the banking-sector restructuring, allowed for monetary policy to pursue its primary goal of price stability. Thus, at an early stage it was made clear that monetary policy would not face the dilemma of trying to comply with conflicting objectives and that it would concentrate on lowering inflation, becoming the required nominal anchor under the floating exchange rate regime.

Low international reserves, mounting fiscal pressures, the weakness of the banking system, and the uncertainty prevailing in financial markets after the collapse of the currency made the discussion of alternative exchange rate regimes irrelevant.[3] The only credible option was to float. Hence, at that time, the most relevant issues were how to implement the necessary institutional and operational innovations on the monetary side to complement the floating exchange rate regime and to reestablish the credibility of Banco de México.

Following the implementation of the enhanced strategy in early April, financial markets recognized the soundness of the measures taken and the commitment of the Mexican government to pay all of its maturing debt. The peso became more stable, and after overshooting to 7.5 pesos per dollar in March (at the time of the initial devaluation in December 1994 the foreign exchange rate was 3.5 pesos per dollar), in May it went back to 6.0 pesos per dollar, regaining some of the ground lost during the weeks of uncertainty. Interest rates began to fall and the stock market returned to its precrisis level. The risk of a government default disappeared as *tesobonos* outstanding were being paid off in dollars and the government demonstrated that it had sufficient resources to accomplish this task in the months to come. The Mexican government, as well as some private banks, regained access to international capital markets soon after the announcement of the program. Because of this, the Mexican authorities used only half of the emergency support provided by the U.S. government, and these loans were repaid in full by January 1997, three years before schedule.

Economic activity recovered rapidly once the comprehensive program was in place, taking advantage of the broad restructuring that the economy had gone through in the previous ten years, which allowed for accelerated growth in exports. Thus GDP grew 5.2 percent on average for the period 1996–99, while consumption and investment also recovered. At the same time, inflation dropped rapidly from 51.7 percent in 1995 to 12.3 percent in 1999.

The conclusion of this section is that even though Mexico had no experience under a floating exchange rate regime, this aspect was not an impediment to achieving stability quickly after the eruption of the crisis in 1994–95, given that a consistent policy framework was adopted at an early stage and that it was maintained in subsequent years.

Monetary and Exchange Rate Policy Since 1995

As a consequence of the devaluation of the peso and the return to a high-inflation environment in 1995, the credibility of Banco de México was seriously damaged. The criticisms concentrated mainly on its supposed lack of ability to tighten monetary policy before, during, and immediately after the crisis. In the aftermath of the crisis it was urgent to correct this deficiency, because after Banco de México dropped the exchange rate as the nominal anchor of the economy and turned to a floating exchange rate regime, monetary policy had to fill the vacuum and become the nominal anchor. Therefore, to understand the success that the Mexican peso float has had since its inception, it is essential to analyze the accompanying and evolving monetary policies.

In theory, under a floating exchange rate regime the central bank acquires control over the monetary base because it does not have to add or subtract liquidity derived from compulsory interventions in the foreign exchange market. By acting directly on the monetary base, the central bank supposedly would be able to influence interest rates and the exchange rate, and through these, the general price level. Consequently, as the central bank reduces inflation by these means, the management of monetary aggregates becomes the anchor for the evolution of the general price level. These were the types of argument that prompted the Mexican authorities to consider quantitative targets on monetary aggregates in early 1995 when designing its monetary program for the year. Specifically, Banco de México established as an intermediate target a ceiling on the growth of the monetary base for the year.

Regrettably, it soon became obvious that this very simple, transparent, and intuitive monetary program was not enough to stabilize inflationary expectations, the exchange rate, and the subsequent evolution of inflation. The rule-based monetary policy failed to perform as expected due to a collection of factors:

1. In a crisis scenario, the velocity of money is very unstable, rendering the relationship between the monetary base and inflation unstable as well;

2. It was not possible for the quantitative target on the monetary base to prevent sudden large exchange rate depreciations (resulting from external shocks or shifts in expectations), and for these to substantially affect inflationary expectations and eventually the price level; and

3. The central bank had (and has) hardly any control over the monetary base in the short run. The evolution of this aggregate is driven by the demand for bills and coins in circulation (given the zero reserve requirement policy in Mexico), which has a very low interest rate elasticity in the short term. In addition, Mexican commercial banks do not hold any excess reserves in the central bank, which further prevents any short-term control over the monetary base.

Therefore, in early 1995 events hinted that a key element was missing in Mexico's monetary framework. At that time, market participants were expecting a strong statement by the monetary authorities that would make credible their stated intentions about reducing inflation, a statement that the monetary-base objectives and the subsequent behavior of such aggregate failed to make. In particular, they were expecting considerable hikes in interest rates to counteract the inflationary shocks that were occurring. Thus, in late March, the central bank temporarily increased the overnight funding rate[4] (by establishing interest rate floors in its open market operations) by up to 100 percent. This discretionary monetary policy action, together with the agreement with the IMF on a strong adjustment program and the availability of resources coming from the Exchange Stabilization Fund (ESF), managed to brake the sharp tendency toward depreciation that the peso showed during the first quarter of the year, to stabilize inflationary expectations and, very soon afterward, to reduce the monthly rates of inflation. By May 1995 the peso began to appreciate and inflationary expectations to fall, which led to a reduction in nominal and real interest rates. This, in turn, mitigated the collapse of economic activity and prevented a further deterioration of the banking system.

The experience just described led the Mexican authorities during the first half of 1995 to modify its monetary policy: from one based solely on quantitative targets on monetary aggregates, to another for which both the rules (on the behavior of the monetary base) and discretion (by influencing the level of interest rates) were incorporated. Such discretion had to be bounded by an ultimate objective: the achievement of the annual inflation objective, and in the medium and long term, the gradual but sustainable abatement of inflation. At this stage, the process of a gradual adoption of an inflation-targeting scheme in Mexico began.

To be able to implement in a transparent fashion the discretionary monetary policy actions, and also to tackle the criticism that Banco de México was too slow and indecisive to adjust interest rates, the central bank decided to adopt a new instrument through which it would signal its desire to have higher interest rates, leaving to the market the determination of the exact variation of them (at least in a first instance). This mechanism gravitates around the zero average reserve requirement[5] for commercial banks that was introduced at that time, and that is still in operation as the cornerstone of Mexico's monetary framework.

Under such a mechanism, the central bank determines the sum of credit to be auctioned each day (at a freely determined interest rate) so that the overall net daily average balance of all current accounts held by banks at the Banco de México—accumulated during the specific accounting period—may close the day at a predetermined amount. If the targeted amount is negative, the central bank puts the banking system in "short" (or *corto* in Spanish), in which case at least one credit institution will have to pay a penalty interest rate of twice the prevailing CETES rate.

When the system is put in short, the central bank exerts upward pressure on interest rates, which can be quite significant. The main reason the short is effective in inducing hikes in interest rates is that, under a floating exchange rate regime, the commercial banks do not have means to create balances in their accounts with the central bank (they cannot credit their balances by selling foreign exchange to the central bank, as they can do under a predetermined exchange rate regime). Therefore the short imposes an unavoidable cost to the banking system. Under such circumstances, the rational response by the banks is to allow interest rates to increase to the level they believe is the target of Banco de México, with the smallest possible short. This is precisely what usually happens when a *corto* is applied or modified.

Banco de México has either adopted or increased the *corto* whenever it detected unforeseen inflationary pressures that could threaten the inflation objective. Usually the market is aware of the nature of the inflationary pressures, particularly when they are related to the behavior of the exchange rate. In those cases, the interest rate response to the *corto* basically corresponds to the one that is necessary to stabilize the exchange rate (and even appreciate it, in case of overshooting). This is the typical policy response that it is required in any country pursuing some sort of inflation objective under a floating exchange rate regime.

Since emerging economies tend to have open capital accounts and their external trade corresponds to a large share of GDP, the pass-through of exchange rate depreciation to inflation tends to be high and quick. Therefore, these economies cannot afford a benign neglect of exchange rate developments if inflation is to be brought under control. As Eyzaguirre (1999) eloquently puts it, "When faced with an external financial shock, floaters will need to renew their credentials as inflation fighters. This will amount to limiting the downward pressure on the currency through hikes in interest rates." This is precisely what Banco de México has been doing by means of the *corto*, which implies that the use of this instrument has become the real nominal anchor of the economy.[6]

Since 1996, all the monetary programs that Banco de México has launched have been based on the elements just outlined. To be more precise, they have included three explicit main elements:

1. *A yearly annual inflation objective.* Established jointly by the federal government and Banco de México, the inflation objective is perceived as the result of a concerted effort to coordinate fiscal and monetary policies. It also helps in the determination of the minimum wage, which by itself reinforces the credibility of the inflation objective.

2. *Rules defined on the behavior of monetary base, together with quantitative commitments on the accumulation on net international reserves and the variation of net domestic credit.* The purpose of these rules and quantitative commitments is to assure the market that Banco de México will not create the most basic source of inflation: excess supply of primary money. This, if it were to occur, would immediately raise the public's inflationary expectations, which would result, in turn, in exchange rate depreciation, interest rate increases, and higher nominal wages and prices of goods and services. This is why the central bank has established the following basic operational rule that ensures the central bank will not create a monetary-base surplus: Banco de México will adjust, on a daily basis, the supply of primary money to match the demand for base money.

3. The possibility for the central bank to adjust on a discretionary (but transparent) basis its stance on monetary policy, in case unexpected circumstances make it advisable. As has already been described, this is done by means of the corto.

The element of the monetary programs described under item 2, aimed at preventing Banco de México from creating any excess supply of the monetary base, is not a full guarantee of attaining the desired abatement of inflation. This happens when exogenous shocks to the price level induce an increase in the demand for money, which, given the basic operational rule, Banco de México could end up validating. Such exogenous shocks could come in the form of an excessive depreciation of the domestic currency, contractual wage settlements above the sum of the inflationary target plus productivity increases, or unexpected adjustments to public prices with the purpose of keeping public finances under control.

Any of these events could cause interest rates to rise, tending to mitigate undesirable inflationary pressures. Nevertheless, the case may be that the automatic adjustment of interest rates might not suffice to maintain inflation's behavior in line with the set objective. Under such circumstances, Banco de México tends to restrict even more the stance of monetary policy by means of the *corto*.

To be more precise, Banco de México adopts or increases the *corto* whenever

1. Exogenous shocks induce future inflationary pressures inconsistent with the attainment of the inflationary target;

2. It is deemed necessary to restore order in exchange and money markets; and

3. Inflationary expectations are deemed out of line with respect to the original target.

From the foregoing it follows that the main challenge Banco de México faces when deciding its monetary policy is to determine the degree to which the institution is able to counteract the inflationary shocks that eventually show up.

To the extent that the monetary-policy response to inflationary shocks is extremely strong, entrepreneurs will find it more difficult to pass on to final prices the higher costs resulting from shocks such as sudden exchange rate depreciations, rises in public goods and services prices, or wage pressures. Profit margins would decrease, along with the possibility of domestic producers' losing international competitiveness. All these elements could lead to lower investment and a contraction in the demand for labor, especially if nominal wages are inflexible downward. Workers losing their jobs, and the unemployed who do not find jobs, would suffer the most from this situation. Therefore, a very restrictive monetary policy can have a strong negative impact on economic activity, employment, and investment. At the same time, such a policy response could have undesirable effects on the health of the banking system, especially if it is weak. These two sets of problems, among others, could even make the gains in the reduction in inflation unsustainable. These types of considerations have induced Banco de México to lean in favor of a gradual but sustainable path of disinflation, a criterion that translates, in most of the cases, into decisions to partially counteract the inflationary shocks. This can be considered a fourth (although not an explicit) element of Banco de México's monetary program.

Since 1994, the monetary authorities have allowed the exchange rate to float as freely as possible. Certainly at different points in time there has been the need for the authorities to intervene in the foreign exchange market. In all of these cases, however, such interventions have been completely transparent to the market, and not directed toward defending particular levels of the exchange rate—thus preserving the main characteristics of a flexible exchange rate regime.

In the aftermath of the crisis, Mexico faced the need to reestablish its international reserves to a suitable level in order to strengthen its external financial position. This would allow the country to enjoy access to international financial markets under more favorable conditions with regard to the cost and maturity of foreign financing. Thus, in July 1996, given the stability that the exchange rate exhibited during the first part of the year and that capital was flowing back to Mexico, the Exchange Commission, which was integrated by officials from the Ministry of Finance and Banco de México and is responsible for determining Mexico's exchange rate policy, considered that foreign reserves at the central bank could be increased without causing disruptions in the foreign exchange market. The commission emphasized that this accumulation had to be done with no effect on the behavior of the floating exchange rate and with no signal of any type sent to the market that could be interpreted as a desired level for the exchange rate. In addition, it was important that the way in which the accumulation of reserves took place would encourage purchases of dollars mostly when there was an excess supply of foreign currency, and discourage those purchases when there was a clear excess demand.

The scheme that was adopted to reach these objectives, still in operation, works as follows:

1. On the last business day of each month, Banco de México auctions rights to sell dollars to the central bank (put options) among credit institutions. These rights can be partially or completely exercised within the month following the respective auction.

2. Holders of these rights can sell dollars to Banco de México at the interbank exchange rate published for the previous business day, if the exchange rate is not higher than the average exchange rate for the twenty business days previous to the date on which these rights are exercised.

3. The expansion of the monetary base caused by Banco de México is completely sterilized. Therefore, the evolution of the supply of primary money is in no way affected by the aforementioned operations.

The mechanism just described went into operation in August 1996 and has accomplished its primary goal of accumulating international reserves without interfering with the functioning of the free float. From table 6.1, the high percentage of exercised options with respect to the total amount auctioned stands out (82.6 percent). An interesting aspect of the options

Table 6.1   Result of the Auction of Options

Date of Auction	Amount Auctioned	Amount Exercised	Percentage Exercised	Date of Auction	Amount Auctioned	Amount Exercised	Percentage Exercised
August 7, 1996	130	130	100.0	March 31, 1998	250	250	100.0
August 30, 1996	200	200	100.0	April 6, 1998	250	210	84.0
September 30, 1996	200	179	89.5	April 30, 1998	250	149	59.6
October 30, 1996	200	200	100.0	July 14, 1998	250	250	100.0
November 29, 1996	200	200	100.0	July 31, 1998	250	0	0.0
December 30, 1996	300	300	100.0	August 31, 1998	250	20	8.0
January 31, 1997	300	300	100.0	September 30, 1998		no auction	
February 21, 1997	300	148	49.3	October 31, 1998		no auction	
February 28, 1997	300	120	40.0	December 30, 1998	250	215	86.0
March 31, 1997	300	300	100.0	January 29, 1999	250	250	100.0
April 15, 1997	300	263	87.7	February 26, 1999	250	220	88.0
April 30, 1997	300	300	100.0	March 31, 1999	250	250	100.0
May 30, 1997	300	20	6.7	April 30, 1999	250	205	82.0
June 30, 1997	300	300	100.0	May 31, 1999	250	250	100.0
July 9, 1997	300	300	100.0	June 30, 1999	250	180	72.0
July 31, 1997	500	460	92.0	July 30, 1999	250	200	80.0
August 29, 1997	500	500	100.0	August 31, 1999	250	200	80.0
September 30, 1997	400	375	93.8	September 30, 1999	250	145	58.0
November 28, 1997	250	250	100.0	October 29, 1999	250	0	0.0
December 15, 1997	250	250	100.0	November 30, 1999	250	250	100.0
December 30, 1997	250	49	19.6	December 29, 1999	250	30	12.0
January 30, 1998	250	0	0.0				
February 27, 1998	250	250	100.0	Total	6,830	5,644	82.6

SOURCE: Banco de México.

mechanism is that it allows the purchase of dollars even if for a relatively long period of time the exchange rate does not show a marked tendency toward depreciation. During 1999, for example, the peso exchange rate did not show a clear trend (see figure 6.3), but nevertheless 80 percent of the auctioned amount was exercised. This indicates that a moderate amount of volatility is enough for the options to be in the money, a fact that is not surprising given that, as volatility of the price of the underlying asset increases, the option written on such price typically increases in value.

Both theory (see Werner and Milo 1998; Werner 1997) and practice have shown that the accumulation of reserves through this mechanism has had no noticeable effect on the volatility[7] and trend driving the exchange rate process. Therefore, one can assume that its establishment did not send any type of signal regarding the preferences of the central bank toward exchange rate changes or volatility.

On several occasions after the adoption of the floating exchange rate regime, liquidity in the foreign exchange market almost dried up when the domestic currency experienced sharp depreciations. Under such circumstances, small changes in the demand for foreign currency led to disproportionate depreciations of the peso. These conditions could lead to devaluatory spirals that could seriously affect inflation and interest rates. In order to moderate these extreme situations, a contingent dollar-sales scheme operated by the central bank was introduced in February 1997. According to this scheme, every day Banco de México calls the commercial banks to an auction of $200 million with a minimum price that is 2 percent above the preceding day's exchange rate. Therefore this scheme is not intended to defend specific levels for the exchange rate, but only to moderate exchange rate volatility by reestablishing a minimum level of liquidity at stressful times in the foreign exchange market.

As a result of the international market volatility generated by the Asian, Russian, and Brazilian crises, this mechanism has been activated on several occasions, amounting to total sales of $1,495 million since early 1997 (most of these sales happened in 1998). However, even during 1998—a year of huge pressure in Mexico's foreign exchange market— Banco de México accumulated international reserves, which proves that international reserves no longer play the role of shock absorber as they did under the predetermined regimes. However, given that Banco de México's contingent dollar-sale mechanism is transparent, it has fostered greater stability and order in the currency exchange market without having compromised an excessive amount of international reserves during these periods, thus proving to be a suitable mechanism to reduce the volatility in the foreign exchange market.

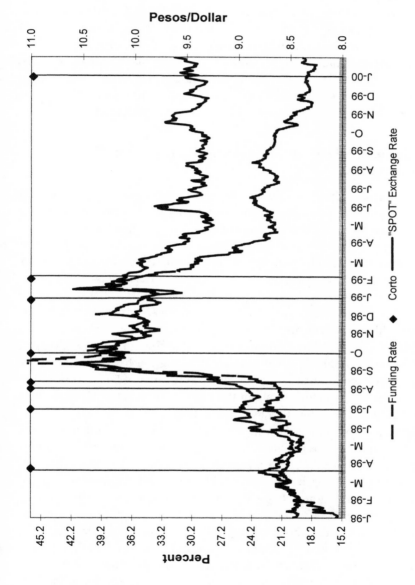

Fig. 6.3 Funding Rate, Exchange Rate, and *Cortos*

An important element that has contributed to isolating the foreign exchange market from significant shocks is that Banco de México has been acting as the counterpart of the government in all its foreign exchange transactions, settling all of them at the market-determined daily fixed exchange rate. In this way, the international reserves act as an absorber to external shocks affecting the federal government's balance of payments, coming mostly from oil price fluctuations and external interest rate variations. In addition, given that the government typically runs a surplus in foreign currency, this practice has been helpful in supporting the explicit policy to increase Mexico's international reserves described above.

Mexico under the Floating Exchange Rate Regime: So Far so Good

After more than five years under a floating exchange rate regime, Mexico is one of the few developing countries where the performance of such a regime can be seriously evaluated. Before we continue along this line, however, it is important to put the Mexican experience in perspective. The adoption of the flexible exchange rate regime in Mexico was not the result of a preconceived plan. The collapse of the peso predetermined exchange rate arrangement was surprising, even though the authorities were aware that it had been under attack for a while. As was pointed out previously, the transition was by no means smooth, particularly during the early stages. The level of uncertainty in the country at that time in both the political and economic arenas was substantial, affecting the behavior of the exchange rate and interest rates. Therefore, it would not be appropriate to reach sweeping conclusions about the performance of the Mexican peso float based on the events that took place during 1995.

Subsequently, in the following years, the consistency of the macroeconomic framework was enhanced, and the positive results obtained in different areas reduced overall uncertainty. This has allowed the floating regime to operate in a relatively stable environment, making a more meaningful evaluation of it feasible. Nevertheless, even though substantial progress has been made in creating and making operational the necessary institutions for a float to work optimally (like in Canada, Australia, or New Zealand), many of them are new and therefore less than totally credible. A point in case would be the credibility of the autonomous central bank. Gradually it has been increasing from very low levels in 1995, but there is still room for improvement.[8] This less-than-optimal credibility of institutions is reflected in the behavior of the exchange rate, in particular in its potential volatility in critical points in time. Having made these provisos, we can now move ahead in evaluating the Mexican experience with a float since late 1994.

As was explained earlier, since 1995 Banco de México's monetary policy has been the nominal anchor of the economy, having as an objective the achievement of a gradual but sustainable abatement of inflation, accompanied by a decent rate of economic growth. This does not mean that economic growth is the overriding objective of monetary policy, but certainly that Banco de México is willing to slow down the short-term abatement of inflation to preserve the growth of the economy. As seen in figure 6.4, this objective of economic policy has been achieved since 1996: The inflation rate fell from 51.7 percent in 1995 to 12.3 percent in 1999, whereas GDP grew at an average annual rate of 5.2 percent in the period 1996–99. The declining trend in inflation has been maintained almost constantly, with a brief interruption in late 1998 at the time of extreme volatility in the international financial markets (more about this event later).

Traditionally, economists have expressed serious concerns about the prospect that a small open economy (or, for that matter, a developing or emerging economy) may adopt a floating exchange regime. Edwards (2000) usefully summarized these concerns as follows:[9]

1. Since emerging countries tend to export commodities or light manufactures, a floating exchange rate would be excessively volatile;

2. Emerging countries do not have the institutional requirements for undertaking effective monetary policy under purely floating exchange rates, being unable to apply the type of feedback rule required for implementing an effective inflation-targeting system;

3. Some authors[10] have argued that in a world with high capital mobility, incomplete information, fads, rumors, and dollar-denominated liabilities, the monetary authorities would be severely affected by a "fear of floating." This is because significant exchange rate movements—in particular, large depreciations—would tend to have negative effects on inflation, the corporate debt, and the banking system. In reality, according to their story, developing countries would be "closet peggers," making every effort through interest rate manipulations to avoid large exchange rate fluctuations.

Note that there seems to be an inconsistency between the last two concerns. In the second, it is hinted that the monetary authorities lack the savvy to influence interest rates to achieve an inflation objective—or

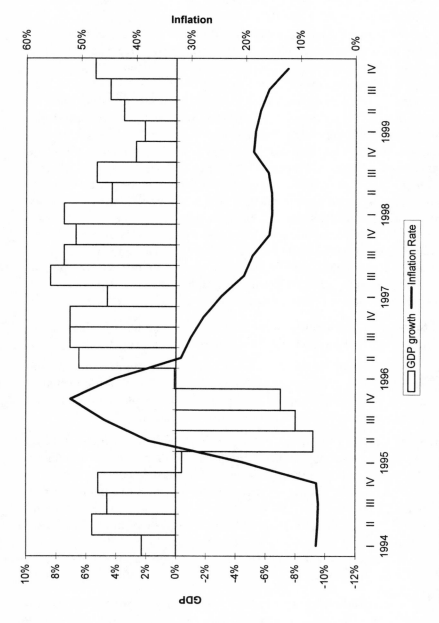

Fig. 6.4 GDP Growth and Inflation

putting it more broadly, for monetary policy to effectively become the nominal anchor of the economy. In the third concern it is implied that authorities have the ability to manipulate interest rates to such an extent that the exchange rate will remain basically stable, becoming the nominal anchor of the economy.

In what follows we will address these concerns for the particular case of Mexico.

Foreign Exchange Volatility and Exchange Rate Risk

Overall, the volatility experienced by the Mexican peso–U.S. dollar exchange rate during its float, once the macroeconomic and financial crises were contained in 1995, has been similar to that experienced by other currencies with floating exchange rate regimes. Since 1996, the implementation of consistent fiscal, monetary, and exchange rate policies with the adoption of programs to restructure the financial system and the accumulation of international reserves by Banco de México reestablished confidence in the macroframework; as a result we have seen usually orderly behavior of the peso (see table 6.2).

The existence of efficient foreign currency derivatives markets in Mexican pesos has been of great use in diminishing the volatility of the exchange rate. According to the sales or purchases carried out in this market, both importers and exporters and, in general, creditors and debtors of foreign currency are able to eliminate or substantially reduce the exchange rate risks they face and thus alleviate pressures on the spot market. Futures, forwards, and options markets for the peso are quite developed and liquid, at least for the shorter maturities.

Peso futures contracts began trading on the Chicago Mercantile Exchange (CME) in April 1995, having immediate success due to the absence of other hedging instruments. During the first months of trading, the initial margin requirements were very high (close to 20 percent of the contract value) due to the volatility of the peso and to the poor credit quality of some of the participants (particularly Mexican banks). However, during the following years the volatility of the peso exchange rate declined and the credit quality of participants markedly improved, giving place to a significant reduction of the margin (to less than 5 percent of the contract value, more in line with other contracts).

In addition, forward contracts are traded out to two years, with very good liquidity throughout the curve. As a matter of fact, the market is at the stage of evolving further into three-year contracts, given the recent

Table 6.2 Exchange Rate Volatility of Some Countries vis-à-vis the U.S. Dollar

	Annualized Volatility (%)									
	1995-I	1995-II	1996-I	1996-II	1997-I	1997-II	1998-I	1998-II	1999-I	1999-II
Mexico	48.56	17.60	5.99	5.31	4.92	10.69	6.68	10.95	9.92	7.05
New Zealand	6.67	5.35	5.56	6.01	5.88	8.61	12.45	14.95	9.54	10.08
Australia	8.86	7.87	6.10	6.70	7.65	10.29	11.91	14.93	12.09	11.92
Finland	12.85	9.13	7.43	7.28	10.04	9.51	8.31	9.17	8.85	9.99
Sweden	12.70	9.91	8.02	7.28	10.26	10.58	9.57	12.59	8.73	9.22
Canada	5.13	5.92	3.64	3.33	5.46	4.24	4.32	6.95	5.72	5.24
Italy	13.97	7.22	5.97	5.73	8.95	9.15	7.82	9.29	8.86	9.99
South Africa	5.64	2.34	13.86	7.20	5.25	4.34	5.35	23.07	12.01	5.66
United Kingdom	10.45	7.41	5.60	6.30	8.13	8.03	7.11	7.33	6.86	7.30
Switzerland	16.67	12.13	7.77	8.84	11.70	9.81	8.70	10.91	9.63	10.88
Japan	14.12	14.04	8.14	7.09	12.56	12.29	12.56	20.08	13.60	12.53
Germany	13.87	10.89	6.28	6.87	9.79	9.76	8.14	9.15	8.87	9.96

SOURCE: Banco de México.

NOTE: The annualized volatility is defined as the annualized standard deviation of the daily fluctuations of the exchange rate placement of three-year CETES by the federal government. Bid-ask spreads are quite competitive (0.1–0.2 percent). As of December 1999, the daily turnover was estimated by Banco de México at approximately $700 million and an open interest of nearly $25 billion. The pricing tends to be quite efficient, given that domestic yields implied by forward prices tend to be similar to CETES yields.

Over-the-counter options are also traded for the Mexican peso. The options market is typically used by foreign participants to help tailor their exposure to exchange rate risk and interest rate volatility. Although this market is also deep, with trading volume close to $200 million per day and liquidity out to one year, most of the market is traded offshore.

With respect to the exposure to exchange rate risk, the government has reduced its own exposure substantially, given that it no longer has internal debt indexed to the dollar and its external debt service is relatively well hedged with its foreign currency income. The large corporate sector does not have significant exposure, given that most of the firms that have access to credit in foreign currency are exporters, as can be seen in table 6.3.

Finally, it is worth noting that the commercial banks are subject to a very stringent regulation related to their open position in foreign exchange (15 percent of their capital) and the amount of indebtedness in foreign currency with a maturity of less than one year that they are allowed to maintain. Banco de México has imposed on commercial banks a foreign currency liquidity requirement. Mexican banks are obliged to hold high-quality sight deposits or other liquid assets denominated in foreign currency to match liabilities with maturity of less than sixty days.

Table 6.3   Mexico's Corporate Foreign Debt

Indicators	Exporting Firms			Nonexporting Firms
	High	Medium	Low	
Total foreign currency liabilities ($ millions)	19,689	9,429	5,241	2,037
Percent of total	(54.0)	(27.0)	(12.0)	(7.0)
Sales abroad/total sales	42.0	17.9	4.7	0.0
Total foreign currency liabilities/ total liabilities	75.0	60.9	43.0	28.8
Sales abroad/foreign currency liabilities	72.1	34.4	17.5	0.0

SOURCE: Bolsa Mexicana de Valores.

Currently, Mexican banks hold $7.9 billion in liquid assets, $4.2 billion in other liquid instruments, and $1 billion in committed credit lines.

Interest Rate Volatility

Although it has been argued that by letting the exchange rate float a country has an additional adjustment variable to confront external shocks and therefore the volatility of interest rates should come down, this is not necessarily true. The adoption of a flexible exchange rate regime precludes the use of its international reserves as an adjustment variable to absorb transitory external shocks. Thus, we should think that when moving from a fixed to a floating regime a country changes its adjustment variables from international reserves and interest rates to the nominal exchange rate and interest rates. Therefore it is not obvious that interest rate volatility should decline when a country adopts a floating exchange rate regime.

To get a feel for the effects of the different exchange rate regimes on interest rate volatility in Mexico,[11] we compare the behavior of interest rates in the 1996–99 period with that observed during 1989–92 (see figure 6.5). In both periods, a similar process of disinflation was underway, but during the

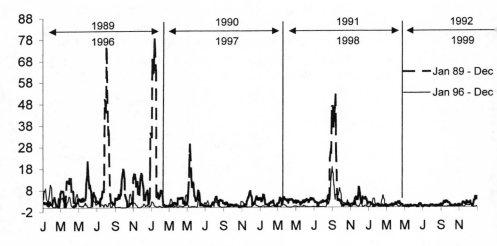

Fig. 6.5   Funding-Rate Volatility
NOTES:
Ten-day moving variance. Last figure: 31 December 1999.
SOURCE:
Banco de México (1999)

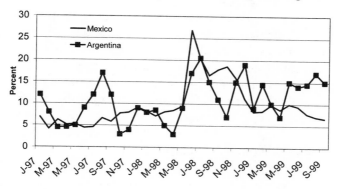

Fig. 6.6   Real Interest Rates for Mexico and Argentina
NOTES:
Figures for Mexico based upon the twenty-eight day CETES rate and inflation expectations for the next twelve months. Figures for Argentina based upon the thirty-day Bank of Argentina Interbank Offering Rate and observed inflation.
SOURCES:
Banco de México and Bloomberg.

more recent period we have had a floating exchange rate regime whereas in the 1988–92 period we had a predetermined exchange rate system.

It is clear that in the current stabilization effort under a floating exchange rate, interest rates have been usually less volatile than they were during the years of the *pacto de solidaridad* (1989–92), the period for which we can safely assume that the predetermined exchange rate regime was credible. If we consider the variation coefficient of nominal interest rates in the period of predetermined exchange rate from 1988 to 1994, and in the most recent one under floating, the former (1.6) is larger than the latter (1.1).

Another comparison that could be enlightening is the one between the real rates of interest in Argentina and Mexico during recent years. Both countries have been subjected to similar external shocks, but the exchange rate regime of one is far removed from the other. As can be seen from figure 6.6, it is not clear that the floating exchange rate regime has a disadvantage with respect to a currency board: Argentine real rates seem to be more volatile and during the last months they have been substantially higher than those prevailing in Mexico.

The Floating Exchange Rate as Shock Absorber and the Possibility of Managing Monetary Policy   Probably the most serious criticism that has been made against the adoption of a floating exchange rate regime by emerging market economies is the supposed fear of floating. This would imply that in the face of a strong external shock the authorities would prevent the exchange rate from adjusting, raising interest rates instead. This action would compound the negative impact of the external shocks, failing the floating exchange rate test as an effective shock absorber. Certainly the event just described could very well happen, but it does not conform to what we have seen in the case of Mexico during the period of a freely floating exchange rate. To substantiate this, it can be helpful to analyze the events that took place during and after the second half of 1998, when the emerging markets faced their most serious threat in decades (due to the Russian crisis, the uncertainty about Brazil, the still-fresh Asian crises, and the long-term capital management scandal, all of which dried up for practical purposes the international financial markets for developing countries). During that period, Mexico was also suffering problems not necessarily shared by other emerging market countries: the sharp collapse in the price of oil, negative shifts in its terms of trade, major indefinitions in the regulatory framework of the banking system, and problems in passing the budget for 1999 through Congress.

Figure 6.3 shows the sharp depreciation that the peso experienced in the second half of 1998, a reflection that the authorities did not prevent the adjustment in the exchange rate. Even though the pass-through of the sharp exchange rate movement to inflation was initially relatively high, this did not preclude the real exchange rate's depreciation, as was to be expected given the sharp contraction in external financing and the adverse performance of the terms of trade. This is apparent in figure 6.7.

The flexibility of the real exchange rate, among other factors, helped Mexican economic activity to remain strong during 1998 and 1999. As a matter of fact, Mexico was the fastest growing economy among the large and medium-sized Latin American countries during the last year. A comparison of Mexico's economic activity and export performance with Argentina's is quite eloquent (see figure 6.8).

Figure 6.3 also shows that interest rates in Mexico increased sharply during the second half of 1998; Hausmann (1999) would take this as a clear indication of Mexico's fear of floating. To be sure, the hike in interest rates then seen was induced in part by the monetary authority. On several occasions Banco de México increased the *corto,* but this was done mostly to limit the pass-through of the exchange rate depreciation to inflation, as was explained earlier, rather than reflecting efforts by the authorities to avoid the exchange rate adjustment. This is one of the actions that the authorities had to take to renew their credentials as inflation fight-

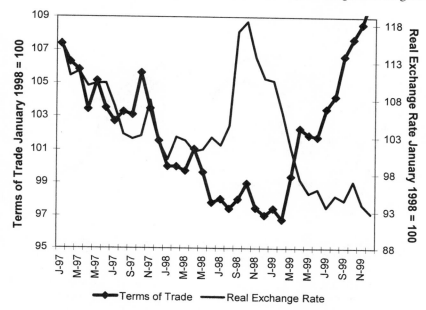

Fig. 6.7   Terms of Trade and Real Exchange Rate

ers under a floating exchange rate regime. The bottom line is what counts: the policy response was successful in stabilizing the nominal variables of the economy, as can be seen in figure 6.9.

It is important to note that part of the interest adjustment resulted from the automatic adjustment mechanism that results when both the exchange rate and interest rates are flexible. The positive correlation between the exchange rate and interest rates is the normal response of the system to an external shock, such as an increase in external interest rates or country risk premiums. Under these circumstances, the downloading of assets denominated in domestic currency will bring about a depreciation of the currency and an increase in interest rates. The simultaneous movements in these variables depresses asset prices, and discourages further selling, stopping the capital outflow. The automatic movements in exchange rates and interest rates increases the price of speculating against the domestic currency. Given the fact that the levels these variables reach during these episodes are inconsistent with the fundamentals of the economy, the currency will recover sooner or later, inflicting considerable losses to those who acquired the foreign currency at a high price and sold their domestic assets at rock-bottom prices. In addition, in an open econ-

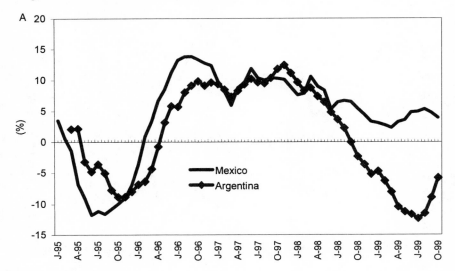

Fig. 6.8   Economic Activity and Export Performance in Mexico and Argentina: Panel A, Industrial Production (three-month moving average); Panel B, Exports Annual Growth (three-month moving average)

omy, the increase in real interest rates that comes with a real exchange rate depreciation does not imply a tightening of monetary conditions, given that the former could only be compensating the expansionary effects of the latter (the currency movement).

This process naturally results in a positive correlation between the floating exchange rate and interest rates whenever pressures are present in the market. In figure 6.10 the moving average autocorrelation coefficient between the exchange rate and interest rates is shown. It is perceptible that such a relationship has frequently been positive, mostly because of the opposite of a fear of floating.

Thinking about Alternatives: Should Mexico Dollarize?

As was mentioned in the introduction, frequent suggestions have appeared regarding the convenience of emerging economies to go to the other extreme of the exchange rate regime continuum—i.e., to dollarize the economy.

The U.S. monetary authorities have on more than one occasion mentioned that they are unwilling to enter into a formal currency union with any country at this stage. This means that for a country such as Mexico the

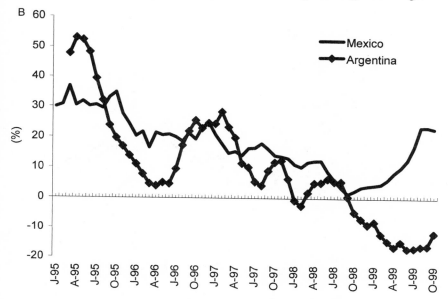

adoption of dollarization (the most extreme of the super-fix exchange rate regimes) would have to be unilateral. This would entail Mexico's losing monetary policy as an instrument, the nominal exchange rate as an adjusting variable, and a lender of last resort for the domestic banking system. Against this backdrop, theory would suggest that the economy would gain from a sharp drop in inflation and in interest rates—the former, to the U.S. inflation level, and the latter, to a level that would tend to be higher than that prevailing in the United States, given that dollarizing eliminates only the exchange rate risk, not sovereign or country risk. In the end, the improvement in terms of lower interest rates depends on how credible the new regime is. If it is considered a solid and credible regime the gains would be large, and therefore adopting such a regime is very likely to be of convenience to the economy. There are other potential benefits that the country could reap from dollarizing; for example, the cost in international trade transactions could fall, stimulating trade. Nevertheless, these benefits tend to be of second order with respect to the benefits in terms of disinflation and lower interest rates, provided that the adoption of the dollar as legal tender is a credible action.

Therefore, for a country like Mexico the decision of whether dollarization is desirable at this stage depends on a straight cost-benefit comparison: the key costs would depend on the consequences of forsaking mone-

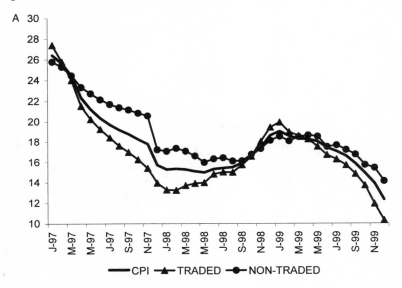

A

Fig. 6.9   Prices and Wages in Mexico: Panel A, Tradable, Nontradable, and CPI (annual growth, %); Panel B, Inflation Expectations for the Next Twelve Months and Wage Settlements (%); Panel C, Inflation Expectations for 1999 and 2000 (%)

tary policy as a stabilization instrument and the exchange rate as shock absorber.[12] The benefits would depend on how quickly inflation and interest rates fall, and if the reduction in such variables is sustainable. The latter, in turn, depends on how credible the new regime is, given such other considerations as the fiscal condition (at present and in the foreseeable future) and the health of the banking system. In what follows we will address these potential costs and benefits for Mexico.

The key costs of dollarization for Mexico are derived from giving up the exchange rate and monetary policy as instruments for macroeconomic adjustment. In principle, the more integrated the Mexican economy is with the American, the lower the costs of dollarization. A close integration would mean that the business cycles in both countries are harmonized, which would mean that the monetary policy in the United States would in most cases be adequate for Mexico, thus making it less costly for the latter to sacrifice such policy. The historical correlation between Mexican and U.S. GDP is relatively low (19.2 percent), which suggest that the adoption of the dollar as legal tender would be rather expensive for Mexico.

Notwithstanding the above, it should be mentioned that for the particular case of Mexico the degree of harmonization of its business cycle with

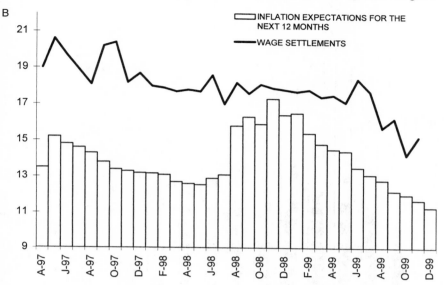

Fig. 6.9B

that of the United States might increase substantially in the future. As Mexico becomes less and less a commodities-based economy, and as the Mexican production cycle becomes more closely attuned to the American one and the financial integration process continues, the adequate monetary policy for the United States might coincide with that for Mexico. Therefore, we expect that within a few years the disharmonization of U.S.-Mexican business cycles will no longer represent an obstacle to Mexico's adoption of the dollar as legal tender.

However, even a tight correlation of business cycles does not mean that external shocks will be symmetric. In the absence of the nominal exchange rate as an adjustment mechanism, the absorption of a severe external shock (terms-of-trade collapse) or an internal one (e.g., salary or real estate price adjustments) will require a prolonged recession and increase in unemployment. The required reduction in economic activity— which would reduce real salaries to restore competitiveness—would have to be smaller the greater the flexibility of wages and the international mobility of capital and labor, and also if there were a scheme of fiscal transfers between countries in the currency union.

Regrettably, in the case of Mexico there is neither free mobility of labor to, nor a fiscal transfer mechanism with, the United States. Even though

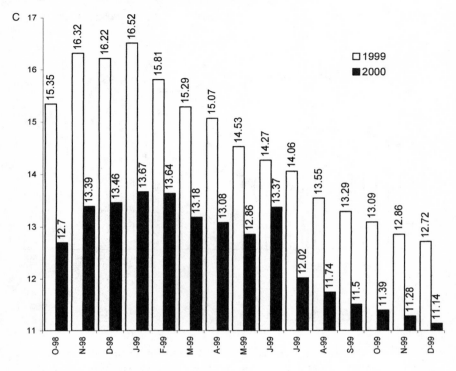

Fig. 6.9C

capital flows freely between Mexico and the United States, the mobility is
not perfect, which means that capital flows are not a perfect substitute for
the management of liquidity by the central bank. In addition, external
shocks tend to be asymmetric between Mexico and the United States
(mostly in the case of the price of oil, which is fiscally extremely relevant
for Mexico). All these elements seem to indicate that at the present time
it would be undesirable for Mexico to sacrifice the floating exchange rate
as an adjustment mechanism. The recent experience of Argentina supports this conclusion.

The asymmetry of shocks between Mexico and the United States is a
reality. Recently, Murray, St-Amant, and Schembri (1999) convincingly
demonstrated that (a) the Canadian and Mexican economies often experience large asymmetric shocks, vis-à-vis the United States, that typically
require real exchange rate adjustment; (b) flexible exchange rates in Canada and Mexico are driven primarily by macroeconomic fundamentals
and adjust appropriately to large asymmetric shocks; and (c) by respond-

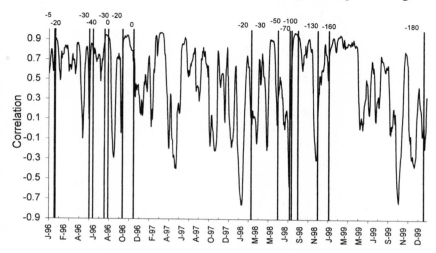

Fig. 6.10   Twenty-Day Moving Correlation Coefficient between Spot Exchange Rate and Overnight Interest Rate

NOTE:

Last observation: 31 January 2000.

ing to shocks in the underlying fundamentals, flexible exchange rates in Canada and Mexico have facilitated economic adjustment.

On the other hand, the perceived benefits from dollarization would come mostly from the credibility bonus it produces, canceling the possibility of monetary mismanagement and devaluations of the local currency. Through elimination of the capability to pursue an active and independent monetary policy, the adjustment of inflationary expectations is triggered, thereby promoting wage and price discipline. This, in turn, gives rise to a rapid fall in inflation. This factor, together with the abatement of the foreign exchange rate premium (it does not disappear completely due to the possibility of a policy reversal) induces a rapid reduction in local interest rates, converging to dollar interest rates except for sovereign risk considerations. For all these reasons, dollarization could stimulate financial intermediation, productive investment, and economic growth.

A key issue is whether sovereign risk would decrease or increase as a response to the adoption of dollarization. There are arguments that run in both directions. One element that would tend to reduce sovereign risk is the fact that the elimination of speculative pressures on the exchange rate would allow for lower interest rates, which would in turn improve the government public finances and the health of the banking system; another is that dollarization implies forsaking the option of reducing the domestic debt burden through inflation and/or a devaluation. Other factors, however, that would increase such risk are the following:

1. The elimination of the possibility of the central bank to perform the role of lender of last resort increases the vulnerability of the financial system to bank runs, a particularly serious problem if the banking system is fragile. Furthermore, given that the adjustment to balance-of-payments problems will take place only through adjustments in interest rates, the financial system could find itself subject to excessive pressures.

2. In addition, the sudden conversion of a sizeable stock of domestic currency debt could test the limits for demand of dollar-denominated debt, thus pressuring spreads.

3. Finally, bunching of amortizations in public debt (if any) might lead to runs.

An interesting comparison illustrates the potentially ambiguous effect of dollarization on sovereign risk. Panama dollarized a long time ago, but the spread of its external debt is still quite large, reflecting mostly sovereign risk. As can be seen in figure 6.11, in recent months it has been even larger than Mexico's spreads, even when these include exchange risk on top of sovereign risk.

The bottom line is that to provide the credibility bonus that dollarization is meant to deliver, the adoption of such a regime should be credible. In turn, this will not be the case if the banking system is in disarray, the public finances are not strong on an intertemporal basis, and the internal debt has important maturity bunchings. Mexico does not fulfill these basic requirements for the successful adoption of a super-fix regime in the near term. Given the fiscal situation, the weakness of the banking system (although improving quickly), and the term structure of the public internal debt, Mexico at present does not really have the option to choose its exchange rate regime.[13]

As we have shown in the previous section, the floating exchange rate regime has worked well in Mexico, and therefore there is no pressing need to modify it. However, this does not mean that in the future dollarizing would not become an optimal choice. The harmonization between the U.S. and Mexican business cycles hints in that direction. Therefore, the optimal strategy for Mexico in the future is to pursue the convergence in the key economic indicators with its main trading partner, which would grant it the freedom to choose. Convergence should be pursued in terms

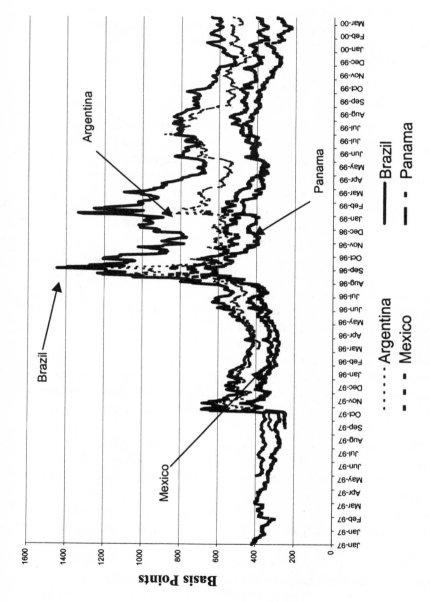

Fig. 6.11   Spread over Equivalent-Duration Treasury Bonds

of fiscal strength, banking-sector health, inflation, debt structure, and basic market regulations.

Once convergence is achieved, it is very likely that the floating exchange rate regime might perform better than it is today, which might mean that, after all, it might be better to stick with the float. The difference is that then it would be Mexico's choice.

Conclusion

Recent crises have reignited the debate on the optimal exchange rate regime for emerging markets. There is now a widespread agreement that the costs of policy mismanagement have increased significantly and in several occasions were not proportional to the policy slippages undertaken on the crisis countries. Therefore, independent of the choice of exchange rate arrangements, the recent financial market crisis underscores the importance of maintaining a consistent macroeconomic framework to avoid financial and balance-of-payments crises and achieve long-lasting stability.

In relation to the conduct of monetary policy, it is clear that assigning multiple objectives to this single policy instrument has led to the collapse of several predetermined exchange rate regimes. Because of this, one of the most important steps undertaken after the collapse of the Mexican peso in 1994 was to spell out clearly that monetary policy was going to focus exclusively on attaining its medium-run goal of price stability, and that the banking-sector problem was going to be addressed by specific programs the cost of which was going to be assumed by the fiscal authority. In this regard, the recent Mexican experience highlights the importance of following consistent macroeconomic policies to accomplish long-lasting stabilization.

The evolution of monetary policy since the adoption of the floating exchange rate regime has converged on a framework that includes three main elements: an annual inflation target, the establishment of rules with respect to the evolution of the base money, and the use of discretionary measures to affect interest rates in the pursuit of inflation targets. It should be added that Banco de México has pursued a gradual process of inflation abatement, with the intention of minimizing as much as possible the costs of disinflation. This mixture of rules and discretion has worked well in recent years. On the one hand, the establishment of rules and quantitative commitments described in this chapter has been helpful in guaranteeing the public that Banco de México will not create the most basic source of inflation: excess supply of base money. However, due to the high pass-through of inflationary shocks, the instability in the demand for base money, and the difficulty in affecting monetary aggregates in the short run, the strict application of rules does not guarantee that the inflation target will be met. Therefore, to be in a position to react quickly to inflationary shocks, Banco de México has the discretion to adjust its monetary-policy stance to influence the behavior of the interest rates in pursuit of its inflation target. Therefore, as time has passed, the inflation objective, supported by discretionary actions, has become the nominal anchor of the economy.

In the discussion on exchange rate arrangements for emerging markets, experience has shown that the Mexican peso has been as stable as other floating currencies, contrary to the original forecasts of several analysts. Therefore, this exchange rate regime has not represented an obstacle in our disinflationary efforts and has contributed significantly to the adjustment of the economy to external shocks and to discourage short-term capital inflows. Thus, the floating exchange rate has become a very important element of Mexico's current macroeconomic policy framework.

At the present time, Mexico is in no position to dollarize its economy, given the weakness in the banking system and in the intertemporal fiscal outlook, the bunching of maturities in its internal debt, the lack of harmonization between the United States' and Mexico's business cycles, and the asymmetry of external shocks vis-à-vis the United States. For the near future, Mexico should concentrate on pursuing the convergence in most economic dimensions with its main trading partner, so that in a few years it could be in a position to choose its optimal exchange rate regime, which might not be the same as today's.

Notes

1. An attempt to implement a controlled movement in the ceiling of the existing currency band was unsuccessful, because it lasted only one day.

2. Mexico suffered in early 1995 an incipient run on the external liabilities of its commercial banks. The central bank, through FOBAPROA (the former deposit insurance institute), provided last-resort credit to financial institutions. At its peak in April 1995, the total amount of such credit reached $3,900 million. The adoption of a credible adjustment program, the penalty rate charged on such credits and the renewed access to capital markets in the second half of 1995, allowed for all these emergency credits to be paid in full by September 1995.

3. It is important to acknowledge that during the first months of 1995, the success that the Argentine currency board had shown since 1991 induced the Mexican corporate and banking sector to lobby strongly in favor of the adoption of a super-fix in Mexico. Sufficient consideration was given to this alternative, but for the reasons that are spelled out later in this chapter, such an option was quickly abandoned.

4. After the Mexican and Asian financial crises erupted, a bulk of literature appeared questioning the capability of interest rates in stabilizing the exchange rate in the face of a banking crisis. This hypothesis is difficult to prove econometrically, given endogeneity and causality issues. Applying the methodology proposed by Basurto and Ghosh (2000), which in principle manages to circumvent these problems, Garcés (2000) proves that the increases in interest rates effectively contributed to the stabilization of the peso exchange rate in 1995.

5. By means of this scheme, Banco de México established accounting periods of twenty-eight days during which banks seek to post a zero daily average balance in the current accounts they hold in the central bank. Banks strive to obtain said balance because, should the daily average balance be negative, the bank in question would have to pay a penalty interest rate equivalent to twice the prevailing twenty-eight-day CETES rate on the respective balance. On the other hand, should the daily average balance be positive, the bank would lose the returns it could have obtained had it invested in the market the respective funds.

6. This contrasts with a convoluted reaction function based on the management of the base money that Edwards (2000) identified as the supposed nominal anchor in Mexico. Such a reaction function does not exist, since Banco de México does not have the control of the base that Edwards claims. In addition, the relationship that he identified breaks down completely in 1999.

7. Probably in the only instances when the existence of the option mechanism temporarily increased the volatility of the exchange rate were when, after the exercise of the options, there was a sudden and large depreciation of the peso generated by an exogenous factor, given that the commercial banks' foreign exchange position was depleted and could not perform as shock absorber.

8. An encouraging sign has been that in early 2000, the difference between the official inflation objective for the year as a whole and market expectations was at its all-time lowest level. At the beginning of the year such a difference was less than one-half of 1 percentage point, whereas in 1999 it was more than 3 percent.

9. Edwards (2000) does not subscribe to the thesis that under no circumstance should an emerging economy adopt a float.

10. Mostly Guillermo Calvo and his associates; see Calvo (1999).

11. A thorough econometric analysis of the impact of the exchange rate on the level and volatility of interest rates is a surprisingly difficult task. The main problem is how to disentangle endogeneity and causality. For a formal discussion see Kraay (2000).

12. Another cost that could be important is the disappearance of seignorage, but for Mexico this would not be that important.

13. Taking for granted the undesirability of the intermediate exchange rate regimes.

References

Banco de México. 1999. Política monetaria: Programa para 1999. Mexico City: Banco de México.

Banco de México. Various issues. The Mexican economy.

Banco de México. 1998. La política monetaria en la coyuntura actual y para el desarrollo económico de largo plazo: Retos y posibilidades. Mexico City: Banco de México. Mimeograph.

Basurto, Gabriela, and Atish R. Ghosh. 2000. The interest rate–exchange rate nexus in the Asian crisis countries. IMF Working Paper no. 00/19. Washington, D.C.: International Monetary Fund.

Calvo, Guillermo. 1999. On dollarization. University of Maryland, Center for International Economics. Mimeograph, April.

Cohen, Benjamín J. 1996. Phoenix Risen: The resurrection of global finance. *World Politics* 48 (January).

Edwards, Sebastian. 2000. To float or to super fix, that is the question: Argentina, Mexico, and Panama. University of California, Los Angeles. Mimeograph, January.

Edwards, Sebastian, and Miguel Savastano. 1998. The morning after: The Mexican peso in the aftermath of the 1994 currency crisis. NBER Working Paper no. 6516. Cambridge, Mass.: National Bureau of Economic Research.

Ericsson, N., and Gordon de Brouwer. 1998. Modeling inflation in Australia. *Journal of Business and Economic Statistics* 16 (4): 433–49.

Eyzaguirre, Nicolás. 1999. Statement on exchange rate regimes in an increasingly integrated world economy. Washington, D.C.: International Monetary Fund. Mimeograph.

Garcés, Daniel. 2000. Aplicación al caso de México del modelo Basurto-Ghosh (Applying the Basurto-Ghosh model to the case of Mexico). Mexico City: Banco de México. Mimeograph.

Ghosh, Atish R., and Steven Phillips. 1998. Warning: Inflation may be harmful to your growth. *IMF Staff Papers* 45 (4): 672–710.

Hausmann, Ricardo. 1999. Should there be five currencies or one hundred and five? *Foreign Policy* 116 (Fall): 65–79.

Heyman, Timothy. 1999. *Mexico for the global investor: Emerging markets theory and practice.* Mexico: Editorial Milenio.

Kraay, Aart. 2000. Do high interest rates defend currencies during speculative attacks? World Bank Working Paper. Washington, D.C.: World Bank.

Lucas, Robert. 1996. Nobel lecture: Monetary neutrality. *Journal of Political Economy* 104 (4): 661–82.

Meltzer, Alan H. 2000. Report of the International Financial Institutions Advisory Commission. U.S. Senate Committee on Banking, Housing, and Urban Affairs.

Murray, John, Pierre St-Amant, and Larry Schembri. 1999. Revisiting the case for flexible exchange rates in North America. Bank of Canada. Mimeograph.

Werner, Alejandro. 1997. El efecto sobre el tipo de cambio y las tasas de interés de las intervenciones en el mercado cambiario y del proceso de esterilización. *Documento de Investigación* no. 9707. Mexico City: Banco de México.

Werner, Alejandro, and Alexis Milo. 1998. Acumulación de reservas internacionales a través de la venta de opciones: El caso de México. *Documento de Investigación* no. 9801. Mexico City: Banco de México.

Chapter Seven

Blueprints for a New Global Financial Architecture
Charles W. Calomiris

> I fear that I must not expect a very favorable reception for this work. It speaks mainly of four sets of persons . . . and I am much afraid that [none] will altogether like what is said of them. *Walter Bagehot (1873)*

Introduction

This paper considers current problems in what is often termed the *global financial architecture* and proposes a set of solutions to those problems. The solutions take the form of redesigning (in combination) rules governing domestic-bank safety-net policies, lending by the International Monetary Fund (IMF), international competition in banking, and government debt management policies.

The next section, "The Weak Foundations of the Current Global Financial Structure," outlines the problems the proposal is meant to address. "Principles on Which to Build a Global Financial System" describes the principles that should guide reform. The fourth section, "A New Institutional Structure for Credible Loss Sharing," discusses details of how to implement those principles, including specific rules governing domestic-bank safety nets and IMF lending policy. These would replace not only the current IMF but other lending programs as well, including the Exchange

Charles W. Calomiris is the Paul M. Montrone Professor of Finance and Economics at Columbia Business School, a visiting scholar at the American Enterprise Institute, and a research associate of the National Bureau of Economic Research.

Discussions with Allan Meltzer inspired this paper. Discussions with Stan Fischer, Jeff Sachs, John Heiman, Ross Levine, Glenn Hubbard, Ernest Patrikis, Jerry Caprio, Michael Bordo, Barry Eichengreen, Athanasios Orphanides, Michael Adler, Dick Aspinwall, Bob Litan, and Kenneth Kuttner have also been helpful.

Stabilization Fund (ESF) and ad hoc emergency lending by the World Bank and the Inter-American Development Bank. The fifth section, "The Political Economy of Financial Reform," discusses the political economy of the new set of rules and whether enforcement would be credible. The sixth and final section provides some concluding remarks.

Economics normally provides rather dismal news, emphasizing difficult choices and trade-offs among objectives. In the redesigning of the global financial architecture, however, such is not the case. It is not difficult to construct a set of mechanisms that resolve problems of illiquidity (by providing a responsive quasi-lender of last resort facility) while avoiding the governance and incentive problems attendant to counterproductive bailouts of risk takers. The claim that it is possible to deliver liquidity assistance without bailouts presumes an economic definition of liquidity assistance, a concept with clear and narrow meaning. Politicians and bureaucrats, in contrast, often define *liquidity crises* and *liquidity assistance* broadly and vaguely to disguise transfers of wealth that have nothing to do with true liquidity assistance.

In essence, my proposal would replace ex post negotiations over conditions for IMF lending with ex ante standards for access to IMF lines of credit and restrictions on the manner in which the IMF lends to its members. These rules and restrictions would automatically constrain the circumstances under which assistance would be provided, and at the same time make potential assistance much more rapid and effective. Proposed criteria for access include rules that impose market discipline on banking systems to limit government abuse of liquidity protection.

A credible reform of bank-capital regulation that ensures market discipline makes it possible to construct an effective domestic-bank safety net in the form of a deposit insurance system, which addresses liquidity problems attendant to banking panics. These domestic safeguards, along with restrictions on the way the IMF would lend, ensure that IMF protection would not be abused. Requiring that IMF members meet standards that ensure market discipline in their banking systems and protection against domestic banking panics makes it possible for the IMF to fulfill its proper role in global financial markets: preventing unwarranted speculative attacks on member countries' exchange rates. Private market discipline, therefore, is the linchpin of effective domestic and international safety-net reform.

The Weak Foundations of the Current Global Financial Structure

Financial crises are the defining moments of the problems that confront policymakers. This section reviews and interprets the recent history of crises and the factors that are alleged to have produced them. The list of problems includes (a) fundamental policy-design flaws in banking systems and in international assistance programs that subsidize risk and foment fundamental bank and government insolvency, and (b) inherent problems of financial systems that aggravate those shocks through four different channels (which are referred to collectively as liquidity problems).

The last twenty years—and particularly the last decade—have witnessed an unprecedented wave of financial collapses. The magnitude of the losses incurred by banks during these collapses is staggering. The negative net worth of failed banks in the United States for the years 1931–33 was roughly 4 percent of gross domestic product (GDP). Nearly a hundred crises with losses of this or higher magnitude have occurred over the past two decades. Twenty of those crises have resulted in losses in excess of 10 percent of GDP, and ten have produced losses in excess of 20 percent of GDP.

Another novelty of the new crises has been the simultaneous collapse of banks and fixed exchange rates. Exchange rate collapses historically were sometimes associated with banking-system collapses, but the two occurred together much less often than they do today, and the historical exchange rate collapses were less severe.

What is driving these crises? The literature has produced a number of explanations, which are not mutually inconsistent. Since the purpose of this paper is to devise solutions (not only for the sake of devising them, but also in the hope of fostering change) I do not prejudge the weights that should be attached to the various views. A proposed set of reforms to the global financial architecture, in order to attract supporters, must encompass a broad spectrum of views.

Problem 1: Counterproductive financial bailouts of insolvent banks and their creditors and debtors by governments, often assisted by the IMF, have large social costs. Bailouts are harmful for several reasons.[1] First, they entail large increases in taxation of average citizens to transfer resources to wealthy risk-takers. Tax increases are always distortionary, and serve to accentuate the unequal wealth distribution. Second, by bailing out risk takers, local governments and the IMF subsidize (and hence encourage) risk taking. Moral-hazard incentive problems magnify truly exogenous shocks that confront banking systems. Excessive risk taking by banks results in banking collapses and produces the fiscal insolvency of governments that bail out banks, leading to exchange rate collapse. Banks willingly and knowingly take on more risks—especially default risks and exchange risks—than they would if they were not protected by government safety nets.

Risk taking often follows a two-stage process. Initially, macroeconomic shocks (e.g., a decline in the terms of trade) reduce bank capital and raise the possibility of currency devaluation. That changes both the incentives for banks to take risks and their opportunities to do so subsequently. The incentives to take risk rise both because bank capital is lower and because banks seek to protect their loan customers (who sometimes also own the bank) from the effects of the adverse macroeconomic shock. The opportunity for taking on risk during a downturn is higher both because of increases in the credit risk of borrowers and because of increased exchange rate risk. Furthermore, a rising risk of depreciation lowers the relative cash flow cost of borrowing dollar-denominated funds, which can make borrowing in dollars attractive to distressed firms and banks. Banks that borrow short-term dollar-denominated funds economize on the current cash flow cost of those borrowings, but take on a large risk of capital loss if the exchange rate peg collapses.

In the absence of safety-net distortions that encourage risk taking, macroeconomic shocks would encourage the opposite behavior—a reduction in bank risk exposure to reassure bank debt holders.[2] However, overly generous protection of banks insulates them from market discipline and makes them willing to increase their asset risk in the wake of adverse shocks. Banks are willing to do so because potential losses will be borne by taxpayers through government-sponsored bailouts of the banking system.

The risks in these banking systems constitute off-balance-sheet liabilities of their governments, since governments either explicitly or implicitly guarantee to bail out banks that fail. Thus bank risk and fiscal risk grow together, which explains the simultaneity of banking and exchange rate collapses. The differences between emerging market financial crises of the last two decades and historical crises—the larger size of current banking-system losses, and the coincidence of banking-system and exchange rate collapses—are attributable to the new link between private risk taking and public financing of the losses produced by those risks.[3]

Banks are not the only entities protected by government safety nets. Large, politically influential firms other than banks often receive implicit protection from the government on their debts, which encourages a similar tendency to bear exchange risk and to rely on short-term dollar-denominated funds, particularly in the wake of shocks that raise the risks of devaluation.

The moral hazard problem also can exacerbate the extent of devaluation during exchange rate collapses. Domestic banks that bet against devaluation prior to the exchange rate collapse (by borrowing dollars or entering forward exchange contracts) can magnify the extent of the collapse by adding selling pressure to the market once the collapse begins. As banks experience initial losses on their open exposures to exchange risk, they may be forced to sell their positions suddenly, which magnifies short-term devaluation pressures. In Mexico, this process of unraveling excessive bank (or nonbank) exposures to exchange risk (in the form of dollar-denominated borrowing and derivative positions) contributed to the severity of the exchange rate collapse in 1995. Garber (1996) argues that the dumping of derivative positions and the scramble for cash by Mexican banks in response to large losses on those positions led banks not only to liquidate their long peso positions, but also to dump their short-term government securities (*tesobonos*) on the market, which put added pressure on the peso in early 1995 and contributed to government problems in rolling over maturing treasury debt.

In addition to the immediate economic costs (tax increases and moral hazard) associated with bailouts, there is also a longer term cost from the way bailouts affect the political process domestically and internationally. Domestically, bailouts encourage crony capitalism in emerging market economies and thus help stunt the growth of democracy and reform. Bailouts also undermine democracy and economic competition in industrialized countries. Bailouts (whether channeled through the IMF or the ESF) are often a means for the U.S. treasury to provide subsidies to international lenders and foreign governments without congressional approval, under the guise of liquidity assistance.

IMF policies exacerbate all these problems.[4] The IMF's role in bailouts is threefold. First, it provides a small wealth transfer (via the interest subsidy on its loan). Second, and more important, it encourages countries to bail out international lenders that are often complicit in excessive risk taking. Third, the IMF helps ensure that domestic taxation (to finance the bailout) will occur, by lending legitimacy to the bailout and by requiring increased taxation as a condition of IMF assistance.

So far I have argued that moral hazard is the key villain in the recent, unprecedented wave of financial system collapses. That is not to say that *all* the costly consequences of financial crises are the unavoidable results of moral-hazard-induced fundamental bank insolvency and its fiscal consequences.

If the only costs of financial system collapse were the *direct* costs of fundamental insolvency—that is, the amount of wealth lost directly through the actions of protected banks and borrowers—then the only threat to the global financial system would be safety-net protection itself. In that case, the best solution to redesigning the IMF arguably would be simply to abolish it, as Schwartz (1998) suggests. The argument for reforming the IMF, rather than abolishing it, revolves around the view that there are important indirect costs attendant to liquidity problems that magnify the direct costs to fundamental bank and government solvency. The potential importance of these indirect costs, and the potential for the IMF to mitigate them, underlies the argument for preserving the IMF. Concerns about liquidity costs can be divided into four additional problems, which are discussed separately below.

Problem 2: Asymmetric information about the incidence of observable shocks within the financial system, especially when combined with short-term debt finance, can magnify the economic consequences of fundamental shocks by leading to a liquidity crisis. The historical evidence on banking panics in the United States and elsewhere suggests that panics resulted from observable economic shocks with unobservable consequences for individual financial intermediaries. The vulnerability of financial intermediaries to crises reflects the fact that the values of their assets are difficult to observe (loans are not marked-to-market) and their debt is very short term (often demandable). Those characteristics are intrinsic to the value-creating functions of banks, but they also make banks vulnerable to crises. Small fundamental shocks to aggregate banking-system solvency can promote widespread disintermediation from banks, leading to a contraction in credit, a decline in economic activity, price deflation, and fire-sale losses as banks and their loan customers scramble to gain liquidity.

Asymmetric-information-induced runs on banks prompted by fundamental shocks to bank asset values characterized the panics of 1873, 1884, 1890, 1893, 1896, and 1907. The weeks and months prior to these banking panics witnessed uniquely adverse combinations of the growth of business insolvencies and declines in equity prices. Previous and subsequent financial panics, both within and outside the United States, have been similarly traced to observable fundamental shocks with unobservable consequences for individual banks and bank borrowers.[5]

Because bank panics result from bank vulnerability to asset-value shocks, bank diversification can be extremely useful in forestalling panics. The peculiar propensity for banking panics in the United States reflected the fragmentation of U.S. banks by location, which made bank loans less diversified than in other countries. That observation suggests that an important ingredient in reducing banking risk in today's global economy is to encourage banks to operate branches throughout the world, and to hold an internationally diversified bundle of securities in their portfolios. The entry of foreign banks into a developing country's market also imposes new competitive discipline on domestic banks, which may be an even greater stimulus to banking stability. Lack of bank competition and diversification has been shown to be a major contributor to bank instability in emerging market economies in recent times, as Caprio and Wilson (1997), Wilson, Saunders, and Caprio (1997), and Kane (1998) emphasize.

Problem 3: The expectations of speculators can exaggerate the effects of adverse shocks, and can even precipitate self-fulfilling financial collapses when weakened financial systems are also illiquid. Current IMF assistance is inadequate to deal with this problem because it offers too little assistance and attaches too many conditions to that assistance at the time of the loan request, which delays the availability of funds. There is both a "Sachs version" of this alleged liquidity problem and a "Mahatir version." The Sachs version (outlined in Sachs, Tornell, and Velasco 1996 and Cole and Kehoe 1996) recognizes that economic fundamentals still drive crises to some degree (which, e.g., explains why Singapore did not come under speculative attack in the Asian crisis). The Mahatir version, predictably, sees speculative attacks as conspiracies that victimize the innocent.

My own view is that the evidence does not support placing much weight on multiple-equilibrium explanations of current financial crises. The Mahatir version has been contradicted by recent empirical studies of the behavior of hedge funds and other institutional investors (see Brown, Goetzmann, and Park 1998 and Choe, Kho, and Stulz 1999). The Sachs version, which is plausible on theoretical grounds, is weak on empirical support. As a general theory of crises it should apply not only to the current wave of disasters, but to historical cases as well. My reading of the available evidence on the history of financial crises does not lend support to Radelet and Sachs (1998), who interpret historical crises as being explicable as bad equilibria within the context of the Diamond-Dybvig (1983) or the Sachs models of multiple equilibria.

Furthermore, Sachs and others search for multiple-equilibrium explanations mainly because they find little evidence of extreme fundamental weakness in macroeconomic flow indicators (e.g., conventional measures of government deficits or current account deficits). As argued above, however, this may be the wrong place to look for evidence of fundamental weakness. Expectations of future government expenditures, not current expenditures, often drive crises. Financial-sector imbalances (expected government costs of a bank bailout, or the bailout of an underfunded pension system) produce fiscal imbalance through the off-balance-sheet contingent liabilities of the government, not through measured flows that show up in today's current account balance or current taxes and expenditures. In a world in which banking-sector collapses often produce fiscal costs in excess of 20 percent of GDP, and in which government expenditures move smoothly compared to changes in off-balance-sheet liability exposures of governments (since banking-system losses can occur very quickly), a focus on macroeconomic flows as measures of fundamentals may leave the prince out of the play. Burnside, Eichenbaum, and Rebelo (2001), for example, show that the fiscal shocks from bank bailouts were a crucial element in the Asian financial crisis.

Despite these objections, there surely is something to Sachs's argument if it is rephrased as the simple claim that a country with very low international reserves is more vulnerable to speculative attacks on its exchange rate or banking system than are others. Furthermore, as Garber (1997) points out, it is very difficult to reject rational-expectations, multiple-equilibrium explanations econometrically. For these reasons, for the purposes of developing my proposed reforms I will assume that the Sachs and Mahatir views have some validity, and that it would be desirable for a global safety net to address the potential for self-fulfilling financial crises to emerge from a combination of small fundamental weaknesses and low liquidity (i.e., low bank and central bank reserves relative to short-term obligations).

Problem 4: "Contagion" across countries in securities and loan markets should be contained. Some researchers have noted that correlations in asset returns are higher across emerging market countries during crises than at other times, and even government bond yields move together to an unusual degree during financial crises. There are several explanations for this contagion. One is irrationality on the part of investors; a second is rational portfolio rebalancing by international investors—if portfolio investors (like banks) target a given default risk on the debt they issue, then they will endogenously shrink asset risk in one country in response to capital losses or exogenous increases in asset risk in another country. A third explanation revolves around linkages in international trade that can transmit economic decline, which is then reflected in asset prices. A fourth explanation revolves around multiple equilibria (either through changes in speculators' views about the probability of bad equilibria, or through reductions in central bank liquidity following a global flight to quality). To the extent that cross-country contagion reflects irrational speculation or multiple equilibria, policies that would solve those problems would also eliminate cross-border spillover effects.

Problem 5: Government debt management sometimes leans too much on short-term debt. There are good reasons (incentive compatibility) for governments to shorten their debt maturities during times of fiscal uncertainty. Indeed, governments have been doing so for centuries.[6] This practice, however, might promote self-fulfilling attacks on currencies (following the multiple-equilibrium reasoning of Cole and Kehoe 1996 and of Sachs, Tornell, and Velasco 1996). Mexico's financial crisis is often held up as an example of such a problem. Although these authors may overstate the empirical evidence in support of that view (particularly in Mexico, where weak fundamentals in the banking system and in central bank policy were evident by late 1994, and persisted afterward), there is a version of this view that is reasonable: A short-term structure of government debt probably aggravates liquidity problems that have their origins in other fundamental shocks (fiscal risks associated with banking-system collapse), as in Mexico during the *tesobono* sell-off of 1995.

There is another reason to be concerned about the short-term structure of government debt. Governments suffer a moral hazard problem with respect to the maturity structures of their debts because IMF protection removes the cost of taking illiquidity risk through the shortening of government debt term structure. In an environment where the IMF cannot credibly say no to bailing out governments that abuse its protection, the IMF may be encouraging financial fragility by not penalizing government debt structures that rely excessively on short-term obligations.

From the perspective of these five challenges to financial-system stability, current IMF policies are woefully inadequate and, indeed, are part of the problem. When a country suffers a banking-system-cum-exchange-rate collapse, its government protects politically influential domestic stakeholders by bailing out banks, their debtors, and their creditors, all at the expense of taxpayers. IMF loans to countries suffering financial collapse serve as bridge loans to permit the rescheduling of debt. The conditions imposed by the IMF along with its financial support help ensure that tax increases to finance the bailouts will be forthcoming, making the IMF an accomplice to the transfer of wealth from taxpayers to domestic oligarchs and global lenders. Banking reforms, promoted by the IMF as a condition for assistance, are inadequate and there is no credible mechanism for ensuring that mandated reforms will be carried out.[7]

Furthermore, IMF assistance is provided only after an agreement is reached, and funds are released in limited amounts over several months. That way of providing assistance is not effective in solving liquidity problems, which require large amounts of funds to be available on very short notice. Thus, current IMF assistance is a non-starter, both from the standpoint of limiting moral hazard problems and from that of reducing the risks of liquidity crises.

We can do much better. Public policy cannot eliminate unavoidable shocks to the financial system. However, thoughtful policy can reduce the five avoidable risks listed above, which magnify the costs of exogenous shocks that buffet banking systems and government finances.

Principles on Which to Build a Global Financial System

In light of the discussion in the previous section, the central twofold objective of policy is to avoid moral hazard problems that give rise to imprudent banking practices while also protecting against the four liquidity problems that can magnify fundamental shocks. A careless approach to providing liquidity assistance results in excessive and counterproductive assistance—a tendency to throw money at fundamental problems, which aggravates problems of imprudent banking and encourages unwise fiscal, monetary, and debt management policies.

Finding the right balance between liquidity assistance and market discipline is the crux of the policy problem. A financial-system safety net will not achieve that balance by making it impossible for banks to fail or for exchange rates to collapse. A system that would eliminate the possibility of collapse would also encourage poor management of private and public affairs. Banks should sometimes fail, exchange rates should sometimes depreciate, and governments should sometimes have trouble rolling over their debts.

Although finding the appropriate balance requires care, I will argue that constructing a balanced safety net does not pose an intractable economic dilemma. It is not the case that policymakers confront an inevitable, dismal trade-off between higher incentive costs from the safety net and greater benefits from safety-net protection against liquidity crises. It is possible to capture the benefits of legitimate liquidity insurance without suffering the costs of moral hazard.

How can financial-system safety nets provide systemic insurance against illiquidity without engendering moral hazard? To achieve that goal, credible ex ante rules must properly allocate ex post losses to private agents, local governments, and international agencies. A global financial safety net, therefore, must define more than the IMF's lending policy; it must define the tranches of risk that are credibly assumed by parties other than the IMF as well as the risks the IMF assumes.

This goal is not new. In fact, it underlay Walter Bagehot's (1873) classic policy prescriptions for domestic central banking: to lend freely at a penalty rate on good collateral. Bagehot argued that an elastic and immediate supply of liquidity was essential to an effectively structured lender of last resort, and that appropriate loss-sharing rules in the form of collateral requirements and penalty interest rates would discourage abuse of the safety net.

Successful lenders of last resort historically have had in common an ability to set credible risk-sharing rules that minimize moral hazard while maximizing the ability of the system to provide liquidity during crises. In the United States prior to the Civil War, for example, three states (Indiana, Ohio, and Iowa) successfully operated mutual insurance systems for member banks that revolved around that principle (Calomiris 1989, 1990, 1993). These were imitated by the New York Clearing House and by other private clearinghouses (Cannon 1910; Gorton 1985). Member banks were constrained by rules and credible monitoring arrangements that limited the riskiness of their debts. Insolvent banks were ejected from coalitions that provided liquidity protection for solvent banks. Enforceable rules requiring the pooling of risks during crises to solve liquidity problems ensured sufficient collective protection. These systems provide examples worthy of imitation today. All successful historical safety-net systems revolved around credible arrangements for limiting moral hazard by clearly defining how losses incurred by members would be allocated.

The appropriate allocation of risk in global safety-net policy requires a credible segmentation of risk into three tranches: the private tranche (exposures to loss incurred by private claimants of individual financial institutions), the domestic government tranche (exposures to loss assumed by local-government bank safety nets, and hence by local taxpayers), and the IMF tranche (exposures to loss assumed by the IMF). The other key design feature of the global safety net is determining how the IMF's financial positions are financed (i.e., how risks taken by the IMF will be passed on to other parties).

The role of financial-system regulation, which includes the rules for IMF lending, is to clearly define when and how the IMF lends, and how losses are allocated within the financial system to maximize the effectiveness of protection against illiquidity while minimizing the moral hazard costs of protection. To be effective, those rules not only must make economic sense, but must be *transparent* and *credible* as well. In other words, the rules governing the global safety net must qualify not only as economically sensible, but also as politically robust.

A New Institutional Structure for Credible Loss Sharing

Without a credible first tranche of private loss, moral hazard will plague any attempt to provide liquidity, from either domestic governments or the IMF. What is needed is a set of transparently credible rules that impose a margin of private loss on bank claimants, which limits the exposure of taxpayers to bailout costs ex post and, in so doing, limits banks' willingness to undertake risks ex ante. Putting those safeguards into place should be a requirement of access to IMF credit. Qualifying members would be eligible for IMF liquidity protection—loans from the IMF that are specifically designed to resolve liquidity problems, not to bail out insolvent banks.

By setting clear, credible criteria for IMF membership, and devising rules for IMF lending that guard against liquidity problems without providing bailouts (that is, without absorbing bank solvency risks), the IMF and its loan programs would help stabilize global financial markets. What sorts of rules would work to accomplish these objectives? The rules divide into three types: (a) domestic regulations required as a condition for IMF membership, (b) rules governing IMF lending to members, and (c) rules defining the way IMF loans are financed.

Credible Bank Regulation: Subordinated Debt, Liquidity, Insurance, and Free Entry

The bank regulatory requirements that should be mandatory for IMF borrowers include four components: (a) capital requirements (including, in particular, a subordinated-debt requirement as part of the capital requirement), (b) reserve requirements (minimum ratios of assets in cash), (c) the explicit insurance of some bank deposits, and (d) "free banking" (unlimited chartering of banks conforming to common regulatory standards, and unlimited investment by foreigners in banks, conforming to the same standards as domestic investors).

A key function of capital regulations is to provide a credible first tranche of private loss by ensuring that uninsured bank claimants (stockholders and subordinated debt holders) will lose wealth when banks suffer adverse shocks to the values of their risky assets. Minimum cash-reserve-ratio requirements serve a similar function (effectively ensuring a margin of protection for insured debt), and also enhance bank liquidity. A minimum amount of global securities—domestic and foreign marketable instruments—adds to the transparency of bank balance sheets and helps diversify bank risk. Thus restrictions on asset holdings and on the composition of bank liabilities provide crucial buffers that ensure the privatization of bank losses, and thus make it easier for local governments and the IMF to provide cost-effective liquidity protection. These regulatory requirements are a first line of defense that reduces the risk of bank failure, the potential for costly bank bailouts, and the liquidity risk that banks face.

Free entry into banking by foreign investors provides an important source of capital (to meet regulatory capital requirements). It also helps diversify both the ownership base of banks and their asset portfolios (since foreign banks naturally hold more globally diverse portfolios), which makes banks more resilient in the face of adverse domestic shocks. Finally, foreign banks provide important competitive pressure that improves the quality of domestic bank management (Demirgüç-Kunt, Levine, and Min 1998; Kane 1998).

Because of the importance of credibility and transparency, bank capital and portfolio regulations must be designed carefully. Credibility and transparency require a reliance on market discipline to enforce bank regulations (Keehn 1989; Wall 1989; Flannery 1998; Berger, Davies, and Flannery 2000). In capital standards, the devil is in the details. A key flaw in the Basel capital requirements to date has been their emphasis on government supervisory standards when measuring capital. Book value equity is measured by supervisors who often have little skill, and even less incentive, to report bank asset losses accurately. Second, the Basel standards imply an arbitrary link between their measure of asset risk and book value capital, while the true asset risk of the bank can differ from the Basel measure of "risk-weighted assets." The mandated 8 percent capital requirement is insufficient if banks assume very high asset risk, and the measurement of risk-weighted assets under the Basel standards leaves much room for bank manipulation of risk (see Shadow Financial Regulatory Committee 2000).

The Basel capital requirements can be substantially improved by incorporating into their framework a minimal (say, 2 percent) subordinated-debt requirement, as a means to ensure a credible relationship between capital and asset risk via market discipline. This approach was first proposed by the Chicago Federal Reserve Bank (Keehn 1989) and the Atlanta Federal Reserve Bank (Wall 1989) in response to the U.S. savings and loan (S&L) and banking crises of the 1980s. The approach outlined here is a modified version of the Chicago Fed plan, and includes elements described in Calomiris (1997, 1999), Calomiris and Litan (2000), and Shadow Financial Regulatory Committee (2000).

As part of their capital requirement (e.g., the 8 percent Tier 1 and Tier 2 requirement under the Basel standards, which apply to internationally active banks), banks would be required to issue at least 2 percent of their assets in the form of a new class of subordinated debt. That debt would be subordinated to (that is, junior to) other bank debts. Unlike equity holders, subordinated debt holders do not benefit from asset substitution (increasing asset risk in order to exploit the implicit put option value of deposit insurance). Thus subordinated debt holders would be a conservative force for restricting bank risk taking, and protecting relatively senior bank deposits. Because subordinated debt is easy to measure (unlike the book value of equity), a minimal subordinated-debt requirement avoids the problems of relying on domestic bank supervisors to measure compliance with equity standards. Furthermore, the yields on the debt are observable, which provides a continuous and transparent market opinion about bank risk and constrains supervisors' ability to postpone enforcement of prudential standards (so-called *forbearance*).

Subordinated debt can be offered through various means to ensure institutional flexibility, and to prevent discrimination against banks that lack access to public debt markets. Banks could issue subordinated debt in the form of interbank deposits, private placements with nonbank creditors, or public offerings. To be successful, however, subordinated-debt issues should be restricted in several ways. To ensure that it serves its role as a source of market discipline, subordinated debt must be credibly subject to loss, and must be held at arm's length. The details of how to design an appropriate subordinated-debt standard are discussed in Calomiris (1999) and Shadow Financial Regulatory Committee (2000).

The subordinated-debt requirement is designed to encourage prudent behavior by banks ex ante (since, on the margin, they are always subject to market discipline), and to encourage appropriate adjustment of asset risk to adverse shocks ex post. Unlike many banks currently, banks subject to a subordinated-debt requirement would not deliberately increase risk in the wake of losses. Instead, banks would have strong incentives to reduce asset risk and cut dividends (or find alternative ways to raise capital) in the face of losses, much as banks did before safety nets changed their incentives to react appropriately to shocks.

Because subordinated debt holders bear risks that come from both on-balance-sheet and off-balance-sheet asset risks, they would also discourage attempts by banks to avoid regulatory capital standards by placing transactions off banks' balance sheets. Subordinated debt holders also encourage banks to develop clear reporting procedures and effective tools for risk management.

A banking system governed by a credibly uninsured subordinated-debt requirement is self-equilibrating. Banks may have difficulty rolling over subordinated debt in response to severe shocks (given the proposed yield spread limit on subordinated debt). The failure to roll over subordinated debt mandates a contraction of risk-weighted assets (e.g., a contraction of loans). That contraction itself reduces asset risk, eventually allowing the market spread on subordinated debt to fall within the prescribed limits of the regulation.

Restrictions on bank asset composition are also desirable, both to promote liquidity for the system as a whole and to provide a transparent safeguard against bank default risk in addition to requiring subordinated debt. Argentina's high reserve requirements were extremely useful in helping Argentine banks weather the tequila crisis in early 1995. Argentina also showed creativity in the way it allowed banks to meet those reserve requirements. Banks were encouraged to hold up to 50 percent of their reserves offshore in private commercial banks, and to hold much of their reserves in the form of standby arrangements with foreign commercial banks (for which the Argentine banks paid a fee) rather than in the form of actual dollar deposits. Like a subordinated-debt requirement (also a feature of the Argentine system) this arrangement rewarded low-risk banks that were able to pay low fees for their standbys.

I propose a similar requirement as part of the mandatory minimum reserve requirement for banks—a 20 percent reserve requirement relative to bank debt, with half to be held offshore (partly to protect against government confiscation of bank resources). Banks can satisfy the 10 percent offshore reserve requirement by maintaining standbys in that amount with any AA-rated international bank.

Some bank debts other than subordinated debt (i.e., a class of senior deposits) should be insured by the government. Doing so would reduce the risk of banking panics due to asymmetric-information problems (problem 2, discussed earlier) or multiple equilibria (problem 3).

The argument in favor of government deposit insurance is primarily a political, rather than an economic, one. Arguably, private methods of protecting against banking panics may be superior to government deposit insurance. Because governments tend to be incapable of credibly committing not to provide insurance ex post, however, it is impossible to construct effective private systems.

Explicit government insurance is superior to implicit government insurance. Although there are some theoretical and empirical arguments in favor of "constructive ambiguity" in deposit insurance that might favor implicit over explicit insurance, those arguments are not convincing. Implicit insurance does not provide as much protection against runs. Also, making insurance explicit allows governments to charge insurance premiums for the protection, and helps government actions conform better to stated government policy (surely a desirable principle in a world where reputation building has value).

In the presence of the other prudential regulations (the subordinated-debt requirement and the reserve requirement), deposit insurance should not be very costly. In a world where market discipline constrains bank behavior, there are likely to be few bank failures, and small losses from insuring some deposits.[8]

These four regulations—subordinated-debt requirements, minimum reserve ratios, free banking, and deposit insurance—constitute a *minimal standard,* which should be required as a condition for establishing lines of credit at the IMF. I would recommend that countries go beyond that minimal standard when devising their bank regulations. A detailed set of recommendations is provided in Calomiris and Powell (2000). Although it is desirable to improve bank regulation by including regulations in addition to the four minimal standards, some regulatory standards should vary across countries. Furthermore, a subordinated-debt requirement and the market discipline it brings arguably subsume other regulatory standards and make additional measures less important. If banks have to satisfy market discipline, markets will informally impose safeguards against market risks, insider lending, and other potential problems, because banks will have to satisfy market perceptions about their overall risk profiles.

By keeping the list of required regulations short and simple it will be easier for the IMF to credibly enforce the rules it sets (see the section on "The Political Economy of Financial Reform"). By vigorously enforcing these rules the IMF will return reason and balance to international banking, and prevent its own protection from being a source of financial instability.

A reformed global banking system will also reduce the riskiness of emerging market securities. Banking systems as a rule have been run inefficiently in emerging market countries, and banks often pursue opportunities more on the basis of insiders' interests than a proper valuation of loans. For that reason there are many viable projects that should be financed by banks rather than via securities issues (i.e., projects that require ongoing monitoring and discipline by banks through concentrated local holdings of claims on borrowing firms), but are pushed into securities markets for lack of a local means of bank finance. In a properly functioning global banking system, those projects would be financed by banks, and banks would be more internationally diversified to permit them to deal with the risks that arise from those risky projects.

These four core banking regulations would ensure a properly functioning global banking system. Free entry, competition, and credible market discipline would encourage proper diversification, prudent management of risk, and an efficient allocation of bank capital. They would also make it possible for the IMF to do the job it was chartered to do—that is, to provide liquidity insurance—without the destabilizing side effects of moral hazard.

Other IMF Membership Requirements

Thus far I have focused on the structure of banking systems, and on proposed mandatory bank regulatory requirements for IMF membership. That emphasis is appropriate given the important role that banking-system losses and moral hazard have played in exchange rate collapses and IMF-sponsored bailouts. Of course, it may also be desirable to place additional limits on prequalification to discourage further abuse of liquidity assistance.

In addition to the mandatory bank regulations, the IMF could require that countries meet minimal standards in their fiscal policies (e.g., some sort of modified Maastricht criterion). It might also be desirable to encourage countries to adopt minimal standards for government debt maturity structure (to limit liquidity risk from excessive reliance on short-term debt by governments), and monetary or exchange rate policies that limit the risk of exchange rate collapse. One can argue that it is appropriate for the IMF to set such standards for debt-management, fiscal, and monetary policies, as well as banking practices, since the IMF will provide liquidity assistance to overcome short-term balance-of-payments disequilibria or to facilitate debt rollover.

Nevertheless, despite the potential desirability of encouraging prudent policies, to prevent abuse of IMF lending, it is also possible to argue against too many prequalification criteria, particularly when those criteria do not lend themselves to being codified in clear rules. The difficulty in constructing meaningful rules can lead to excessive intrusion (micromanagement) by the IMF into countries' fiscal affairs. Furthermore, the greater the discretionary latitude, the more room for politically motivated forbearance by the IMF in enforcing rules.

Finally, in addition to prequalification, to prevent abuse of IMF liquidity assistance, the IMF should lend funds on a senior basis at a bona fide penalty rate (a large markup over its lagged sovereign yield in the market). Countries seeking bailouts from the IMF to benefit their domestic taxpayers (as distinct from liquidity assistance) will not borrow at a penalty rate from the IMF because doing so would not transfer any subsidies to them.[9] Of course, setting penalty rates as markups on lagged interest rates can be a problem if sovereign risk is prone to sudden (daily) jumps. However, the main source of a dramatic, rapid deterioration in a country's sovereign default risk (i.e., a severe deterioration over a matter of days, which could undermine the effectiveness of penalty-rate lending as an incentive device, as described below) comes from the government's contingent liabilities for protecting the banking sector. Thus, so long as the banking sector is solvent, and the IMF lends as a senior creditor at a penalty rate set as a markup over the immediate precrisis borrowing cost on sovereign debt, moral hazard from access to IMF credit should be minimal.

I propose a few simple rules, in addition to the four governing the banking sector, that are easily defined and enforced and minimally intrusive. As in the case of mandatory banking regulations, rules should be as few and as simple as possible, and should be designed to make compliance with them easily observable to the IMF and to third parties.

To limit liquidity risk in sovereign debt, countries could face a ceiling on the proportion of short-term sovereign debt they issue. For example, members could be required to maintain ratios of short-term debt that were no more than 25 percent of the previous year's export earnings, and no more than 25 percent of total sovereign debt.

Countries should not be required (or even encouraged) to maintain fixed exchange rates, but if a country does peg its exchange rate, then it would be desirable to require it to meet two additional standards. First, it should maintain a minimum ratio of reserves to high-powered money. Economic theory has little to say about the right reserve ratio for a central bank to maintain, except that the right minimal proportion of reserves depends on the confidence the market places in fiscal and monetary policy. Countries operating currency boards maintain ratios of nearly 100 percent, but there are many examples of countries (the United States prior to 1933, for one) that have been able to maintain exchange rates for long periods of time with much smaller reserve ratios. Rather than requiring everyone to hold 100 percent reserves, or trying to set standards for reserves that depend on hard-to-observe fiscal and monetary fundamentals,

I propose requiring a low minimal reserve ratio (25 percent) and encouraging countries to manage their reserve policies properly by making it clear (by enacting the aforementioned reforms to IMF lending policy) that the IMF will help resolve *only bona fide* liquidity problems.

Second, member countries with fixed exchange rates should be required to permit banks to offer deposits denominated in both domestic and foreign currencies. Doing so (as Argentina did when it adopted its currency board) helps insulate banks from the risk of devaluation; funds can flow out of the domestic currency without flowing out of the banks. Bank deposit accounts in both currencies also provide continuous market information about the risk of devaluation. Domingo Cavallo, the Argentine finance minister, has argued that observing interest rates in both currencies gives domestic policymakers a valuable signal of market perceptions of government policies that bear on the maintenance of the exchange rate (Cavallo 1999).

Observing interest rate differentials prior to a speculative attack also would give the policymakers valuable information, which may be useful in judging the causes behind a speculative attack or preventing one. Government accountability is also enhanced. If the perceived risk of devaluation (reflected in the interest rate differential) rises gradually over a matter of months, while the government makes little effort to diffuse market concerns through increases in reserves or fiscal reforms, then it is difficult to blame the speculative attack on multiple equilibria or irrationality.

I do not include any membership requirements with respect to capital controls, fiscal or monetary policy, or devaluation policy. Although I recognize that such criteria might be desirable, I cannot think of simple, general rules to cover these areas; moreover, the appropriate policies with respect to capital controls and the appropriate circumstances for a devaluation should be left to governments to decide for themselves.

Many economists have rightly argued that the proper alternative to bailouts is a functioning bankruptcy code that can distribute loss according to clearly specified rules. I agree with that point of view, but do not attach it here as a condition for IMF lending for two reasons. First, it would be difficult to specify the terms of that bankruptcy code in an uncontroversial way (the Swedish code is my personal favorite). Second, it is probably not necessary to add bankruptcy reform as an additional requirement of IMF lending. A banking system that is responsive to market discipline will be a powerful force for creating bankruptcy reform endogenously. The same can be said for the endogenous reform of commercial law, collateral registration procedures, and accounting standards.

IMF Lending Policy

Thus far, I have outlined the criteria for borrowing from the newly constituted IMF. Access to IMF assistance depends on satisfying four bank regulatory requirements (free banking, market-based capital standards, reserve requirements, and credible deposit insurance) and three additional
policy requirements (limits on short-term government debt, and two additional rules for fixed-exchange-rate economies: a minimal central bank
reserve requirement, and the requirement that banks be permitted to offer accounts denominated in both domestic and foreign currency). Countries that do not satisfy these requirements would be ineligible for lending
from the IMF.

Of course, it would be necessary to allow a phase-in period for establishing these standards. Five years would be a reasonable time frame for
countries to adopt the necessary reforms.

What function would IMF lending serve, and what rules would apply to
that lending? The goal of the IMF would be to mitigate problems of illiquidity, as described above. Note that many of the problems listed in the earlier section on "The Weak Foundations" are addressed by IMF prequalification requirements. Problems associated with bailouts, and banking
panics resulting either from asymmetric information about bank loan portfolios or multiple equilibria, are mitigated by the requirements that mandate market discipline in banking, and that ensure against asymmetric-
information panics (i.e., the credible insurance of bank deposits). Problem 5
(government debt rollover risk) is addressed by limiting short-term sovereign debt issues, which also prevents governments from free-riding on
IMF insurance against liquidity risk.

To provide liquidity protection while avoiding abuse of IMF loans, I
propose that the IMF provide lines of credit to sovereign borrowers on a
senior basis at a penalty rate. The proposed lending policy is based on
Bagehot's (1873) rule: lend freely during crises on bona fide collateral at
a penalty rate. Bagehot's rule was designed to create appropriate incentives for banks borrowing from the central bank. Banks facing an illiquidity crisis benefit by borrowing at a penalty rate, but insolvent banks do not.
If an insolvent bank were to borrow from a senior creditor at a penalty
rate, it would weaken its fundamental portfolio value slightly (because of
the penalty rate) and would also aggravate the losses to its junior depositors and stockholders because of the pledging of collateral to the senior
creditor. By *penalty rate* I mean a rate higher than the pre-crisis market
rate for the borrower.

In the case of sovereign borrowing from the IMF, physical collateral is an impractical means for ensuring seniority. Not all sovereign borrowers possess state-owned enterprises that export primary commodities for which collateralization would be feasible. Indeed, requiring collateral might even create an undesirable incentive for governments to retain control over export industries rather than privatize them. Thus, despite the desirability of lending against physical collateral (as described in Calomiris and Meltzer 1999), this approach suffers from major practical problems. Instead of relying on physical collateral, establishing the clear legal seniority of IMF lending, and limiting the amount of IMF loans in order to make seniority meaningful would serve the same function—providing the incentive for the country to access the credit line only during bona fide liquidity crises. For additional discussion of this point, see International Financial Institutions Advisory Commission (2000).

To be concrete, a government that is a member in good standing would be able to borrow up to a maximum amount of dollars or other hard currencies from the IMF for a short period of time (say, for one year, with one rollover permitted). The interest rate would be 2 percentage points above the sovereign yield in the market one week before the request for an IMF loan.

The new IMF discount window would provide significant protection against short-term liquidity problems. Governments would be able to convert large amounts of their bonds into cash on short notice, provided that they satisfied prequalification standards and IMF lending rules. Assistance would be available on short notice, without the delay (and intrusiveness) from setting ex post conditions.

Of course, this discount window would not protect a country against persistent balance-of-payments outflows, and it should not attempt to do so. Persistent outflows, which would lower central bank holdings of hard currency and hard-currency-denominated securities, would be a sure sign of fundamental weakness. IMF lending should not try to lend to prop up unsustainable currency pegs. It should lend freely, however, to ensure that sudden, self-fulfilling speculation does not undermine an otherwise sustainable peg.

It is worth emphasizing that a Bagehotian lender of last resort cannot provide much protection against banking panics that are caused by asymmetric information about bank loan quality. That is why it is necessary to combine a Bagehotian lender of last resort (like the reformed IMF lending facility envisioned here) with credible protection against asymmetric-information problems in the banking sector. Deposit insurance reduces depositors' incentives to run banks when they become concerned about the value of loan portfolios. Credible market discipline (through a subordinated-debt requirement and a reserve requirement) reduces the incidence of such asymmetric-information problems and provides strong incentives for banks to control loan risk, which eases the funding burden of providing deposit insurance protection, and fosters deposit insurance credibility.

How would the IMF finance its lending to central banks? IMF senior lending at a penalty rate would be self-financing. Funds for loans could either be made available through credit lines with hard-currency-issuing countries, or through private market debt issues, as suggested by Lerrick (1999).

Transition Problems

Some of the world is very far from meeting the conditions specified above for IMF membership. Over the five years allowed for transition to the new arrangements, how difficult would it be for countries to satisfy the eight membership requirements, and what transitional policies could facilitate that process?

The central bank reserve requirement, the limits on government debt maturity, and the requirement that banks be permitted to offer accounts in domestic and foreign currency would be relatively easy to satisfy. The main difficulty is transforming the banking systems of many countries (including those in some Western European countries, as well as the vast majority of those in developing economies) into competitive, market-oriented systems. The problem is not mainly an economic one; if governments opened their banking systems to foreign entry and imposed the regulations suggested above, efficient banking systems would develop quickly. The problem, however, is the politics of banking—the resistance of entrenched special interests to reforms that would erode the rents they currently enjoy. The challenge reformers face is to find a way to placate that political opposition.

The resistance to market discipline can be found even in relatively efficient banking systems (like that of the United States). U.S. banks consistently opposed a subordinated debt requirement in recent years, predictably preferring to maintain the implicit subsidy from the taxpayers. But for a brief moment before the passage of the 1999 Gramm-Leach-Bliley Act, some of them (notably members of the Bankers Roundtable, which represented the largest 150 U.S. banks) were calling for safety net reform because they saw credible market discipline, and a subordinated-debt requirement in particular, as means of permitting an expansion of bank powers (Bankers Roundtable 1998).

Deregulation is one way of buying support for market discipline, but in many developing economies (where banks already enjoy broad powers, and where bank owners would have great difficulty meeting market-enforced capital standards), it may be necessary to buy support more overtly through a government-financed recapitalization of existing banks. That recapitalization would make it easier to swallow the pill of market discipline, and if a one-time subsidy would set the stage for credible regulatory reform (on the lines described above), it would be well worth the cost.

Such a recapitalization must be carefully designed, however, so that it is cost effective and does not undermine market discipline in the future. One approach to providing government subsidization of bank recapitalization without undermining the effectiveness of market discipline is proposed in Calomiris (1998a, 1999). Assistance would take the form of subsidized government purchases of bank preferred stock for a short period (say, five years). Those purchases would occur on a matching basis with arm's-length public offerings of new common stock. To qualify, banks would have to agree to other provisions, including the suspension of dividend payments on common stock during the period in which the government holds preferred shares. The one-time recapitalization subsidy is designed automatically to target assistance toward the relatively strong, and to help make subordinated debt requirements feasible.

The World Bank and other development banks could help during the transition process in two ways: by providing financial assistance to encourage countries to implement credible market discipline (and thereby qualify for IMF membership), and by offering advice on how to structure complementary institutions and laws (including commercial laws, accounting codes, and bankruptcy laws). Too often, World Bank loans have crowded out private lending and removed incentives for countries to adopt the fundamental reforms of property rights on which private lending depends. World Bank loans to China are the clearest example of such misdirected lending. However, in some cases the World Bank has successfully targeted its assistance to encourage privatization of financial institutions and the creation of credible market discipline. Its loan subsidies to Argentina to help pay for the privatization of provincial banks are an example. The World Bank and other development banks could help ensure broad-based membership in the new IMF by redirecting loan subsidies toward government programs that restructure banking systems to encourage adherence to market discipline.

Large Macroeconomic Shocks

No matter what the stated commitment to market discipline, time-inconsistency problems will tempt governments to provide assistance to banks during severe macroeconomic downturns. Banking systems that respond properly to market discipline will necessarily magnify recessions by curtailing the supply of loanable funds when they experience losses on their loan portfolios. Governments will be tempted to relax market discipline to prevent the aggravation of cyclical downturns.

A better approach is to maintain market discipline through the subordinated-debt requirement but subsidize private bank recapitalization (using the preferred-stock-matching subsidy described above) to counteract especially severe economic downturns. I am not arguing that bank recapitalization is desirable economically; rather, I am arguing that if government intervention into the banking system is politically inevitable, it is better to intervene to help banks meet the standards of market discipline, rather than simply repealing those standards.

Waiving the Prequalification Requirement

What would happen if a liquidity crisis in one country that had not prequalified for IMF lending threatened the stability of many neighboring countries, and of global capital markets more generally? It is probably beneficial, and in any case, probably unavoidable, to allow the IMF to waive prequalification requirements for lending if a sufficiently severe liquidity crisis erupts. Granting waivers too freely would weaken the incentives for reform in banking systems and other government policies; but that need not imply significant moral hazard from IMF lending. The IMF would still lend on senior terms at a penalty rate, implying that accessing IMF funds would not provide subsidies for bailouts of governments or banks. Indeed, it would be desirable to make the penalty rate even larger to nonqualified borrowers (say, 3 percent above the precrisis yield) to further ensure that IMF loans do not channel fiscal subsidies to borrowing countries.

The Political Economy of Financial Reform

Politics poses challenges for any attempt to bring economic reason and market discipline to bear on the regulation of the global financial system. Politicians and regulators are jealous of their power, tend to prefer systems that rely on discretion rather than rules, and are more comfortable managing cryptic decision-making processes (the proverbial smoke-filled rooms in which IMF policies are determined today) than engaging opponents openly in public fora.

Thus, the reforms I advocate—the abolition of the ESF and a sweeping reform of the IMF—will likely not be very welcome in Washington or in the treasury departments or finance ministries of many nations. That does not mean that reform is impossible, but it certainly will be an uphill battle.

Consider, for example, the problem this proposal poses for the U.S. treasury department. It has frequently used the ESF (Schwartz 1997, 1998) and the IMF as means to provide foreign aid under the guise of liquidity assistance. These mechanisms have the advantage that they avoid the unpleasant and inconvenient requirement of seeking congressional approval for such aid. Also, the costs of aid are shared with other countries. Another convenient aspect to multilateral lending is the inability to trace the political deal underlying the flow of aid.

The political obstacles to rationalizing the current system are formidable but the distortions in decision making created by those obstacles also are motivating a redoubling of effort in some quarters to reform the system. Simplifying the IMF's role and decision-making process by setting simple, meaningful, and publicly observable membership criteria, and placing strict bounds on how and when the IMF provides assistance, would be a welcome means of reducing politically motivated distortions from the process of providing necessary liquidity assistance. These reforms would also remove the IMF from the uncomfortable position of dictating the details of macroeconomic and microeconomic policy to its member nations (see Feldstein 1998). Aside from IMF membership criteria (see table 7.1 for a summary), according to my proposal, no conditions would be attached to IMF liquidity assistance.

The prospect of a world where the power to allocate risk would be less abused, and where political puppeteers would find the strings of the financial system beyond their reach, fires the imagination and invites the effort to see such a project through. The recent failings of IMF–U.S. treasury policies in Mexico, Asia, Russia, and Argentina, and the chorus of criticism facing the IMF and the treasury, provide a window of opportunity for reform. Congress is now poised—for the first time in U.S. history—to thoroughly evaluate the process of decision making within the IMF.

Table 7.1 Elements of the Reform Plan

Regulation	Details
Membership criteria for the IMF	
Bank regulations	Capital standards (but without restrictions on sub-ordinated-debt/Tier 2 capital)
	2% subordinated debt requirement (with rules on maturities, holders, and yields)
	Credible, funded deposit insurance policy
	20% cash reserve requirement
	Free entry by domestic and foreign investors into banking
	Bank recapitalizations permitted, but strict guidelines must be met (and must follow preestablished rules, as in preferred-stock-matching program)
Other criteria	Limits on short-term government securities issues
	If fixed exchange rate, 25% minimum central bank reserve requirement
	If fixed exchange rate, banks offer accounts in domestic and foreign currencies
IMF lending rules	Loans are provided only to members that qualify for lines of credit (those following the above rules).
	Loans are senior and short-term (say, for one year, with one possible rollover).
	The interest rate on the loan is set at 2% above the yield on sovereign debt observed one week prior to the loan request.
Other emergency lending	IMF, World Bank, Inter-American Development Bank, and others would make no additional emergency lending available.
	The ESF would be abolished.

Conclusion

A global financial architecture can be defined as the set of institutions, contracts, and incentives that determine how financial risks are taken and how losses and gains from taking those risks are allocated. This paper offers an ecumenical proposal for reforming that architecture. I have followed the working assumption that there is some truth in virtually every argument that is made about the problems facing the global financial system, and have argued that it is possible to design a global safety net that properly allocates risk, eliminates (or at least substantially reduces) problems of moral hazard, and still provides protection against illiquidity problems. I have argued that the imagined system would be simple to operate, and would be more credible politically (more time consistent) than many alternatives. It would also permit the IMF to provide elastic liquidity assistance to help members defend their exchange rates from unwarranted attacks.

The proposed changes would also avoid IMF micromanagement in the midst of crises, which has been criticized as an abuse of power (Feldstein 1998), an ineffectual means of financial-system reform, and counterproductive to the provision of rapid liquidity assistance. Focusing the IMF's mission on true liquidity assistance would transform it from an agency that balances political interests to one that solves well-defined economic problems, which would do much to rebuild the shattered reputation of the fund.

Others, no doubt, will find ways to improve this proposal. By being concrete—drafting blueprints rather than only outlining broad principles—I do not mean to suggest that mine is the only imaginable way to proceed, but rather I hope to stimulate specific discussions.

These reform proposals assume that the defining objective of the IMF is to provide the global public good of liquidity at least cost. Others may wish the IMF to perform additional functions—both political and economic—including the handling of all manner of emergencies, assisting in the restructuring of sovereign debt, and managing the reform processes of emerging financial markets. Still others will think that the IMF should be a force limiting sovereign debt contracts and forcing countries to limit short-term capital flows. However, the IMF's record in debt management, and in managing reform, has been quite poor (International Financial Institutions Advisory Commission 2000; Calomiris 2000). The first step to effective IMF reform is to rein in its ambitions, and narrowly define a set of economic objectives that it can address effectively.

Notes

1. For more details, see Calomiris (1998a) and Meltzer (1998a,b).

2. For a discussion of the responses to loss by New York banks during the Great Depression, see Calomiris and Wilson (1998).

3. For details on the moral-hazard costs of safety nets over the past two decades, see Caprio and Klingabiel (1996a,b); Lindgren, Garcia, and Saal (1996); Demirgüç-Kunt and Detragiache (1998); Calomiris (1997, 1998a); Meltzer (1998, 1999); and Kane (1998) for summary analyses; De la Caudra and Valdes (1992) on the Chilean crisis of 1982–83; De Krivoy (1995) on the Venezuelan crisis of 1991–93; and Wilson, Saunders, and Caprio (1997) on the Mexican crisis of 1994–95.

4. For details, see Calomiris (1998a) and Meltzer (1998, 1999).

5. Calomiris and Gorton (1991) review models of banking panics and provide empirical evidence on their causes. See Mishkin (1991) and Wicker (2000) for

complementary evidence. Bordo (1985), Calomiris and Schweikart (1991), Calomiris (1993, 1994), and Calomiris and Mason (1997) provide similar perspectives on the Panic of 1857, the Penn Central Crisis of 1970, historical banking panics outside the United States, and the Chicago Banking Panic of June 1932.

6. For a review of the use of short-term debt finance by the United States historically, see Calomiris (1991).

7. IMF conditionality is not always ineffectual. Banking reform is a protracted process, however, and cannot be accomplished easily through IMF pressure (see Calomiris 1998a).

8. For historical evidence supporting this view, see Calomiris (1989, 1990, 1993).

9. It is possible, of course, that government officials would use access to IMF resources for selfish purposes, and leave taxpayers to foot the bill, and it is hard to imagine IMF lending rules that could prevent this. The alleged "disappearance" of large sums of IMF assistance in Indonesia is a case in point. No seniority or penalty rate rule could prevent such abuse. This possibility reinforces the desirability of prequalification criteria, which constrain the potential for fradulent abuse of borrowing by limiting prospective bailout costs.

References

Bagehot, Walter. 1873. *Lombard Street.* London: Henry S. King.

Bankers Roundtable. 1998. Market-incentive regulation and supervision: A paradigm for the future (April). Washington, D.C.: Bankers Roundtable.

Berger, Allen N., Sally M. Davies, and Mark J. Flannery. 2000. Comparing market and regulatory assessments of bank performance: Who knows what when? *Journal of Money, Credit, and Banking* 32 (3, part 2): 641–67.

Bordo, Michael D. 1985. The impact and international transmission of financial crises. *Rivista di Storia Economica* 2:41–78.

―――. 1990. The lender of last resort: Alternative views and historical experience. *Economic Review* 1 (January/February): 18–29. Federal Reserve Bank of Richmond.

Brown, Stephen J., William N. Goetzmann, and James Park. 1998. Hedge funds and the Asian currency crisis of 1997. NBER Working Paper no. 6427. Cambridge, Mass.: National Bureau of Economic Research, February.

Burnside, Craig, Martin Eichenbaum, and Sergio Rebelo. 2001. Prospective deficits and the Asian currency crisis. *Journal of Political Economy* 109 (6): 1155–1197.

Calomiris, Charles W. 1989. Deposit insurance: Lessons from the record. *Economic Perspectives* (May): 10–30.

―――. 1990. Is deposit insurance necessary? A historical perspective. *Journal of Economic History* 50 (June): 283–95.

―――. 1991. The motives of U.S. debt management policy, 1790–1880: Efficient discrimination and time consistency. *Research in Economic History* 13: 67–105.

―――. 1993. Regulation, industrial structure, and instability in U.S. banking: An historical perspective. In *Structural change in banking,* ed. M. Klausner and L. J. White, 19–116. Homewood, Ill.: Business One–Irwin.

———. 1994. Is the discount window necessary? A Penn Central perspective. *Review* Federal Reserve Bank of St. Louis 76 (May/June): 31–56.

———. 1997. *The postmodern bank safety net.* Washington, D.C.: AEI Press.

———. 1998a. Historical and contemporary perspectives on banking instability, deposit insurance, and prudential regulation and supervision. Columbia Business School. Working Paper.

———. 1998b. The IMF's imprudent role as lender of last resort. *Cato Journal* 17 (Winter): 275–94.

———. 1999. Building an incentive-compatible safety net. *Journal of Banking and Finance* 23 (October): 1499–519.

———. 2000. When will economics guide IMF and World Bank reforms? *Cato Journal* 20 (Spring/Summer).

Calomiris, Charles W., and Gary Gorton. 1991. The origins of banking panics: Models, facts, and bank regulation. In *Financial markets and financial crises,* ed. R. Glenn Hubbard, 109–73. Chicago: University of Chicago Press.

Calomiris, Charles W., and Robert E. Litan. 2000. Financial regulation in a global marketplace. In *Brookings-Wharton Papers on Financial Services,* ed. Robert E. Litan and Anthony M. Santomero, 283–323. Washington, D.C.: Brookings Institution.

Calomiris, Charles W., and Joseph R. Mason. 1997. Contagion and bank failures during the Great Depression: The June 1932 Chicago banking panic. *American Economic Review* 87 (December): 863–83.

Calomiris, Charles W., and Allan H. Meltzer. 1999. Fixing the IMF. *The National Interest* 56 (Summer): 88–96.

Calomiris, Charles W., and Andrew Powell. 2000. Can emerging market bank regulators establish credible discipline: The case of Argentina, 1992–1999. In *Prudential supervision: What works and what doesn't?* ed. Frederic S. Mishkin. Chicago: University of Chicago Press.

Calomiris, Charles W., and Larry Schweikart. 1991. The panic of 1857: Origins, transmission, and containment. *Journal of Economic History* 51 (December): 807–34.

Calomiris, Charles W., and Berry Wilson. 1998. Bank capital and portfolio management: The 30s capital crunch and scramble to shed risk. NBER Working Paper no. 6649. Cambridge, Mass.: National Bureau of Economic Research, July.

Cannon, James G. 1910. *Clearing houses.* National Monetary Commission. 61st Cong., 2nd sess. S. Doc. 491. Washington, D.C.: GPO.

Cavallo, Domingo. 1999. Policymakers roundtable. *Journal of Banking and Finance* 23 (October): 1535–41.

Caprio, Gerard, Jr., and Daniela Klingabiel. 1996a. Bank insolvency: Bad luck, bad policy, or bad banking? In *Annual World Bank Conference on Development Economics, 1996,* ed. M. Bruno and B. Pleskovic. Washington, D.C.: World Bank.

———. 1996b. Bank insolvency: Cross-country experience. World Bank Policy Research Working Paper no. 1620. Washington, D.C.: World Bank, July.

Caprio, Gerard, Jr., and Berry Wilson. 1997. On not putting all your eggs in one basket. World Bank Working Paper.

Choe, Hyuk, Bong-Chan Kho, and René M. Stulz. 1999. Do foreign investors destabilize stock markets? The Korean experience in 1997. *Journal of Financial Economics* 54 (October): 227–264.

Cole, Harold L., and Timothy J. Kehoe. 1996. A self-fulfilling model of Mexico's 1994–1995 debt crisis. Federal Reserve Bank of Minneapolis Staff Report no. 210, April.

De la Cuadra, Sergio, and Salvador Valdes. 1992. Myths and facts about financial liberalization in Chile: 1974–1983. In *If Texas were Chile: A primer on banking reform,* ed. P. Brock, 11–101. San Francisco: ICS Press.

Demirgüç-Kunt, Asli, and Enrica Detragiache. 1998. The determinants of banking crises: Evidence from developed and developing countries. *IMF Staff Papers* 45 (1): 3.

Demirgüç-Kunt, Asli, Ross Levine, and Hong-Ghi Min. 1998. Opening to foreign banks: Stability, efficiency, and growth. In *The implications of globalization of world financial markets,* ed. Seong-Tae Lee. Seoul, Korea: Bank of Korea.

Diamond, Douglas, and Philip Dybvig. 1983. Bank runs, deposit insurance, and liquidity. *Journal of Political Economy* 91 (June): 401–19.

Feldstein, Martin S. 1998. Refocusing the IMF. *Foreign Affairs* 77 (March/April): 20–33.

Flannery, Mark J. 1998. Using market information in prudential bank supervision: A review of the U.S. empirical evidence. *Journal of Money, Credit, and Banking* 30 (August): 273–305.

Garber, Peter. 1996. Managing risks to financial markets from volatile capital flows: The role of prudential regulation. *International Journal of Finance and Economics* 1 (3): 183–95.

Gorton, Gary. 1985. Clearing houses and the origin of central banking in the U.S. *Journal of Economic History* 45 (June): 277–83.

International Financial Institutions Advisory Commission. 2000. Report of the International Financial Institutions Advisory Commission, Allan H. Meltzer, Chairman, March.

Kane, Edward. 1998. Capital movements, asset values, and banking policy in globalized markets. NBER Working Paper no. 6633. Cambridge, Mass.: National Bureau of Economic Research, July.

Keehn, Silas. 1989. Banking on the balance: Powers and the safety net, a proposal. Federal Reserve Bank of Chicago. Monograph.

De Krivoy, Ruth. 1995. Lessons from financial crises: Evidence from Venezuela. Proceedings of the 31st Annual Conference on Bank Structure and Competition. Chicago: Federal Reserve Bank of Chicago.

Lerrick, Adam. 1999. *Private sector financing for the IMF: Now part of an optimal funding mix.* Washington, D.C.: Bretton Woods Committee.

Lindgren, Carl-Johan, Gillian Garcia, and Matthew I. Saal. 1996. *Bank soundness and macroeconomic policy.* Washington, D.C.: International Monetary Fund.

Mason, Joseph R. 1997. Reconstruction finance corporation assistance to banks during the Great Depression. Drexel University. Working Paper.

Meltzer, Allan H. 1998. Asian problems and the IMF. *Cato Journal* 17 (3): 267–74 (Winter).

———. 1999. What's wrong with the IMF? What would be better? *Independent Review* 4 (2): 201–15.

Mishkin, Frederic S. 1991. Asymmetric information and financial crises: A historical perspective. In *Financial markets and financial crises,* ed. R. Glenn Hubbard, 69–108. Chicago: University of Chicago Press.

Radelet, Steven, and Jeffrey D. Sachs. 1998. The East Asian financial crisis: Diagnosis, remedies, prospects. *Brookings Papers on Economic Activity,* Issue no. 1: 1–90.

Sachs, Jeffrey D., Aaron Tornell, and Andres Velasco. 1996. Financial crises in emerging markets: The lessons from 1995. *Brookings Papers on Economic Activity,* Issue no. 1: 147–215.

Schwartz, Anna J. 1997. From obscurity to notoriety: A biography of the exchange stabilization fund. *Journal of Money, Credit, and Banking* 29 (May): 135–53.

———. 1998. Time to terminate the ESF and the IMF. Foreign Policy Briefing no. 48. 26 August, The Cato Institute.

Shadow Financial Regulatory Committee. 2000. *Reforming bank capital regulation.* Washington, D.C.: American Enterprise Institute Press.

Wall, Larry D. 1989. A plan for reducing future deposit insurance losses: Puttable subordinated debt. *Federal Reserve Bank of Atlanta Review* 74 (July/August): 2–17.

Wicker, Elmus. 2000. *Banking panics of the Gilded Age.* Cambridge: Cambridge University Press.

Wilson, Berry, Anthony Saunders, and Gerard Caprio Jr. 1997. Mexico's banking crisis: Devaluation and asset concentration effects. Working Paper. Washington, D.C.: World Bank Policy Research Department.

Chapter Eight

Roundtable: Institutions for the New Millennium
Matthew Bishop, T. Britton Harris, John Lipsky, Allan Meltzer, and Guillermo A. Calvo (moderator)

GUILLERMO A. CALVO: As pointed out this morning by Auernheimer in his introduction, we started with papers whose titles contained question marks, and we then moved on to papers with more assertive titles. It seems to be now the time to put your cards on the table and play hard.

We have a wonderful panel for the discussion of the institutions for the new millennium. Matthew Bishop, our representative of the specialized press, is the finance editor at the New York Bureau of *The Economist* and one of the authors of the recent survey on taxation and globalization. We have two representatives from the private sector: T. Britton Harris IV is the president of Verizon Investment Management Corporation, which oversees more than $80 billion in investments for Verizon Communications and its employees, with a portfolio encompassing more than forty countries, so he is a real private-sector man. The second is John Lipsky, who is the chief economist and director of research of the Chase Manhattan Bank, so he's private sector but still one step removed from the real money. [Laughter]

Last but not least, Allan Meltzer, who really does not need much introduction. He is a professor at Carnegie-Mellon University and has been

Matthew Bishop is the New York financial editor of *The Economist*. Guillermo A. Calvo is Distinguished Professor of Economics at the University of Maryland and an associate of the National Bureau of Economic Research. He is currently Chief Economist at the Inter-American Development Bank, on leave from the University of Maryland. T. Britton Harris is the President of Verizon Investment Management Corporation. Allan H. Meltzer is the Allan H. Meltzer University Professor of Political Economy at Carnegie-Mellon University and a fellow at the American Enterprise Institute. John Lipsky is chief economist of Chase Manhatten Corporation and the director of research of Chase's Global.

associated with many other institutions and think tanks, particularly with the American Enterprise Institute since 1989. And, of course, he has become now the man in the news, together with the other members, as the chairman of the International Financial Institutions Advisory Commission, which has very recently issued their important and widely publicized report.

Since the report of the Advisory Commission coincides precisely with the topic of this roundtable, I am going to ask Allan to start off and then the other members of the panel will follow in alphabetical order. Each of you will have ten minutes for your initial remarks, with the idea of maximizing interaction within the panel and with the participation from the floor. So, please, Allan . . .

ALLAN MELTZER: Thank you very much. It's a great pleasure to have an opportunity to talk about the work the commission has done. Today the topic of this panel is the institutions for the new millennium, and the day is Economics Day at Texas A&M; I had the rather unique privilege of chairing a commission designed to look at these institutions, and, as you will see, what the commission proposes really fits both of those titles.

The commission worked very hard. We met approximately every two or three weeks, and we were constantly receiving, reading, and rereading papers from people who had thought about these issues a great deal. It was a wonderful opportunity to come up to date and learn a great deal about the legal, institutional, and economic aspects of the problem. There were eleven members in the commission—this afternoon you heard one of them, Charlie Calomiris. Of the eleven members, six were economists, and that is why this is a report that is appropriate to the Economics Day at Texas A&M. This was a report drafted by economists; and as economists we centered the analysis on where are the externalities and the public goods involved, and what, as a result, it is that these institutions should be doing.

We began with the idea that the postwar order in the world had benefited substantially for twenty or twenty-five years from the presence of institutions like the World Bank and the International Monetary Fund. In this period more people in more countries had their standards of living rise by larger amounts than ever before in the history of the world. These institutions were productive, in various ways, for both the countries that received aid and for the countries that gave aid. That a stable financial order and a mechanism to help lift countries from poverty and encourage market reforms through the World Trade Organization was tremendously important in making the postwar period as successful as it was, but in the view of the commission, these institutions have now gone off in different directions and are much less successful.

You have heard Charlie Calomiris, who was a member of the commission, and I think you can gather from the way he presented his material that we had very lively and interesting discussions of substance. Jeffrey Sachs was a member of the commission, and there were other very good economists, so the discussions really were very substantive and to the point. We tried to concentrate on how these institutions could be reformed to provide the public goods that were necessary to carry the world through the next twenty-five or fifty years of economic development. And we thought, at least I thought, that if we could reform these institutions to do as well for the next twenty-five or fifty years as we had done for the past twenty-five or fifty years, that would indeed be a remarkable achievement.

I am going to talk mostly about the International Monetary Fund [IMF]. There were seven institutions that we had to consider in a six-month period. We spent most of our time on the International Monetary Fund and the development banks. The first and largest problem is of course that there had been crises, extraordinary crises, as Calomiris emphasized in his discussion. The second most important problem is that the World Bank functions much less effectively than anyone—certainly anyone other than Jeff Sachs in our commission—had any reason to believe before we began our work.

At the start of our work we identified three public goods, or externalities, that we thought needed attention. One was the role of the fund as a quasi–lender of last resort, where the emphasis should be on the quasi–lender of *last* resort. We cannot do without that lender of last resort, but we want it to be a standby lender, as Guillermo Calvo pointed out in his talk earlier today. Countries that aren't members of the elite group of countries that can issue debt in their own currencies need to borrow in foreign currencies; and they can't create foreign currencies, so when they have a crisis and it's a foreign exchange crisis, they need some place to get the foreign exchange. We need to find a way to provide that foreign exchange without creating the problems of either moral hazard or some of the others that came up at the end of Charlie Calomiris' paper.

The second is the provision of information. If we are going to rely primarily on market-based solutions, then markets will function best if the information provided to the markets is timely, adequate, and up to date—and correct, of course.

And third, we thought that there was a problem of technical assistance.

We not only have to provide countries with information, but we have to see that the information that exists is constructed and disseminated in a proper way.

What did the commission do? It identified three main reasons for recent crises. One is pegged exchange rates—we heard about that earlier today. Second is weaknesses of the financial system so that the worst crises, the ones that Calomiris talked about a little while ago, were crises that occurred when both the exchange rate and the financial system collapsed at the same time, so that the whole banking system went down. We needed something to avoid that, and the question was what should be done. In most of these crises the banking systems were undercapitalized and depended excessively on short-term capital flows. The third problem that we wanted to address, or the third main reason for these crises to occur—here again, Calomiris talked about that—was the long time that it took while the IMF negotiated out all the conditions to be put on the loans that they were going to make. Crises got worse during that period. We wanted to shorten the length of time between the time the crisis occurred and the time that they solved it, while at the same time providing some remedy for the first two problems.

We came up with three solutions. First, countries should have either a hard peg or a floating exchange rate. There has been a lot of talk about that and my time is limited, so I will not say more about it. Second, for the financial system, we came up with four preconditions for assistance. The treasury and other people labeled this as radical and extreme. I'm going to go through those four preconditions and you tell me which of these you think is radical or extreme. First, capital adequacy—that is, to apply something like the Basel standards, or better than the Basel standards (but nevertheless, a capital adequacy standard). Second, competitive foreign banks admitted into the country. That is from the World Trade Organization's General Agreement on Trade and Services, Protocol number 5. Fifty countries have already accepted that, so how can that be considered a radical change? Third, an adequate fiscal policy. That is not a radical change either—it might be a radical change for some of these countries, but it is hardly a radical proposal. And fourth, countries must publish the maturity structure of their sovereign debt, so that people will know how much they owe and how much is going to come due in a very short period of time.

Those were our recommendations. Those are the ex ante conditions the country would have to meet. These ex ante conditions would replace the current ex post conditions that sometimes run up to fifty or more conditions, which are ever changing, and most of the time are not observed. The purpose of having ex ante conditions was, first, to push these countries into having better financial systems and better economic policies, and second, to speed up the process between the crisis and the time that assistance would come forward, by making the assistance automatic or quasi-automatic. The way in which we chose to implement it was to develop a Bagehotian lender of last resort, that is, to basically take Bagehot's rule and make it apply to an international system. There would be collateral or senior status for the debt and a penalty rate. The idea is that if the country has a problem and it has a collateral, it can go to the marketplace to borrow. That's why it's going to be a standby lender of last resort with a penalty rate, because countries will only choose to pay that penalty rate when the market isn't operating. On days when the market operates they'll be in the marketplace; on days when the market doesn't operate, then they'll be at the IMF. And as soon as the market begins to operate again, they'll like to get out of the penalty rate by rolling the loan into a market-based loan. That is why it can be short-term assistance, and that is why it is a "standby."

Now, what about countries that don't meet the standards? Imagine what is going to happen if these rules were adopted. There are going to be two lists of countries, the A-list and the B-list. The A-list would contain all those countries that have met the four preconditions. The B-list would have all those countries that haven't met the preconditions. How much money do you think they are going to get from the private capital markets if they are on the B-list? The incentive that is going to drive governments to meet these prequalifications is that if you're not on the A-list you're not going to get much money from the private market, and you're certainly not going to get it for long periods of time. The markets are going to ask, "How come you are not on the A-list? Why don't you meet the standards?" It is not the penalty rate that is going to drive them into good behavior. It's the fact that no one in his right mind will want to be on the B-list if he can possibly avoid it. And we gave them five years in which to move from one to the other. Maybe that is not sufficient time, perhaps it ought to be eight years, and that can be discussed further. But the idea is that we are going to give countries an incentive to behave properly, to have a good, open, and competitive economy.

My time is limited, so let me say that there is much more to the story. I just want to react to a couple of other things and then I am going to stop. Many people have said that this is a program to destroy the IMF. Nothing could be farther from the truth. It *shrinks* the IMF in a certain sense. Most of the people at the IMF work on Article IV consultations, that is, they work to provide information which is very useful to the market. In our proposal we continue the Article IV consultations—we just take away financing tied to Article IV consultations. The reason we shrink the IMF is because we eliminate the source of crises. If most crises are the result of bad exchange rate policies and bad financial systems, and we get rid of the bad financial systems and we get rid of the bad exchange rate policies, then we still have crises—no one can promise that crises disappear—but we will have fewer crises. We will not need the IMF as much. That is why we can put it on standby, relying on the market when the market can work and relying on the IMF when the market cannot work.

Finally, let me just say two or three sentences about the World Bank, which takes up a big part of our report. We discovered, in the process of our work, using World Bank data, that 70 percent of the bank's loans go to countries that have investment-grade ratings and borrow in the capital markets. If you look at the list of these countries, lo and behold, they happen to be U.S. client countries or countries that we would like to make clients of the U.S. Seventy percent of the money goes to these countries. Now, the critics of our reports say "Well . . . You are going to take the money away from a country like China, which has most of the poor people in the world." That's true; China does have most of the poor people in the world, but it also has $160 billion worth of foreign exchange reserves and it borrows in the capital market, on average, $60 billion a year, as compared to less than a billion dollars that it gets from the World Bank. It can finance any poverty-alleviation program that it wants to finance. How much more valuable would that billion dollars be if we reallocated it from China to those countries that have no access to the capital market, where they have poor people without the resources to be able to solve some of their problems? So, concerning the World Bank, the main part of our recommendation is to do just that.

Let me close by saying that the great interest of the United States in these institutions is not because we are going to increase trade or we are going to increase our standard of living by changing their behavior. We, above all, have been providing public goods in the whole postwar period. The public goods that we provide have produced greater stability and greater spread of democracy than at any time in the past. If we reform these institutions, we will continue to see greater stability, greater spread of democracy; and that is in the interest of the United States. The interest of the United States in these institutions is not because we are going to gain commercially. The interest of the United States in these institutions is because we're going to help have a more stable, more democratic world order, which is the high challenge, and to a considerable extent the high achievement of the U.S. in the postwar period. Thank you.

CALVO: Thank you Allan. I'm sure that we are going to revisit most of these topics. There's one issue that kept ringing in my ears as you spoke, and I don't know if the other panelists wish to address it. The problem I have with the IMF as you seem to envision it is that it looks a little bit like a central bank, but a very non-independent central bank.

MELTZER: Now or under our proposal?

CALVO: Certainly not now, but I would like to hear your comments about independence under your proposal, because moving countries from the A-list to the B-list and vice versa is going to be politically charged. Under the present circumstances it would be very difficult to stop the hand of the treasury from interfering in the process, and I wonder how difficult it would be under the proposal.

Let's proceed with our second speaker, who in alphabetical order will be Matthew Bishop.

MATTHEW BISHOP: I am Matthew Bishop and I am glad that you and the conference organizers have used the phrase *institutions for the new millennium* rather using than the expression *global financial architecture,* so much in use nowadays.

MELTZER: I hope we would avoid that expression.

BISHOP: Yes. At *The Economist* we have had a lot of debate about using the expression. I actually prefer the phrase *global financial infrastructure* if we are going to use a phrase like that at all. The term *architecture* reveals for me a sort of planning mentality, as if there is some blueprint that one can come up with that will provide all the solutions, whereas *infrastructure* is more of an enabling sort of thing rather than a complete solution. And I think it is very striking that many of the financial institutions now under discussion were created at a sort of high point of the planning mentality within capitalist countries. In fact, the greatest British economist, Keynes, was simultaneously introducing the idea of planning macroeconomic policy and also planning global recovery and stability; and it is notable that his macropolicies have been largely kicked out, but some of the ideas on institutions have continued despite a record that I think is not much better.

My concern about the planners, even though many economists use this dreadful phrase *global financial architecture,* is the assumption that in practice there is some predictable, orderly solution out there that bright people like them can come up with. And they sort of ignore the human factor and the fact that people just don't fit into the blueprint. Even politics means that people don't actually behave as you would like them to, and investors are often catching the blueprint authors by surprise. I think this even affects the proposals from this commission, in terms of the crises that we are talking about and the institutions to deal with them. I think it is very striking how inherently volatile financial markets are, and the idea that you can actually manage to avoid crises by any ingenious system, I think, maybe lulls people into a false sense of security, when the message should be that everyone (including countries) has to be prepared to accept that shocks are going to come along. I was very struck by the experience of the financial crisis of the autumn of 1998, which I had the privilege of covering for *The Economist.* It started with the Russian default, then the long-term capital problem and so forth, and soon things happened that everybody's financial model said shouldn't happen. And partly as a consequence of leverage, partly as a consequence of inadequate information, and partly because of strong financial incentives and overconfidence about their own brilliance amongst the financial community, the result was complete paralysis and fear and lots of chief executives of investment banks on Wall Street going crazy and demanding that their risk models be rethought and withdrawing from risk-taking activities. And actually I think it is now becoming clear that the risk models that are used by all those banks actually exacerbate the problems of volatility in financial markets in certain circumstances and maybe we need to expect crises of liquidity more often than ever before. Soon after, *Time* magazine published a cover with pictures of Larry Summers, Allan Greenspan, and Robert Rubin on the front, named as "the committee to save the world." And I think it's also worth bearing in mind that, in fact, most of what went on was, I think, domestically motivated, having to do more with problems of potential bankruptcies on Wall Street than with dealing with worldwide problems. The Fed made it very clear that it was willing to stand ready to provide liquidity to insure the system survived. We had a series of interest rate cuts, again, primarily justified by restoring confidence on Wall Street. Fannie Mae and Freddie Mac bought a vast number of mortgage bank securities that were being used for hedging by hedge funds to fund speculative activities, and equal pressure came from America on the international institutions to lend, to try and again restore confidence on Wall Street. This resulted in a huge amount of moral hazard and probably the stock market rising, and talk of something called *the Greenspan put option,* which people now felt is underwriting the stock market. In other words, we are talking about international institutions but in fact a lot of the activity concerning the need for reform has been generated by domestic pressures, I would argue.

So then, countries need to be prepared. There is no perfect global blueprint, and the real challenge is how do we get countries to be prepared so that surprises and shocks don't turn into crises. Which brings us to the report of the Meltzer Commission. Reading it, it's a damning indictment of the IMF, the World Bank, and the Regional Development Banks. And in fact I think what they essentially argue for is scrapping the IMF and the World Bank. The conclusions of the report are that you stop the IMF and the World Bank from doing what they are currently doing and create entirely new things for them to do, in the case of the IMF this lender-of-last-resort insurance function and in the case of the World Bank this new and more generous institution investing in poverty alleviation infrastructure and using the private sector to ensure greater efficiency and to encourage less corrupt behavior in the country receiving aid, which would only be the world's poorest countries.

Now, I think, as these reforms go, that they are pretty attractive in many ways. The liquidity proposal that Calomiris explained seems to make a lot of sense to me, but I must admit, it just seems too perfect and too much economic sense to be workable. . . . [Laughter] I'm just trying to think of some finance minister going to his people when there is a run on his currency and his bonds are rapidly deteriorating in price and saying, "Well, I'm afraid this is a structural problem, not a liquidity problem, so I can't go and use this credit facility that we have at the IMF." And his voters go, "What? There's this money sitting here! Why aren't you taking it?" The temptation to take the money and call an election before the money runs out must be quite high. And then there is the question of whether it is actually possible to know, when you are the government, whether you're in a liquidity crisis or a structural one. These things are very hard to tell, the markets often catch these politicians by surprise. They don't really understand the financial markets and maybe they'll make mistakes.

And if it works, there are the problems involved with this prequalification idea. If the prequalification standards really are tough, will anyone that qualifies actually ever be the victim of a liquidity crisis of this sort? And if that's the case, is the plan that you create this institution that does absolutely nothing beyond the prequalification period? Or maybe it will spend all its time following up people to see if they are really prequalified or not. And wouldn't all of this get us back into all the problems of the IMF taking decisions on specific issues about policy in particular countries?

And are they really going to push someone off the A-list onto the B-list, given that that is going to actually create some kind of crisis in the financial markets and leading to the bonds of those governments being devalued? This is a huge question given also the fact that, as you know, people love working for the IMF and they are often interfering, so you have gigantic incentives to overcome.

As for the World Bank, I think the basic proposal of the commission is a great idea, but that requires a huge increase in international giving—let's hope it takes place. In passing, I think that the Bank for International Settlements got off quite lightly in the report. I know it was mentioned that the way they calculate capital requirements is not perfect, but I actually believe that it was a very serious cause of the problems that led to the Asian crisis. But, in any case, I like the reforms proposed for the banks. They are innovations, and the only real problem I have is what chance they have of being implemented. Here, we have two big institutions, with the IMF unable to get beyond the point of how to select a leader, except for the argument that he is a German. [Laughter] When you think about the innovator's dilemma, it is a huge question, one that is on the desk of every corporate chair of America. How on earth does one innovate given the intense inertia within any organization and the fear of cannibalization? And in this case you haven't even gotten an IMF dot.com banging on your door. [Laughter] You have just got this organization that has absolutely no accountability to speak of and no pressures to change. So I am afraid that though the ideas are in many ways very attractive, I'm left feeling quite depressed by the whole process and feeling that the likeliest outcome is that we just will get a lot more of the same: more crises, more money being wasted, and more moral hazard. And if only there was some way to scrap these organizations, maybe we could have a world where there wouldn't be any rescues, but there would be a kind of ad hoc rescue, and politicians would at least have to account for themselves to their electorates, which you don't have with IMF.

Those are my thoughts.

CALVO: Thank you very much. I think we are going back to the issue of IMF governance and the effectiveness of that governance. And I guess you have put your finger also on the incentives from the borrowing side, an issue that Mike Dooley and other brought up before. I am sure that this topic will be revisited.

We have now Britton Harris.

T. BRITTON HARRIS: Thank you very much. I have to tell you that when I saw who my fellow panelists were, my obvious question was, "Why am

I on the panel?" And I told myself, "The answer is that you are the only one who actually invests real money in the real world, and your job is to represent investors and talk about how these financial institutions influence them." So, I am going to do that.

And so the first thing I would tell you is that you're probably overestimating the degree of knowledge that the average investor has about these international financial institutions in general. And as I thought about this, I found that the whole thing is rather confusing. I read Stanley Fischer, who says the IMF is the most important way through which the international community promotes good macroeconomic policies around the world. Then he goes on to point out how small their staff is relative to the size of the typical regional U.S. Federal Reserve bank. Then, Larry Summers says the IMF is one of the most cost-effective investments we can make in the defense of America's core interest. I also thought he was very profound when he said that the best way for a country to reduce poverty is to make itself richer—[Laughter]—which is certainly very prescriptive. And then President Clinton said that we now have as much to fear from nations that are too weak as we do from nations that are too strong—and that is a very huge change from the way people thought twenty years ago. So, here I have Fischer, Summers, and Clinton all in support of the IMF, and therefore the IMF must be good. And I thought I would hear the same all over this conference of economic professionals, but I didn't hear it once.

On the other hand, George Schultz proposes to abolish the IMF outright, as an institution that is swollen beyond any defensible purpose and actually does more harm than good. And then, this morning, Professor Bordo said something that for investors is a massive statement: countries that went to the IMF for funding had subsequent real GDP growth that was either lower or no better than those that did not. For an investor that is a huge statement to make. The Heritage Foundation says that data for the past three decades demonstrate conclusively that most of the less-developed countries receiving IMF loans have the same or lower per capita wealth today than they had before receiving these loans and many of them are actually worse off. And then we get to Professor Meltzer himself with his report. The professor has everybody up in arms. So, Schultz, Professor Bordo, the Heritage Foundation, and Professor Meltzer oppose the IMF, and therefore the IMF must be bad.

So, as an investor I am confused. As a sort of confused investor, you try to go back to your pillars and your fundamentals, and you then remember that there are four issues that are important to investors. One of them is confidence, the second one is stability, the third is growth, and the fourth is fairness, or ethics. Therefore, as investors, we are very much in favor of pretty much anything, anyone, anywhere, that produces more confidence, more stability, and higher growth within a fair and ethical structure. Then, for investors, the key question with regard to the IMF and these other institutions is, "Do these institutions contribute to these four key pillars of attractive investment?" I think the bottom line is that the record is mixed, and like most things, the IMF's reputation with investors waxes and wanes, and at the moment I would say it is below average.

From an investor's perspective, there are six things that I would like to mention. First, that with all said, at the margin I think investors would prefer a properly structured, properly constructed lender of last resort. But this lender of last resort should be considered what I would call an *economic paramedic*. When my son was injured two or three weeks ago at a ski slope, everything went into disarray. His parents were destabilized, there were no doctors, there was nothing that could be done for him until a small team of paramedics showed up on the scene, carried him down from the mountain, put him in the ambulance, drove the ambulance safely to the hospital, dropped him off and everything turned out fine in the end. There was no one, during that time gap, that was capable of handling the problem. With that said, I should also tell you that we got a huge bill, and that we never saw those paramedics again—which is a key part of the analogy.

The second thing is, don't compete with us in private markets. The IMF should not be a source of low-cost financing for countries with ready access to financial markets—a point that I think has been made repeatedly. And in addition to that, it should not be a long-term supporter of countries that cannot break bad habits. The IMF should then be a bridge, that should not be very long, for countries to get back to the private markets.

Third, I think we all would be in favor of a premium price charged for services, but charges for this kind of service should not be below, and certainly not substantially below, what you would pay otherwise, just because you are in the club.

The fourth thing is that we need a much higher graduation rate from these countries. The main message from the Heritage Foundation and other critics is that the idea should be to produce productive, growth-oriented, stable investment opportunities for global investors to access on a long-term basis. If that has not been the case, the best scenario that you can paint is that you have not hurt anybody, but at the end of the day you also have not helped anyone.

The fifth point is that one of the most effective and simple things the

IMF could do would be to produce standardized, accurate, periodic reports for all countries. The fund has access to information that is not properly disseminated at this point, and it would be very helpful to investors if it were.

And the sixth and final thing—and I'll end before I get the red card—has to do with a subtlety that exists behind all of this. Investors, particularly large investors, are investing in the whole asset class. They're not just investing in Argentina or just investing in Mexico or in Thailand or in Russia. They are investing in all these countries at the same time, because they are looking for a diversification benefit. That makes it extremely important to contain contagion for them to be able to capture that diversification benefit.

CALVO: Thank you very much. Our last panelist, in alphabetical order, is John Lipsky.

JOHN LIPSKY: Thank you. I first have a few introductory remarks, and then I will concentrate on some of the comments that have been made, trying not to repeat those that I agree with—I thought, for example, that a lot of the things that Britton said were very sensible.

First of all I want to take an opportunity to publicly congratulate Allan Meltzer and Charles Calomiris and their colleagues on the excellent work that they did in producing this commission report in a very short period of time, covering a very broad spectrum of issues and at the same time generating a focus on what I hope will be a very useful and productive way. I am sorry I missed this morning's discussions, and I hope that some of my remarks won't be completely repetitive.

I find it very interesting, and I'm not going to deviate from this tendency, that the discussion generated by the commission's report has focused almost entirely on the IMF, an institution that the commission did not suggest should be eliminated in any way, shape, or form, but adapted. I did think that the remarks the commission made on the World Bank and the development banks were extremely powerful, and I have been surprised that they have not elicited more discussion. I would recommend a rereading of the commission's report in that regard, because I think there are serious issues that need to be rethought.

Going back to the main line of the discussion—the IMF—before going on I should note, because of truth in advertising, something that Professor Calvo didn't mention, and it is that I started out during the first ten years of my career with the IMF, before going to Solomon Brothers in 1984. If there is a part of the comments that we keep hearing about the IMF that makes me a little uneasy, it's what I would consider a lack of sensitivity to the structural and legal role of the IMF and the actual role that has performed since it was founded. The report suggests that the functioning of the IMF had three assumptions underlying it. First, that the world economy would remain on a system of fixed but adjustable exchange rates. Second, in the words of the commission, that after an initial postwar economic adjustment, payments for goods and services would be free of exchange controls. And third, in short, that the capital account transactions would be under the complete control of individuals, with the provision of the legal basis for a multilateral, nondiscriminatory payment system in which prima facie it would be considered illegal to interfere with current payments for balance-of-payments purposes. And the way that they thought would be supportive of that, would be the dollar exchange system. Yet, conventionally it is claimed that the IMF was created to run the fixed exchange rate system and it has morphed into an organization that is primarily in charge of crisis control and that makes large emergency loans. And I would say that this conventional claim is missing the point.

At the time the articles of agreement were signed, hardly anybody didn't interfere with current payments for balance-of-payments purposes. In essence, in signing the articles of agreement, countries said, "We are all sinners, but we will make ourselves free from sin over time through the good offices of the executive board of the IMF." And what is amazing is that it worked. That is essentially what has happened. And we should therefore recognize that the lending role of the IMF was always considered completely subsidiary to it is basic role of creating this system free of controls of payments for current transactions. And further, that the Article IV missions that have been much maligned and much misunderstood are not simply fact-gathering or interfering missions, but were designed to provide the surveillance by the international community of the compliance of individual countries with their obligations under the articles of agreement. There is no other institution that provides this role. This is a role that only the IMF can accomplish, and if you took away those things like the Article IV missions, you have to ask yourself, "How are we going to guarantee compliance with the countries' legal obligations?" or "How is the fund going to conduct surveillance?" I wish there was a little more sensitivity to that role of the fund which is absolutely critical and absolutely unique and not covered by any other institution. And this leads me to another question that I will put on the table before I turn to the commission's report itself.

The interim committee of the IMF, which in spirit is a kind of executive committee of the board of governors, is a political board that was created to propose changes in the structure of the IMF, and it was endorsed in the annual meetings in Hong Kong three years ago, that the articles of agreement be extended to include the goal of creating capital account convertibility—in other words, that freedom of capital movements be given the same legal status of the freedom of current account movements. And the idea was not that freedom would be decreed overnight, but that the same process would take place for creating a liberalized world of capital markets that was implemented successfully under the IMF in the postwar era in which current account payments were effectively liberalized. I also wish that the commission had dealt with that decision which the interim committee already has endorsed and that I happen to think would provide a basis for substantial reforms, not only of the IMF itself, but of successful liberalization of the capital account of the world. I think that by understating the structural and legal role of the fund, which is unique, the commission has overlooked what I would consider an important avenue toward further reform and improvement of the stability of the international system in a way that I suspect most of the members of the commission would approve of. I wish they had addressed that because, in fact, the interim committee has endorsed that proposal but it is very clear that subsequently they have backed away from it, thanks to the kind of criticism that I would consider well intentioned but misdirected, and to arguments about the need for allowing countries to unilaterally place controls over capital movements, what today are perfectly legal under the articles of agreement.

Let me turn now to just a couple of quick remarks on the commission's report. I do not want to run out of time, but I can't resist, after what Matthew Bishop said about economists, to remember the only good economist's joke I think I ever heard, and that was by Ronald Reagan. He said that an economist is a kind of person who, when he sees that something works in practice, he thinks that the real question is whether it works in theory. [Laughter] He actually said that.

MELTZER: It was probably more profound than he realized.

LIPSKY: Exactly.

Let me conclude then with my short remarks, that unfortunately will be quick and will involve argument by assertion. The commission report talks about the fact that problems come from currency pegs and we've heard all about how you can't have pegged rates because they lead to problems. All well and good. As a former fund official, I would say that the problem is that you're in a crisis, they have a pegged rate, then what do you do? The commission is quite silent on how do you get out of that problem once you are in it. It's nice to say, as in another economist's joke, "Assume we have a can opener," or "Assume we have floating rates," but the question is that the fund needs and has always tried to develop ways to get out of a bad peg once you're there.

I think that Britton Harris's remarks hint that the idea that moral hazard is absolutely critical to the problems of the fund is dramatically overstated. One fact that suggests this is that although it is alleged that moral hazard was one of the explanations for large amounts of short-term lending in recent crises, the question has to be asked of "Why was that lending so uneven across banks from different nations in different areas?" In other words, if there was moral hazard, somehow it was not perceived equally by banks in different regions, which suggests that maybe that is not a complete explanation.

There is a lot of picking on conditionality in the report, and I think in a somewhat misleading way. When you say that the fund program conditions are not kept, and this means that they have no impact, it's not a logical conclusion. You have to ask the counterfactual "What would have happened in absence of conditionality?" I don't think that is a very easy question to answer, and my experience tells me that this is not the right way to look at the question.

Concerning prequalifications, I think there is an important issue here. I am sure this lender-of-last-resort issue is a big question, and I'm not going to solve it in two seconds here. But I should mention that the report tends to pick on conditionality as involving excess discretion, and it strikes me that the prequalification ultimately is going to involve a lot of discretion as well, and it doesn't scape that problem. Further, the lender-of-last-resort solution as suggested by the commission doesn't fully meet all the Bagehot conditions, one of which is access to unlimited amounts of liquidity at a penalty rate. The commission said very clearly that there should be limits and that does not meet the Bagehot conditions for the successful lender of last resort.

I think that some issues were not well addressed concerning the question of adequate fiscal policy—things like auditing and accounting standards, creditor rights, and legal systems, which I think legitimately impinge on stability of financial systems. And since they ought to do with the question of prequalification, they get us right back into the world of discretion, because you will end up asking how does the broad principle apply in a particular country's case and in the particular country's institutions. Again here I don't think we escape from discretion.

Finally, the commission suggested a large expansion of the role of the

Bank for International Settlements [BIS] in terms of setting standards, and I frankly didn't understand where that came from or why the BIS should be considered the logical seat of that kind of operation, that struck me as belonging squarely with the IMF. The other factor that doesn't eliminate discretion in the proposals of the commission is that if there is a crisis in a not prequalified country that is deemed to have systemic implications, the lending is to be made available. And if that is the case, again, we are way back into the world of discretion and politics, along with the issue that others have mentioned, namely, once somebody is qualified, how do you unqualify him?—basically a decision to invite a crisis.

As a final word, I am actually quite optimistic. I guess Matthew is not so optimistic. I think that the better performance of the U.S. economy in the past few years, among other things, has not been an accident, but a result of better policies and more liberalized markets. I believe that the message has been taken home by many countries, not that the U.S. is some paragon of virtue, but that better policies pay, and that we are in an era in which policy is improving around the world. One thing that has been taken on board is a concentration by central banks on price stability, without much qualification, and I think they're having success. That, plus the move toward greater liberalization market after market and economy after economy around the world make me think that in fact, there are reasons for optimism and not pessimism about the way forward. Thank you.

CALVO: Thank you very much, John.

Well, Allan, you have your hands full with the questions and so we would like to hear from you. Let me add just one small thing, a clarification rather. On the set of preconditions, I did not hear a direct reference as to what one might call vulnerabilities—short-maturity loans, bonds, etc. I know that you want the countries to publish the maturity structure. Is that enough? Should we also worry about the vulnerability that, for example, a short-maturity debt structure would bring about?

MELTZER: I'm obviously not going to take up all of these points, but I will try to group them and answer generally and then we can open up the discussion and those who are not satisfied can come back.

I like the first question that you asked, Guillermo, right after I finished, in which I think you put your hand on what is probably the single most important problem: if these institutions—the fund, the World Bank, and the others—are going to operate effectively, then they have to be more independent of the U.S. treasury than they have been. And that is the central issue. I think a lot of the criticisms of our report have nothing to do with what is in the report. Obviously, there are criticisms that have to do with the report, but the central criticisms have to do, as Charlie has pointed out in a paper that is partially written, with the question of whether the IMF and the banks are going to be independent of the U.S. treasury. And that is a question where I think, and hope, the facts will be on our side. When I give this talk on the fund and the bank and the reforms proposed by the commission in Europe, or other places outside of the United States, and even inside the United States, and when I talk about freeing the IMF and the bank from the control of the U.S. treasury, the heads nod. Even in the case of civil servants who are very circumspect about those things, those heads nod.

There really is a desire to see this happen, partly because the Cold War is over. Everyone knew that Mobutu was a crook, but he was our crook, that is, as opposed to being a Russian crook. Everyone knew that the Suharto family was corrupt, but they were our crooks. Now they're on their own. The same is true of many others. Now, why is that happening? Partly, as I said, because the Cold War is over, partly because the domestic political pressures in the United States are against foreign aid—certainly against ineffective foreign aid. When the public reads that the IMF gave the money to the Russian central bank and we don't know what happened to it, that is a true statement. People think that it is not a very good way to conduct business. When they read that the Suharto family or the Mobutu family steals the money, that is not very popular, so we need to have reform. And I think the major thrust of the reform, the reason that people are interested in our report, is because it goes to the heart of questions which people in the U.S. are concerned about: namely, the question about corruption, the question about ineffectiveness, the question about the fact that these institutions are big and long lasting, and finally—and very important—that while the last crisis occurred at a time when the U.S. was very strong and doing very well, nevertheless, we had to absorb a current account deficit of something like $150 to $200 billion. We are not going to be willing to do that all the time. That is partly the reason why the labor unions complain about the fund. That is why they have become much more anti–foreign trade and anti-IMF.

When we wrote our report, three people didn't sign it, two of them principally because they wanted the report to say that there should be worker rights, that is, some form of protection for labor unions, which of course would involve restricting trade.

I think that tells you something about what is happening to the domestic political consensus in the United States. And if the consensus is not there to support international institutions and foreign aid, and if the United

States doesn't take leadership, it's hard to know where the consensus in the world is going to come from.

The question of whether we are going to get reform involves much more than the kinds of issues which are in our report, and it does involve the question you started with, of whether these institutions are going to be effective. In order to be effective they must become more independent of the U.S. treasury. They are now used largely as slush funds for the treasury, to solve international political problems. They are only going to be effective if that influence, which may not be removed, becomes much more limited than it has been before. You only need to look at the list of countries that are principal beneficiaries of World Bank loans to get the idea that the countries are not a randomly selected group of countries. It's China, Argentina, Mexico, Brazil, countries which are important politically and in other ways to the U.S. That has to begin to change. I think that the point that you raised at the beginning, about independence and nonindependence, is the critical issue on which reform will succeed or fail. That is, we have to get the treasury to accept these changes and that is the hard part of the battle.

Let me now just say briefly a few things about the other comment. Much comment is about whether we will generate a crisis when we move countries from A-list to B-list. I think that's a very important point. I respond by saying that we have tried to set that up not so that it becomes a dramatic event, but so that it becomes like a corporation having its bond rating moved from AA1 to AA3. It is a wrench, but not something that is going to be completely unforeseen. Why is that? Because the principal job of the International Monetary Fund under our arrangement is not going to be crisis management—we expect our proposals would reduce the number and the intensity of crises—but it will be to collect timely and accurate information and to publish the Article IV reports. People will be able to read the Article IV reports and decide, and the comments will be, "This one doesn't look too good; it looks as though they are going to get a rating change coming along, so we should get out of there." And somebody else will say, "Well . . . At the current interest rate, I'm willing to go in." And that is the way in which the market smooths the effects of the change, when it finally takes place. And that is why, if the proposed reforms are carried out, the problem can be handled. It would be a problem if we suddenly, without any previous signaling or warning, get the announcement that there is about to be a crisis and we don't think that Thailand can hold on to its exchange rate. That does produce a crisis. But if over a period of time some problems have been observed, and we say that Thailand is running larger deficits than can be sustained and they have to do something about it, that is going to produce different kinds of response in the market. I believe it would work the way bond-rating-changes announcements of companies work. If the markets are developed and resilient then we should be able to get through those problems without much concern.

BISHOP: Although the IMF was a good six months behind the curve in the Asia crisis.

MELTZER: Right. That is why the principal job of the IMF has to be to collect and timely publish information and work on the Article IV consultations—which is what most of the IMF employees now work on anyway. We have read many of the Article IV reports and they are not always right, but they are certainly carefully done, thoughtful, analytical reports. I expected them to be the kind of stuff that says this went up and that went down—what I call the ups and downs of economic life—but they were not of that kind. They were analytic reports, not always right, but serious and analytical. And releasing those reports is going to provide the market with a great deal more information than it now has, and therefore is going to let the market work more efficiently. Will it work perfectly? No, it will not work perfectly. We don't expect it to work perfectly. We don't expect that there will be adequate information about Burkina Faso or Senegal, but there isn't going to be a lot of capital involved in Burkina Faso or Senegal, either, so that is unlikely to produce a major crisis.

Now, John gave me a long laundry list of objections. I'm not going to refer to all of them; I already responded to some on how adjustments are to be made. I want to pick up on the question of discretion. This is a rule-based system, but there is some discretion—this is true of any rule-based system except in systems in which you are on automatic pilot. If you adopt an inflation-targeting system, for example, it is going to be a rule-based system, but you have to make some judgment about whether the inflation rate is going to go up or down and make some judgments and forecasts, so there is room for discretion. But in the system we propose there is not quite as much discretion as you alleged. After all, we do know something about capital standards, and it is not so hard to look at the books of these banks or countries to see whether they have met the capital standards or not. It isn't so hard to decide whether there is competition in the banking system. Of course, there will always be complaints and charges of discrimination, but by and large we can decide whether the country is complying with the preconditions or not. On the fiscal side, yes, it is hard to define a precise standard. The commission sort of punted on the question of trying to define the fiscal standard, because if we had tried to do that we would have been there for a much longer time than we had. This I'll grant you. And the precondition of releasing information on the maturity distribution of their debt is going to be a pretty straightforward kind of thing. So, I'll grant you that there is a little room for discretion but it is not nearly as bad as you allege.

Finally, there was the question, "Do we distinguish between a liquidity crisis and a solvency crisis?" We ask for collateral; if they come with collateral and they come at a penalty rate, then we say that it is a liquidity crisis, because we are going to get paid, whatever happens. If they can't come with collateral, then we're going to say that this is a case in which there is no way in which we can bail them out without an outright transfer, so that is a solvency problem, and that is going to be the cutoff point.

CALVO: I just need clarification. What if the collateral is, "We are going to make an adjustment, and will increase taxes"?

MELTZER: No, "We are going to give you a loan, and you are going to back it by collateral." These can be things like receipts in foreign exchange—

CALVO: I see. You would not take future tax revenues as collateral.

MELTZER: That is right. You are not going to give us a promise. That is not collateral. We are using the term *collateral* in the sense that a banker uses it. That is what Charlie meant when he talked about a senior obligation; the repayment is going to be ahead of all the other obligations and it is going to be backed with some kind of collateral.

CALVO: I think that is a very important clarification, because it seems to me that is quite different from the way the fund operates now. The collateral they get is a promise that they will make an adjustment. You wouldn't take that as collateral.

MELTZER: No; we would not. Let me just pick up on your point, and then I am going to stop. The deficiency in the present system is that the Russians or anybody else know that they can promise the fund anything, even when they have no intention or ability to carry it out. They know that then, three months or later, maybe the fund will rap them across the knuckles and tell them that they are not going to renew the loan. But both—the fund and the country—know that the fund has a vested interest in seeing the country "succeed." And the country knows that, and they also know that at the end of three or four more months the fund is going to be back there, making another agreement, in which the country does the same thing that it did before. That is what we want to get out of. That is why we want the preconditions and not the ex post conditions.

Let me make one last remark; I know that I have said "finally" four times now, but this is the final "finally." After Anatoly Chubais came to the United States and negotiated the $22 billion bailout for Russia, there was a private dinner for him in which I was one of the guests. And I congratulated him because, I said, "You know, you're the only man I ever knew who came to borrow twelve billion dollars and ended up with twenty-two. If I am ever in debt or have a problem, I want you to be my negotiator." And then I asked him, "Do you think that the twenty-two billion dollars will actually get you out of your problem?" His answer was, "This is the best chance we ever had," to which I said "That is not exactly an affirmative answer," and he repeated, "But it is the best chance we have ever had. . . ." So much for conditional lending.

CALVO: Thank you, Allan. Perhaps other panelists would like to make some very brief remarks? Would you, John?

LIPSKY: Yes, I would, actually. It will be brief because I want everybody else to have a chance. I don't want us to get lost in an argument over how to run the liquidity facilities and if that is the right way to do it, and if this really represents such a difference as it is claimed with regard to what the fund is doing now, and so on. I just want to give a little warning because I think, once again, that the discussions are taking place with a little bit of a lack of sensitivity to the legal structure of the fund and its importance. And that is, the notion that somehow the fund's staff ought to be put at work as economic investigators and informants to the investing public; that is not the legal structure of the fund.

MELTZER: Let's change it.

LIPSKY: Well . . . That is an important question. But the legal structure of the fund, of course, is that the staff works for the executive board, and the executive board is the political authority of the fund. The analyses under the Article IV are designed specifically to judge the adequacy of the performance of the member countries under their obligations of the articles of agreement to be considered before their fellow country members. To say now that we should take that and use it as a report for investors is to profoundly change the nature of the relationship of the consultation of fund staff with member governments, to the benefit of investors.

MELTZER: No—to the benefit of the member governments.

LIPSKY: There is nothing today that prevents a member government from releasing an Article IV discussion paper related to that country. The member government always has the option to do that, at its discretion. That is the country's own prerogative and it can always do it. but to make it mandatory is to change the nature of the relationship of the fund staff to fund members, and whether that is good is not immediately obvious to me. There is a difference between making data available and requiring information on the facts to be disseminated, and to make public, as a matter of course, the opinion of the fund staff and the nature of their discussions with member governments. This is a step that has consequences—that is not obviously or ambiguously good—and I think should be treated with great caution. Data dissemination obviously is another issue.

CALVO: Matthew?

BISHOP: If I may quickly jump in for a couple of points. The first, in connection with Chubais's response about the best chance they've ever had for Russia. I wonder whether similar possibilities, or chances, may apply for a country that is on the verge of default and where it is sufficiently difficult to tell whether it is a liquidity problem or an insolvency problem, that it may be worth the gamble to exercise the facility, because that will give the IMF approval that it is a liquidity crisis, so that the country can go to the markets and meanwhile refinance everything before the crisis happens.

MELTZER: We get collateral, right?

BISHOP: Well . . . All you are doing with collateral is becoming senior debt, which means everyone else's bonds become more risky and the consequences. The question is that there can be a gamble for the country, in which by taking your senior debt it sends a message of the situation being a liquidity problem rather than something else, even though it may actually be a structural problem. It just buys them time, and it is a gamble. And if countries start to take this debt as a gamble, it may actually lead to a deeper crisis in the long run.

The other point that I would just love to hear from Allan is how you actually think the process of reform is going to happen in these institutions.

CALVO: There are several questions from the floor. I would ask each speaker to please be short and ask questions, if possible, rather than offering long comments. Charles?

CHARLES W. CALOMIRIS: I just wanted to make a couple of clarifications. First, we have been talking about collateral and lenders' priorities. We talk about the desirability of collateral, but there are many practical questions and we need to be very careful. Second, and with respect to a couple of things that John said: He said that unlike the Bagehot, we want to limit lending. The Bagehot conditions refer to unlimited collateralized senior lending, but to say this is the same is to say that you cannot have unlimited amount of senior lending since you cannot have an unlimited amount of good collateral. Just as how a lender of last resort can lend to a bank is limited by the bank's good collateral, there is a limit to how much can be lent to a sovereign country. John also mentioned that the World Trade Organization [WTO] seems to be taking over the role of legal enforcer of rules, not only on trade, but also on financial services and capital markets. My vision is also that the WTO is taking over those functions, as you described. Another question for John is, why do we need to subsidize exit strategies for pegged exchange rate systems? And then, finally, concerning the state of counterfactuals, Michael's study—I guess he might wish to talk about it— and also the study by Mohsin Khan, they are explicitly counterfactual studies about IMF access.

CALVO: Pablo?

PABLO GUIDOTTI: I want to make two comments. The first is about the issue of collateral, which you partially clarified. I understand the concept of seniority, but the question there is how it would differ from the preferred-creditor status, which I think currently the fund has. With respect to collateral in particular, if you are not considering real physical assets or something very similar to that, considering having a collateral on current tax revenues or on reserves is equivalent to not providing the funds, because the country would need to set them aside and not use them in case of a liquidity crunch, right? I don't understand how that concept really works.

The second comment is with respect to the issue of independence from the U.S. treasury. The fund is an organization that essentially makes decisions on public money, and the U.S. is the major shareholder—for that reason, it has influence. Then the question is what do we mean by "independence from the U.S. treasury?" Do we mean by providing less authority to the U.S. treasury relative to other governments?

MELTZER: No, by making more rule-based decisions.

GUIDOTTI: Well . . .

CALVO: That is the answer. Continue. [Laughter]

GUIDOTTI: That doesn't really solve the problem, right? I think that the shareholders will want to have a say in the decisions of the fund, and my impression is that in fact the influence of the U.S. treasury, perhaps with the exception of the case of Russia, has not been a bad thing in the functioning of the IMF. I think that were it not for that influence, some of the emerging markets today would be significantly worse off than they are thanks to that influence.

CALVO: I gather that you are alluding to the time-inconsistency problems that some of these countries have, in which (because of the issue of sovereignty) sometimes the very countries may want to limit themselves. It is interesting to see if you thought of some way of taking that into account.

Next in my list is Agustín Carstens.

AGUSTÍN CARSTENS: Thank you. At the board level of the fund, where I belong, the Meltzer Report has been received with a very positive attitude. I think the institution needs to reflect on itself, and this type of interaction certainly stimulates the discussion. There is no doubt that many aspects of the report are positive and we should try to act on them, but it is also true that there are other aspects which can be subject to criticism—certainly what John said about the basic legal aspect is an extremely important issue.

Going a bit into the origins, the report said that part of the mandate of the fund was to address the issues of fixed exchange rates with adjustable parities, and in this respect my comment will be tied with something that John mentioned. I will say, first, that more than 100 of the 182 country members of the fund, at least, are still on a fixed exchange rate system. What John said goes precisely to the point, and it is how, now that we apparently have the consensus that we need to move to the extremes, are we going to move all those countries to the extremes? I think that a huge contribution that the fund can make—and here I take a comment by Britton Harris—is to provide confidence in that transition. And I believe that many of the standby arrangements that the fund provides have been extremely successful in promoting that transition in an environment of confidence.

I have a lot of problems with what has been said on the impact of IMF programs on some economies. Certainly there is the study by Mohsin Khan, but there are many other cases where the counterfactual is difficult to make. Just take the case of Mexico; Mexico certainly would have not been where it has been in the last five years without the fund program.

Concerning the issue of conditionality, I should say that it is true that conditionality sometimes has not been compiled with, but you have to put that in perspective. Most of the fund programs—in fact, all of them—include some clauses saying that after a certain period of time there will be reviews of the program. This is so because those programs are tackling economic situations that involve a lot of uncertainty, and the situation that the economy will face in the near future will change and will require adjustments of conditionality. Therefore, if you adjust the statistics of compliance with the fact that events have induced changing conditionality, I don't think that the record of the programs is so bad.

There is also a lot of talk about intrusiveness in the report. My own perception is that the system of preconditions proposed in the report, especially given that there would be no further conditionality required, would be far more intrusive than the conditionality we have right now. Therefore, I don't think that those issues are resolved in their commendations.

Thank you.

CALVO: Michael Bordo?

MICHAEL D. BORDO: My comment relates to something that John Lipsky said. I did a paper with Harold James for the Meltzer Commission, which is on their Web site, which I think took a sort of middle-of-the-road, neutral position. We didn't have an axe to grind at all. What we did was to focus on the issue of how the role of the IMF evolved since the breakdown of the parity system, and we concluded that the evolution really reflected demands by the members—especially the United States, then Europe, then the less developed countries—to deal with perceived problems as they came along. Those were the problems brought about by the breakdown of colonialism, oil price shocks, the debt crisis, opening up of capital markets, the breakdown of the USSR, and so on. In a sense, then, the fund and the fund's staff evolved to deal with the problems as they were presented to them and expanded in response to those issues. Then, when we get to the question of the reform of the fund or the other international financial institutions, the question—and I think this is a big think issue which we cannot resolve here—is who is going to deal with these problems as they come along. The view that we took in that paper was (although this was not said directly) that in a sense the IMF was supposed to be a sort of economic United Nations. And, somehow, that is how the United States and a lot of other countries saw it; so the question is, when you do the reform, how are you going to replace this?

CALVO: No more questions for the floor?

BISHOP: I have another question. In terms of the size of these institutions and in terms of the number of people they employ, do you see the IMF and the World Bank as being much smaller than they are now, if these reforms take place? As you have said, political Americans have mixed motives and mixed interests as to whether they want to provide support to these institutions and support for these reforms. I think that most of the other countries don't have a lot of enthusiasm for the reforms; the IMF and World Bank are famously a place where you can send a lot of your promising young people off for jobs for a few years—sons of the prime minister and all that kind of thing. Therefore, a lot of countries are going to resist that kind of reform. Assuming America does want to lead, is there anything that can be done to actually force reforms of the kind you are proposing? I am thinking, for example, that not paying the dues to the United Nations didn't make much difference, and Britain didn't have any impact on the International Labor Organization when it withdrew for a few years because it didn't like what that organization was doing. Do countries have any devices available to try and ginger out the reform process?

Calvo: John, do you have any short responses? I will let Allan speak at the end.

Lipsky: Let me try to make a couple of remarks here. I find this fascinating—I guess this is a bit as with interpretation of works of art—that the artist, in this case, describes the important message of the report as one of independence of the institutions from their political authorities.

Meltzer: No; it is the message that the political authorities see as the most important.

Lipsky: Oh, all right, then. Because I thought that the really powerful message of the report is that the institutions have to be focused, that they have become baroque in their responsibilities as well as overlapping and that we need to get back to the basics and rethink what we want them to do. I think that message is extremely valuable and that is why this report is going to have an echo and it is going to have an impact and be really useful.

I am made uneasy, however, by the suggestion that what you're proposing is a rule-based institution to replace a non-rule-based institution. The fund is a rule-based institution and spends a lot of effort trying to make sure that the specific interpretation of the general rule in case A is equivalent to the interpretation in case B. It has been said that politics get in the way, which underscores the fallacy that the fund is an independent operation with the staff divorced from the political authorities that control it. Of course it is not, and it can't be, and I suspect that to try to make it that would be equivalent to making it irrelevant. The political authorities that fund these institutions will not support, I think, a structure they felt was a group of totally independent agents. At least not now, not at this time. I believe we understand what you're getting at, which is the issue of focus and clarity, and I certainly agree with that. But to put it in terms of the notion that we're talking about—rule-based versus non-rule-based—is, I think, a little harsh and a little extreme.

A couple of specific things. Charles, I don't agree with the idea that the WTO has taken over the role of adjudicating the openness of capital markets. The WTO talks about whether foreign agents can operate in markets, not whether those markets themselves are open and anybody can do transactions.

CALOMIRIS: I meant trade, though. Trade and financial services with the banks. My point is that, if we were to do what you're suggesting, why wouldn't the WTO be the place?

LIPSKY: I think that the WTO, by its very nature, is very ill suited for those kinds of very big legal judgments. Probably we should talk about this later.

Also, when you ask why should we support exit strategies for bad pegs, I'm only saying that in practice, faced with crises, the fund is often confronted with a bad starting point. In other words, it is like the old joke about the city slicker lost in the countryside in New England and asking the old crotchety mean farmer how to get to Boston, and the farmer's answer is "Well, if I were you I wouldn't start from here." [Laughter] In practice, the fund spends a lot of time in situations like that.

Professor Bordo, when you said what reform would replace the fund—

BORDO: What I said was, if you're talking about major reform of the IMF, how do you get at this issue that the fund, in a sense, serves as this sort of economic United Nations and does many things that the members don't want to do themselves. How are you going to replace that? It is a political problem—we are talking about politics now, and not economics. How do you deal with that?

LIPSKY: My image is not that the IMF is the United Nations of economics, my view is that it has become the investment banker of international financial institutions, always looking for the opportunity to make a buck and jumping on it. And that is how we have ended up with good intentions have led to a somewhat baroque role, and that is why I believe it is time for a rethink. But I suspect you wouldn't want to scrap the flexibility that the fund has, and thus you wouldn't want to do away with an institution like the interim committee. I don't know if that really answers the question, though.

CALVO: Allan, you will now have the last word.

MELTZER: I have a limited amount of time. I first want to thank many of you for all the comments, particularly from the people on the panel, who made many thoughtful suggestions. I'm going to be critical of John Lipsky, because he testified before the commission and if he was going to alert us to this serious problem of legal structure, that was the time to tell us about it. Maybe you did. Do you remember that?

LIPSKY: I appeal to this umpire over here.

CALOMIRIS: This was a big theme in his discussion but he didn't, I think, make a specific recommendation. [Laughter]

LIPSKY: You have a great future as a diplomat. [Laughter]

MELTZER: He does.

Let me say that I'm not as concerned about that question as you are, although perhaps I should be. The function of the IMF has changed a great deal, so its legal structure has to change to reflect that. Keynes, throughout his life, and White to a considerable extent also, was a firm believer in capital controls of one kind or another. When he was working on the bank and the fund problem, he wrote something like "I don't think we'll have to go as far, in England, as to open the mail to enforce capital control." This was supposed to be from the great liberal economist: he is not going as far as opening the mail, but would do anything short of that. We are in a very different world now, and we have to change the legal structure to reflect that.

LIPSKY: I agree.

MELTZER: The principal reform of the IMF now, it seems to me, has to be to have a focus. I absolutely agree with that, and the report is certainly strong on that, but the focus has to be how we can provide an infrastructure that will permit the capital markets to operate more efficiently, more effectively, than they have operated before. If we are going to rely on the capital markets to develop a hundred times or more the amount of lending which is going through the international financial institutions, then we're going to have to make those capital markets work better or there is going to be a problem. And one of the ways we make them work better is to have a Securities and Exchange Commission [SEC] function performed. That is what the IMF does, but it has to do it in a more thorough way than the SEC, because the problem is bigger. And that is really what the release of the Article IV report was all about. People will like that or not like it. It is quite a critical step toward making the markets able to evaluate information. People like you will look at the information and make marginal adjustments. That way we are going to avoid the big jumps that occur when we suddenly release information and have a crisis. We would like to avoid all crises, which is impossible—but we are going to make them much less frequent. That seems to me to be critical and that is an assumption which certainly I carried into this discussion.

I would like to respond to the question by Matthew Bishop of what will bring reform. As a member of the media, you can help. That is what newspapers and magazines can do, namely, is to keep the issue alive. And that is what some of the members of the commission have been doing: to try to keep the issue alive. I don't share your pessimism and I don't agree with you about the attitude outside the United States. It is true that Europeans are far less vocal about this, but I've just come back from talking to central bankers and government officials, and I am going to do more of that in Canada. What I get is lots of people who say "Gee . . . This is a starting point for reform, and reform is overdue." People say things like "We missed the opportunity at the fiftieth anniversary of Bretton Woods. We should've been taking up those issues then. Your commission has raised exactly the right issues; we don't agree with everything you say, but we think that is the starting point for reform." So, there is a lot of support for the idea of reform and a lot of people endorsing it, and I believe that Phil Gramm, who will talk tonight, is one of the people who is beginning to do that. They've already held hearings in the Senate. They have held hearings in the House, and the Senate is beginning to draft legislation. We of course don't know where all that will go and how it will finally work out, but there are a lot of things happening and quite a lot of people who have come up and volunteered either by e-mail or in person to say "Yes, we think that this is the basis for a reform that is long overdue." And that was the view of the *New York Times,* the *Wall Street Journal,* the *Financial Times,* your own publication, *The Economist,* and a large number of others. I think there is a sense of wanting to go ahead, and you as members of the press can help us by keeping the issue alive and pointing out how important it is to get these reforms.

The other avenue through which reforms are going to come is with reference to what Agustín Carstens said concerning the attitude within the IMF. When Stanley Fischer testified before the commission he agreed with us on most of the major points. He didn't agree with us about everything, and he didn't agree with us about every detail of our recommendations, but the IMF, unlike the World Bank, has been very supportive of the direction of change. For example, moving toward preconditionality is something that I think there is a distinct possibility that the fund is going to do without being pressured. That would be a big step forward. They don't agree with us about ex post conditionality and I don't expect them to implement that on their own, but preconditionality and a Bagehotian type of lender-of-last-resort arrangement with a real penalty rate are ideas which they like. And, of course, the best kinds of reform will be those that they do themselves because they are convinced that they are in their best interests and will make the organization more effective. I really admire the positive attitude we have seen at the IMF, and at the same time deplore the very negative attitude that we have seen at the World Bank, where in fact the reforms are much more overdue and much more needed.

Obviously, I am not going to have time to answer all of the other questions. What will happen to the size of the institution? Well . . . I don't think very much would happen to the fund. The fund is a relatively lean institution and runs rather effectively. Many of the people who are there are working on things like Article IV consultations, which we want to continue, so they might actually grow in numbers because they have to implement more of them. The development banks have 17,000 people and about half a trillion dollars in capital. There is a lot of trimming that could be done there, because they duplicate each other. And the shrinking should be done so as to make them more effective, more efficient, and less subject to corruption in the countries that receive their assistance. Those are the things I think the public would endorse.

Let me stop here, and again thank all of you for your many comments, particularly the people on the panel, but also the people from the floor.

CALVO: Thank you very much, Allan. I'd like to thank the panelists and the audience for helping us flesh out the complexities of the new institutions for the new millennium. The good news is that we have a whole millennium ahead of us to take care of them. Thank you very much.

Contributors

Leonardo Auernheimer
Department of Economics
Texas A&M University
College Station, TX 77843-4228
leonardo@econ.tamu.edu

Michael D. Bordo
Department of Economics
Rutgers University
New Jersey Hall
75 Hamilton Street
New Brunswick, NJ 08901-1248
bordo@economics.rutgers.edu

Charles W. Calomiris
Columbia University Graduate School
of Business
7W Uris Hall
New York, NY 10027
cc374@columbia.edu

Guillermo A. Calvo
Inter-American Development Bank
1300 New York Ave., NW
Washington, DC 20577
gcalvo@iadb.org

Agustín Carstens
Secretarìa de Hacienda
Palacio Nacional
06066 Distrito Federal
MEXICO
acarstens@shcp.gob.mx

Michael P. Dooley
Department of Economics
University of California

Santa Cruz, CA 95064
michael.dooley@db.com

Pablo E. Guidotti
School of Government
Universidad Torcuato Di Tella
Miñones 2177, C1428ATG
Buenos Aires
ARGENTINA
pguidotti@utdt.edu

Guillermo Ortiz
Banco de Mexico
5 de Mayo #2
06059 Distrito Federal
MEXICO

Andrew Powell
Department of Economics
Universidad Torcuato Di Tella
Miñones 2177, C1428ATG
Buenos Aires
ARGENTINA

René M. Stulz
Department of Finance
Ohio State University
800 Fisher Hall
2100 Neil Avenue
Columbus, OH 43210
stulz@cob.ohio-state.edu

Carl E. Walsh
Department of Economics
University of California
Santa Cruz, CA 95064

The letter *n* after a page number indicates an endnote, *t* indicates a table, and *f* indicates a figure.